Thomas Howard Fourth Duke of Norfolk

NEVILLE WILLIAMS

Thomas Howard Fourth Duke of Norfolk

BARRIE AND ROCKLIFF
LONDON

© 1964 by Neville Williams

First published 1964 by
Barrie and Rockliff (Barrie Books Ltd.)
2 Clement's Inn, London WC2

Printed in Great Britain by
Robert Cunningham and Sons Ltd
Alva, Scotland

TO A. B. E.

CONTENTS

		Page
Introduction		xi
One:	Kenninghall Palace (1538-47)	1
Two:	The Wheel of Fortune (1547-58)	23
Three:	Premier Peer (1558-9)	36
Four:	The Affair of Scotland (1559-60)	52
Five:	The Duke in his Country	65
Six:	The Bid for Power (1561-6)	80
Seven:	Family Fortunes	104
Eight:	Mary Queen of Scots (1567-8)	126
Nine:	Privy Conspiracy (1569)	146
Ten:	Rebellion (1569-70)	169
Eleven:	Howard House (1570-1)	189
Twelve:	Westminster Hall (1571-2)	217
Thirteen:	The Tower (1572)	238
Epilogue		255
Notes to Chapters		262
Index		275

LIST OF ILLUSTRATIONS

Thomas Howard *frontispiece*
  Reproduced by permission of Lord Rothschild

Lord Treasurer Norfolk *facing page* 18
  Reproduced by gracious permission of Her Majesty the Queen

Surrey *facing page* 19
  Reproduced by permission of the Duke of Norfolk

Mary FitzAlan *facing page* 114
  Reproduced by permission of the Duke of Norfolk

Norfolk to Cecil, 1559 *facing page* 115
  Crown copyright

Margaret Audley *facing page* 130
  Crown copyright

Cipher found at Howard House, 1571 *facing page* 131
  Crown copyright

INTRODUCTION

THOMAS HOWARD was one of the half-dozen principal actors on
the Elizabethan stage, yet no life of him has previously been
attempted. This is the more remarkable since he is, perhaps, the
earliest Englishman outside the ranks of royalty for whom a full
biography is possible. This is due in part to the novel practice
whereby important individuals wrote many of their letters themselves, instead of entrusting their entire correspondence to clerks,
which is an aspect of the notable growth of literacy in the sixteenth century; in part to the enlargement of government activity
in the Tudor state, which has left details of many transactions that
had previously gone unrecorded; and also to the fact that in his
last months many of Howard's private archives were either copied
or confiscated by the Crown, while other family muniments have
passed with the estates down an unbroken line. Every stage of
the fourth duke's life, even the childhood years, are well docu-
mented; we know the exact time both of his birth and of his
death. Enough of his own letters survive to depict his personal
life; sufficient private accounts to make clear his changing financial circumstances, as well as a mass of state papers and other
official records for portraying his political life with some certainty.

For almost as long as I can remember I have been thinking
about Howard for, like him, I was born in the pleasant village of
Kenninghall. The fields where his great palace had once stood
were shown me by kindly neighbours but they could not, or
would not, tell me any more than that the duke had been a great
man long, long ago. So when I could read I looked him up in
the books in our house and found out, after some difficulty, that
he had been executed for high treason in 1572. It sounded remarkably exciting and I wanted to know more. Later on it seemed very
odd to me that a man whose name occurred twice in a *Child's
History of England* should not have a book to himself. My interest

waned a bit after that, though I did work out the ingenious theory
that I had been given my baptismal name in Kenninghall Church
because Thomas Howard's sister, Jane, Countess of Westmorland,
'the last of the Nevilles', had been buried there! During the rest
of my schooldays, after we had moved from Kenninghall, I hoped
periodically that somebody, some day would write Howard's
life.

Fifteen years ago I began to return to the charge myself, when
I undertook my first piece of original work at Oxford. Political
history was rather out of fashion and my interests in Tudor East
Anglia were steered towards economic history. I am thankful
that I did not attempt this biography as a novice, and in those
fifteen years much detailed work by Tudor historians has helped
to make the task less exacting. It was Dr A. L. Rowse who suggested to me in 1949 that I might write a book on the county of
Norfolk, parallel to his own classic *Tudor Cornwall*, in which the
House of Howard would loom large. Alas, other commitments
prevented more than the occasional gathering of material. It was
in 1956 that the late Professor Conyers Read firmly told me that
whatever other publisher's commissions might come my way I
must see to it that I did not neglect the fourth Duke of Norfolk.
It is no small regret for me that he has not lived to see it.

His Grace the Duke of Norfolk generously allowed me to work
among his family muniments at Arundel Castle and to reproduce
three of his pictures; and I am indebted to his Librarian, Mr
Francis W. Steer, for his invaluable assistance. I am grateful to
the staffs of the British Museum and the Bodleian Library for their
courteous help and in particular would mention Dr G. R. C.
Davis and Dr W. O. Hassall. Most of the original sources for a
study of this nature are in the Public Record Office and I am indebted to several of my colleagues over the years for sharing with
me their specialist knowledge of the records. Mr G. D. Ramsay
made some helpful comments on an early draft of chapter seven,
while Mr Geoffrey Robinson, to my great profit, read the entire
typescript. In the choice of illustrations I have had the benefit of
Mr David Piper's advice. Mr N. Long-Brown, the Registrar,
kindly showed me round the Charterhouse.

Unpublished material in the Public Record Office in which
Crown copyright is reserved is printed by permission of the Controller of Her Majesty's Stationery Office. Part of Chapter Ten

appeared in an article in vol. xxii of *Norfolk Archaeology* (1959) and I am grateful to the editor for allowing me to reprint it.

For the sake of clarity, in all quotations from contemporary documents I have altered both spelling and punctuation to conform with modern usage.

While writing this biography I have had the constant encouragement of the friendliest of publishers. Mrs D. Steer once again typed my manuscript with her customary skill. Finally, my wife not only provided valuable help in proof reading but at every stage has shared my enthusiasm.

N.W.

Hampstead Garden Suburb
St Edmund's Day, 1963

Chapter One

KENNINGHALL PALACE
1538-47

IN the spring of 1538, as the monasteries were falling, Frances Howard, Countess of Surrey, gave birth to a son at Kenninghall Palace, the principal country house of her father-in-law, Lord Treasurer Norfolk. Apart from princes of the blood, the exact dates of birth of very few Englishmen of the earlier Tudor period have come down to us, but the case of Thomas Howard is unique in that the precise hour of his delivery is known. The child's father, Henry, Earl of Surrey, poet and soldier of renown, directed an Italian astrologer who was in residence to cast the baby's horoscope. The man did his best, though he made a grave error in assuming the latitude of Kenninghall was 51° 38′ north, which must have upset his curious calculations. The final result was not at all pleasing to his patron. He foretold that Surrey himself would meet with an untimely death and that his infant son would be doomed to a life of sorrow and misfortune, owing to the un-favourable position of the stars at thirty-six minutes and seven seconds past two o'clock in the morning of 10th March 1538.[1]

The Lord Treasurer was less superstitious. He was overjoyed that his eldest son now had a son to guarantee the succession to the dukedom of Norfolk and was delighted that he was himself in residence at Kenninghall for the event, which occurred some five weeks earlier than predicted. Four days later he wrote to Thomas Cromwell, Lord Privy Seal, who was at Westminster, asking him to pass the good tidings to the King.

*These[2] shall be to advertise you that it hath pleased Almighty God
to send me so good a fortune that my daughter of Surrey is brought
a bed of a son; and notwithstanding that she looked not to have been
delivered until[3] after Palm Sunday [14th April] yet, God be
thanks, the child is as lusty a boy as needeth to be of that age if she
had gone her full reckoning and then had a son. I intended to have
sent to the King's Highness to have beseeched him to have had it
christened in his name and in likewise to your good Lordship to
have been another godfather, but because she was so long delivered
before her reckoning, the women here would not suffer me to let
the child be so long unchristened. Surely my good Lord, I am not
a little joyful to see my two sons to have two sons[4] of [an] age,
meet to await on my Lord Prince; trusting that when time convenient shall be, the King's Majesty will be content they shall be
of the first sort that shall be appointed to await upon him, which
to see shall be more to my comfort than I can with my pen express.*

Horoscopes apart, it was an anxious time. The plague, which
was rampant in Norwich, had spread to the neighbouring market
towns and at any moment some member of the great household
at Kenninghall might fall a victim. The Duke had hoped to
evacuate some of his staff to healthier spots, but the sickness had
now cut him off from his houses at Castle Rising and Bungay.
The church accounts of a Norfolk parish of this time reveal the
great number of burials and the pitifully few churchings of
women. The old duke had seen all four children which the Lady
Anne, his first wife, had borne him, die young and now he was
fretting about his grandson. He worried, too, about himself, for
at sixty-five the third duke was by Tudor standards a very old
man and, characteristically, the Lord Treasurer of England pondered his own financial affairs. So he continued his letter by asking
Cromwell to send him down his will, which he kept sealed in a
box at Westminster – perhaps for adding a codicil in favour of
his new grandson, but certainly for making various changes, 'for
my substance in money and plate is not so good now as it was at
the making thereof by more than £2,000. A man cannot have
his cake and eat his cake.' For some time now he had realised that
building and maintaining Kenninghall had been eating up too
much of his substance.[5]

The Palace at Kenninghall, twenty miles south-west of Norwich, off the road leading through New Buckenham to Bury St Edmunds, was one of the stateliest of homes. The village of Kenninghall was a mile from the porter's lodge which led into the seven-hundred acre park. On succeeding his father in 1524 the third duke had pulled down the old moated hall and replaced it by a fine residence of ornamental brick-work, a little to the north-east. He hoped his buildings here and in Norwich would outshine the houses of his enemy, the Cardinal, at York Place and Hampton Court. The same taste for self-advertisement which prompts a modern millionaire to have his own initials on the number-plates of his cars, led Thomas Howard to build Kenninghall Palace in the form of a letter H, fronted east and west. The bar of the H divided it into two courts, Ewery and Shelfhanger. Everything about it was in 'the grandest manner'.

From the beginning Kenninghall was planned as a family home, with ample space for all the Howards of each generation to have suites of their own; even the old dowager duchess was sometimes tempted away from Horsham for a few weeks in the year. The House of Howard, closely-knit, living in a world of its own, was essentially a patriarchal society, with the authoritarian, conservative duke at its head. Delighting in pomp and ceremonial, he dressed his household servants in a livery of black and tawney velvet. Howard's widowed daughter, the Duchess of Richmond spent months on end at Kenninghall. There was only one absentee. Because of the duke's infidelities, Duchess Elizabeth had separated from him; she had tried without success to persuade Henry VIII to grant them a divorce, and since 1533 had been living at Redbourne in Hertfordshire, so she only heard of her grandson's birth by a side wind.

The duke's own lodgings were on the second floor, over the chapel, and on the floor above, leading off a short gallery, were the apartments in which he had installed Elizabeth Holland, his mistress, the daughter of his steward. Howard's sons and their families had quarters on the other side of the building in Ewery Court, with the Earl of Surrey's rooms on the first floor. The walls of the bedroom in which young Thomas was born were decorated with tapestry hangings 'of imagery'. A crimson and white canopy stood over the great bed, hung round with curtains of yellow sarcenet. Strips of Turkey carpet – a luxury not to be found in the palaces of Henry VIII – covered much of the floor.

Visitors to the Countess of Surrey's bedside sat in chairs covered with Bruges satin, made tolerably comfortable by white and yellow cushions.

So extensive were the buildings and so splendidly furnished the rooms that it was only fitting to designate Kenninghall a palace. The chapel where Thomas was christened can have been little smaller than the chapel royal at St James's. The staff included six domestic chaplains and a full complement of lay clerks and choristers in the charge of a master, who was provided with 'two pair of organs'. While the Countess was in labour a litany would have been said; but now all was rejoicing. For a christening and family thanksgiving the finest pieces of the chapel plate would be displayed, even though it was Lent, and the richest vestments would be worn by the priests; in oak presses in the vestry were over forty copes. Over the high altar was a picture wrought upon the wainscotting of Christ's birth, passion and resurrection – a picture soon familiar to the Howard children through regular attendance at the chapel services. The great hall, presence chamber and other rooms were on a similar scale of magnificence as the chapel.[6]

Thomas was Surrey's second child. He and Lady Frances Vere, daughter of John, Earl of Oxford, had been married in the summer of 1532. Both of them were then only fifteen and, as was the custom, did not begin to live together for another three years. Jane, their eldest child, was born in 1537 and other children now followed fairly quickly. Katherine was born during 1539, Henry in the following February, and Margaret in January 1543. The Surrey nursery was a lively place.[7]

The 'old nursery' at Kenninghall was on the ground floor of the first court, appropriately next to the wash-house, but it is rather doubtful whether the Surrey children ever lived in these two rooms as their grandfather was using them to keep various clothes in, as his 'second wardrobe'. Probably from the first the children were quartered near their parents in Ewery Court. By 1546 we know that Jane and her sisters had rooms on the ground floor near the kitchen, while Thomas and his brother were on the floor above, next to their father's suite. The boys' room was gay with hangings of red cloth and curtains of green and yellow sarcenet. Unlike their sisters they had no carpet. There was space for three beds and in the oriel window was a desk. The surveyors who made an inventory of the room in 1547 noted a broken chair – evidence, perhaps, of some boisterous pranks.[8]

Kenninghall Palace was to be 'home' for Thomas throughout his life, the favourite house of the considerable Howard inheritance, yet even as a child, as later in life, only a proportion of each year was spent there. There were the regular visits to the family mansions and smaller manor houses that were dotted all over East Anglia, all of them being made more sumptuous in Thomas's earliest years as a result of the spoil of the monasteries. The Lord Treasurer's palace in Norwich was largely rebuilt out of stone from St Benet's Abbey, and his son, not to be outdone, was building Mount Surrey, a fine Renaissance mansion, on the ruins of St Leonard's Priory, and a smaller residence, Surrey House, on the north side of Great Newgate Street. The manor house at Thetford was another windfall of the Dissolution. Castle Rising on the Wash had a much longer connexion with the house of Howard, but without a doubt the most ancient of ancestral homes was Framlingham Castle in Suffolk. [9]

Since the plague constantly threatened the capital, the Howard children's visits to London were few, though Margaret, Thomas's youngest sister, was in fact born at the duke's principal town house. No doubt the children were very occasionally taken to Horsham to see the Dowager Duchess of Norfolk, their great-grandmother, and also to Richmond Palace to see their aunt Mary, the young widow of Henry Fitzroy, King Henry's natural son. We may assume that young Thomas was presented at court to another aunt, Queen Catherine Howard with her hazel eyes and auburn hair, before the wrath of his royal godfather overthrew her. Catherine's trial and execution for adultery (at the Howard house in Lambeth), coming when he was nearly four years old, sounded the first note of tragedy in Thomas's life.

Life was never dull in the Howard world. There was so much for the children to see at Kenninghall, so much that they could learn from the servants of the household and estate, whether it was Mr. Controller or a dairymaid, a kennel-boy or the head game-keeper. The duke's own mill, forge and brewhouse, his fishponds and his pheasant yard were fascinating places. As they grew older the girls learnt the lore of the kitchen, the pastry and the still-room and joined their brothers for riding lessons in the paddock, hawking and hunting in the park, and archery in the butts; the name Butts is still kept green by a cluster of tiny cottages today, whereas all other parts of the old Norfolk estate have vanished, leaving no trace in the names of the leafy, winding lanes or of the flat fields of sugar beet.

Katherine, with Thomas and Henry as her nearest playmates, grew up to be a thorough tomboy. She became a brilliant shot with the long bow and was an expert falconer. Later in life she always kept 'a cast or two of merlins, mewed in her own chamber to the detriment of her gowns and kirtles'.[10] Thomas's early lessons on coursing the hare in Kenninghall and Winfarthing parks led him to write a treatise on the subject, which became a standard work and was still being reprinted a century ago. The armourer taught him and his brother how to use small arms and the elements of fencing; together they followed the hounds, saw calves being born and watched their elders play royal tennis. But as Thomas would one day be master of Kenninghall he was singled out for instruction in the rudiments of running a great household and spent long hours in the company of the controller, the treasurer, and the auditor, on the principle that a good master must 'understand his estate' better than any one of his trusted officials.

The Howard children's more formal education was not neglected. Their father, Surrey, was a scholar of distinction in the liberal, Renaissance tradition. In contrast to his contemporaries who rarely strayed from theological controversy, the Earl's own religious writings went no further than verse paraphrases of parts of the Book of Ecclesiastes and of various psalms. The man who undertook a verse translation of two books of the *Aeneid* as a labour of love and was as much at home in classical Greek as in Italian and Spanish, planned that his children should have a thorough grounding in scholarship. Before Thomas was six his father had brought to Kenninghall Hadrianus Junius, a scholar of European reputation; he features in the household accounts as 'physician', though he was in fact the children's tutor. Down to his death the Earl allowed him fifty angels a year, which was twice the sum that Henry VIII gave to Roger Ascham.

Jane, the eldest child, profited most by this schooling. John Foxe thought her knowledge of Greek and Latin so exceptional 'that she might well stand in competition with the most learned men of that time, for the praise of elegancy in both' languages. Hadrianus also kindled in Henry, her younger brother, a love of learning between his fourth and seventh birthdays that was to lead him in after years to deliver Latin lectures at Cambridge in rhetoric and civil law. Compared with these two prodigies, Thomas Howard was undistinguished, and became an educated man of affairs with no pretensions to scholarship. In years to come he was almost unnecessarily 'ashamed of my unskilfulness' in writing the language of Cicero and Livy and once, when he found himself presiding at a meeting of the Privy Council, he had to ask a colleague to take charge of the negotiations with the Spanish Ambassador 'because his own Latin tongue was not ready'. Another pupil of Hadrianus at Kenninghall was Thomas Churchyard, a page and protégé of Surrey's, who was to become a prolific and uneven court poet; unlike the master he so much admired, Churchyard was to live 'quite long enough to see the greater part of his multifarious writings consigned to oblivion'.[11]

★   ★   ★

The Norfolk peerage stretched back majestically through lines of Howards, Mowbrays and Bigods to the aftermath of the Norman Conquest, the very dawn of recorded history in England, when Ralph the Staller lost his East Anglian lands. The Bigod earls of Norfolk had left Framlingham Castle as an impressive monument to their power in the Angevin and early Plantagenet kingdom; and when the last of the Bigods died without heirs, the earldom passed to Thomas, the youngest of King Edward I's sons, known from his Yorkshire birthplace as Thomas of Brotherton. From 1397 the title had been a dukedom, held by Mowbrays, and with the death of John de Mowbray, the last of the line, in 1476, the Norfolk dukedom became extinct, though only for a few months. John's five-year-old daughter, Anne, was soon married to Richard, Duke of York, Edward IV's younger son, and in contemplation of the marriage the boy was created Duke of Norfolk. Little Anne had already died before Richard was sent by his uncle, the hunchback, to join his elder brother in the Tower on 16th June 1483, and was seen no more. Before the murder of the Princes Richard III had granted the dukedom to a zealous supporter, John Howard of Stoke Neyland, who as Constable of the Tower was probably in league with their murderers.

John, the first duke of the Howard line, was slain on Bosworth Field, where he commanded Richard's vanguard of archers. His eldest son, Thomas, Earl of Surrey, who was taken prisoner during the battle, lost his estates and spent four years in the Tower. On his release he was restored to the earldom of Surrey and was sent as general to the Scottish border. Not until he had given twenty years of loyal service both in the field and also as lord treasurer, did King Henry restore him to the dukedom. He became second duke in 1514, in recognition of his victory over the Scots at Flodden the year before.

Thomas, the third duke and builder of Kenninghall, had risen to power as the opponent of Wolsey. A Venetian ambassador commented on 'his very great experience in political government' and noted that 'he aspires to fresh elevation'. He was 'small and spare in person and his hair black'. Such was the man we can still see from the portrait which Holbein painted of him in the year after Thomas Howard's birth, with his thin lips and long nose, his expression giving nothing away except his concern for his health, for he was a martyr to both rheumatism and indigestion. He is clutching the Lord Treasurer's white staff which he had still clung to, despite the execution of his niece, Queen Anne Boleyn, at whose trial he had presided. When there was a rumour at court that he was being sent to the Tower he scotched it with the remark that it would be no more likely to happen than 'Tottenham shall turn French'.

Norfolk it was who arrested Thomas Cromwell, his grandson's godfather, in the Council Chamber and sent him on his way to the block. He tried to consolidate this victory by arranging for another niece, Catherine Howard, to marry King Henry, but the sordid business of her trial and execution for adultery in 1542 brought him disgrace and threw the whole Howard family into disrepute. He went off to Kenninghall and licked his wounds; thereafter, despite the high offices he held, the duke was never one of the King's inner circle of advisers. But he was still too useful a servant to be cast aside and later that year found himself commanding the army which was harrying the Scottish border. He had been with his father at Flodden and now inflicted the defeat of Solway Mcss on the Scots. Two years later, though over seventy, he was appointed lieutenant-general of the army in France and though he succeeded in capturing Boulogne, he almost lost it again through tactics which provoked a rebuke from his master as severe as anything Henry ever wrote. He had acted 'so clean discrepant from our commandment. . . . We cannot but marvel that men of such experience as we know you to be' should take such risks, and ordered Norfolk 'to seek no more indirect excuses to cloak your ill-favoured retreat, but rather study and be as to see our honour, herein somewhat touched, redubbed'.[12]

Though he had suppressed the Pilgrimage of Grace, had scoffed at the priests' '*old mumpsimus* and superstitions', and had shared in the scramble for monastic lands, Norfolk was essentially a conservative. He was, with Stephen Gardiner, bishop of Winchester, joint architect of the religious reaction after Cromwell's fall, but it was for political and dynastic, rather than religious reasons that he abhorred Protestantism and despised the New Learning. For some years he had marked down Edward Seymour, Earl of Hertford, as his principal enemy, for Hertford was uncle to Prince Edward, heir to the throne, and the Seymours were to the Howards an upstart family, grasping for position and power, privilege and plunder – a far greater affront in Norfolk's eyes than that they were Protestants. The Seymours and their supporters were trying to oust the older nobility from their traditional place in the counsels of state, as Wolsey, the butcher's son, and Cromwell, the smithy's boy, had tried. Old Norfolk was also dismayed that Hertford should win the final laurels for the war in France, and in the last year of the King's life he escaped from the factions of court whenever he could to his palace at Kenninghall where he alone was king.

The Earl of Surrey, even more than his father, hated 'the new men', who had come to power during the turbulent years of the Breach with Rome. Proud, self-willed, rash and hot tempered, he always said what he thought in vigorous terms; thus Cromwell was 'that foul churl', Hertford 'the upstart'. Surrey lacked his father's political cunning, yet took no pains to acquire the polished manners of a courtier. Bred to high estate, he had at an early age been singled out for favours. The King chose him as the companion for his natural son, Henry Fitzroy, Duke of Richmond, first at Windsor and then for a sojourn at the French court. Both Anne Boleyn and Pope Clement VII in turn regarded Surrey as a most suitable husband for Princess Mary, and Richmond married his sister. In 1537 Surrey had ridden with his father to suppress the Pilgrimage of Grace and when, afterwards, a courtier at Hampton Court repeated a rumour that he had sympathised with the rebels, the earl had struck him in the face. For this indiscretion he was confined to Windsor Castle for a few weeks just before Jane, his first child, was born.

Surrey's attitude to the *nouveaux riches* was well known. A conversation between John Barlow, dean of Westbury, and George Constantine, a servant of Cromwell's, in the summer of 1539 showed what men were thinking. Mr Dean described the earl as 'the most foolish proud boy that is in England'. 'What, man', asked his companion, 'he hath a wife and a child and ye call him a boy?' 'By God's mercy', replied the dean, 'me think he exceedeth.' 'What then? He is wise for all that, as I hear; and as for pride, experience will correct well enough', rejoined Constantine. But experience, alas, did nothing to correct the earl. He needed taking down a peg, but instead honour after honour was lavished upon him.[13]

This is the Surrey of Holbein's portraits. In one a scarlet cap, worn at a jaunty angle, with a large white feather, emphasises the oval, clean shaven face; in another the scholar holds a book, a valuable jewel on his finger; in a third the brilliant soldier has his hand on the pommel of his sword. Tall, stately, every inch a lord: such was the image conveyed by the artist and it was the image Surrey wanted.

At jousts he was the apple of King Henry's eye and the idol of the ladies. The Garter, which Norfolk had torn from Cromwell as he left for Traitor's Gate, came to Surrey, and he became high steward of Cambridge University at an incredibly early age. The disgrace of his cousin Queen Catherine Howard failed to halt his progress. But the next year, when his son Thomas was four-and-a-half, Surrey's temper landed him in prison. Having quarrelled with a man from Stockwell he challenged him to a duel and as a result was sent to cool his heels in the Fleet Prison for a fortnight, from which he wrote letters of apology to the Privy Council, half blaming 'the fury of restless youth', yet half excusing himself in a rather grand third person, for 'he is not the first young man to have enterprised matters that he afterwards regretted'. He was released on entering a recognisance of 10,000 marks to keep the peace, but the lesson was not learnt.[14]

After a season spent harrying the Scots, Surrey returned to London and celebrated his return with gay abandon. He became the leader of a gang of high-spirited youths, Thomas Wyatt, the

poet's son, amongst them, who smashed windows of churches
and of aldermen's houses and attacked people in the streets at
night with 'stone-bows'. One night they rowed on the river and
'shot at the queans on the Bankside' with pellets. The identity of
the ringleader of these escapades soon became known. Surrey's
headquarters were at Mistress Arundel's cookhouse in St Lawrence
Lane, where she kept him and his companions well supplied with
meat, even though it was Lent. But one day a butcher told the
authorities what he had heard about her and her customers and
so Millicent Arundel was examined at court. It came out that she
had told her kitchen-maids how cross young Surrey was about
the purchase of some cloth and had burst out, 'I marvel they will
thus mock a prince'. 'Why,' asked one of the girls, 'is he a
prince?' 'Yea, mercy he is,' answered Mistress Arundel, 'and if
ought should come at the King but good, his father [Norfolk]
should stand for King', for the earl had told her as much. This was
the first hint of Surrey's pretensions to the crown, but the Privy
Council thought it no more than woman's gossip.[15]

On 1st April 1543 he and two others were called to St James's
before the Council; his father thoughtfully absented himself.
Surrey claimed he had a special licence for eating meat during
fasts, but admitted that he had broken the peace by breaking windows and shooting at prostitutes. It had grieved him, he said with
as straight a face as he could, to see the licentious manners of
Londoners 'which resembled the manners of Papal Rome in her
corrupted state'. To the Fleet he was sent a second time, and spent
his imprisonment writing *A Satire Against the Citizens of London*.

> London! hast thou accused me
> Of breach of laws? the root of strife!
> Within whose breach did burn to see,
> So fervent hot, thy dissolute life . . .

When he was released he stole away from court to Norwich
where Thomas, then five, and his other children saw more of him
that summer than at any time in their lives.[16]

In October he returned to the King's favour and joined the
force under Sir John Wallop which was aiding the Emperor
Charles V against Francis I. Next June he was in France with the
English army and was wounded at Montreuil; but after the surrender of Boulogne he became lieutenant-general of the English

forces on the continent, with his headquarters in the captured
seaport.

Leading raids beyond the enemy's line was the kind of soldiering he loved and he even relished the King's reproof from
needlessly exposing himself to danger. Then, in January 1546,
came his first reverse when he was defeated at St Etienne and the
casualties were heavy for so small an operation. Surrey had slipped
over to England on leave in the previous July and stayed for a
few days at Kenninghall. That autumn he asked whether his wife
and children could come out to join him at Boulogne, but the
reply had been unfavourable. In March he repeated his request
but Henry thought it was not right 'now that time of service
which will bring some trouble and disquietness, unmeet for
women's imbecilities, approacheth, that your lordship should
send for my lady your wife'. To sugar the pill Henry granted him
a licence to eat meat in Lent (or was that a dig at the past in
Mistress Arundel's kitchen?). The next week Surrey heard he was
being superseded by Hertford, but he ended his military career
with a typical skirmish at Etaples which (as he told Paget) 'proved
that the Frenchman can run as fast away up the hill as the Englishman not long ago ran down'.[17]

With the help of Hadrianus Junius, the children had written a
pompous little letter in Latin to their father, rather belatedly
complimenting him on his victories. Thomas, who was only
seven, can have had little share in the composition, which was
clearly very much Jane's work. The letter, even in translation,
shows more than anything how distant Surrey was from his
children:

> *No tongue can declare how joyful we all are – your children, our
> noble grandfather, your revered sister the duchess, your dear wife,
> our parent, in short all your household – at your unexpected return.
> The sides of this little body cannot certainly express it. All con-
> gratulate you on your return after defeating the French so often and
> vindicating the royal authority so well. We also applaud the King
> and his whole realm for having had you for a vice-roy in Boulogne…*

No warmth of feeling here, no touching endearments. Merely a
dutiful letter, as was expected of them by the great man they so
rarely saw; a diplomatic letter even, written at their tutor's
prompting, with no hint of St Etienne, or loss of command, to

placate Surrey before he arrived at Kenninghall and stalked into the schoolroom to learn of their progress.[18]

For the next few months the earl lived quietly in London and Norfolk, and much of the time he spent overseeing the embellishments to Mount Surrey. One of his few appearances at court was for the reception given to the French Embassy, led by the Admiral of France in August. He now had leisure to write verse again. He sat for the Dutch painter Guillim Scrots and, as with so much associated with Surrey, the picture set a new fashion in English portraiture. Statues, cherubs, masks and arms in true Renaissance style flank an arch, under which the earl stands in gorgeous Italianate costume, hand so surely on hip, a Renaissance prince to his finger-tips. It is all of a piece with the architecture of Mount Surrey and with the poems modelled on Petrarch. But the coat-of-arms in the portrait were to cause trouble before many weeks.[19]

During the summer Norfolk had decided he must attempt a *rapprochment* with Hertford. He even asked the King to help him arrange a match between his daughter, the Duchess of Richmond, and Hertford's brother, Sir Thomas Seymour. This, he hoped, would be the first of a series of alliances between the Howards and the Seymours. Young Thomas, aged eight, was already with his sisters a pawn in the dynastic game. 'Whereas my son of Surrey has a son and divers daughters, that a cross marriage might be made between the Lord Great Chamberlain and them.' Nothing came of these schemes, though Surrey continued to press his sister to favour Seymour. More than this, he was deep in a plot for Mary Fitzroy to become her royal father-in-law's mistress.[20]

In the autumn the King's old trouble with his leg returned. He became extremely ill and, even when his condition improved, it was clear to those in the inner circle of the court that he would never recover. Hertford had returned to the Council table very much the hero of the late war and was supported by John Dudley, Lord Lisle. Quarrels in the Council became frequent. Once Lisle struck Bishop Gardiner in the face and had to retire from court for a month. Wriothesley, the Lord Chancellor, and Paget, the Secretary of State, seeing the way the wind was blowing deserted Gardiner and Norfolk for Hertford. The Council began to meet at Hertford's house, instead of at Whitehall Palace and Norfolk, fearful for his own safety, did not attend after 1st November 1546, but withdrew to Kenninghall. On every hand there was scheming and speculation about the regency for governing the realm after Prince Edward's accession. Early in December Sir Richard Southwell, a Norfolk M.P. who had risen to power as Cromwell's eyes and ears at the Dissolution, informed the Council that 'he knew certain things of the Earl [of Surrey] that touched his fidelity to the King'. Throughout his career Southwell had bowed to every wind of change, hitching his fortunes to the man of the moment, and now he had thrown overboard the earl, who was both his neighbour in Norfolk and his old comrade in arms at Boulogne. Surrey understandably wanted to fight Southwell 'in his shirt'. For the moment both of them were detained in Wriothesley's house.[21]

Norfolk was sent for and when he arrived in London on Sunday 12th December he was taken by barge to the Tower. A dozen years back he had said shrewdly to Sir Thomas More 'By the mass, Master More, it is perilous striving with princes', and now his own position made its wry comment. That day Surrey, too, was moved to the Tower while Southwell was released. The wildest rumours were afoot. Some said the Howards had planned to murder all the Council, others that they aimed at the custody of Prince Edward. The Imperial Ambassador reported, 'They are said to have entertained some ambitious designs when the King was ill at Windsor, six weeks ago, to obtain control of the Prince and of the country; and their chance of liberation is small.'[22]

Just before dusk on that Sunday afternoon Southwell left London for Norfolk at the order of the Council. John Gates and Wymond Carew, two officials of the court, went with him. The weather was against them as they rode and they did not reach Thetford until very late on the Monday night, having covered no more than eighty-four miles. There they rested in the duke's house and left at dawn to ride the remaining seven miles to Kenninghall. On arrival they found the steward, Robert Holdyche, was away taking musters, so they called the almoner, Sir Henry Symondes, before them, and Southwell told him of the arrests of the duke and of the earl. He was ordered to bar the park gates and all the doors, back and front, of Kenninghall Palace.

The visitors then summoned the Duchess of Richmond and

Elizabeth Holland, Norfolk's mistress, to the dining chamber to cross-question them. It was a remarkable situation. Here was Surrey's principal accuser coming down to his house to examine his relatives; it was a procedure that was part and parcel of the process of judicial murder on which the anti-Howard faction had decided. The ladies had only just risen. The Duchess of Richmond was 'sore perplexed, trembling and like to fall down'. On her knees she declared her affection for her father whom, she was convinced, was a faithful subject, but her brother Surrey 'she noteth to be a rash man'. She agreed to put on paper all she could remember. Southwell's companions found very few valuables in her rooms – 'all being very bare' – as she had sold her jewels to satisfy creditors.

Elizabeth Holland was garrulous. She was prepared to do anything to save herself and her possessions. The visitors searched her and found all kinds of precious jewels concealed on her person. Orders were given for her own new house in thirty-six acres at Framlingham, once the property of Corpus Christi Guild in Diss, as well as the Howard mansions in Norwich and elsewhere, to be put under lock and key until complete inventories had been made. Both ladies were to be ready to leave for London on the morrow. Southwell then made the almoner produce a list of the staff left at Kenninghall, and their names were called over – sixteen gentlemen, six chaplains, twelve servants of the chapel, fifty-two yeomen and sixty-one grooms in the duke's service and six gentlemen, eight yeomen and five grooms on Surrey's establishment. As only the Countess of Surrey and her children with their attendants were now left, Southwell asked in his letter to the King the same evening whether he was to dissolve the rest of the household and close down part of the palace. For all practical purposes Kenninghall Palace had already been confiscated by the Crown.[23]

A few days later in London Mary Fitzroy deposed that her father had wished her to marry Sir Thomas Seymour, 'which her brother also desired, wishing her withal to endear herself so into the King's favour, as she might the better rule here as others had done and that she refused'. In the Howard household there had been heated arguments about the tactics for dealing with Hertford and his supporters and according to the duchess her brother had said, 'These new men loved no nobility, and if God called away the King they should smart for it.' She revealed, too, that Surrey had made an alteration in his arms and had replaced his coronet with a crown, and underneath the arms was a cypher 'H.R.' She denied there was any hint of disloyalty in her father.

Elizabeth Holland related various remarks of the duke's about his unpopularity in the Council. None of them loved him 'because they were no noblemen born themselves' and the King no longer confided in him 'because he was too much loved in his country'. The duke, she said, had not liked Surrey's changes in his arms and had forbade her to embroider them in his house.[24]

Others now came forward to tell what they knew about the earl. Edward Rogers recollected in great detail various dark sayings of Surrey's in the spring about who should govern after King Henry's death, which had been passed on to him by Sir George Blagge. He also mentioned the story told him by Sir Gawen Carew 'that my lady of Richmond had discovered unto him as strange a practice of her brother as ever he heard of'. Carew was sent for and swore on oath that he had heard from the duchess herself about Surrey's advice to marry Seymour and 'although her fantasy would not serve to marry with him, yet, notwithstanding, she should dissemble the matter, and he would find the means that the King's Majesty should speak with her himself. But that she should in no wise utterly make refusal of him, but that she should leave the matter so diffusely that the King's Majesty should take occasion to speak with her again; and thus by length of time it is possible that the King should take such a fantasy to you that ye shall be able to govern like unto Madame D'Estampes', the mistress of Francis I of France. In this way she should help herself and her relatives. 'Whereupon she defied her brother and said that all they should perish and she would cut her own throat rather than she would consent to such a villainy.' Carew himself had heard Surrey say, 'Note those men which are made by the King's Majesty of vile birth hath been the destruction[25] of all the nobility of this realm.'

Sir Edmund Knyvet, the King's serjeant porter, deposed that during a recent conversation when he had charged Surrey with malice towards him, the earl had replied, 'No, no, cousin Knyvet, I malice not so low; my malice is higher . . . These new erected men would by their wills leave no noble man on life.' Knyvet also felt it his duty to mention that Surrey kept in his household an Italian named Pasquil 'as a jester, but more likely a spy', and another Italian named Peregrine; the latter was probably the man who drew up Thomas Howard's horoscope. Sir Edward Warner talked of Surrey's 'pride and vain glory' and in particular of his bearing the arms of Edward the Confessor.[26]

Garter King of Arms was then called in. He deposed that some while back, before Surrey had gone to Boulogne, Richmond Herald had asked him to speak with the earl about his arms. In the gallery of the Howard house at Lambeth Surrey had shown Garter 'an escutcheon of the arms of Brotherton and St Edward, and Anjou and Mowbray, quartered. I asked him by what title, and he said that Brotherton bare it so, and I showed him it was not in his pedigree. And he said that he had found it in a house in Norfolk in stone graven so, and he would bare it.' Clearly, Garter was reluctant to take up the matter with his master, the Earl Marshal. In the end it was to be for the heraldic offences that Surrey was to be tried, and it was not to be a matter for the court of Chivalry, but a trial for high treason before his enemies sitting as special commissioners. Fresh evidence was to come out about his instructions to a Norwich glazier for putting the Confessor's arms into a window at Mount Surrey, his purchase of a stamp of the same arms for engraving his plate and of his having them painted at Kenninghall Palace on 7th October – the royal arms 'azur a cross fleury between five martlets gold', belonging to King Edward and his progenitors in right of the Crown of England.[27]

The duke's mistress and his daughter each had an axe to grind, but apart from Garter, what sort of men were the other accusers? Sir Edmund Knyvet had been at daggers drawn with the Howards for some years. When in 1541 he had struck a friend of Surrey's in the royal tennis court and drawn blood he had been sentenced, under the provisions of a recent, barbarous statute, to lose the offending hand but had persuaded the judges to let him keep his right hand so that he could the more readily serve his king. Of late there had been a law-suit about some land in Old Buckenham over which he had aroused the duke's wrath and Surrey's un-kindness, 'the which I had so long and so heavy borne', that he had at last ceased to visit his neighbours at Kenninghall. The Howards had also upset Sir Edward Warner and for his share in their fall he was to be rewarded with a grant of the duke's property at Castle Acre, while Edward Rogers, a protégé of the Seymours, was to be knighted at Edward VI's coronation. Another witness, Sir George Blagge, a gentleman of the bedchamber, was a fervent Protestant and only the King's intervention had saved him in July from being burnt at Smithfield when Bishop Gardiner, Norfolk's ally, had kindled new flames of persecution. Finally Sir Gawen Carew was a friend of Southwell, the man who had begun the witch-hunt. Such witnesses do not inspire confidence. Yet from the very beginning there was not the slightest doubt that Surrey would be found guilty of high treason and his father suffer an attainder; the Howard house, divided against itself could not withstand the onslaught of its enemies. Moreover every possible attempt was made to implicate Gardiner in the conspiracy and by the end of the year Hertford had succeeded in having the Bishop's name expunged from the list of councillors named in Henry VIII's will.

The King, ill though he was, took the greatest interest in the case, so nearly touching his dignity and honour. Notes were prepared for him, memoranda drafted and amended in his own hand, difficult though it was for him to hold a pen. 'If a man compassing himself to govern the realm do actually go about to rule the King and should for that purpose advise his daughter or sister to become his harlot ... what this importeth?' he wrote. In the end the charges about Surrey's proposals to his sister were dropped from the trial, for there was more than enough meat in the armorial offences.[28]

There is a story that Surrey attempted to escape from the Tower. He persuaded his servant, Martin, to smuggle in a dagger inside his breeches and to arrange for a boat to be ready in St Katherine's Pool. The earl's room overlooked the river and he planned to lower himself through the window when it was low water. At midnight, when the water was still two feet deep, he decided to wait no longer, but was in the instant surprised by the guards. His trial was hurried forward. A Norfolk grand jury found a true bill against him for high treason at Norwich Castle on 7th January and on the 13th twenty-four jurors from the neighbourhood of Kenninghall came to London, of whom twelve were old acquaintances of the accused like Sir William Paston, Sir James Boleyn, Sir Richard Gresham, Sir William Woodhouse, Christopher Heydon and Nicholas L'Estrange. The trial was to

Lord Treasurer Norfolk. Portrait by Holbein

Surrey. Portrait by Scrots in Arundel Castle

take place not in Westminster Hall, but in the Guildhall and Surrey was escorted thither soon after dawn by three hundred halberdiers; 'it was fearful to see the enormous number of people in the street', wrote a Spaniard.[29]

Proud to the end the earl had demanded that the Lieutenant of the Tower should provide him with a new coat of satin, furred with black coney, for the trial. The proceedings in the Guildhall lasted eight hours and, though the verdict was a foregone conclusion, Surrey fought fiercely at his accusers. He lashed out at Paget, the Secretary, whose father had been a constable. 'Thou Catchpole, what had thou to do with it? Thou hadst better hold thy tongue, for the Kingdom has never been well since the King put mean creatures like thee in the government.' When the sentence of hanging and mutilation had been given, he made a final outburst: 'I know that the King wants to get rid of the noble blood round him, and to employ none but low people.' There was no hope of a reprieve, but the sentence was mitigated to one of simple beheading. Surrey went to the block on 19th January and was buried in All Hallows, Barking, the church in Tower Street. Thus was the first part of the astrologer's prophecy fulfilled.[30]

Technically, Surrey was guilty of high treason, and it was on this technical point that his enemies had fastened and would not leave go. As a descendant of Edward I, through Thomas of Brotherton, Surrey had a perfect right to bear the royal arms, but they should have appeared in the second quarter and he had been rash enough to have them depicted in the first. As son of the Earl Marshal, he should have realised the seriousness of the step, but rash, overweening, he had chosen this way deliberately, as a challenge to his opponents who were bent on keeping the regency of the young Edward to themselves, by proclaiming that he and his family had a better title to the government of the realm than anyone.[31]

*   *   *

The Duke of Norfolk, compromised by his son's indiscretion, was at the mercy of his enemies. Searching questions were asked of him in the Tower, but he persisted in maintaining his loyalty. He told the Council, 'I have had great enemies' – the Cardinal, the Duke of Buckingham and Cromwell, and members of his

TH C

own family. 'The malice borne me by both my nieces whom it pleased the King to marry is not unknown to such as kept them . . . ' He hoped desperately that the Council would show this profession of a loyal servant to the King, but Henry was in no mood for mercy.[32]

On 12th January, the day before his son's trial, he drew up a confession. He agreed he had concealed high treason in keeping secret the fact that Surrey had improperly used the Confessor's arms. Moreover, he admitted that he himself had borne for twenty-two years in the principal quarter of his arms 'the arms of England, with a difference of three labels of silver, which are the arms of my lord the Prince'; this was an offence which he now admitted was high treason. The old man begged for mercy and added that his confession had been quite voluntary, 'without compulsion, without force, without advice or counsel'.[33]

Within a few days a bill of attainder was brought into Parliament against both Norfolk and Surrey; it was the only act of that sessions and passed through all the stages of enactment speedily, for Surrey had already been executed, and the duke had already confessed. On 27th January King Henry appointed Wriothesley, Hertford and other peers as commissioners to give the royal assent to this bill, which was duly performed in the Lords the same day. During that night Henry VIII died and Norfolk's life was saved. The commission for the royal assent to the attainder had the appearance of legality, though as the King was too weak to sign it himself his Secretary, Paget, had used his wooden stamp. No one will ever know whether the stamp was used with the King's full knowledge, to send so eminent a servant to the block. Hertford knew Henry was near his end but had no reason to think that he would not survive another week during which Norfolk's sentence could be carried out. But the demise of the Crown posed more pressing problems for him than the position of the old duke.[34]

If it is true, as some have said, that Hertford had no wish to begin his rule with bloodshed, it is also true that he had not the time. For three days he delayed announcing Henry's death until he and Paget had completed making their dispositions. Their principal enemy, Surrey, was dead; Norfolk was powerless in the Tower and had already played into their hands by beseeching the King to settle his estates, from Kenninghall downwards, on

Prince Edward. The new rulers had seized power without having
to put Norfolk to the axe and the old man was to be allowed to
live out his days in captivity, while the Seymours plundered the
Howard treasures.

The Howards had fallen largely because their house was divided
against itself; husband against wife, brother against sister, son
against mother. Family quarrels had been exploited by astute
opponents who feared the Howards for being too close to the
throne in blood, and had brought the monarch to share their fear.

The fall of the house of Howard, so sudden and so complete,
astonished the courts of Europe when Hertford's and Paget's
accounts of the high treason were made known. The conspiracy
of father and son seemed to Dr Nicholas Wotton, ambassador to
France, 'the most execrable and most abominable intent and
enterprise'. Thirlby, Bishop of Westminster, then with the
Emperor Charles V in Wurtemberg, pondered the fate of 'those
two ungracious *non homines*, the Duke of Norfolk and his son,
the elder of whom I confess that I did love, for that I ever supposed
him a true servant to his master . . . Before God, I am so amazed
at the matter, I know not what to say.'[35]

Already the household at Kenninghall had begun to break up.
Before Surrey's execution Hadrianus, the tutor, had settled in
London and was cautiously searching for fresh patrons. One day
he was penning a dedication of his Greek-Latin lexicon jointly to
King Henry and Prince Edward, the next he was persuading the
imperial ambassador to accept an inscribed copy of his latest
translation from Plutarch. He was to leave England in the spring
and would not be heard of at court again for twenty years, when
he began to seek Cecil's patronage.[36]

Thomas and his brother saw the King's men making detailed
inventories of their grandfather's jewellery, plate and clothing
and of their father's possessions. Rooms were sealed up, locked
chests and caskets removed. Mount Surrey and the other family
houses were similarly ransacked. Most of the loot went to Hertford – rings, brooches and bracelets, chains, collars and girdles,
jewelled ornaments and pictorial tablets of gold, a hoard of family
heirlooms worth a million pounds. The Lord Protector pilfered
Surrey's Parliament cap, his spurs and even two pairs of stockings,
while another Seymour pounced on his shirts. A list was made of
every horse in the stables, each with its pet name and its markings.

It was a nightmare for the steward, for the King's men played havoc with the place; there was no privacy and the ordered life of Kenninghall Palace slowed down to a standstill. Thomas's home was no more, his inheritance had been usurped, and he was made to understand that through his father's attainder his own blood was corrupted.[37]

The shock of her husband's arrest and trial had a disastrous effect on Lady Surrey. When she first heard the news of his going to the Tower she was already great with child, and she was fortunate to survive the miscarriage which it brought on. Too ill to be moved from her bed for weeks to come, she was in no position to care for her children, and with Hadrianus and the Duchess of Richmond both gone, there was no-one for them to turn to.[38]

The tragedy of January 1547 left an indelible mark on Thomas Howard. He had inherited his father's haughty pride, and now his own utter mistrust of the self-seeking upstarts, personified by Hertford, who had spilled noble blood in their thirst for power, was intensified. Hertford now assumed old Norfolk's offices of Lord Treasurer and Earl Marshal and within a few days would be created Duke of Somerset and seize power as Lord Protector. In later life the memory of this *coup d'état* would make Howard suspicious of the Cecils and Dudleys and their hangers-on, and persuade him to shun the court whenever he could. In cheating his father of his life the Seymours had deprived him of his rightful position as a regent of the realm and governor of the boy King. Thomas Howard was not to see Kenninghall again for another five years. Perhaps, before he left, he took one last look at the now mutilated Arms of England over his father's bed, which had caused all the trouble. In years to come he would himself be led by events to make a bid for the Crown, and regard it as his birthright.

Chapter Two

THE WHEEL OF FORTUNE
1547-58

In the long gallery at the duke's palace in Norwich there stood a 'little table, with a printed paper thereon, with a hand to be twirled about, called the Board of Fortunes', perhaps an invention of Surrey's Italian astrologer. It was the only game in the palace except chess and in happier days Thomas Howard must have played with it now and again, to while away the time. But now the wheel of fortune was turning in reality, and the next twelve years were to see some surprising changes.

Thomas was only eight when his father was executed on Tower Hill. No letters have come down to us from Surrey to his children, similar to the touching testaments written by Thomas himself, twenty-five years later. Indeed he scarcely knew his father. Away on the King's service in France and Scotland, and when in England spending more time in the capital than at Kenninghall, Surrey was to his children a rather remote figure. They heard of some of his exploits at second-hand and much that they heard was too difficult for them to understand. It was perhaps an even greater shock to them that their grandfather, Lord High Treasurer and Earl Marshal – and in their eyes the very ruler of the realm under the King – was in the Tower, than that their father had gone to the block as a traitor.

Kenninghall Palace was, as a matter of course, confiscated by the Crown and was very soon assigned to Princess Mary. The heir to the throne was as much a prisoner as the heir to the duke-dom. The bailiff's accounts from the spring of 1547 contain

various items of expenditure for 'making the house of Kenninghall close', with new doors or locks at the entrance to Shelfhanger
Court and on the doors at the foot of each staircase, to prevent
Mary's escape. A plan of the palace, made by the carpenter, was
sent up to the Council. The Princess was not stinted of Lenten
fare, for Parker, the carrier, brought from Thetford quantities of
salt fish and fresh oysters at twopence per hundred. Much of her
brother's reign Mary stayed at Hunsdon in Hertfordshire, but
whenever she and her attendants came to Kenninghall they were
treated with great respect by the villagers and by the neighbouring
gentry. Out of loyalty to the old duke in the Tower, tenants now
and again risked their lives to help smuggle a priest into the house
so that Mary could hear Mass. Their own church of St Mary had
most of its precious altar furnishings confiscated and was left with
only the smallest bell of a peal of six.[1]

The blow of Surrey's attainder and execution was hardest for
Thomas, for he was at once separated from his brother and sisters.
They were taken from their mother's care and placed under the
nominal guardianship of Lord Wentworth, though in fact their
immediate custodian was Thomas Gawdy, an East Anglian lawyer
who was an old friend of the family. But Thomas Howard was
placed with Sir John Williams, the treasurer of the Court of
Augmentations. His keeper was kept by business in London most
of the time, while the boy lived quietly at Ricote, Williams's
charming manor house near Thame. By a touch of irony, when
the Howards eventually returned to power in the next reign,
Thomas's cousin, the Princess Elizabeth, was to spend a similar
period of confinement at Ricote.[2]

After a difficult year the children were reunited, for the Privy
Council decided to place them under the guardianship of their
aunt, the Duchess of Richmond. Mary Fitzroy was not only a
cultivated woman but was well known as an ardent supporter of
the Reformation. Scholars and divines were always welcome at
her London residence, Mountjoy House in Knight Rider Street.
The Howard children were not, however, to live in London, but
at Reigate Castle, which became their home for five impressionable years. They were joined there by Charles Howard, their
second cousin, two years older than Thomas. He was the son
of Lord William Howard and was destined to win fame as
an admiral. Probably on Lord Wentworth's advice, the Duch-

ess of Richmond engaged John Foxe as tutor to her charges. Foxe was at this time living in London in great poverty. There is a tale that as he 'one day sat in St Paul's church, spent with long fasting, his countenance thin and eyes hollow, after the ghastly manner of dying men, every one shunning a spectacle of so much horror, there came to him one whom he never remembered to have seen before, who, sitting down by him and saluting him with much familiarity, thrust an untold sum of money into his hand, bidding him be of good cheer, adding withal, that he knew not how great the misfortunes were which oppressed him, but supposed it was no light calamity; that he should, therefore, accept in good part that small gift from his countryman which common courtesy had forced him to offer; that he should go and take care of himself and take all occasions to prolong his life, adding, that within a few days, new hopes were at hand and a more certain condition of livelihood ... Certain it is, however, that within three days after the transaction the presage was made good. Someone waited upon him from the Duchess of Richmond, who invited him, upon fair terms, into her service.'[3]

It seems incongruous that the man who had earlier resigned a fellowship at Magdalen College, Oxford, to avoid persecution for his faith and was in due course to write a detailed account of the sufferings of English Protestants in a book popularly known as the *Book of Martyrs* should have become tutor to Norfolk's grand-children. The Lord Treasurer and the Reformer were about as different in outlook as any two men can be. In 1540 the duke had up-braided a clerk in the Exchequer for marrying an ex-nun, and when the man quoted Scripture to justify his action, Norfolk replied: 'I have never read the Scripture, nor never will read it. It was merry in England afore the new learning came up; yea, I would all things were as hath been in times past.' Yet the Scriptures and the new learning formed a large part of the curriculum at Reigate Castle.[4]

Residence at Reigate gave Foxe sufficient leisure for writing. His pupils would have been taken through his treatise on excom-munication and made to construe his *Comoedia Apocalyptica*. Tutoring the Howard children gave him practical experience for compiling *Tables of Grammar* (1552), which he hoped might be-come a standard text book, to replace the older continental grammars. Soon Foxe's teaching extended beyond the walls of the castle, for in 1550 he was ordained deacon to enable him to convert the townsmen from idolatrous ways to the Protestant truth. The young Howards listened to his fiery sermons and saw him stamp out the devotions made at the shrine of a local madonna, Our Lady of Ouldsworth, which was credited with miraculous powers of healing. Surrey's children were almost drowned by the high tide of Protestantism; yet in these very months mass was still being celebrated in the chapel at Kenninghall Palace, while Princess Mary was in residence.[5]

There were occasional holidays away from Reigate. On one of them Foxe took Thomas and Henry down to a family manor in Dorset, not far from the coast; and while visiting Lulworth he agreed to look after the sea chest of a pirate captain for a day and a night, no doubt to the great excitement of the boys.[6]

There was excitement of another kind in Thomas's native county when Ket's Rebellion broke out in the summer of 1549, beginning as a protest by small tenant farmers against the enclosure movement. Tenants from the former Howard estates at Castle Rising and Beccles joined the army of insurgents on Mousehold Heath, where for six weeks Ket held the city of Norwich in subjection. Eventually Thomas would have heard accounts of Warwick's arrival with twelve thousand men, including German mercenaries, and of the street fighting in the city he knew so well, before the rising was stamped out. Perhaps, too, he learnt about the rebels' capture of his grandfather's faithful servant, Thomas Gawdy, and of 'little Sir Roger' Woodhouse, who had acquired his father's house in St Stephen's parish, being imprisoned in his other mansion, Mount Surrey. With the duke in the Tower there had been an unseemly struggle amongst the new men for the position he had occupied for so long in the affairs of the county. Had Norfolk been still at Kenninghall the rising would have taken a very different turn. The moral of Ket's rebellion was not lost on his grandson. Whatever the shortcomings of his bailiffs, when he inherited the property, he was a good landlord. Unlike the new class of landlords who were exploiting to the full the abbey lands they had wrested from the Crown, the fourth duke did much to foster good relations with his tenants; long afterwards their grandsons were to remember him with affection as 'the good duke'.[7]

Now and again the question of the custody of the Howard children was raised. For an outsider their wardship would have

been a most profitable form of investment; yet in turn both Protestant Somerset and the Duke of Northumberland agreed to leave
the arrangements as they stood. Edward VI knew 'no better place
for their virtuous education' than with their aunt of Richmond.
At Christmas 1551 she was granted an annuity of £100 towards
their maintenance and the next year was given a further £100.

The children heard nothing of their old grandfather who had
played so large a part in their earliest days. When he had lived
through one year of considerable hardship he was allowed a new
feather-bed, bolster, pillow and blankets and then, in 1549, the
exchequer relented even further and allowed him £80 a year
'spending-money'. Sir John Markham, the Lieutenant of the
Tower treated him in later years less strictly that the Protector
imagined, and in 1552 Norfolk's former secretary, John Clerk,
joined him there. Clerk had been brought before the Council
and accused of 'lewd prophecies and slanders', which he fervently
denied, and was also asked questions about certain books of
necromancy found in his lodgings. He persisted in his denial and
Northumberland thought him better under lock and key.[8]

$$* \qquad * \qquad *$$

The death of Edward VI brought about a revolution in the
Howard fortunes. Queen Mary, fearful of plots against her, fled
from Hunsdon to shelter at Kenninghall 'where she has the
support of several gentlemen and others who are devoted to her',
but as soon as she arrived there she learnt of Lady Jane Grey's
accession. On the advice of Norfolk retainers she rode on next
day to Framlingham Castle, which could stand a siege if necessary.
The royal standard usurped the Howard banner at the castle until
the crisis was over, and then she rode to London, accompanied
by the Duchess of Norfolk, to take up her residence in the Tower
until Coronation Day. Before then, the old duke had been released
from his close confinement in the Tower and at the Council
meeting on 10th August was restored to the Order of the Garter.
Although nearly eighty he was soon back in harness, preparing
as Earl Marshal for Mary's coronation. His grandchildren's sojourn at Reigate was also over. Thomas Howard soon joined him
in London and at the end of the month the Countess of Surrey was
ordered by the Council to have the rest of her children brought
from Reigate Castle to Mountjoy Place 'where they shall be re-

warded by the Duke of Norfolk'. It was a time of great rejoicing
and the Duchess of Norfolk, separated from her husband for the past
twenty years, entered fully into the spirit of the family reunion.[9]

On Michaelmas Day Thomas was made a Knight of the Bath
at the Tower, the youngest of those created, and with his fellows
kept solemn vigil over their arms in St John's Chapel in the White
Tower throughout the following night. Next day they rode with
the Queen through the city to Westminster Abbey for her
coronation.

Coronation Day, 1st October, proclaimed the triumphant return to power of the House of Howard after six years of political
exile. The duchess accompanied the Queen's litter in the procession from the Tower and carried her train in the Abbey.
During the service the duke, as Earl Marshal, was little less
important than Bishop Gardiner of Winchester who crowned
Queen Mary; but afterwards in Westminster Hall he was supreme,
for in addition to being Earl Marshal he had made good his claim
to serve as Lord High Steward of England at the Coronation
Banquet. In view of his advanced years and of his great duties
Norfolk was assisted both in the Abbey and in the Hall by his
fifteen-year-old-heir – an invaluable experience for young
Thomas which enabled him to act with such authority at Elizabeth's Coronation five years later. To Norfolk House, after the
ceremonies were over, went the customary perquisites; the
Queen's palfrey, with its rich hangings, the tablecloth from the
high table in the Hall and the cloth of estate.[10]

A new Parliament was summoned for 5th October, and it
required little active electioneering for East Anglia to send
Howard supporters to Westminster; there, for instance, as one
of the members for Norwich was Thomas Gawdy, serjeant-at-
arms. Early in the sessions a private act was introduced declaring
the supposed attainder of the third duke to be void by the common laws of the realm. He was restored to his titles and lands,
though provision was made in the act to safeguard the rights of
those who had been sold or leased certain of his properties under
Edward VI. During the debate in the Lords he agreed to abide
by the valuations of these properties (apparently they were worth
£926 a year) and of the arrangements for his compensation,
which were to be suggested by eight members of the Privy
Council. At the same time another private act was brought in 'for

the restitution in blood of Sir Thomas Howard, otherwise Thomas Howard, Earl of Surrey'. It was unquestioned that his father had been legally attainted, so he stood 'a person in blood corrupted'. In its final form the act restored the earldom of Surrey to him and his heirs; although he was empowered for the future to inheirt land and liberties, he was specifically debarred from claiming the properties which had become forfeit to the Crown on his father's execution.[11]

The Coronation over, the old duke decided that his grandsons must be taken in hand. He was grateful for the care with which his daughter of Richmond had discharged her duties towards them, while he was a state prisoner, and on this account left her £500 in his will; but the doctrines instilled in the boys at Reigate Castle were anathema to him, and on practical grounds made them ill-qualified for service at the court of a Catholic queen. Foxe's teaching of classical languages had been sound enough, and in this the boys had been fortunate, but the calculated heresy which they had been imbibing for five years must be eradicated before it was too late. Norfolk discussed the matter with Stephen Gardiner, who agreed that for the moment Thomas should join his household as a page. There is a tale that shortly before Foxe escaped to the continent he used to come 'by a back way' to Thomas Howard's rooms in the Bishop of Winchester's house in Southwark, to visit his old pupil. The bishop, informed of these visits by a false brother, might once or twice have instantly apprehended him, if the circumstances of person and place had not dissuaded'. Another version of the story has it that Gardiner when visiting Howard at Norfolk House found Foxe with him. On Foxe's withdrawal, the bishop asked who he was. 'My physician,' replied Howard, with a blush. 'I like his appearance', said Gardiner, 'and will on occasion employ him.' These stories, first written down a generation later, probably have some basis in fact: that Thomas under Gardiner's tutelage, continued to see something of his old master, who was recognised by the bishop and took the hint to leave England while he could. At any rate Foxe was soon safely in Flanders, while Howard had before long moved on to another episcopal household.[12]

Thomas, now joined by his brother, continued his instruction in the London house of John White, a priest as unbending in his devotion to papal principles as Bonner, or Gardiner himself. Like

Norfolk, White had been in the Tower in the late reign. He already occupied prebendal stalls at Lincoln and Winchester and under the new regime was marked out for high preferment. In March 1554 he was elected Bishop of Lincoln and within two years was to be translated to Winchester, as Gardiner's successor.

The Howard brothers passed bewilderingly from the extreme Protestantism of Foxe to the stern Romanism of the Counter Reformation. They heard their old preceptor denounced as a heretic and saw their new master preside at Ridley's trial. They exchanged the Second Prayer Book of Edward VI for the Roman Missal, forsook communion in both kinds, and learnt once more to regard the invocation of saints as a laudable, nay very necessary, practice. Images of the Virgin Mary and gorgeous vestments, censers and sanctus bells, returned to the whitewashed churches and chapels. The boys saw those who persisted in denying the doctrine of transubstantiation burn at Smithfield. They were themselves young enough to recant the errors of five summers without feeling that they were mere time-servers. Loyalty to the established order in church and state was second nature to them and they took it for granted that unquestioning acceptance of the tenets taught them by Bishop White and his chaplains would lead to freedom and advancement, while obstinate rejection might lead to imprisonment, and even death.

About this time the Countess of Surrey faded out of her children's lives by remarrying. Her husband was Thomas Steynings, a country gentleman from Earl Soham in Suffolk, where she now spent most of her time. The manor of Earl Soham was her own property, but the old duke had granted her for life nine manors, including Rising, worth £353 a year. Now and again she came to court, as a peeress in her own right, and in July 1554 was Queen Mary's representative at the christening of the French Ambassador's son. After Thomas had succeeded his grandfather it was suggested to Bishop Gardiner that Lady Surrey should 'have the ordering of her daughters, Ladies Jane and Margaret Howard', but they stayed on at Kenninghall. A more important duty fell to her in December 1557 when she acted as chief mourner at the funeral of her sister-in-law, the Duchess of Richmond. A great procession wound its way through the streets of Norwich to the cathedral: the dean and canons of Norwich, the mayor and aldermen of the city, the chief officers of the duke's household with white staves, Garter King of Arms and the heralds following the great Howard banner, and after the coffin the Countess, with her daughter Katherine bearing her train. The service over, the heralds rode with the small burial party to Framlingham, but Dowager Countess Frances returned with the mourners to the duke's palace for the funeral feast; but for the rashness of Surrey ten years back it would have been her palace. As chief mourner she sat in the hall under a cloth of estate of black velvet. Thus she discharged her debt to the woman who for five difficult years had acted as foster-mother to her own children; it was one of her last duties to the House of Howard. Six years later she acted as chief mourner once again; this time at the funeral of her son's second duchess, going through the same sombre ritual in the cathedral and the great hall of the palace. It was only a Howard death that brought her out of the shadows. Her second marriage proved happier than the first and she soon bore Thomas Steynings a son. She lived quietly in Suffolk, watching at a distance the fortunes of her five children by Surrey. She died at Earl Soham from an ague in 1574, almost, but not quite, forgotten.[13]

Howard was not to remain in Bishop White's household for many months, for his presence was needed at court. Even before Mary's Coronation there had been a rumour about his being sent on a diplomatic mission to the Emperor, but with the Queen's marriage he was now appointed one of the seven gentlemen of the chamber of her consort, Philip of Spain. As Earl of Surrey he was the senior in rank; he was heir to a dukedom but the other gentlemen were but sons of earls. They were all at Portsmouth to welcome their prince and, as the Spanish fleet approached, they set out in a boat to be introduced to Philip aboard his galleon by the Spanish ambassador. Five days later Thomas was present in Winchester Cathedral for the royal wedding, and throughout Philip's residence in England was expected to remain at court.[14]

At last on 25th August 1554, after six weeks of failing health, his grandfather died at Kenninghall in his eightieth year and Thomas succeeded to the title as fourth Duke of Norfolk and hereditary Earl Marshal of England.[15] In the past few months he had been gradually taking over the administration of the vast estates and now he was busy preparing for the burial at Framlingham and making suitable arrangements for the wardship of his sisters. Bassingbourne Gawdy rode post haste to London with

letters for Lord Chancellor Gardiner and returned as speedily as
he could to Norwich. The escheator of Norfolk held a formal
inquisition at the Shirehouse, Norwich to survey the great
Howard inheritance, of fifty-six manors, thirty-seven advowsons
and 'many other considerable estates', which passed for the present
into the hands of the Crown, as Thomas was still a minor. He in
due course would inherit the property, but under the terms of the
old duke's will his brother and sisters were to receive 1,000 marks
each on coming of age, or marriage. A last minute bequest of
£100 was made to Jane Goodman, a young girl living in Norfolk's
London house when he made the final changes to his will in the
previous July. She may have been a natural daughter; at any rate
she was still a member of the Howard household in 1571. Nothing
was left to his mistress, Elizabeth Holland, even though her father,
by now the duke's secretary, wrote out the will at Norfolk's
direction 'in his great chamber at Kenninghall' and sealed it with
the duke's signet, after reading it over to him. This important document was witnessed by no less than eight trusted servants headed
by Thomas Gawdy. The executors included the Lord Chancellor,
the Chief Justice of the Common Pleas, the Bishop of Worcester
and the Controller of the Queen's household. Queen Mary was herself appointed supervisor of the will and was bequeathed £100.[16]

A month after her grandfather's death Katherine Howard, the
younger of the sisters, married Henry, Lord Berkeley, at Kenninghall. This turned Norfolk's mind to matrimony, and six months
later he married Mary FitzAlan, daughter of Henry, Earl of
Arundel, who was Lord Steward of the royal household. This
alliance had been planned in the lifetime of the old Lord Treasurer, who was to have granted Thomas his home at Castleacre and
twelve other manors, producing an income of £240, but now
he had inherited the dukedom he could expect £2,489 a year,
once he was out of his minority. The bride was fifteen years old,
the bridegroom seventeen and as a ward of the Queen he had to
obtain her permission to marry. Theirs was the great social event
of the spring of 1555 – 'all the Council being busy' over Norfolk's
wedding, the business of government slowed to a standstill. To
enable him to support his bride a private Act was passed through
Parliament enabling him to sell and lease certain of his lands,
notwithstanding his minority, with the advice of the Lord Chancellor, the Bishop of Ely and his father-in-law. The wedding

probably took place in St Clement Dane's, the parish church of Arundel Place, the Lord Steward's town house, which had formerly been the London residence of the Bishops of Bath and Wells. No doubt Mary continued to reside with her family for a further year, until Norfolk brought her to his own mansion. After her marriage she continued her scholarly pursuits, garnering passages in verse and prose from Greek and Latin authors, which she wrote out in a singularly beautiful Italic hand.[17]

A portrait of Thomas painted at this time, now at Arundel Castle, shows a tall, handsome youth, arrogant in his stance and his expression. He appears every inch as Surrey's son, and were it not for the face and the fashion of the clothes one might imagine one were looking at a portrait of the poet as a youth. Thomas wears his plumed cap with a swagger and his left hand he places proudly on his hip. Here is the young courtier, in his fashionable Italianate dress, which emphasised his height. His face is oval, with a sensitive mouth and trusting eyes; and his youthful moustache and trim beard were auburn – they were to become much darker.

It had almost been a double wedding for in mid-April 1555 Mary's brother, Henry FitzAlan, married a young widow. The girl was, alas, a widow again before long. While on an embassy to the King of Bohemia young FitzAlan caught a fever and died in Brussels. His death without heirs, followed twenty years later by the death of his childless elder sister Jane, Lady Lumley, was to merge the Arundel earldom into the dukedom of Norfolk.[18]

In view of this later history it was fitting that Duchess Mary had chosen Arundel Place for her lying-in, where all was prepared for the arrival of an heir in June 1557. At this anxious time Norfolk had the misfortune to cause the death of a trusted servant, when he was out riding his black gelding from Newington to Tottenham. One of his retainers, Thomas Baynes, 'a man well liked by and in good repute with him, sported with him in a friendly and joking manner'. Suddenly, as the party was riding up Stamford Hill, the duke's horse foundered and as he went down Norfolk knocked his pistol on his saddle. The gun was loaded and Baynes was shot through the head at point-blank range. Norfolk's horse, thoroughly frightened, knocked its brains out. The coroner's inquest was held later the same day and in due course the duke was pardoned for manslaughter.[19]

Within a fortnight, on 28th June, his son was born and four days later was christened at Whitehall Palace, by Nicholas Heath, the Archbishop of York and Lord Chancellor. The two god-fathers, Philip of Spain, after whom the boy was named, and the Earl of Arundel, his grandfather, were present in person for the ceremony. The dowager Duchess of Norfolk, as his godmother, held her great-grandson over 'a font of gold, made of purpose and kept in the Treasury only for the christening of the princes of the realm'.[20]

But rejoicing soon gave way to bitter grief. The son so swiftly christened after delivery lived to become Earl of Arundel, but the mother never recovered from his birth. She lingered for eight weeks, but never left her bed at Arundel Place. On the anniversary of the day on which Norfolk had succeeded to the dukedom three years back, Duchess Mary died, a girl of seventeen. She was buried in St Clement Dane's church with full funeral pomp. Bonner, Bishop of London, and the last Abbot of Westminster together conducted the service, while the choir of St Paul's sang dirges. All the heralds were present for the interment of the Earl Marshal's wife, 'with many banners and banner rolls borne about her'. There had been eighty torches at her little son's christening, but there were twelve dozen in her funeral procession; what a difference from the funeral of Norfolk's second wife, six years later, when it was noted there was neither torch nor taper. Her sister, Lady Lumley, was chief mourner. Young Mary FitzAlan was by all accounts a sweet-natured and pious girl. 'All who knew her could not but love and esteem her much.' Her death was the second great tragedy in Norfolk's life.[21]

Norfolk remained a widower until the end of the reign. It was not a simple matter for the premier peer of England to find a suitable wife and when he made his choice there seemed endless legal difficulties. As is often the case of young widowers, he chose a young widow, Margaret, Lady Dudley, aged eighteen, whose husband had been killed at the Battle of St Quentin. She was the sole surviving child of Lord Audley (Henry VIII's Lord Chancellor) and consequently the heir to a rich inheritance. Of more immediate importance she was also a cousin of Norfolk's, and it was necessary to obtain a papal dispensation before the marriage could be contracted.

In the spring of 1558 Norfolk sent Nicholas Mynne, an East

Anglian lawyer, as his agent to Rome, but the Papacy was famed for its delays and its costs, where dispensations were concerned. First Mynne had to await the return of Cardinal Carafa from the Council of Trent, and it was not until 7th May that he was able to begin the suit. A month passed and still the dispensation was 'as nigh now as it was at the beginning'. The negotiations with the canon lawyers dragged on until the autumn and Queen Mary's death. With the accession of what he regarded as a heretic to the English throne, it was obvious that the Pope would not permit a relaxation of the church's law for so high a subject as the Earl Marshal.[22]

Norfolk's patience had been strained to the utmost. Gossip in some quarters had it that the Pope's obstinacy was really a blessing in disguise, for the Duke would now be free to marry another cousin – none other than the Queen herself. But rumour also had it that his father-in-law, Arundel, had a stronger candidature. The Duke, however, remained faithful to Margaret Dudley, and, casting doubts about the Book of Leviticus to the winds, he married her, very quietly at the end of November, 1558. His bride was nearly nineteen.[23] The following March the Duke obtained Parliamentary ratification of his marriage 'of long time prohibited and letted by reason of certain decrees and awards of the Pope's law'. Margaret brought as her marriage portion Cree Church Place, the mansion in Aldgate Ward, London, which her father had built on the site of Holy Trinity Priory. This was to be Norfolk's principal town house until in 1565 he purchased the Charterhouse, and it was soon being termed 'the Duke's Palace'.[24]

With a fresh marriage and a new reign, the last days of 1558 mark the end of a chapter in Norfolk's life. He was nearly twenty-one and had completed his apprenticeship at court. The coming Coronation, for which he was busily preparing during his first days with Margaret, would see him in his full grandeur as hereditary Earl Marshal of England. The first peer of the realm, he was connected by descent or alliance with the whole body of the ancient nobility; even the new Queen, as the child of his aunt. Anne Boleyn, was his cousin. Pre-eminent in degree and in wealth, 'the right high and mighty prince Thomas Duke of Norfolk', as he styled himself was singled out for high public service, and with unique opportunities for exercising power and influence both at court and in the country at large, all England lay before him.

Chapter Three

PREMIER PEER
1558-9

THE first few weeks of the new reign found Norfolk extremely busy. Within an hour of Mary's death at St James's on 17th November he was mustering his heralds for proclaiming Elizabeth Queen of England, France and Ireland at the Holbein Gate of Whitehall Palace. It was a peaceful accession: there was no seizure of power, as there had been on Henry VIII's death, no pretender to the throne as in 1553. The duke was too busy to ride out to Hatfield to pay his court to his sovereign, as so many were doing, but stayed in the capital with Lord Treasurer Winchester, Shrewsbury and Bedford, awaiting instructions.

In a day or so Winchester was sent a list of such nobles 'as Her Majesty thinks good to attend upon her to London', and on 23rd November, when she left Hatfield, the premier peer was at the head of 'a thousand and more lords, knights, gentlemen, ladies and gentlewomen', who formed her escort to the Charterhouse, the sumptuous house in Smithfield belonging to Lord North which had until recently been the Carthusian Monastery. Five days later Norfolk waited on his horse in the courtyard of the Charterhouse to take his place in the royal cavalcade to the Tower, and as the only duke of the realm he took precedence immediately below the Queen.[1] Within six years he was to purchase this mansion, fit for a queen, from North's executors.

Those were exciting days for Norfolk. He had had no time for a honeymoon after his marriage to Margaret Dudley, for he commanded all the pomp and pageantry which heralds brought to state occasions. But first he had to attend to Mary's obsequies. Her body lay in state in the Chapel Royal until 13th December when it was brought to Westminster Abbey. Over her coffin was a painted effigy, crowned and bearing a sceptre. Beside the hearse was a guard of honour bearing torch staves and behind it walked one hundred poor men in black gowns. The late queen's personal standards were in evidence: the Falcon and Hart, the Lion and Falcon, and the White Greyhound, while the officers of arms bore her crests, mantles and shields. Next day a requiem mass was sung in the Abbey.[2]

Elizabeth had asked Dr John Dee to choose an auspicious date for her Coronation and the astrologer had selected Sunday 15th January, which gave Norfolk and the other officials little time for making arrangements. In preparation for the Coronation the heralds and pursuivants were brought up to strength by creations first at Somerset House and then, on 13th January, at Norfolk's own house. The Queen, who was then once more residing in the Tower, drove down to Cree Church Place, Aldgate for creating John Cook as Lancaster Herald. Seven commissioners had been appointed for sitting as a coronation court to hear and determine all claims to service at the crowning in the Abbey and at the banquet in Westminster Hall which followed. The Earl Marshal, following the precedent of his grandfather in 1553, stood down from the commission, as he had a claim to make himself. He appeared before the commissioners in the Star Chamber, just before Christmas, to claim the office of Chief Butler of England at the Banquet, by virtue of his tenure of the manors of Kenninghall, Buckenham and Wymondham, which was fully admitted.[3]

Elizabeth's Coronation was, in fact, to be even more of a Howard family affair than Queen Mary's. Norfolk's father-in-law, Arundel, was appointed Lord High Steward of England for Coronation Day, from sunrise to sunset, and was also to serve as Lord Great Chamberlain on the previous day, with power to create thirty Knights of the Bath. The duke's great uncle, Lord Howard of Effingham, had already been confirmed in his appointment as Chamberlain of the royal household. In the long procession from the Tower to Westminster on the Saturday, with many halts for formal speeches and informal acclaim, Margaret, the new Duchess of Norfolk, rode side by side with the Duchess of Lennox. These two were the principal ladies of honour and, as such, their white palfreys with gorgeous red side-saddles trotted immediately behind Lord Robert Dudley, the Master of the Horse, who followed the Queen's chariot.

On Coronation Day itself Norfolk walked in the great procession from Westminster Hall to the Abbey in front of the Queen, bearing St Edward's Crown. A few paces behind was his duchess, who carried Elizabeth's train. A splendid blue carpet had been provided at a cost of £145 to cover the route from the upper end of the Hall to the choir door of the Abbey, but 'as Her Majesty passed the cloth was cut by those who could get it'; the intrepid souvenir-hunters who braved the cold early morning air to get their fill of pageantry, nearly tripped up Duchess Margaret as she walked behind her sovereign.[4]

The problem of finding a bishop to crown Elizabeth had been difficult since, apart from the archbishopric of Canterbury, no less than eight sees were vacant. Of the remainder White of Winchester had been confined to his house by royal command for his sermon at Cardinal Pole's funeral. Eventually Owen Oglethorpe, Bishop of Carlisle, was appointed to perform the ceremony as suffragan of Heath of York. The Queen had an especial enmity towards Bonner of London and with a touch of irony she had ordered him to lend his richest vestments to Oglethorpe. After the customary annointing and investiture the bishop placed St Edward's Crown on her head to the sound of fanfares and then made his own homage to her. Norfolk followed him, as the first of the lords temporal; he knelt before her and with a kiss on her left cheek promised to become her liege man 'of life and limb and of earthly worship'. Significantly Elizabeth had made the other twelve bishops present, who had each refused to crown her, wait until after the lords temporal had finished before making their homage.[5]

While the procession was reforming ready to file slowly out of the great West Door, Norfolk and Arundel were busy in Westminster Hall seeing that all was prepared for the banquet. As Chief Butler the duke was particularly concerned about the wine to be served. Together they excluded many interlopers, inspected the kitchens as well as the tables, and then changed from their Coronation robes of velvet crimson and ermine into 'short capes according to the Spanish fashion'; Arundel's was of cloth of gold, Norfolk's of silver tissue lined with sables. As the guests entered the Hall they were seated according to strict precedence, and 'all was performed under the directions of the officers of the college of arms'. The duke and his father-in-law 'went about their victuals' before anyone else had begun to eat, to be ready for further ceremonial when the Queen, now in violet velvet, sat down at the high table a little after three p.m.

The Earl Marshal and High Steward now mounted their chargers. Norfolk's was covered 'with white lions rampant'. He was bare-headed and carried a silver staff to indicate his office. They rode into the Hall amidst the cheers and fanfares to announce each course and also to present the Champion, Sir Edward Dymoke 'who rode in full armour and threw down his gauntlet, ready to do battle against anyone who might dispute the Queen's legal right to her crown'. The celebrations lasted till one in the morning. An Italian who was present thought all the ceremonial was splendid, in contrast to the music, which 'not being remarkable, and having heard better, I will say nothing about it'. Norfolk and his heralds had clearly rehearsed their difficult parts very carefully and the court was to see more of his superb horsemanship within the next few days.[6]

There was to have been a joust in the tiltyard at Whitehall on the Monday, but as the Queen was still very weary from the ordeals of Coronation Day it was postponed until the Tuesday, when Norfolk, Lord Robert Dudley and Sir George Howard were the challengers. They had 'as many hits as the adventurers and the judges therefore could not award the prize which, as they jousted for love, was a diamond'.

The festivities following the Coronation, with banquets, masques, dancing and other entertainments arranged at court by the Master of the Revels, provided the duke and duchess with a honeymoon. After the gloomy months of the end of Mary's reign life at court seemed one long party – so much so that a Mantuan visitor lifted a reproving finger at 'the levities and moral licentiousness practised at the court in dances and banquets'. One night, he reported, a double mummery was played, when 'one set of mummers rifled the Queen's ladies and the other set, with wooden swords and bucklers, recovered the spoil'. In the dance which followed Elizabeth chose Norfolk, clad in 'superb array' as her partner. Now that the Coronation was over he could relax, for he was not as yet a member of the Privy Council, and he attended the opening of Parliament on 25th January to discharge his duties as Earl Marshal rather than to take an active part in the discussions in the Lords while the Elizabethan settlement in Church and State was being forged.[7]

He had wanted to take his bride to Kenninghall, but his attendance was still needed at court, sometimes to accompany the Queen to hear a sermon at Paul's Cross, sometimes to entertain a foreign envoy. On 23rd May, for instance, Norfolk had welcomed the French embassy, led by Montmorency, which had come to settle the terms of peace. The Frenchmen had come to the Tower from Gravesend by barge and here Norfolk escorted them to Whitehall, where there was a banquet in their honour in a temporary banquetting hall under the long gallery, 'closed in with wreaths of flowers'. The Duchess of Norfolk was also in attendance and enjoyed the dancing which lasted till late in the evening. In recognition of his services, Elizabeth elected the duke a Knight of the Garter on St George's Day at Whitehall. As that day was a Sunday the St George's Feast was postponed until 6th June when Norfolk and the other new knights, Dudley, Northampton and Rutland, were installed at Windsor by the Earl of Pembroke, as Her Majesty's deputy, and the communion service in the chapel on that day was for the first time celebrated in English. After a few further days at court the duke was at last free to go into the country where he stayed until the autumn.[8]

*   *   *

It was not only as England's sole duke that Howard was first subject in the land. The authority which he exercised as Earl Marshal gave him exceptional power and prestige quite independent of his peerage title. It was much more than the performance of his ceremonial duties at coronations, tournaments and other state occasions, for which his annual fee of £123 14s. might have seemed a gross over-payment. To his officers at the College of Arms belonged the right to decide which arms a newly created peer should bear and by what title he should be known; even a Leicester or a Hunsdon had to abide by their decisions and pay for their advice. The presence of a herald was essential at any peer's marriage or burial and the High Court of Chivalry, in which the Earl Marshal pronounced judgment in armorial disputes, was no empty title, but a powerful tribunal. The regular visitations of the counties by the provincial Kings of Arms, or their deputies, to determine claims to bear arms, to register titles, investigate descents and pronounce on pedigrees made old aristocracy and new gentry alike conscious of my Lord Grace's close control on progress from one rung of the social ladder to another.

The College of Arms, as founded by Richard III, had fallen on evil days. Old Lord Treasurer Norfolk, burdened with other duties, had given little attention to the work of the heralds, who, left to their own devices, had bickered amongst themselves, struggling for position like a chapter with a non-resident dean. As a result, the authority of the College as a whole had suffered. To add to the difficulties the library in the heralds' office at Coldharbour, down by the River Thames, had suffered the same fate as so many collections of manuscripts and records in the decade of the Dissolution. In 1530 a violent dispute had broken out between Garter and his provincial kings, Clarenceux and Norroy, over the former's claim to make visitations. Henry VIII had then issued a commission putting the whole machinery of visitations on a new basis, yet Garter had refused to obey and the conflict of authority continued. Litigation about this was to drag on into the reign of Elizabeth. In the face of these internal troubles the system of regular visitations of each county failed to take root.

The fourth duke secured a new royal charter of incorporation for the College in 1555 which brought the heralds a permanent home at Derby House, a site which they have occupied ever since, though the original buildings were destroyed in the Great Fire. But it was Howard rather than Queen Mary who was (in the present Garter's words) the 'real second founder of the College', for the new charter was only the first step in a considerable reform of the college, which he undertook so his officers might be in a position to discharge their duties effectively. In particular he set in motion the regular progresses of Clarenceux and Norroy into the counties, which were to endure until the Revolution of 1688. In each county warrants would go out to the bailiffs of every hundred requiring them to summon 'the gentlemen and others' named in accompanying lists to appear before the heralds on a certain day with their arms, descents and evidences. While Norfolk was Earl Marshal the first complete cycle of visitation of the southern province was made and much of the northern province was systematically covered. During the 1560's there were visitations of no fewer than twenty-five counties, including Norfolk, in 1563, by William Harvey. The most difficult counties were Yorkshire, visited by William Flower, Norroy, in 1563-4, and London, undertaken by Robert Cooke, Clarenceux, in 1568.[9]

The duke's reforms of the administration of the Heralds' College were embodied in his constitutions of 'the ancient manner and order of officers of arms', of which the following points are of especial interest. The supremacy of Garter was established beyond question; he was to preside at chapter meetings and to be responsible to the Earl Marshal. The three Kings of Arms, six heralds and four pursuivants were to decide in full chapter how the accommodation at Derby House was to be assigned, though one room, Norfolk insisted, was sacrosanct. The lower room, on the south side of the gate, where the records were kept must remain as 'a library or office for the safe custody and preservation of the records'. Nothing was to be removed from this library unless all three Kings of Arms had given their consent, though Clarenceux and Norroy might take with them on their visitations such records as they needed, provided they returned them to the library without fail at the end of a visitation.

Visitors who came to use the library were to be supervised and a roster of duties was to be drawn up, so that one month the senior herald and the senior pursuivant were on duty together, the second month the next herald and pursuivant in seniority, and so on. This concern of Norfolk's for the College's records is as remarkable as it was important. The sixteenth century has a poor reputation for the preservation of public records. The muniments of many monasteries had been carted off as waste parchment and Leland has left a pitiful account of priceless documents lying in the gutters of the High at Oxford. It was not until the early years of the next century that a State Paper Office was established. Hitherto, as we have seen, many valuable evidences belonging to the College had been lost through negligence by heralds taking documents to their homes, but Norfolk as a great landowner knew the importance of records remaining in proper custody, and it was fundamental that these evidences should remain on record if the system of registering arms and pedigrees, by visitations and by personal application to Derby House, was to be effective. Thanks to his orders the duke may be regarded as the founder of genealogical research in England.

The respective provinces of Clarenceux and Norroy, for long a thorny problem, were clearly defined once and for all. In recent years there had been too many disputes about which officers were to attend the funerals of particular peers, spiritual and temporal, but Norfolk's constitutions laid down precisely the procedure to be followed for peers of each degree. Moreover the executor of every individual who had borne arms was to furnish a death certificate to the heralds. All search fees were to be paid into a common chest which was to be distributed among the officers each month according to a scale proportionate to the seniority of each, 'as the Prince's largesse is done'. No herald or pursuivant was to declare any pedigree or to issue any arms or crest without the permission of one of the Kings of Arms. In all their work, the Earl Marshal insisted, the highest standards of scholarship were to be maintained, and chapters were to be held regularly at which debatable points of heraldry were to be discussed. As a result of these reforms there was a new spirit abroad in the College, even when the duke was in the country, and when Clarenceux, Norroy and their deputies visited the counties they carried with them the Earl Marshal's enhanced authority.[10]

★   ★   ★

Norfolk was proud to show Margaret the glories of Kenninghall. Brought up at Cree Church Place and Audley End, she was used to spacious rooms filled with lovely things, but the riches of Kenninghall seemed on a different plane. Even though the house had been ransacked in 1547 much had been recovered on the third duke's restoration and his grandson had been steadily acquiring precious objects. At this time his latest acquisition was a group of gold pictorial tablets which the dowager duchess had bequeathed him; they included one of Christ with the Apostles, one of the Battle of Pavia, and a third 'with a naked woman painted therein, being a Mirror of Death'. The Long Gallery really became a portrait gallery with a series of pictures chiefly of foreign royalty. There was Louis XI, Francis I and Charles IX of France, Ferdinand of Spain, the Queen of Hungary and the Count of Nassau; the only English sovereign in the gallery was Richard III, who had brought the dukedom to the House of Howard, looking down from 'a little picture'. But a portrait of the third duke, 'with a curtain of silk to hang before the same', had pride of place and next to it was the poet Surrey. Among the pictures in other parts of the house were a painting of 'Lucretia' and 'A Woman with a Child in her Arms'. Most of these items can still be identified in the collection at Arundel Castle.

Howard had enriched other state rooms since the old Lord Treasurer's death with various new tapestry hangings. One series of eight was devoted to scenes in the lives of David and Saul, another series depicted Jonah, while there were hangings commemorating philosophers as well as warriors, Greek gods as well as English country sports. As befitted the home of the Earl Marshal, some of the walls were decorated with painted shields, standards, the Queen's arms, St George's crosses and a 'rich arras from the Hall of the Coronation, of Our Lady and some of the Apostles'. Most curious of all was a map of the world in an eagle, set in a wainscot frame.

Kenninghall was the first house in England to boast a room actually called a bathroom, where there were 'twelve pieces of copper, great and small, to bathe in', and the walls were hung, apparently, with a tapestry of ladies bathing and playing instruments. Norfolk could afford to be prodigal in his purchases of Turkey carpets from Antwerp, which the Queen allowed him to import duty-free, and these were rapidly replacing the coarser 'English carpet work'.

It was a musical household. There were sets of viols, lutes and zithers, flutes, a shawm, three pairs of virginals and a regal, or portable reed organ. Thanks to the chapel there was a resident professional choir. Apart from service books, anthems and 'other books where certain songs be double-pricked', there were collections of songs, 'singing songs and ditties', some for five, some for eight voices, carols, and music for dancing the pavan and the galliard.

The Chapel was not so very different from the days of Norfolk's youth, yet the parish church, two miles away, had lost many of its treasures, including some glass, during the high tide of Protestantism under Edward VI. Duchess Margaret took a personal interest in the church and felt it needed embellishing. As a result the duke provided a number of stained-glass windows depicting the arms of the Howard and Audley families. A few years later he began rebuilding the tower, but never completed the work. It remains a squat structure, 'its head being shortened by the misfortune of its founder'.[11]

His palace at Norwich was, in a way, even more remarkable. A century later it was still the greatest mansion to be found outside London and Westminster, and in the duke's day it boasted as fine a collection of tapestries as were to be found in private hands. There were series devoted to Abraham, to Solomon, to Massinissa and, most splendid of all, the 'eight fair pieces of hanging of the History of Pyramus and Thisbe', a tale of Ovid's popularised by sixteenth-century writers long before Shakespeare made a burlesque of it. For some reason here, as also at Kenninghall, was a picture of King Peppin. In the presses in the Council Chamber were Norfolk's Latin books; his Italian books he kept in the closet at the end of the gallery. Much of the furniture for his own rooms was new, and he was particularly fond of walnut, even for chessmen. Of the buildings themselves (which are described in a later chapter)* two amenities are worth special notice – the bowling alley and the playhouse. The bowling-alley was the first of its kind and since it measured 180 feet by 26 feet, was easily the biggest in England; the tennis court was later to lend point to one of Norfolk's most famous *dicta*. The playhouse showed Norfolk's keen interest in the drama.[12]

As a patron of the drama in the formative years linking the medieval mystery play with the Elizabethan theatre, the duke played a prominent role. His grandfather had supported a dramatic company which gave occasional performances at Norwich and Thetford, but it was the example of his uncle, John de Vere, Earl of Oxford, that encouraged him to revive his patronage. In 1555 the Earl's players began regular tours of the provinces. Next year the duke's newly-formed company played in Norwich and soon we hear of their performances in Cambridge and Ipswich, and then further afield, in Exeter and Bristol. By Queen Elizabeth's accession the Duke of Norfolk's Players had become one of the four principal dramatic companies. Howard later had under his patronage a bearward, who went the rounds of the larger towns baiting his bears. As in most great households, the choristers at Kenninghall and Norwich would act simple plays in the great hall on red-letter days, while host and guests were digesting their feast, and the boys also performed when the Duke entertained the Norwich City fathers at Christmas. A list of clothes for masks and interludes mentions 'five toppened hats of slight cloth of gold

* Below, pp. 68-70.

and cloth of silver, with tassels of crimson silk and gold in the tops of them'; a Prologue's cap; visers; 'caps and faces' of cats and white foxes, and jerkins with checkered satin sleeves. The robes for the Lord of Misrule and his train – red coats and caps and toy wooden halberds – were kept in a special chest in the wardrobe at Kenninghall.[13]

During that summer the Norfolks stayed for a while at Audley End, on the outskirts of Saffron Walden, the home of the duchess's widowed mother, Elizabeth Lady Audley. In summer weather, when the roads were firm, they could ride over from Audley to Kenninghall in a day. Margaret was often to stay with her mother and it was Audley which she was to choose for the birth of her eldest child in August 1561 – Thomas, who would become Lord Howard de Walden and, like his great grandfather, another Lord Treasurer of England who would spend a fortune in rebuilding his birthplace.

Occasional residence at Audley suited Norfolk, for from there (as Charles II was to find a century later) he could easily visit Cambridge, a town very much under his protection. Three days after his grandfather's death, Howard had written to Cambridge University, asking that he might succeed him as high steward ; but he was too late, as the post had already been offered to Lord Paget, who had deputised for the third duke when he was in the Tower. Later in 1554 the burgesses of Cambridge, anxious for a powerful patron, appointed Howard as high steward of their town – a typical way, too, of town cocking a snook at gown. The new high steward was disappointed when he tried to foist a Parliamentary candidate of his own on the borough in 1557, since the burgesses declared Sir Nicholas L'Estrange, chamberlain of the ducal household, ineligible under an ordinance a century old, which provided that the town's member must be a resident. The duke was more fortunate in his high stewardships at King's Lynn and Great Yarmouth, as we shall notice later. Meanwhile he nursed Cambridge, by personal visits and by watching over the town's interests at court, while the burgesses dutifully sent him the customary offerings of freshwater fish, marchpane and hippocras. He was to remain high steward until 1569. A benefactor of Magdalene College, he was to arrange for his sons to attend the University after his death.[14]

After an absence of eight months in London there was a great deal of domestic administration for Norfolk to oversee, problems of his estates to settle, and improvements to his properties to plan. His position in the county involved considerable entertaining. There were, too, matters of local government for him to attend to as we shall see in a later chapter, and he was soon immersed in the training of the militia, the condition of Yarmouth harbour, and the state of the Norwich clothing industry. Inevitably he was out of touch with wider political events. The London post came to Kenninghall via Newmarket and Thetford and took between three days and a week; but it was fitful. Important letters from court came by special messenger, and the duke's agent in London would sometimes send one of his staff with important information. A breakdown in postal communications today through a strike, enables us to appreciate the difficulties with which a courtier of Elizabethan days, on leave from court, was constantly troubled. At the end of August 1559 Norfolk heard of the Queen's recovery, but until then he had been quite ignorant of the fact that she had been ill. He penned a letter to Cecil, saying how glad he was to learn Her Majesty was better, and told him of the 'quiet state of our country here, which at this day is in as good order and obedience as at any time heretofore'.[15]

Another letter of that autumn was more cheerful. His old tutor John Foxe, after cautiously waiting to see the shape of Elizabeth's religious policy, had landed in England. He sent a copy of the first part of his *Church History*, which was published in Basle in September. This was the English section of a great European history of ecclesiastical affairs which he had planned to write, and was dedicated to the duke, 'all powerful and pious . . . my Maecenas'. It brought tears of joy to Norfolk's eyes. He wrote to Foxe, who was in London in great poverty, and as their letters crossed he wrote again: 'To my right loving schoolmaster John Foxe.'

> *I have received your letter, my excellent master, from which I learn your affection for me, which is very acceptable. If my servants had not returned before my letters were ready you would already have been on your way. For I wrote to them they should so provide you with all things that you might speedily come to me, which would have so happened, had they not returned more quickly than I expected. But now, since I shall be in London shortly, I wish you to*

await me there, when, as I desire and am bound to, I will look to
you. In the meantime I bid you farewell, from my house at Ken-
ninghall, 30th October 1559.

Out of deference to Foxe, Norfolk had written in Latin, though
he later admitted he had not penned a Latin epistle for five years.
For the rest room was found for Foxe and his family in Christ
Church, Aldgate, and once he was settled, the scholar began to
collect material for his martyrology. Deprivation and exile had
seriously affected his health and in the following spring Norfolk
invited him to stay in the country and later found a niche for him
in Norwich.

Perhaps, too, John Capon and the other bond tenants of the
duke at Framlingham who had fled to distant parts during the
religious persecution of Mary's reign, had returned home.[16]

Whenever the duke left Norfolk for the capital a 'worthy
company' travelled with him. The Queen had licensed him to
retain a hundred men in his service, in addition to members of
his household staff and officials of the College of Arms, notwithstanding the Act against Retainers. Five miles outside London
he would be met by heralds, who escorted their master with due
pomp on the last stage of the journey. To watch the duke's
entourage go by was one of the sights of the season. The duke's
year followed a regular pattern: to London every autumn, returning to Norfolk for Christmas, setting out again for court
towards the end of January and back again to his county for the
high summer. In the villages through which he passed labourers
stopped work to cheer his procession; for they dearly loved any
lord, but Norfolk was their premier peer. Even in London where
pageantry was a commonplace of Tudor life, the duke's arrivals
and departures in state attracted much attention. Foreign envoys
and London diarists never failed to note his coming with his
duchess to Aldgate 'with a hundred horse in his livery' and all in
velvet coats.[17]

The duke and his duchess returned to London in the autumn
of 1559 to find the Queen seemingly infatuated with Lord Robert
Dudley. Idle gossips elaborated stories to the discredit of both and
even so staid a man as Bishop Jewel told a friend that Elizabeth
would reject the suits for her hand being made by foreign princes
as she was 'probably thinking of an alliance nearer home'. During

Norfolk's absence from court the favourite had gone from strength to strength and he was alarmed at what he heard and saw on his return. He was quite outspoken on the subject of Dudley in his conversations with fellow courtiers. He found his friend Sussex equally perturbed, the other peers bewildered, while Cecil seemed out of his depth and, for once, quite unable to influence the Queen.

At first sight everything had pointed to friendship between Norfolk and Dudley. From Elizabeth's accession the Earl Marshal and the Master of the Horse were together a great deal, presiding at state occasions and welcoming foreign envoys in the Queen's name. Both were elected to the Garter on the same day. There was a family connection, too, for Norfolk's second duchess, Margaret, was the widow of Lord Henry Dudley, Robert's brother, and Robert's own wife had come from Wymondham, a few miles from Kenninghall. But wives counted for little when their husbands' dispositions were so different. Norfolk soon came to regard Lord Robert Dudley with the same haughty disdain with which his own father had in his day regarded Edward Seymour and John Dudley, Lord Robert's father, as newcomers to the ranks of the peerage, with whom it was as well for a Howard to be rather distant. Norfolk felt sure that Lord Robert was playing a dark game and he wanted no part in it. Dudley, in his turn, reciprocated this suspicion. The ill-feeling between the two was nicely captured years afterwards, in that strange work *Leicester's Commonwealth*, where one of the characters heard from a servant of Norfolk's reports of 'strange things from the duke's own mouth, of my Lord of Leicester's most *troublous* dealing towards him, for gaining of his blood' and of Lord Dudley's utter contempt for 'the ancient nobility' in general.

As Lord Robert rose in eminence he interfered in East Anglian affairs. It was through his influence that John Appleyard, Amy Robsart's half-brother, was appointed high sheriff of Norfolk and Suffolk in the autumn of 1559 in place of Norfolk's candidate, and this poaching on his preserve was a snub which the duke was slow to forget. Appelyard's sister had married a Flowerdew of Wymondham and when Dudley appointed him his steward the duke had the uneasy feeling that all kinds of local gossip, true and false, about the inmates of Kenninghall were eventually served up at Cumnor Place and Leicester House.[18]

There was another matter than rankled. In August the tax
collectors, two hard-headed London merchants, demanded £160
from Norfolk as his first instalment of the Parliamentary subsidy.
All peers had been individually assessed by Lord Keeper Bacon,
Lord Treasurer Winchester and Arundel on the value of their
personal estate. With two exceptions the duke had to pay more
heavily than anyone else in the Kingdom, but Dudley managed
to wriggle out of paying a single penny. He was not even assessed
for the tax but produced a writ of discharge from the Queen.
Possibly Lord Robert openly boasted of his good fortune; at any
rate Norfolk heard about it from his father-in-law. This made the
duke decide against paying his dues until he was really pressed.[19]

Alvarez de Quadra, Bishop of Aquila, who was Spanish
Ambassador until 1564, was extremely well informed about events
at court, though he was somewhat given to exaggeration in his
reports home. It is from his pen that we first hear of the growing
enmity between Norfolk and Dudley at the end of October 1559.
De Quadra soon caught wind of the duke's anxiety in his conversations with others and found an opportunity to talk matters
over with him. On 29th October he told the Duchess of Parma
in the Netherlands that: 'A plot was made the other day to murder
Lord Robert and it is now common talk and threat. The plot was
headed by the Duke of Norfolk, the Earl of [Sussex] and all the
principal adherents of the scheme for marrying the Queen to the
Archduke. The Queen and Lord Robert are very uneasy about
the Duke of Norfolk as he talks openly about her lightness and
bad government. People are ashamed of what is going on, and
particularly the duke, as he is Lord Robert's enemy. The Duke
is a great friend of ours.'[20]

That murder was contemplated is out of the question; probably
the 'plot' was no more than an ill-defined scheme for taking Lord
Robert down a peg or two – at the least that they should press
him to support the Archduke's candidature. But Norfolk must
have been extremely angry when he discussed Dudley and his
pretensions with the Ambassador, for the latter to have written
as he did. What De Quadra wrote to Philip II a fortnight later is
probably what he should more accurately have written to the
Duchess of Parma: 'The Duke of Norfolk is the chief of Lord
Robert's enemies, who are all the principal people in the Kingdom and that he had said that if Lord Robert did not abandon his

present pretensions and presumptions, he would not die in his bed ... I think his hatred of Lord Robert will continue, as the Duke and the rest of them cannot put up with his being King.'

Norfolk made it his business to talk to Dudley on this delicate subject as Christmas approached, before he left the court for Kenninghall. He 'spoke out so plainly', advocating Elizabeth's marriage with the Archduke Charles that 'they separated abruptly and Lord Robert told him he was neither a good Englishman nor a loyal subject who advised the Queen to marry a foreigner. Things are very strained between them', continued De Quadra, 'and the duke has gone home in dudgeon . . . ' Not even Norfolk felt he dare take the matter further by tackling the Queen. He hoped that by January, when he expected to be in London again, the Queen's infatuation would have passed. As it happened he never left London for Kenninghall that Christmas, as a result of critical developments over Scottish relations. Undoubtedly the duke had embarrassed Dudley by his unrelenting opposition and it is hard to resist the conclusion that he was appointed Lieutenant General in the North, on Christmas Day, to get him as far away from court as possible.[21]

Chapter Four

THE AFFAIR OF SCOTLAND
1559-60

WHEN news of Mary's death reached France, four days after Elizabeth's accession, Henry II had proclaimed his daughter-in-law as Queen of England and Ireland. Mary Queen of Scotland and of the Isles and Dauphine of France had soon begun to quarter the royal arms of England on her own, at first privately, later in public. Within a month of England signing peace with France and with Scotland in the spring of 1559 the Dauphin's heralds were wearing the arms of England for all the world to see, and when Throgmorton, the ambassador in Paris, complained about this to the Constable of France, the great man shrugged his shoulders. He knew nothing about it, he said, as at the time of Mary's marriage to Francis he had been in prison, and in any case the ambassador must not forget that Queen Elizabeth still styled herself Queen of France and quartered the fleur-de-lis on her arms.

An escutcheon of Mary's offending arms was brought over from France in June, a month before the Dauphin succeeded to the throne as Francis II and it was passed to Norfolk, as Earl Marshal, for examination. He consulted Garter and the other officers at the Heralds' College who shortly reported that they had 'perused this escutcheon of arms delivered by your Grace and we find the same prejudicial unto the Queen's Majesty, her state and dignity'. Despite the line of succession through her grandmother, Margaret Tudor, as a collateral heir Mary Queen of Scots 'cannot nor ought not to bear any escutcheon of the arms of England'. To clinch the matter the heralds found the escutcheon 'falsely marshalled, contrary to all law and order of arms'.

Strange that Norfolk should first have dealings with Mary, then seventeen years old, on a technical point of high heraldry. Her claims were also translated into verse:

> The arms of Mary Queen Dauphine of France
> The noblest Lady in earth, for till advance
> Of Scotland Queen and England, also
> Of Ireland, as God hath provided so.

Within ten years he and she were to be attempting a marriage which would aim at fulfilling the prophecy of those lines.[1]

The sudden death of Henry II on 10th July made Elizabeth's position even more critical. Francis II and his wife were puppets controlled by the Guises, who were bent on re-establishing Mary's power in Scotland and on supporting as effectively as they could her claims to the crown of England. Never had the 'Auld Alliance' presented so alarming a situation, as when Henry of Guise and the Cardinal of Lorraine ruled France while their sister Mary was Regent in Scotland. Better, thought Cecil, to oppose the French over the border than delay until they became strong enough to invade England. As a first step Sir Ralph Sadler was sent north with £3,000 to wean the Protestant lords from Mary of Guise. Other money followed. To avoid open trouble with France all was done with such secrecy that even the English coins were changed into French crowns. Meanwhile reports came from Paris of great preparations for pouring French troops and munitions into Scotland. And then, in October, the Lords of the Congregation, inspired by John Knox, deposed the Regent, at Edinburgh's market cross. For the moment she shut herself in Leith, yet the Scots, divided, disorganised and short of supplies, were powerless to expel the French troops. Though it was 'against God's law to aid any subjects against their natural princes', Elizabeth was persuaded that in self-defence she must send an army to the border, and she was hopeful that its presence might decisively influence the course of events in Scotland, without a shot being fired and her own neutrality prejudiced.

When the command of this army was first offered him on 15th December the duke would have liked to have declined it. He felt very strongly that the war was an unnecessary one and told Cecil and Bedford as much. They replied that there was no alternative left and that 'if peace could be had otherwise they would sue for it on their knees', yet Norfolk still held to his opinion. Later in the day Elizabeth sent for him and (according to what he told the Spanish ambassador over supper) entreated him not to desert her in her danger. Howard reiterated that a far better course than meddling in Scotland would be for Her Majesty to marry the Archduke Charles; if she would only do this she should find Philip of Spain would help her out of her difficulties with the French. Norfolk knew that the Privy Council were divided over the Scottish question and he also sensed that his cousin was herself wavering, as she so often wavered. Nonetheless he had to stay at court instead of keeping Christmas in the country.

For another ten days the matter was discussed from every angle until Cecil had brought the Council to accept his policy, and in the end Norfolk came to realise that he had no alternative but to accept the command with a good grace. A week or so later he was to remind Cecil that he had learnt the principal lesson of life at court when still a youth: 'never at the Prince's hands to seek charge nor never to refuse which it shall please him to command me.' On Christmas Day 1559 he was appointed Lieutenant General 'of all the north from the Trent northward'. Unknown to him that very day two detachments of the Regent's troops under D'Oysel had driven the Protestant Lords from Stirling. There was no chance now of the duke being in Newcastle by New Year's Eve, but he arrived there a week later.[2]

The duke, with Berwick-on-Tweed as his headquarters, was to assemble an army of 4,000 men on the border, ready for action. The command of the army in the field was to be given to Lord Grey of Wilton, who was in general to be subordinate to Norfolk. The Queen's revised instructions were far less militant than those sent by Cecil. He was to aid the Scots 'as might serve their turn to expel the French *and yet not* to have any open hostility shewed on our part' – at least not for a month or two to come. This secret aid in trained captains, guns, powder and money, was to be sent very largely by sea and until Admiral Winter's fleet arrived Norfolk was to borrow such money as he could from the merchants of Newcastle.[3]

Howard had never been so far afield. Though he owned isolated lands in Shropshire and Devon and even a small coalfield in South Wales, his principal properties were concentrated in

East Anglia, Sussex and London, and he had rarely been further from Kenninghall than the capital and the Home Counties. Scotland was to be the only foreign country which he ever visited. His journey north was, in consequence, something of an education. The character of the north country in wealth, population, social structure and political outlook, no less than its physical geography, was so very different from the duke's East Anglia or the regions of southern England which he had visited. This was the feudal, Catholic, 'inly-working North' of the ballads, with its own loyalties, traditions, almost its own code of law. He noted that the country beyond York was 'far out of order in matters of religion, and the altars standing still in the churches' and hoped that Cecil would instruct the Dean of Durham 'to see these things reformed in such sort as shall answer to the advancement of God's true religion'. And as Norfolk reached the Scottish Marches and the domains of Percy, Neville and Dacre, the contrast with the south which he had left behind was at its greatest; this was, indeed, a different world. Had he not travelled thither in the first week of 1560 it is unlikely that his sister would have married a Neville or he himself a Dacre; and in less than a decade his own political strength was to lay in this territory which he now viewed as a stranger.[4]

His own county furnished 1,650 men and these included some of his own retainers. His Norfolk neighbours did not hesitate to answer his call to arms; Sir William Buttes, Thomas Drury, Henry Knyvett and Francis Woodhouse were all serving as captains of foot in Grey's army, and Thomas Gawdy was captain of 100 demi-lancers. The controller of the duke's household, Thomas Timperley, and two of his stewards, William Cantrell and Peter Bannister, took the field with their master.[5]

Admiral Winter's arrival was the one gleam of hope in a cold, gloomy month. Encouraged by the duke, he sailed on from Berwick to the Firth of Forth and took the French quite by surprise. They thought his ships were the long awaited supply vessels from France, and before they had discovered their mistake he had made off with two of their transports and effectively cut the line of communications between the fort at Leith and the French army in Fife. In an hour the campaign on the north side of the Forth was over. Winter remained in command of the Firth, but the French convoy he hoped to intercept never came; some of the

ships had foundered in a gale, the rest, crippled, turned back
to France.

For Norfolk, too, the period of waiting seemed interminable,
until, after many preliminary moves, Ruthven and Maitland of
Lethington, as representatives of the Scottish lords, came to
Berwick to treat with him. The offensive and defensive alliance,
which was signed on 27th February, was in its way a masterpiece
of treaty-making, and the articles show Norfolk as a skilled
diplomatist. Had Cecil not been three hundred miles away at the
time, the unsuspecting might have fathered the treaty of Berwick
on him, for it is a remarkable performance for a man of twenty-
one. Undoubtedly the duke left the formalities in the document
to Gregory Railton, a clerk in the Signet Office, who had been
seconded to be Secretary of Norfolk's Council at Berwick; at the
end of the year Railton was to become prothonotary of the
Chancery, whose duties included treaty-making.

Elizabeth having understood, both by the information given
by the Scottish nobles and also by the manifest proceedings of the
French, that the latter intend to conquer Scotland, suppress its
liberties and unite that Kingdom to the Crown of France for
ever, had at the request of the Scots taken over the protection of
their realm and its civil and religious liberties so long as the
marriage between the Queen of Scots and the King of France
endures, and one year besides. The Scots for their part agreed to
aid England with 2,000 foot and 1,000 horse in the event of any
French invasion of England. Norfolk further declared that his
mistress had been moved to action only 'upon respect of honour
and neighbourhood, for the defence of the just freedom of the
Crown of Scotland from conquest, and not of any other sinister
interests'. He made it abundantly clear that it was Scottish inde-
pendence that was being upheld; it was not Mary's sovereignty
that was being abrogated.

For the due performance of their side of the treaty the Scottish
lords handed over six sons of noble families as hostages. Rather
shrewdly they asked the duke to press Elizabeth to see that places
were found for the boys 'either in Cambridge or Oxford'. Before
the treaty took effect it had to be sent, at the request of the Scots,
to Elizabeth for ratification under the great seal. The impossible
had happened. The English and Scots for once in the long, bitter
history of the border were going to fight side by side against

France. The duke whose father, grandfather and great grand-father had each in turn harried the Scots, had broken the 'Auld Alliance'.[6]

There was another five weeks of inactivity, as Elizabeth still favoured further negotiations with Mary of Guise. To Norfolk's dismay she was still bent on applying pressure short of war itself to gain her ends. But at last, with the power of the Guises under-mined by the Conspiracy of Amboise, the time for delay was over. On 4th April Grey brought his army to join the Scots at Prestonpans. The very next day a special envoy from Philip II arrived at Whitehall to persuade Elizabeth to sign an armistice to a war in which scarcely a shot had been fired, but Cecil insisted that the phase of negotiation had passed.

This was no ordinary campaign, but a 'phoney' war that at times degenerated into sheer pantomime. English and Scots made uneasy allies. There were the Lords of the Covenant who indi-vidually seemed remarkably lukewarm in prosecuting the war, the Lowlander 'neutrals' who saw little point in joining an alliance in which they would be denied their traditional plunder, and their counterparts on the English side of the Marches, like Dacre, who above all wanted Norfolk and his army out of the way so they could resume their private feuds on both sides of the border. The presence of Mary of Guise complicated the scene still further. At the outbreak of hostilities she left Leith for Edinburgh and was permitted to take refuge in the Castle with her maids of honour and some few servants, yet Queen Elizabeth insisted that Grey should not attempt a siege of Edinburgh on the grounds that it would show lack of reverence to the Queen Mother! Every now and then the Regent would send forth a herald to negotiate with Norfolk at Berwick, but he soon saw through her schemes: 'her blubbering is not for nothing'; concealing 'her bloody sword in a scabbard of peace', she was trying to put into practice Elizabeth's own tactics. The next messenger to Berwick often brought fresh instructions from court which countermanded previous orders, for Elizabeth blew hot and cold on the campaign according to the temperature of international politics. The day after Norfolk's troops had finally moved forward there was a letter from the Queen back-pedalling; she had 'condescended' to his advance into Scotland but he was to do all he could to gain his ends without resort to force. How 'we now stand between war and peace' changed almost daily and Grey's reports from the camp before Leith were bewilderingly contradictory.[7]

It was not an easy command. From the beginning there was a serious shortage of essential military stores at Berwick, too few troops and a lamentable lack of money. Even in peacetime the Berwick garrison swallowed up vast sums and the pilfering that had gone on there was a byword. In a conversation at Whitehall Palace, in the gallery by the privy garden, Elizabeth had told Norfolk her suspicions about maladministration and once he reached the border he saw for himself how bad things were. He eventually discovered that the villain of the piece was Sir James Crofts, the captain of Berwick, whose cheating and thieving had made heavy inroads in the armoury and elsewhere; there was scarcely enough gunpowder for a royal salute. Corruption spread down the ranks and the taking of musters was farcical. 'Dead pays', the iniquitous system by which fictitious names were kept on the roll, already had a long history, but at Berwick 'the pilling and polling of the Queen's Majesty', complained the duke, 'will let no true muster be made. They say it is not the fashion to be mustered all in a day, and by that means one helpeth to deceive the Queen's Majesty and their country one day, and another the other.'

Norfolk's attempts to end these and other irregularities were unpopular among the men whose pay was always in arrears. 'You know well enough', he wrote to Cecil, 'how mutinous Englishmen be when they cannot have their ordinary necessaries.' Life was even harder for the troops than usual, for as they were not at war with Scotland they were forbidden to loot over the border. Even when money arrived it was in such low denominations that the carts that had set out from Berwick to carry it to the English camp before Leith were so weighed down that they stuck in the muddy roads and so it had to be sent by sea. 'For God's sake whenever you send us more money', the duke wrote, his patience almost at an end, 'let it be sent in gold, or else in new silver. This [last consignment] was in pence, twopence and old testoons.' Having to pay the messengers less than their normal wages made them slack in their duties, so Norfolk's letters to Whitehall took much longer than he thought possible and this was the more serious in a political war when the commander had his hands tied and was always waiting on instructions from court.[8]

But manpower was the chief problem. In the end Norfolk succeeded in increasing his force to 8,813 foot, 1,990 horsemen and 1,663 pioneers, gunners and carters, 'made up of sundry shires of the realm', recruited piecemeal over five months. At one time Elizabeth had hoped that the Scottish lords of the lowlands could be persuaded to do all the fighting, but it was clear to Norfolk that he must at all costs have a proper army. He sent instructions into the Midland Counties for troops to be levied and the draught-horses for pulling the guns into position came from as far afield as Northamptonshire. Such troops were, of course, raw and undisciplined. He made up for his lack of sappers by impressing Durham miners to help to undermine the defences of Leith.

Because Mary Queen of Scots and the Dauphin had borne the arms of England, this war in the north was called by some 'The War of the Insignia', and it was appropriate that the lieutenant-general should be the Earl Marshal. In sixteenth-century warfare heralds still played their ancient role of carrying messages between the opposing commanders; and in this campaign of negotiation, persuasion and threat they were very active. Chester Herald and Rougecroix Pursuivant were both with the duke, and Berwick-on-Tweed at this time had its own pursuivant-at-arms. And when, finally, a peace treaty was signed the French gave way over the question of the insignia.[9]

Lord Grey of Wilton, who commanded the army besieging Leith, was by no means an ideal choice. To Norfolk's dismay he did not reach Berwick until 5th February and once operations started he became increasingly disappointed in Grey and feared that through lack of initiative Leith never would be taken. 'He sheweth himself forward enough', the duke reported, 'but all is not in him that hath been thought . . . It is a shame to lie so long at a sand wall.' Had Norfolk been at Leith himself he would have 'lain in the ditch for shame', he said 'if the town resisted his assault.' The fault was that Grey 'hath not his wits and his memory faileth him'. To make matters worse Crofts, the deputy to Grey, deliberately hampered operations and actively discouraged the Scots from joining in the campaign.

There were 'hot skirmishes' before Leith from 6th April onwards, but the joint army began to dwindle to half-strength through desertions, chiefly on the Scottish side. Then on 14th

April the French sallied forth from the town and broke through the English trenches, killing two hundred men. What was planned as Grey's grand assault on 7th May failed miserably; 'marvellously ill-handled', was Norfolk's phrase for it. Between eight hundred and a thousand Englishmen were killed and honour was saved only by the bravery of Sir Henry Percy's son. Grey now declared that Leith was impregnable and rather dishonestly blamed the duke for insisting on the attempt.

In his despatches to the court Norfolk said what he thought and his judgments on men were forthright. He hoped Cecil would moderate, if he thought fit, 'whatever his rash head writes on the sudden' into more politic language. He spoke his mind about Lord Grey and Sir James Crofts, as we have seen, and he did not hesitate to brand Dacres as 'the undutifullest subject of England'. He had an eye for a loyal servant, like Bowes or Sadler, and his judgment about whom he could trust implicitly and whom he dare not rely on never failed him at Berwick, and this particularly impressed Cecil. In years to come, alas, Norfolk's judgment of men and affairs was to desert him at the most critical moments.[10]

At the end of March the duke had been cheered by the arrival at Berwick of his friend and servant, Sir Nicholas L'Estrange, who had brought the ratification of the treaty with the Lords of the Congregation – far too important a document to be entrusted to an ordinary messenger. To stamp out corruption Norfolk appointed him muster master of the army. Thereafter L'Estrange travelled between the border and London twice more, and on his return was able to give Norfolk the latest news from Court, especially about Dudley. Rumour had it that Lord Robert was 'laying in a good stock of arms and every day is assuming a more masterful part in affairs. They say that he thinks of divorcing his wife.' And when Cecil himself had left for negotiations in Scotland there was no-one left at court to rival the favourite. It was reported that the Queen and he spent days shut up together 'without coming abroad' and that under his spell she was unable to concentrate on matters of state. 'Not a man in England but cries out at the top of his voice this fellow is ruining the country with his vanity.'

Behind Norfolk's back there was a good deal of malicious gossip about his leadership. The failure to take Leith was attributed by

some to incompetence, by others to lack of loyalty; still other
critics began to accuse him of wanting to continue the war for
his own ends – the same accusation as had been made against his
father in 1545. Even De Quadra, who was his friend, felt he must
report that Elizabeth was 'in great doubt of the duke of Norfolk
and is sorry she gave him the command'. So in his letters to the
court Howard reiterated that he was faithfully fulfilling his duties.
'Whatsoever the Queen's Highness shall command me to do
during my life I will either accomplish, or else it shall be seen
that care of my own carcass is not the let thereof.'

The pilferers and profiteers were, of course, anxious for the
'continuance of this brute life. But so [long] as the Queen's
Majesty and this realm was delivered with honour and good
success in their enterprises, and I at home in Kenninghall, I care
not in what other country they had their fill' of war. Sir Peter
Carew, who was sent from court to report on the state of the
army, had no criticism to offer against Norfolk. The failure at
Leith had been Lord Grey's, and had he lived in a later age Grey
would doubtless have been court martialled for incompetence.[11]

Early in June Norfolk and Cecil met at Alnwick. A new phase
had opened with the arrival in England of a special French envoy
to treat for peace and after preliminary exchanges Elizabeth had
somewhat reluctantly appointed Cecil and Dr Nicholas Wotton
as her special commissioners to negotiate with the French representatives – Monluc, the Bishop of Valence and Charles de
Rochefoucauld, Sieur de Randan – at Newcastle. As soon as he
heard of this the duke offered the Secretary 'and mine Uncle
Wotton' the use of his house at Newcastle. After a first session
there on 8th June Cecil rode off for a few hours' talk with Norfolk. The frequent letters that had passed between the two of
them since the beginning of the year had deepened their respect
for each other. Both were by nature aloof, but correspondence
had broken down the barriers and they greeted each other in
Northumberland's castle at Alnwick as old friends. Back at Newcastle next day Cecil persuaded the others to agree to the removal
of the peace conference to Edinburgh. His hopes of a satisfactory
treaty were high, for Mary of Guise was mortally ill and had,
indeed, died before the commissioners re-assembled in the Scottish capital. Meanwhile Norfolk was to continue the siege of
Leith, taking over from Grey in the field if he thought necessary,

as the best means of exerting diplomatic pressure, and he convinced Cecil that he must have more men and money to gain this objective.[12]

We need not follow the protracted negotiations. Right up to 6th July, when the treaty was signed, there was the threat of Norfolk's army marching on Leith. England, to Elizabeth's dismay, failed to get Calais restored, but on every other point her demands were met. The French troops were to leave Scotland and their fortresses at Dunbar and Eynemouth, as well as Leith, were to be rased to the ground. For the future no Frenchman was to hold office in Scotland, while Francis II and his Queen were to abstain from using the style and arms of England and Ireland. In general the clauses of the treaty of Cateau-Cambrésis of the previous year were to remain in force. Until the return of Mary Queen of Scots the kingdom was to be governed by a council of twelve, seven of whom were to be chosen by Mary and five by the Estates, to 'temper' the honour of the Crown. Thanks to Cecil's tact the alliance between Elizabeth and the Lords of the Covenant, which Norfolk had forged, remained firm, though it was too delicate a matter to be mentioned in the peace treaty.[13]

The signing of the treaty of Edinburgh was a great relief to Norfolk, who at this time was far from well, and it pleased him to see East Anglian vessels like the *Peter* of Dunwich, which had come to the Firth of Forth for the salt trade, being used for transporting French soldiers back to Calais. Even though the fort at Leith was to be demolished the duke was adamant that the garrison at Berwick must be brought up to strength, the fortifications there improved and the place left in the hands of a capable commander. The objective of his own command had been achieved, and Cecil saw no reason why the duke should tarry any longer in Berwick, 'having no lodging there meet either for him or ... for my poor countenance. It is miserable to behold what pain he hath sustained.'[14]

The operations, true enough, had not been glorious. From start to finish the campaign had been nothing more than a series of diplomatic moves; a statesman's war, not a general's. At times, when the incessant rain depressed him, Norfolk must have sighed for such a chance to prove himself in the field as his father had often been given in France. But when all was over he could take his share of the credit for what was to prove one of the major achievements of the whole of Elizabeth's long reign. For Scotland 6th July 1560 was the 'central point in her history'; for England the final breaking of the 'Auld Alliance' was the first of a chain of events that would lead to the Union of 1707.

Before he left Berwick he held three investitures to knight Sir Arthur Grey and ten other English captains; he had already knighted that stalwart of the north, George Bowes, and felicitously had chosen St George's Day for the occasion. Mindful of heraldic matters even when commanding an army, the duke noted that two of the men he had honoured (Sir William Babthorpe and Sir Walter Aston) had 'no crests'. Neither Elizabeth nor anyone else questioned his power to create these knights, whereas the Earl of Essex was to earn a considerable rebuke for his dubbings forty years on.[15]

In the end Norfolk's return south was postponed for a few days further owing to an attack of rheumatism that gave him so much pain that he could neither eat nor sleep. He was utterly sick of the climate of the borders and in a heartfelt phrase said that 'this country and I can ill agree'. The worst over, he returned to London by way of Kenninghall and then proceeded to Farnham, where the Queen was staying in mid-August to make his report. At court, as he knew, the articles of the Treaty of Edinburgh were already being belittled, and its architect blamed for allowing Calais to remain lost. The duke encouraged Cecil to stop his ears to the malicious criticisms of the uninformed. 'Blind men can show no colours', he wrote. 'Perchance they that make most of their painted sheath will never do such service to the realm as you have done in concluding this peace. I dare in argument stand with them all, that the Queen's Majesty could not have bought this agreement too dearly. Perchance they will say with deferring we might have had Calais. But I will rather think that we might had sped like the dog in Aesop's fables, which having a bone in his mouth and seeing the shadow in the water, gaped to have fetched it and so lost both.'[16]

Throughout his eight months at Berwick Norfolk had been close to Cecil, and their many letters to each other that have survived for this period show a real affection developing between them. Cecil was particularly upset that the duke's service was inadequately recognised by the Queen. 'Alas, Mr Throgmorton', he complained to the ambassador in Paris, 'what comfort is there to be hoped when my Lord of Norfolk, a rare nobleman, *columen familiae reginae*, is thanked and not rewarded, sent home with no allowance neither in credit nor promise. I dare not write it, I might speak: God send Her Majesty understanding what shall be her surety.' Norfolk, too, regarded himself as the pillar of the royal household. He had no complaint about not being paid his expenses, as Cecil had, for he was allowed £12 12s. 2d. a day for himself and his retinue while at Berwick; nor did he expect extensive grants of Crown lands, as did Cecil. The least Norfolk expected was to be taken into the Queen's confidence and given the power for which his service in Scotland showed he was fitted.[17]

Chapter Five

THE DUKE IN HIS COUNTRY

As England's sole duke and her greatest territorial magnate Norfolk's influence in his native county was little less than absolute, for the county, the city of Norwich, and the five corporate towns were largely governed from Kenninghall Palace. Many of his lands formed a private franchise, 'the Liberty of the Duke of Norfolk', which had been founded by Edward IV for John, the third duke of the Mowbray line, and continued intact with privileges unabridged despite the upheavals of the Reformation. Since the Duchy of Cornwall, and the Duchy of Lancaster had both been merged with the Crown estate the Norfolk Liberty remained as the greatest lay private franchise in the realm. In his county, as he boasted to Queen Elizabeth, Thomas Howard was monarch of all he surveyed, and it was a demesne worthy of its lord.[1]

Elizabethan Norfolk was 'a populous and fruitful country, mostly open and plain, very rich and stored in itself of all things necessary for the sustenance of man's life'. Norfolk corn and Norfolk wool were each quality products. On the sandy loam of the north-east was grown the best barley in England, while the boulder clay of the central area produced fine crops of wheat. The chief grazing lands were in the marsh country of west Norfolk and the north-western coastal strip. There was a higher proportion of freeholders to copyhold tenants than in any other county but, since Norfolk was populous, the average holding was small. Even before the Dissolution some of the larger landlords were converting arable to pasture, to make quick profits from wool, and the more unscrupulous among them then turned

common grazing lands into private sheepwalks, enclosed with
quickset hedges. This had provoked Ket's Rebellion. Ten years
later arable was still holding its own against pasture and on the
ducal estates there was a careful balance between the two types
of farming. In the south-east, near the Suffolk border, dairy
farming predominated and small farmers were clearly gearing
their production of butter, cheese and bacon to meet the needs of
London's larders. Compared with other parts of rural England
few of the open fields had been enclosed.[2]

Norfolk was prosperous largely because it was a maritime
county, well served by a system of inland waterways that led to
one of the two principal ports, King's Lynn and Great Yarmouth.
In addition to their importance as centres of foreign trade, both
were key distributing centres in the coastal traffic with other
English ports, especially London, and both were headquarters of
a fishing industry, the one specialising in cod, and the other in the
herring. Lynn, on the Wash, was the gateway to a fifth of England.
From it left the barges which passed along the Ouse, or the Nene,
or the Welland, and their tributaries, into eight counties. Merchants from such different towns as Cambridge, Huntingdon,
Bedford, Northampton, Peterborough, Lincoln and Leicester all
regarded King's Lynn as their natural port. Thetford, on the
Little Ouse, handled goods for Kenninghall Palace that had come
from Lynn.[3]

The chief traffic was on the Great Ouse, between Lynn and
Cambridge, the least tortuous of all the channels in the Fens. The
wine that stocked the cellars of the colleges, even books for the
study and such articles as sets of virginals, as well as the fish, coal
and salt that supplied the needs of the growing town and the
neighbouring shires, came upstream in keels and lighters which
returned to Lynn laden with corn, butter and cheese. Apart from
this regular trade carried on throughout the year, there was renewed activity each September when Sturbridge Fair was held
in the fields, hard by the Cam, a mile or so to the north-east of
the town. Sturbridge was, for William Camden, 'the most famous
fair in all England'; thither came merchants from 'all parts of the
realm' – Merchant Taylors and Grocers of London were jostled
by men from Bristol and clothiers from the West Riding. Earlier
in the century there had been much friction between the corpora-
tions of Cambridge and Lynn about the rights of the former to be

free from paying local tolls at the port and in the reign of Edward VI the Court of Star Chamber in a test case had upheld their rights. Fortunately for the duke, who was high steward of both Lynn and Cambridge, the controversy had died down. But the traffic on the Ouse grew greater each year.[4]

The state of Yarmouth harbour, three miles from his seat at Caister Castle, was one of the duke's greatest worries. As he and other local commissioners reported in 1565, Yarmouth was 'the only port for the city of Norwich [and served] also for the relief and help of the most part of Norfolk and Suffolk ... by three great rivers, descending to the same by the space of twenty miles and more'. The Rivers Yare, Waveney and Bure were the normal channels of trade for much of East Anglia. A lighter of thirty tons could use the Bure as far as Aylsham; the Waveney served Beccles, Bungay and Harleston, and without the Yare Norwich could never have developed as a great industrial city. We shall never know the exact courses these rivers followed in Tudor England as they meandered down to find their outlet in the North Sea together at Yarmouth. In a telling phrase Fuller remarked that the Yare was 'so wanton that it knoweth not its own mind which way to go', but the holiday sailor on the Norfolk Broads today can easily appreciate the significance of cheap water-carriage in past centuries, thanks to which so many village smithies got their Wealden iron and Tyneside coal.[5]

In this corner of England rivers were, indeed, far more important than roads, even though two of the half-dozen great roads of medieval England passed through Norfolk. There was the 'Pilgrims' Road' to Walsingham, through Waltham, Ware, Newmarket and Brandon Ferry, which took the duke most of the way from London to Kenninghall; and secondly, the east coast road to Yarmouth, passing through Colchester, Ipswich, Woodbridge, Snapesbridge, Blythburgh and Beccles. It was clearly the latter highway that James I had in mind when he said he wished all Norfolk was cut out into roads to supply the rest of the Kingdom. By contrast the road from Norwich, by Wymondham and Thetford, which joined the 'Pilgrims' Road' at Mildenhall was poor and sections of it were impassable in the winter. The rest were little more than bridle-paths that were always in a hopeless state of repair and made travelling 'very noisome and cumbrous'.[6]

The better roads had linked the chief religious houses, and their

TH F

dissolution provoked the greatest change in the landscape. Norwich Priory had become the Cathedral church, but the Rule of St Benedict had been abolished. St Benet's Holme, Buckenham Priory, Thetford Nunnery and Wymondham Abbey, once a cell of St Alban's, were no more. The great house of Austin Canons at Walsingham, custodians of the famous shrine of Our Lady, and the smaller foundations at Thetford and at Beeston, near Cromer, were derelict. In Norwich the sites of the former colleges, friaries and hospitals that had covered so much of the old city had been used as quarries for building material by Surrey and lesser men who followed his lead. All over the county lead had been ripped from the roofs of monastic refectories, much stained glass had been smashed and many monuments been mutilated. Thomas Howard belonged to the first generation that had not known the monasteries; everyone older than him could remember their last days and the manner of their dying. His own staff of domestic chaplains at Kenninghall, which included two ex-religious, was the largest body of ecclesiastics in the county, with the exception of the chapter of Norwich Cathedral.

Norwich, with its castle and ducal palace as well as its cathedral, was the capital of East Anglia and rose during Norfolk's short lifetime to be second city in the Kingdom. Thanks to his efforts Flemish immigrants settled in the city and both revolutionised the clothing industry and revitalised the entire community. Norwich was no longer a port in its own right, as it had been in earlier times, but the river trade with Yarmouth was busier than ever before. The market held in the shadow of the castle was still the hub of the week's business and the two annual fairs, the Tombland Fair, beginning on Good Friday, and the Whitsun Fair, were lively centres of trade for half a dozen counties.

A disastrous fire in 1508 had destroyed much of the medieval city, and for a time the deserted market place had been covered with weeds. There was little immediate rebuilding and the Dissolution of the Monasteries added to the city's decayed appearance. And then, as Thomas Howard grew to manhood, a revival began in earnest. New buildings altered the landscape and, even in the smaller alleys, timber and thatch were giving way to brick and slate.

The most extensive of all the new buildings was the palace, begun by the third duke on a grandiose scale, but enlarged by his grandson through acquiring neighbouring properties which he demolished. This mansion was in the parish of St John Maddermarket, covering an area between the River Yare on the north and the High Street on the south. The buildings formed a quadrangle, in the middle of which ran an aqueduct. The north and south sides were three storeys high, the others four storeys. In the centre of the south side was the great gateway, leading onto the High Street, with a gatehouse over it. Along the first floor of this wing ran a gallery, at the eastern end of which was the duke's closet, at the other end his duchess's.

On the west was the great hall and presence chamber, both on the third floor, and fifteen other rooms, including the quarters of the duchess and those of her children. Opposite, in the east wing were the duke's bedchamber and the rooms of his steward and other principal officers; his own study lay under the lantern tower. The dining-hall was on the north, or river, side. This was a splendid wainscoted room, three storeys high, with two stone windows. Nearby were the pantry, the kitchen and pastry, and below was the still-room. The duke's private quay on the river led through the water gate to the wine cellars, the granary, the woodyard and the fish-house; Norfolk's own waterman, Robert Godfrey, was the most important man on the river and became elected a freeman of Norwich under special terms. Also in the north block was the armoury, well stocked with arquebuses, powder, pikes, pole-axes and armour. The stables contained, besides horses, a variety of caparisons for the duke's own use – saddles of black velvet, fringed with gold and black silk, saddles of crimson and gold, and harnesses. There were litter-chairs and trappings for his duchess and furnishings for a hearse here in Norwich which were duplicated (such was the uncertainty of life in Tudor England as Norfolk had cause to know), at Kenninghall and the Charterhouse. Besides the great tennis court and playhouse, there was a bowling-alley, 180 feet by 26 feet. This mansion, no less than the ducal residence at Kenninghall, was indeed a palace.[7]

Norfolk entertained lavishly at Norwich. In the summer of 1561, for instance, 'a great many lords and knights with their ladies' stayed as his guests for several days, and their entertainment included a tattoo on Mousehold Heath. Some of these guests were probably assigned logdings in the 'Crown' Inn, next door to the palace. This was the best hotel in Norwich, for the judges of assize generally stayed there and the owner was a tenant of the duke's. There were regular feasts for the mayor and aldermen, banquets for the high sheriff and the judges of assize twice a year, and an occasional dinner for the justices of the peace. There was venison in plenty from deer, caught in Rising Chase and Framlingham Park. Bishop, dean and canons, rectors of city parishes and also, on lowlier benches in the hall, incumbents of livings under the duke's patronage, would expect to enjoy his hospitality from time to time. The bowling-alley and the tennis court were sacrosanct, but now and then quite humble folk used to be admitted to the playhouse and drink free ale in the kitchens afterwards. There were always beggars and destitute women and children waiting for the almoner's staff to begin their daily distribution of loaves and meat, now that the relief offered of old by the religious houses had ceased.[8]

Norwich had suffered as severely as anywhere in the country during the years of commercial depression in the middle of the century. On top of the great slump in the worsted industry came Ket's Rebellion and its legacy seriously hampered recovery. The more far-seeing citizens realised that the only way of halting the decline lay in the introduction of a new industry, fashioned to meet the needs of the contemporary market. News that skilled refugees from the Low Countries, fleeing from Alva's persecution, had settled successfully in Sandwich and London, prompted the mayor to ask if a colony could come to Norwich. Howard was converted to the idea and gave his whole-hearted support to the mayor's petition to the Queen, which spoke of the utter decay of the worsted trade and of the consequent unemployment and distress in the city. Thanks to Norfolk's backing a licence was issued to the mayor in November 1565 permitting thirty alien weavers to come over, with their families, and settle on the condition that they made bays, says, mocadoes 'and other outlandish commodities . . . not heretofore made in the city'. On Christmas Eve the duke was writing to Archbishop Parker to arrange for the Huguenots to be assigned a church in the city.

The settlement was as peaceful as the occasion for it was bloody, and in a short time the immigrants invigorated the whole commercial life of the region. Two Dutch boys were pressing their parents to come and join them. They would be supplied with all the tools necessary for weaving: 'There is a great trade doing ... when you come to Norwich you shall have gold.' Another refugee wrote back to his wife on arriving to report very favourably on his prospects: 'There is a good trade in bays and I will look for a house as quickly as I can to get into business, for it will be easy to make money. I will get the gear for making bays against your coming ... May God give you the same loving peace and riches as we have here in Norwich.' The call was irresistible. By 1569 there were nearly 3,000 strangers in the city and further arrivals had to be strictly controlled. Even though the great plague of 1579 took a heavy toll there were over 4,600 aliens there in 1582.[9]

Each immigrant became licensed by the mayor to manufacture new types of cloth, and manufacture they did. The first year, 1566-7, they made 1,200 bays. In the succeeding four years they annually doubled their output and from 1574 their production averaged 30,000 cloths a year. There was a fairly rigid distribution between the New Draperies made by the Dutch and those made by the Walloons. The latter made grograms, carrels and mocadoes, which were all 'dry woven goods', while the Dutch kept to coarser types of cloth, principally bays. Both communities made silken fabrics and woollen stockings.

From the first the men of Norwich had insisted that the newcomers should share the secrets of their techniques with them; they were either to work with Englishmen or shut up shop. Soon numbers of English lads were serving apprenticeships with the Dutch settlers for learning the art of weaving bays. The city fathers also made regulations for controlling the sale of the aliens' cloths, subjecting them to inspection and sealing in the cloth halls. This bone of contention was not finally settled until the middle of 1571. In the face of competition from the settlers the Norwich clothiers kept their looms busy and the output of woollen stockings by the Russell Weavers Company leapt ahead. Prosperity spread well beyond the city walls, for hundreds of cottagers within a twenty-mile radius of Norwich spent every minute they could spare spinning yarn.[10]

Not surprising that after a while relations between the citizens and the aliens became strained. The latter sensed they were being exploited, when they realised that the properties for which they were made to pay £14 rent a year had not been let at £2 before their coming. Some who had welcomed the refugees with open arms, by stages grew extremely suspicious of them. Thomas Whall, mayor in 1567-8, even tried to have them expelled, but the duke was adamant. To many it seemed as if the newcomers alone were prospering. One Norwich merchant noted how wealthy they became from their skill and hard work; they cornered all the best wool in the county for their looms so there was 'no trade but of their commodities'. In a crisis their rise to prosperity produced violent clashes and the rebels in the city and the county who plotted to overthrow the government in 1570 were to make the expulsion of the aliens as one of their battle cries, and it took time for the shouting to die down.[11]

The establishment of the New Draperies, soon to play so vital a part in the balance of trade, survived these bickerings. The trade on the River Yare, the city's lifeline, grew to such a volume that a new quay had to be constructed. Along the river from Yarmouth were brought the quantities of food, drink and luxuries – wine, sugar, fruit, fine glassware and *objets d'art* – for which there was a keen demand in the city; the immigrants had their own drinking tastes and imported barrel upon barrel of aquavitae. The river keels also brought raw materials for the clothing industry – woad, madder, fullers'-earth, soap, alum, Spanish wool and woolcards. Downstream, towards the sea, went practically nothing but the cloths and worsted stockings which symbolised the commercial significance of Norwich. By 1600 it had become the second city in the realm, in wealth and population:

> This city, self-supplied, should England need
> A capital, might fairly take the lead.[12]

There is another aspect of the rise of Norwich in which the fourth duke took an equally important part. For as long as he could remember he had heard about the sad state of Yarmouth harbour; like the rise in prices and the growth in unemployment, it seemed a perennial problem. As high steward of Great Yarmouth and as lord of Caister, Thomas Howard was most concerned that every effort should be made to solve this problem. He sat on two royal commissions which went into the matter very thoroughly and contributed handsomely towards the special fund for saving the harbour, and saved it was. This was in its way a triumph of engineering and Yarmouth was transformed from a decayed fishing town into a thriving port. Had these endeavours failed, Norwich could not have developed as a great industrial city at nearly so phenomenal a rate.

Tradition has it that Yarmouth is situated on a sandbank which had formed across the Bure-Waveney estuary. Certainly in the early middle ages there had been two entrances to the river, of which the northerly became choked with shingle in the course of time, and thus the original bank became part of a continuous spit, which presented a great hindrance to navigation. For two centuries from 1347 the men of Yarmouth made a number of unsuccessful attempts to cut this spit, aiming to bring the mouth nearer the town. The sixth attempt was made in 1549 by Thompson, the chief engineer of Dover, but as his new cut neared completion a party of rebels under Nicholas Byron arrived from Mousehold Heath. The men failed to capture the town but before being routed did untold damage to the works, and to cap this misfortune Thompson died shortly afterwards.

When Thomas Howard succeeded to the dukedom the prospects were still grim. The old mouth was stopped with sunken ships, the piers were strengthened and rather primitive dredging was constantly in progress. A northerly gale in the winter of 1557 cheated the inhabitants of possible success by flooding the town with marsh water and wrecking weeks of patient endeavour. Trade was almost at a standstill, as few ships could pass in or out of the port, and to prevent the loss of their voyages some crews dragged their vessels over the Dunes to the sea with capstans. A determined effort would have to be made if Yarmouth were to remain a port. At last, as a result of the recommendations of the first commission on which the duke sat, it was decided to cut the new channel at the position in which it still remains.

Men, women and children turned out in the spring of 1560 to dig the new channel, but the wooden bulwarks, which had been constructed to keep the current from running into the old one, were not strong enough. The problem needed an expert. Sir William Woodhouse thought he had found one in 'a very expert man in sea works' from Emden, but the task proved too great for him. The whole venture again hung in the balance and for nearly four years a quarter of the inhabitants of Yarmouth were called out every day by the constables, bringing with them shovels, baskets and staves. A second royal commission, after inspecting the works and questioning witnesses, reported in 1565 that the piers were inadequately maintained and that the harbour was always silting 'by the violence of the sea casting into the same great quantity of sand and gravel, so as ships . . . cannot have their safe course'.

Two years later, on the advice of Henry Manship, the leading Yarmouth merchant of the day, the bailiffs brought over Joyse Johnson, a very experienced Dutch engineer. Thanks to his skill the harbour, 'having a lust to run again to the southward, was substantially set upon by great cost wrought with very great works . . . and was brought into one certain course to run out into the sea between two great piers. Which thing', Manship proudly added, 'our predecessors could not compass or attain unto.' The foundations were sunk twenty foot deep, the piers were long enough to give a very wide entrance, and there was seventeen foot of water on the bar at high tide. It had been a most costly operation and the maintenance of the new harbour continued to swallow up a very considerable sum of money. The county was not rich in woodlands, but the duke gave generously. Thanks to his influence the Queen remitted to the town's use all the sums contributed by its inhabitants to subsidies.

Yarmouth was not the only harbour needing money. To raise funds for general repairs the government resorted in 1567 to the strange expedient of a state lottery. Each lot, costing 10s., was to stand a chance of winning a first prize of £5,000 and other prizes totalling over £100,000, and the profits of the scheme were to be applied 'to the reparation of the havens and strength of the realm'. But the public was so slow to subscribe that Cecil sent circulars to all mayors and J.P.'s commending the lottery. In the end, alas, only a twelfth of the anticipated sum was subscribed and the prize money dropped to £9,000. The lots were drawn at the west door of St Paul's between January and May 1569. None of the entries made by Yarmouth Corporation was successful, not even the lot bearing on the back the couplet:

> Yarmouth haven God send thee speed
> The Lord he knoweth thy great need.

What happened to the proceeds of the lottery remains a mystery, and Cecil incurred a good deal of odium up and down the country for what many subscribers regarded as pretty sharp practice as regards the profits of the venture and also for the reduced prize money and the method of drawing lots. His unpopularity on this score made the men of Norfolk all the more ready to rise a year later to demand the duke's release from the Tower and the execution of Her Majesty's 'evil advisers'. Significantly, in the local plots of 1570 it was at Yarmouth that Alva's invading army was to land.[13]

*   *   *

The duke's political patronage was the decisive factor in elections. There were five Parliamentary boroughs, each returning two members, of which three, Norwich, King's Lynn and Great Yarmouth, were ancient creations. Norfolk was high steward of both the coastal boroughs and his influence in each was paramount. From his palace in the city he was able to dispose of one and on occasion of both of the Norwich seats, though his part in the election of the two Knights of the shire in the county court is less apparent and may have been negligible. Thetford and Castle Rising were both ducal pocket boroughs which had been enfranchised during the heyday of Lord Treasurer Norfolk, the former by Henry VIII, the latter by Queen Mary. In both boroughs there were Howard residences and for a manor house, Thetford was of spacious proportions, with an inner and an outer court, a hall and a chapel, 'a great chamber with a bedchamber within it' and forty rooms besides. Norfolk's chamberlain, Sir Nicholas L'Estrange, regularly sat for Castle Rising.[14]

In December 1558, when the writs for the election of Elizabeth's first Parliament went out, Norfolk reached a typical concordat with the mayor and corporation of Lynn. They 'have condescended', noted the town clerk, 'that my Lord of Norfolk shall at his own request have the nomination of one of the burgesses of the next Parliament for this town [and] that one of the town shall be the other burgess'. In such cases the patron's payment of the members' expenses was the chief attraction for the borough, as the 'independent' member for King's Lynn himself admitted during a debate on residentiary qualifications for borough candidates in 1571. Robert Bell, who had already made his mark as a lawyer and was to become Speaker in the next Parliament claimed that some boroughs had not among their residents men of sufficient wealth or ability to send as their representatives to Westminster; but he so little approved of the duke's exploitation of his borough's weakness that he proposed that each borough electing a member on a nobleman's nomination should be fined £40.[15]

Rather surprisingly the duke exercised little patronage in the Suffolk boroughs and no more than an occasional member for Dunwich, later to become a byword for electoral malpractices, can be traced as a Howard dependant. But in Sussex the position was very different. Long before the merger of the earldom of Arundel with the dukedom the Sussex boroughs had come under the Howard sway. The borough of Horsham and the lordship of Bramber had descended to the dukes of the Mowbray line, so that even in 1465 it was noted that 'my Lord of Norfolk maketh burgesses of the Parliament' at Lewes, Shoreham, Horsham, Reigate, Bramber and Gatton, and this considerable inheritance of political patronage passed in time to the dukes of the Howard line. In the reign of James I, Thomas Howard's grandson was to write to the men of Steyning before an election, reminding them that it was customary for most towns to choose suitable outsiders, 'and herein to have recourse and respect unto the tender made to them of able men by their chief lords. As my ancestors have done unto your predecessors.'[16]

The Howard dependants and followers who were returned for the five or six Sussex boroughs for Mary's and for Elizabeth's first three Parliaments all came from the county of Norfolk. For example Richard Fulmerston, one of the members for Horsham in 1558, was a Thetford man high in Norfolk's service, while John Blennerhasset, the other member, lived near Diss. In the 1563 elections no less than six Norfolk dependants came to Westminster from Sussex seats – William Barker, Edward and Lawrence Banister, Robert Buxton, Robert Harris, and Nicholas Mynne. At each general election there was a general post and some of the former members from Sussex boroughs graduated to seats nearer their home. For the last four years of his life Fulmerston, now knighted, sat as M.P. for his native Thetford, while Blennerhasset was later elected M.P. for Norwich at a by-election. Nicholas Mynne, one of the duke's legal advisers, sat for Bramber in 1558, for Shoreham in 1559 and 1563, and then at last was returned for Castle Rising in 1571. The same family which pro-

vided a member for Dunwich in 1563 provided both members
for Horsham in 1571.[17]

As with other noblemen and notabilities, Norfolk's motive for
getting his nominees returned was one of patronage; the question
of 'packing' did not arise. There was 'nothing sinister' about a
great landowner extending his territorial authority to borough
elections. No ducal borough was completely under his thumb,
or Peter Osborn, the extreme Protestant who had been imprisoned for his faith under Mary, would never have been elected
for Horsham in 1563. The Archbishop of York, the Bishop of
Winchester, the second Earl of Bedford, Sir Francis Walsingham
and other statesmen were all engaged in similar activities to
Norfolk. Their nominees were not 'government' men but dependants, and it would be an anachronism to think they were
trying to form a party, or even a pressure group. 'If we had the
evidence,' considered Sir John Neale, 'we should almost certainly
discover that [the members] themselves asked for seats, and that
in satisfying their wishes the Duke was merely carrying out the
social obligations of his class.' The number of his dependants at
Westminster, shows not the strength of Howard supporters in
the Commons but the strength of the duke in his own county.
'I would have been sorry for my countrymen', he told Cecil, 'to
see that any matter touching the Queen's service in Norfolk or
Suffolk had been committed to any other than myself.' In the
same way the county expected to get the pickings of posts in the
duke's gift and had the post of Marshal of the Marshalsea and
Queen's Bench Prison not gone to a Norfolkman in 1561 there
would have been an outcry.[18]

At the beginning of the reign the duke was Lord Lieutenant of
Norfolk and Suffolk, an office at that time almost entirely military. The Lord Lieutenant commanded the militia in his shire in
times of emergency, and in peace-time he was required to muster
them for training at intervals. Only a man with a considerable
household staff was able to discharge these duties properly; and
often the duke's steward was away from Kenninghall for days
on end mustering contingents in distant hundreds. In January
1559 when England was still at war with France and Scotland,
Norfolk was ordered to call out his men to defend the coasts in
case of an attempted invasion. The lord lieutenant, as the Queen's
representative, had wide powers for preserving public order in a

crisis. In the late autumn of 1559, when the possibility of sending
Norfolk to the Scottish border was already being mentioned,
Elizabeth relieved him of his Lieutenancy duties. 'With the coming of winter, wherein is nothing to be doubted of any like
insolence of disordered people as before', she told him he could
safely lay down his command, and she knew he would be
'grateful . . . to be disburdened of this care'. But it seems that after
his return from Scotland he was again acting as lord lieutenant,
for he was busy overseeing musters in 1561 and 1562.[19]

Until his trial Norfolk was on the commission of the peace for
Middlesex, Norfolk and Suffolk, and also for the Isle of Ely, and
was also a commissioner of sewers for those counties. It was, of
course, normal for a peer to be *honoris causa* on commissions in
the counties in which his principal estates lay and a few great
officers of the Crown, such as Lord Keeper Bacon and Secretary
Cecil, were on all commissions of the peace. But the duke took
his duties seriously and whenever he was not at court he sat at
Norwich Quarter Sessions. The Queen appointed him steward
of the Duchy of Lancaster manors in Norfolk and Suffolk,
steward of the Liberty of St Edmund, with its centre at Bury, and
bailiff of the Isle of Ely – both were offices which brought him
in a few fees but involved his household officials in much hard
work.[20]

Nominations for many local offices came his way. As lord
lieutenant and *custos rotulorum* the appointment of clerk of the
peace was in his gift and after he had been succeeded by Sir
William Woodhouse as *custos* his recommendations to the Lord
Keeper about J.P.s carried great weight. Four of his household
staff were on the Norfolk Commission of the peace, and all were
of the quorum. He regarded it very much his business to recommend whom should be pricked for sheriff, and, as we have
noticed, he resented Leicester's interference on this score very
strongly. Norfolk could also expect to influence the Marquess of
Winchester in the exercise of his patronage as Lord Treasurer in
Norfolk, Suffolk and Sussex, which ranged from highly lucrative
permanent posts in the customs service to the busy and underpaid
office of escheator which no one held for more than a year. Time
and again a member of the staff at Kenninghall acted as tax
collector, while the duke himself did his utmost to regulate the
corn trade; he aided Valentine Browne, the victualler of the

Berwick garrison, in buying grain and even himself interrogated merchants who had refused to show their export licences to the authorities.[21]

Thomas Howard inspired incredible loyalty among his officials, retainers and tenantry. There is no question that his tenants, particularly in South Norfolk, regarded the duke with fanatical affection. After he had been sent to the Tower in the autumn of 1569 a group of tenants staged what amounted to a private rising at Kenninghall for his release. The following summer, when a more professional rebellion was planned at Norwich, the duke's delivery from the Tower remained as one of the planks in the rebels' platform; and when the conspirators had been sentenced and Norfolk was moved from his close confinement to his own Charterhouse, the City of Norwich sent him a jubilant gift of money. Months after his execution in June 1572, when the expression of personal loyalty to a feudal overlord had utterly lost its point, a number of men rose at Sawston in Cambridgeshire, where the Howard standard was proudly carried by 'a lusty gentleman of Suffolk'.[22]

Chapter Six

THE BID FOR POWER

1561-6

FOR the first four years of Elizabeth's reign Norfolk was not a privy councillor. Honours, indeed, were bestowed upon him, as befitted his high hereditary position, but he was not given power. The inner group of ministers on whom the Queen chiefly relied in those early days were Secretary Cecil, Lord Keeper Bacon, Sir Thomas Parry, the controller of her household, and Lord Robert Dudley, master of the horse; the last, though not as yet a member of the Privy Council, was as her starry-eyed favourite in an exceptional position. Even after his service in Scotland, through which he had won his way to Cecil's confidence, Norfolk remained an outsider when questions of high policy were discussed and he picked up what information he could from his friends Pembroke, Howard of Effingham and later from Sussex, and at times he had to be content with titbits of news gleaned from the Spanish Embassy. At any rate, since he chose to spend the greater part of the year in his county, right away from the intrigues of Whitehall Palace and of the court on progress, he was inevitably out of touch with men and affairs.

That Elizabeth should, despite his youth, neglect him in this way rankled and sometimes he would sulk to Cecil that 'Her Highness hardly thinks anything worth bestowed upon me'. Yet because he was by nature aloof, the duke's anomalous position at court made him the independent critic of government policy and thus the focal point of opposition for the rest of the peerage. This first expressed itself in hostility to Robert Dudley, later in mistrust of Cecil. Singly, or in alliance, the favourite and the Secretary down the years were to prevent Norfolk from enjoying for long that power which high rank and family tradition made him feel was his due.

Norfolk's absence in Scotland had not helped to lessen the tension with Dudley. The duke's reaction to the news of Amy Robsart's death at Cumnor on 8th September is not known and the absence of information on this point, on which ambassadors scoured the court for opinions, suggests that he was not among those who openly suspected Lord Robert of foul play. Their enmity went deeper, and although Lord Robert kept away from court for some months, while the cloud hung over him, when he returned their relations had not improved. After Christmas Norfolk was reported to be still 'on very bad terms with the Queen', as a result of this. There were incidents between the two peers' servants in London and in February 1561 Dudley sent the duke a terse note. He understood that Norfolk's servants were declaring that he was the duke's enemy. Was this true? If not, Norfolk should punish the men concerned for idle and scandalous talk. So Howard sent along Sir Nicholas L'Estrange, his chamberlain, to Dudley's house to make diplomatic apologies for any breach of etiquette that men in his livery might have made, and the affair was patched up. But according to De Quadra the Queen was still very cross with Norfolk 'and is determined to humble him when she can ... He on his side is full of boasts, although I do not know how it will turn out when he has to carry them into effect.'[1] For the rest of that year the quarrel simmered rather than boiled and Howard spent most of the time in his county.

A further annoyance for Norfolk was the creation of Robert Cooke as Chester herald. All officers of the College of Arms were appointed for life by the Crown on the nomination of the Earl Marshal. But Cooke, as a protégé of Dudley's, was appointed over the duke's head, which he regarded as an unwarrantable interference in his province.[2]

In the last days of the year Howard was admitted to Gray's Inn. This was a characteristic choice, for of all the Inns of Court at that time Gray's Inn was the one most favoured by peers. The duke's brothers-in-law, Scrope and Westmorland were members, so was his friend Sussex, as well as Northampton, Bedford, Derby, Northumberland and Stafford. It was also Cecil's Inn. But, no more than they, did Norfolk contemplate attending moots or acquiring any expertise in the law. Quite apart from their place in legal education and the organisation of the profession, the Inns of Court were the London clubs of the Elizabethan age and membership of one gave any statesman a good opportunity of informal discussion with men of informed opinions. For a nobleman as aloof as the duke, admission to an Inn was a step of some consequence.

The following January he was admitted a freeman of the City of London through his company, the Fishmongers. A crowd saw him ride through the middle gate, salute the Wardens of his livery, and tie up his horse at the steps of the Guildhall. In the Council Chamber he took his oath before Sir William Harper, the lord mayor, and was admitted free 'in all things, excepting the orphanage of his children'. Afterwards he enjoyed two dinners – one in the Lord Mayor's house in Lombard Street, the other, as guest of the Fishmongers, at the *King's Head* in Bridge Street.[3]

Away in Kenninghall he knew nothing of Dudley's schemings with the Spanish ambassador, De Quadra, during 1561 for gaining Philip II's support for his marriage to the Queen at the price of a restitution of Catholicism. Indeed, the fact that Norfolk and Lord Robert were at daggers drawn led the ambassador to avoid the duke's company when he was in town. But what Norfolk heard in due course from Cecil about Dudley's double dealing confirmed him in his utter mistrust of the favourite, and this mistrust remained mutual. Each of them was a dark horse, withdrawn from the normal groupings of courtiers, and if neither was a member of the small, select Council, then this was a slight they shared with both the archbishops. Yet each was a person to be reckoned with, whose influence could make or mar any scheme, ruin a reputation or block a promotion. Norfolk's opportunism was different in kind from Lord Robert's in 1561 and the year following. Waiting on events, he knew it was only a matter of time before he was admitted to the close circle of advisers round his royal cousin. The crisis of the autumn of 1562 was destined to bring the rivals closer together than at any time in their lives.

That spring there was work for him to do. For some while Elizabeth had been keeping an eye on Temple Newsam, Lennox's house near Leeds, which she knew to be a meeting-place for the Catholic gentry of Yorkshire. The Queen feared that Lady Margaret Douglas might persuade those disaffected northerners, who came to the house for confessions and mass whenever there was a priest in residence, to rise in favour of her son, Darnley's, match with Mary Queen of Scots and even to support his claim to the English throne. She now decided to send mother and son to the Tower to cool their ambitions before it was too late and to despatch a group of trusty noblemen to keep the north country quiet.

Early in March Norfolk was sent to Yorkshire where he was joined by the Marquess of Northampton, the Earls of Huntingdon and Rutland and Lord Hunsdon 'under the pretext of a harehunt'. The idea of a meeting of noblemen for such a pursuit, as a blind for their political task, was probably Norfolk's own; was he not the finest courser in England? Yet the secret of the expedition was not well kept, for De Quadra who was hand in glove with Lady Lennox, had an inkling of the affair. 'It is suspected', he wrote to Cardinal Granvelle, 'that this meeting may be to fall unawares on some of the Catholics who are most feared, but whom they dare not arrest without some such precaution for fear of a disaster.' Yet the duke's presence puzzled the Spaniard. 'There is not a head amongst them worth anything, except that of the duke, and I should be astonished at his entering into such an enterprise as he is not at all attached to the present state of things in religion or otherwise. Quite the contrary.' But lead such an enterprise he did, and the presence of the hunters ensured that the peace was kept. As a further precaution the Earls of Northumberland and Westmorland were summoned to court and, though Darnley managed to slip through Elizabeth's fingers, his mother was sent to London, where she was later joined in the Tower by her husband. Norfolk was too young to remember her spell of close confinement at Kenninghall in 1541 for indulging in a courtship with Charles Howard, Queen Catherine's brother.[4]

When under the terms of the secret Treaty of Richmond, signed with the Huguenot leaders in September 1562, Elizabeth intervened in the third French War of Religion, Ambrose Dudley, Earl of Warwick, was sent to occupy Le Havre. Initially Norfolk may have resented being passed over in favour of Lord Robert's brother, but soon there were rumours that a larger force was to be sent across the Channel under his command. After Michaelmas, as usual, he returned to London from Kenninghall, entering the City with great pomp on 8th October. Two days later he moved to Hampton Court where the Queen was residing, but when he arrived he found her dangerously ill. She had caught smallpox, a disease from which the Countess of Bedford had recently died. For a week there was no sign of the rash and she grew daily more feverish. Death seemed near at hand.

In this sudden crisis the duke was fortunate to be present at court. The problem of the succession over-shadowed all else, and as the Queen was too delirious to be able to name her successor power lay in the hands of those about her. Norfolk had the opportunity of frank talks with Dudley before Cecil, hastily summoned from London, arrived at midnight. Regardless of the fact that they were not privy councillors both the Earl Marshal and the master of the horse took active parts in discussions which went on into the night and were continued by adjournment during the next few days. As premier peer Norfolk could not be ignored at a time like this. In fact the one result of the Queen's illness was that he and Lord Robert were both admitted to the Council on 20th October.

According to the only account we have of the hectic, informal conversations at Hampton Court 'there were nearly as many different opinions about the succession to the Crown' as there were councillors present, though no one, apparently, espoused the cause of Mary Queen of Scots. The two most promising candidates were Lady Catherine Grey, younger sister of Lady Jane Grey, who was descended from the marriage of Henry VIII's sister with the Duke of Suffolk, and on the other hand Henry Hastings, third earl of Huntingdon who was descended on his father's side from Edward III and on his mother's from the brother of Edward IV. Both were protestants, but as the Suffolk claim had been upheld by Henry VIII's will, Lady Catherine was at the outset the favourite of the two. For the moment Norfolk and Dudley agreed to support Huntingdon's title; to them he seemed a more satisfactory candidate than Lady Grey, who was in the Tower on account of her secret marriage with the Earl of Hertford, and both Bedford and Pembroke came to a like conclusion. Cecil did not show his hand, but as the debate continued all chance of unanimity receded. Lord Treasurer Winchester voiced the views of a third group, which wanted to submit the rival claims to lawyers. Others, including perhaps Norfolk, opposed such a scheme as the jurists were all suspected of being Catholics and would probably turn down both Lady Grey and Huntingdon in favour of the claims of Lady Margaret Douglas and her son.

Before anything had been decided Elizabeth recovered and in her first words begged the Council in case of emergency to make Lord Robert Protector of the Kingdom with an income of £20,000 and a suitable title. It was clear to Cecil and others that Dudley's admission to the Council, which this royal pleading foreshadowed, must be balanced by the addition of Norfolk, and from a letter of the duke's of a year later there can be no doubt that Cecil was responsible for his appointment. The rivals, for all their differences still evenly matched, entered political power on the same day.[5]

In London that winter the first in the land continued to discuss the problems of the succession and of the Queen's marriage over their dinner tables. There was much speculation and a wealth of gossip. One week it seemed that Lord Robert's hopes were 'higher than ever and the Duke of Norfolk is, to all appearance, helping him sincerely. There seems a close intimacy between them since their reconciliation', noted Bishop De Quadra. But the next week he reported that Norfolk had altered his mind. A number of peers met at Arundel House and talked till the small hours. The Lord Chamberlain, Howard of Effingham, came out against Dudley and said he could never approve of Huntingdon's candidature and won the duke round to support the Suffolk claim. We are told that a possible inducement was that one of his little daughters might in time be married to Lady Catherine Grey's baby son. Elizabeth was very angry when she heard of the meeting at Arundel's of what was in effect the strongest pressure group in politics for settling the succession in defiance of her prerogative and she upbraided her lord steward for taking part.[6]

In January 1563, four days before Parliament assembled, the Spanish ambassador appeared before the Council to lodge a complaint. He complained he had been unjustly arrested and the locks on the doors of his embassy at Durham Place forcedly changed for harbouring a would-be assassin which had provoked a public demonstration in the Strand. Norfolk was presiding at the Council that day but as he felt unequal to the task of conducting the conference with De Quadra in Latin he called on Cecil to put the Council's case. Some might think this was merely a pretext, to avoid having to deal with a man with whom he had been on friendly terms, but the duke's plea was a valid one and the Secretary was glad of the opportunity of dealing with the troublesome Spaniard himself. As he had his confidential secretary in his pay Cecil knew a great deal about the goings on in Durham Place – the plotting with disaffected Englishmen, the attendances at mass at the embassy chapel and the rest of it. De Quadra was asked to leave Durham Place, which he rented from the Crown, and although his recall to Spain was not actually requested, the bishop faded out of history; he died, heavily in debt in that summer and a successor, de Silva, did not arrive in England until July 1564. As a former gentleman of Philip II's bedchamber, Norfolk was sorry for De Quadra's inglorious end.[7]

Though he attended the House of Lords every day during the Parliament which sat from January to April 1563, we have no means of knowing what part Norfolk played in the business of the House. The Queen had not allowed the great theme of the succession to be developed before the Sessions ended, yet this theme was to be taken up time and again during the next few years whenever two or more councillors were gathered together. Norfolk was convinced that the only solution to the problem would be for Elizabeth to marry the Archduke Charles of Austria, younger son of the Emperor Ferdinand I, and for the next few years he gave his full support to the protracted negotiations for this match. In the first year of the reign Cecil had favoured such a union and Elizabeth herself regarded it as the best match she could make in Christendom. A marriage with the House of Hapsburg would strengthen the old Spanish alliance, the cornerstone of England's overseas trade, and nullify the Franco-Scottish threat as well as increase England's standing in Europe. Since Charles was a younger son there was little danger of England becoming, as a result of a union of crowns, the minor partner; and the marriages of Philip and Mary and of Francis and Mary Queen of Scots provided vivid examples of dynastic alliances of queens with consorts who were heirs to a greater empire.

With such personalities as Dudley and Norfolk it was impossible for divisions in the Council to be healed. Rumours of further trouble at home dismayed Sir Thomas Smith, the ambassador in France, in mid-August. 'That there should be trouble and disagreement in England between my Lord of Norfolk and my Lord Robert, my Lord Admiral and the Earl of Warwick, and

the Council divided in a great jar', increased his worries. Later in
the year the duke's relations with Cecil became strained. The facts
are obscure, but undoubtedly the question of Dudley was at the
bottom of it. Apparently the Secretary felt bound to remind
Howard that he had persuaded Elizabeth to appoint him a privy
councillor as 'a meet instrument to serve her affairs'; yet the
Queen had now complained to him that 'none was so much
against Her Majesty'. Cecil, anxious to hold a difficult team together, had become tired of answering for Norfolk's outspoken
opinions to the Queen, and he even suspected that various rumours being circulated at his expense had been invented by the
duke. Norfolk denied the charge and still signed his cryptic and
allusive letter of reply to Cecil, 'your most beholden'. The
rumours were, it seems, part of Dudley's campaign to discredit
Cecil in the Queen's eyes. Astutely the Secretary succeeded in
turning Elizabeth's wrath away from himself on to his brother-
in-law, Lord Keeper Bacon, who for a time was in danger of
dismissal. Norfolk had played no part in Dudley's intrigues and
his friendship with Cecil survived this period of misunderstanding,
for they were soon united in pressing forward with proposals for
the Austrian match.[8]

Norfolk was in the shadows again during the early half of 1564,
for on 10th January Duchess Margaret died in her twenty-fourth
year. Three weeks earlier she had given birth to her second son,
William, at her own beloved Audley End. She was moved on a
litter to Norwich for Christmas too soon after her delivery, and
died in the palace. The duke was left a widower a second time at
the age of twenty-five, with five children to care for; his eldest
son Philip, and four children by Margaret Audley – Thomas,
born 24th August 1561, Lord Howard de Walden and future
Earl of Suffolk, the inheritor of his mother's estates and destined
to become, like his Howard great-grandfather, Lord Treasurer
of England; Bess, loyally named, born in 1560 who died as a
child[9]; Meg, now a year old, who was to marry Robert Sackville,
second Earl of Dorset; and baby William, the future Lord Howard
of Naworth, nicknamed 'Belted Will'. In his bereavement Norfolk was given leave of absence from court and lived quietly with
his children in the country. For a few years, until he married
again, the children's grandmother, Lady Audley, was to occupy
the same position in the Howard nursery that the Duchess of

Richmond had done in Norfolk's youth. His five years with
Margaret had, by all accounts, been exceptionally happy and her
early death was the third great tragedy of his life – and probably
affected him far more deeply than either his father's execution or
Duchess Mary's death. For six months it made his struggle for
power at court pointless and high politics lost their savour.

*   *   *

Earlier negotiations with the Archduke had long been put on
one side, but in the summer of 1564 they were reopened in earnest
by the envoys sent to the imperial court with Elizabeth's condol-
ences on the death of Ferdinand I. The initiative was undoubtedly
Cecil's, but he had Norfolk's warm support. Soon he was far
more enthusiastic about the match and its chances of success than
Cecil and for the three further years during which the negotiations
dragged on he was the principal protagonist and the marriage
alliance his first political care. In opposition to these schemes,
Dudley, as irresponsible as ever, was soon deeply involved in
Marie de Medici's plans for Elizabeth to marry a French prince
and at the same time was taking every opportunity to further his
own suit with the Queen. Consistent only in her inconsistency,
Elizabeth blew hot and cold on each project as her fancy led her.[10]

August saw the three contestants for power in another setting,
for the Queen was paying a visit to Cambridge. Cecil was Chancellor, Dudley had recently succeeded Paget as High Steward of
the University and Norfolk was High Steward of the town and
visitor of Magdalene College. Elizabeth resided at King's, Cecil
at St John's, his old college, and Dudley at Trinity; but etiquette
required the duke to become a guest of the town and so he stayed
with Alderman Ray in the market place. Providing food for the
enormous entourage that always followed the Queen on progresses had left Cambridge poulterers with little worth buying,
so Norfolk sent a messenger to his wife's estate at Saffron Walden
for capons and chickens to help feed various notabilities in his
lodging, but he made the burgers pay for this favour.

A heavy programme of ceremonies and entertainments began
on the Saturday, 5th August, when the Vice Chancellor, Dr Haw-
ford, called to present the duke with two pairs of gloves, a marchpane and a sugar loaf. He then set out on horseback, with Sussex
and Richard Cox, Bishop of Ely, in scorching sunshine to meet

the Queen who had been staying the previous night at Hasling-field, near Granchester, the home of Worthington, a gentleman pensioner. When the royal party reached Newnham there was a formal welcome by the mayor and burgesses. Orations, disputations, services, plays and feasts filled each of the five days. On the Sunday evening there was even a secular play in King's College Chapel, and on the Tuesday morning the vestry of the chapel was used for a meeting of the Privy Council.

The dons delighted in disputations in the schools, debating in Latin such self-evident propositions as 'Monarchy is the best form of government' and 'Frequent change of the law is dangerous'. On the Wednesday it was the turn of the doctors of divinity to show off their learning and their loyalty, when the proposition was 'Scripture has greater authority than the church'. A lengthy debate was brought to an end by a long oration by the Bishop of Ely, and afterwards the lords in the audience, 'especially the Duke of Norfolk and the Lord Robert, kneeling down, humbly desired Her Majesty to speak something to the University in Latin'. Elizabeth at first refused; coyly she suggested that a speech in her native tongue might suffice, but Chancellor Cecil reminded her that in a formal gathering the University could only be addressed in Latin; three words, he thought, would do. She then floored her hearers by speaking six hundred, *more Ciceronis*, on the subject of diligent study. She was as a result too weary to see *Ajax Flagellifer*, a Latin translation from Sophocles, that was billed for that evening, and Norfolk, who had little love for classics, must have been extremely grateful that the programme was cancelled.

At eight next morning a special Congregation was held for conferring honorary M.A.s on Norfolk, Sussex, Warwick, Dudley and other courtiers, and an hour later the Queen left Cambridge. While escorting her from the town, the duke was persuaded by Dr Kelke, the master, to look back and see the melancholy aspect of Magdalene. His duties over, he returned and saw 'the air of desolation that pervaded the whole college', which Elizabeth had not troubled to visit. Lord Audley's foundation had not prospered, but as he had married the founder's daughter Norfolk was its patron and visitor. That same morning he undertook to give the college £40 a year until the building of the quadrangle should be completed, and also promised to endow the college with lands to increase the number of fellows and scholars.[11]

The favourite's advancement to the earldom of Leicester at Michaelmas 1564 did not improve his relations with Norfolk, for it made him and the rest of the older nobility even more conscious of what a parvenu he was. But in December their names were coupled together in a very different context. The question of a husband for Mary Queen of Scots for a time supplanted the older quest of a husband for Elizabeth and this was inextricably bound up with the succession to the English throne. Elizabeth now suggested that Mary should choose a spouse from one of three Englishmen: her own Leicester, Norfolk, now a widower for a second time, or Darnley. Mary replied that she was prepared to marry either of the latter provided Elizabeth would declare her as her successor – a request that abruptly terminated the negotiations. The Scottish no less than the English queen would marry on her own terms. The next spring Maitland of Lethington, who had taken part in these discussions, was to propose Norfolk as the most suitable husband for Mary. When he was approached he declined the honour and thus opened the way to negotiations with Leicester which Mary was to terminate only by marriage with Darnley in the teeth of Elizabeth's opposition. When three years later Maitland repeated the suggestion, Norfolk by then a widower for a third time was to act very differently. If by 1569 he was to regard Mary's hand as the only path to power, he undoubtedly looked on such a match in 1565 as tantamount to political suicide.[12]

Norfolk was present at the Council meeting on 1st May 1565 and with twelve other councillors signed the declaration to be sent to Edinburgh warning Mary of the dangerous consequences of marrying Darnley.

> *The Queen finding the intended marriage of Queen Mary with Lord Darnley strange has committed the same to certain of her Council, who with one assent thought that it would be unmeet and directly prejudicial to the sincere amity between both the Queens. They desire her so to say and to offer Queen Mary a free election of any other of the nobility in the whole realm or any other place.*

Leicester's name was significantly absent; so was Arundel's. The duke was asked by Cecil to send the latter a copy of the resolution to add his name to it, but he had refused to sign.[13]

Meanwhile there had occurred the incident in the tennis court. Like Drake's game of bowls before the Armada and Raleigh's throwing his cloak on the mire, it was an incident that caught the imagination of later generations, yet no eye-witness account has come down to us. One looks in vain for dramatic reports in the despatches of foreign ministers in London, or for an allusion in a letter of Cecil's or even a chance entry in a courtier's diary. The only contemporary account we have of the affair in the tennis court – probably the one at Hampton Court – comes from Edinburgh. The Earl of Athol told the story to Thomas Randolph, the English agent in Scotland, who passed it on in a letter to Sir Nicholas Throgmorton on 31st March:

> *That early the Duke's grace and my lord of Leicester were playing at tennis, the Queen beholding of them, and my Lord Robert being hot and sweating took the Queen's napkin out of her hand and wiped his face, which the Duke seeing said that he was too saucy, and swore that he would lay his racket upon his face; whereup rose a great trouble and the Queen offended sore with the Duke . . .*[14]

Their antipathy was soon to be intensified by the presence at court of the Earl of Sussex, a relative and close friend of the duke's, who returned from five years' soldiering in Ireland to become the leader of the anti-Leicester faction.

Thomas Radcliffe, third Earl of Sussex, was almost as much of an aristocrat as Norfolk. His mother was a Howard – the daughter of the second duke – and a grandmother was a Stafford. He was already very friendly with Cecil and now that he was again in England he and Norfolk were to be drawn very closely together, despite the fact that Sussex was twelve years older than the duke. Their alliance was founded not so much on ties of kin as on similarity of outlook, and the most striking expression of this was dislike of Leicester. The favourite was, for Sussex, not merely a man to arouse mistrust, but a dangerous man, who could have no principles whatsoever because he was a parvenu. To the end he remained outspoken about Leicester; even on his death-bed he counselled his friends: 'Beware of the gipsy, for he will be too hard for you all. You know not the beast as well as I do.' When the 'Gentleman' in *Leicester's Commonwealth* shook his head at the favourite's disdain of 'all the ancient nobility of our realm, how he contemneth, derideth and debaseth them', it might have been Sussex speaking. The return of Sussex to court was in consequence electric, and his effect on Norfolk profound.[15]

A stronger personality than the duke, he soon took over from him the lead in the campaign against Dudley and their quarrels 'threatened to convert the court into an armed camp'. In a letter that autumn to Sir Thomas Smith, Cecil commented on the fresh groupings of the factions at Whitehall Palace and hoped he could bend them all to Her Majesty's service. With Sussex and Norfolk were now aligned Lord Howard of Effingham and Lord Hunsdon, another cousin of the Queen; and in noting the strong bonds between Sussex and the duke Cecil made plain his own affection and high regard for the latter:

> *My Lord of Norfolk loveth my Lord of Sussex earnestly, and so all that stock of the Howards seem to join in friendship together; and yet in my opinion without cause to be misliked. And for the Duke, I think England hath not had in this age a nobleman more likely to prove a father and a stay to this country, and so I am glad to perceive the Queen Majesty to have him in estimation. He is wise, just, modest, careful, et timens Deum.*[16]

Leicester was, indeed, out of royal favour at the time. He had been making indiscreet advances to the beautiful Lettice Knollys, Viscountess Hereford, a cousin of the Queen's, and Elizabeth retaliated by becoming seemingly enamoured of Sir Thomas Heneage, the perfect courtier. But beyond and behind these flirtations Cecil and Norfolk pressed forward with the Hapsburg marriage scheme, while Leicester and Throgmorton pursued their rival negotiations for a French marriage.

News of the first reactions of the Archduke to the marriage proposals was sent post haste to Norfolk at Kenninghall in mid-July. The new Spanish ambassador, de Silva, hoped he would immediately come to court where his presence would be 'very advantageous, more on account of his rank and standing than any particular influence he has on affairs'. But the duke stayed in his country. A little later, in a conversation with Arundel at Nonsuch, de Silva expressed his surprise that Norfolk should not have been summoned by Elizabeth for urgent talks and thought this was a slight on him. According to one of his secretaries the duke decided against coming to court on his own initiative as he feared the Queen was 'not acting as straightforwardly in the affair as he could have wished'. Arundel apparently shrugged his shoulders and said the duke was still young and may have misjudged Elizabeth's enthusiasm for Archduke Charles's hand. In any case, Norfolk was summoned to London with Arundel, Pembroke, Northampton and certain other councillors in the last week of September for discussing the more urgent topic of Scottish policy. His experience of the Borders in 1560 made his advice valuable, and on the eve of Mary's marriage to Darnley there had been talk of sending the duke as lieutenant-general in the north, ready to invade Scotland. Elizabeth, however, decided to continue to wait upon events.[17]

A day or so later, on 30th September 1565, Norfolk was standing godfather with Archbishop Matthew Parker, at the christening in the chapel of Whitehall Palace of the infant son of Princess Cecilia of Sweden and the Margrave of Baden, who had arrived in England earlier in the month after a journey of eleven months – a matter of days before the Princess's delivery in the Strand. Elizabeth was herself godmother and had chosen the names Edward Fortunatus. Leicester was present at the service, but the fact that Norfolk, not he, was a godfather, is significant.[18]

During that winter the affair of the Archduke Charles proceeded all too slowly. The duke and Cecil were anxious about the long-delayed reply from the Emperor and even more disheartening was the news that Philip of Spain was discouraging the match on religious grounds. While Cecil feared that the Archduke's intention of remaining a Catholic would prove a stumbling block, Norfolk was more hopeful. He was convinced that, despite the weight of French diplomacy being thrust in the scales for Leicester, Elizabeth would never consent to marry him; 'there is no-one else', he wrote, 'but the Archduke whom she can marry'. Norfolk was here the *politique*, prepared to sacrifice principles in allowing Charles the private exercise of his religion as consort (a compromise, such as the privileges to be allowed in the next century to Queens Henrietta Maria and Catherine of Braganza); for him anything was preferable to having the realm 'desperate both of marriage and succession'. He continued to advocate this course for another two years as the only sensible solution to a difficult problem.

There was fresh trouble with Leicester. The whisperings of the rumour-mongers have gone, still less has 'the budget full of pretty inventions' about the two peers been preserved; all we know is that there was 'a great controversy' between them. The Queen's attitude remained unpredictable. When the duke asked her for her leave to return to Norfolk, early in December, he spoke plainly to her about the necessity of marriage, to settle the succession and quieten the realm and once more extolled the benefits of a Hapsburg match. Such, he said, was no personal whim, for he claimed to be spokesman 'of all the principal people in the realm who loved her and whose feelings on the subject he well knew'. Those of her Council, he added, who had advised her to marry Lord Robert, had done so because they imagined that was where her heart lay, 'not because they really thought the match would be beneficial to the country, or good for her own dignity'. Elizabeth did not lose her temper, but thanked her cousin graciously, though she made no firm promises. The same day Norfolk saw Leicester and reminded him that he had promised to drop his suit for good, and it was with this assurance that his colleagues had re-opened negotiations with the Archduke. Leicester, too, kept his temper and when the duke left London, glad to be on his way home again, he was prominent among the gathering of notables to speed him on his way, 'doing him all the honour in their power'. At Norwich he prayed for the success of the negotiations at the imperial court and for a change of heart from her Majesty.[19]

Almost as soon as he reached Norwich came a letter from Cecil, telling of the latest developments with the House of Hapsburg, which Norfolk was 'well enough able to prick out both treble and bass', and hinting that Leicester was still pressing forward with his suit. Cecil also announced, as tactfully as he could, that the Queen had found it necessary to reduce by ten sarplers* the annual amount of wool he was to be allowed to export by special licence.[20] This hurt Norfolk to the quick. He at once 'scribbled' a reply:

> *I am sorry that the Queen's Majesty judges my deserts so far uncomparable to others, when in greater things she grants so frank and lasting licence to some (yea, by hudle), and sticks and stays me*

* The sarpler contained 728 lb.

upon trifles. Well, how hardly so ever I am dealt withal, if ever time come wherein occasion may require my service, the world shall see that no use to me ward can discourage my fervent zeal and love to my Mistress and my Country; and perchance therein will not be behind with them that have speed best in this time.[21]

All hope of reconciliation with Leicester was gone for the sake of ten sarplers of wool!

When Norfolk returned to London in January 1566 the feud broke out again, for he had been angered by Leicester's broken promises about abandoning his courtship of Elizabeth. He told the favourite plainly that he would stop at nothing to oppose him, and each marshalled his forces. To emphasise the divisions at court Lord Robert's supporters started wearing blue (or purple), and Norfolk's yellow. 'I am told that Leicester began it, so as to know who were his friends', wrote de Silva, 'and the adherents of the Duke did the same in consequence of some disagreements they had with them about the aid of the Duke and his friends had given to the Archduke's match.' Arundel it seems intervened to try and keep the peace; outwardly they were all smiles to each other, 'dissembling in the usual English way, but remaining of the same opinion as before'. Could it be otherwise? There is a tale, plausible enough, yet impossible of proof, that about this time an agent approached Amy Robsart's half-brother, to bribe him into denouncing Leicester as the murderer of his wife. This Appleyard (we shall meet with him again later) crossed the Thames at Hampton in his nightshirt to meet a man who suggested his joining those of the Council 'who do mind to charge him [Leicester] with certain things' . . . The atmosphere was as over-charged as ever, yet a truce was called for 24th January.[22]

That winter Charles IX had written to Elizabeth to announce that he intended to invest two of her subjects with the Order of St Michael when his special envoy came to the Court of St James's to receive the Garter on his behalf. He delegated to her the task of selecting the recipients. When she had first heard of the French King's intentions, Leicester struck her as an obvious choice, and after a while she settled on Norfolk as the second. A joint investiture of the two contenders might help to end the dissensions between them. But the duke had not been eager to accept the honour and, according to Sussex, had only done so in obedience to his sovereign. Her design was to prevent jealousy among the nobility if Leicester were to be the only recipient of the St Michael. Accepting the Order, according to one shrewd observer, might well damage Norfolk's reputation for being a true Englishman, 'knowing that the populace were badly affected towards French Kings' – a traditional anti-Gallic prejudice that would in a later age have as its *cri de coeur* 'No Popery and no wooden shoes'. Perhaps, as Sussex claimed, the duke had even told his household of his dislike of having the honour thrust upon him. At any rate he entered London on the eve of the investiture in greater style than ever before, with three hundred horsemen.[23]

In the 'great closet' at Whitehall Palace on 24th January, in the presence of Charles IX's deputy, M. Ramboilliet, his officials, the French ambassador and a gathering of courtiers, the duke and the earl 'embraced each other and communed awhile'. It was ten o'clock and both had fasted. After a while they were both led off to be dressed for the ceremony and reappeared in chapel in 'white velvet shoes, hose, girdle and scabbard; netherstocks of white silk knit, coats, with sleeves on, of cloth of silver, edged with silver lace, and in short gowns of russet velvet, furred with leopards, the sleeves decorated with aiglettes of gold'. On their heads were black velvet caps with a silver band and a white feather.

The Chapel had been prepared by Garter Dethick in consultation with the French heralds. It was hung with rich arras and the altar, its frontal a cloth of silver embroidered with gold angels, was crowded with gilt basins, cups, candlesticks, an ark, a fountain of mother of pearl and other priceless vessels and ornaments. For that morning the dean of the Chapel was subject to the authority of the French King's deputy and to emphasise this the arms of France were placed over his stall.

Norfolk's stall, opposite the dean, was decorated with his own arms beneath a ducal crown. Instead of crest or supporters there was his style written out in full: 'Treshault puissant et tresnoble prynce Thomas duke de Norfolk, Comte Mareshall d'Angleterre, Seigneur de Mowbray, Segrave et de Brus, Chivalier du tresnoble Ordre de la Jarretiere et aussi du tresnoble de Seint Michell.' Leicester's stall was beneath the dean's. For the Earl Marshal the investiture was not only a high honour, it was a matter of exceptional professional interest to see how M. Ramboilliet, M. Dore, St Michael King of Arms, and his Secretary went about their complicated duties, and one of his officials was present to make a full report.

The ceremony over, the two new companions took the Frenchmen to dine in the Council Chamber and later they had an audience of the Queen in the Privy Chamber. Afterwards they disrobed and changed into their normal clothes. The Queen, Norfolk and Leicester 'well rewarded' the Deputy, while St Michael took as his customary perquisites the gowns of the two new knights, who also gave him a chair of gold. For the recipients it was an expensive honour. Next day the French party left for Edinburgh where they were to invest Lord Darnley with the same order. Becoming a Knight of the Order of St Michael placed Leicester and Norfolk on a level with Kings and the consorts of Queens regnant, and undoubtedly helped to feed their respective ambitions at striving for a crown matrimonial.[24]

For duke and earl it had been a day of 'dissembling'. Within the week Howard, as spokesman of the majority of the Council, called on Dudley to have out with him the business of his continued intrigues. Now that they were friends, began Norfolk, he could be frank with him. In everything else he would do what he could to support Leicester, but over his renewed attempts to gain the Queen's hand, he had no alternative but to stand in his way. Elizabeth, the duke continued with assurance, did not intend to marry him, so nothing but trouble could be reaped from his schemes, and as he alone would be blamed by the entire country for further delays in the negotiations with Archduke Charles, he would earn for himself a fatal unpopularity. The only sensible course was for the earl to join with the rest of his colleagues in promoting the Archduke's suit. Leicester characteristically replied that he would certainly do as Norfolk advised if he could so arrange matters that Elizabeth should not think that he was neglecting his suit out of distaste for her, as this 'might cause her, womanlike, to undo him'; and on this understanding the rivals parted.

The Privy Council also debated whether they should collectively or individually approach the Queen on the same topic. Meanwhile Sussex lobbyed de Silva who promised to use his influence with Elizabeth; the duke would have come and discussed tactics with the ambassador himself, but felt it might compromise him in the eyes of Leicester's party, and in any case he and Sussex

'were like one person' in their views. This series of confidential
conversations, whose substance was soon the common knowledge
of all the embassies, had an immediate effect, for when de Silva
had an audience with the Queen at Candlemas, as they walked
in the Privy Garden at Whitehall, she told him of Leicester's un-
selfishness in urging her to marry for the sake of her country, of
herself, and even of himself, for he was being blamed for her
single state.

With the outlook much brighter the duke left London for
Kenninghall, confident that he had saved a crisis and in good
spirits at his success in obtaining the Dacre wardship – a topic we
shall consider in the following chapter.

The Catholic Arundel, who had taken a neutral part in these
discussions, was leaving England at this time for a course of baths
at Padua as a cure for his gout. Before he went he told de Silva
he was sure the Archduke affair would come to nought and that
his son-in-law of Norfolk was as a matter of principle pursuing
the phantom of a Hapsburg match merely 'out of enmity to the
Earl of Leicester'. It was too harsh a judgment. Cecil, undiscour-
aged by the slow progress at the imperial court, applauded the
duke's efforts. In March he wrote to Sir Thomas Smith in confidence that 'My Lord of Norfolk hath shewed himself a very noble
man and wise', throughout the affair. But Leicester's return to
royal favour inevitably provoked fresh trouble with the duke,
who stayed away from court in a huff, and even excused himself
from the St George's Day celebrations at Windsor, where the
Emperor was to be nominated to his father's place in the Order
of the Garter; he pleaded an indisposition, but the truth was he
could not abide Leicester's company. Except for a brief visit to
London to see Elizabeth about the Dacre wardship, he stayed on
at Kenninghall until 13th September and made a point of absent-
ing himself from the royal visit to Oxford at the beginning of
that month, where Leicester as Chancellor of the University
would be playing the principal role. Even while he was away
from court the ill-feeling between supporters of the two rivals
increased apace and there were high words between Lord North
and Lord Clinton, now behind Leicester.[25]

During May 1566, Thomas Dannett had been sent as agent to
Augsburg and Vienna to discuss affairs with the Emperor Maximilian II and the Archduke Charles. On the vexed issue of faith

he reported that the Holy Roman Emperor 'seems not to be hard, but looks that the religion his brother was brought up in should be permitted him'. 'Something must be winked at by the Queen', suggested the envoy, who for his part went out of his way to show the imperial court that an Englishman was open-minded, by accompanying the Archduke to evensong. More encouraging for Norfolk were his reports of the spouse proposed for Elizabeth. He was courteous, affable, liberal, wise and of a good memory, was popular, and an active man who liked vigorous outdoor sports. A recent attack of smallpox had not disfigured him; he was 'of a sanguine complexion and, for a man, beautiful and well faced, well shaped, small in the waist, and well and broad breasted; he seems in his clothes well thighed and well legged'. Because he stooped a little some might think him slightly round-shouldered, but Dannett added that in the saddle he was as straight in his body as any man alive. From this description Norfolk must have thought him no less attractive to women than Leicester himself.[26] At last things were beginning to move and soon Elizabeth would demand a portrait.

That summer the political situation at home was still uncertain and rumours were rife. At a Council meeting Leicester accused Sussex of responsibility for Shane O'Neill's rebellion in Ireland, and when Sussex retorted that it was his accuser who had himself fermented rebellion by his letters to O'Neill, the two nearly came to blows. Recent developments in Scotland began to cast a deeper shadow and were linked inevitably with the problem of the succession. The consequences of Rizzio's murder at Holyrood House in March had become a powerful factor in English politics. A spy of Cecil's in Edinburgh reported in June that Mary had told him of letters she had received from Dacres of the crooked back, Sir Thomas Stanley and others, proffering friendship and she hoped through them to win over Norfolk, Shrewsbury, Derby and the Northern Earls, 'for that she thought them all to be of the old religion which she meant to restore again with all expedition and thereby win the hearts of the common people'. According to Sir James Melville, who hastened from Edinburgh to Greenwich in July to announce to Elizabeth the birth of James Stewart, Norfolk and Pembroke had now declared they would support Mary's claim to succeed Elizabeth; but this is, in fact, most unlikely. The duke was away from court and the views with which Melville credited him were pure hearsay. He was too entrenched in the Archduke affair to be able to swap horses at that moment even if he wanted to.

'There are communications going on among the aristocracy here, which threaten a storm', reported de Silva in the early autumn, 'and I think, considering that the winter is near, that they will not dare to make any open movement.' There was, indeed, an undercurrent of uneasiness both at court and in the country, and men were turning to the duke for a lead, yet he remained aloof. Directly he arrived in London on 13th September he had an audience with the Queen to impress on her once again the need for her to conclude the negotiations with Archduke Charles. He had not time that evening to call on the Spanish ambassador, but sent his Secretary; 'he wishes to show the country that he desires the Queen to marry in a way fitting to her rank ... and he has great influence and many friends, being the most powerful person in the realm', de Silva told Philip II. It was clear that when Parliament opened unprecedented pressure would be brought on Elizabeth to marry. Meanwhile on this pregnant eve of sessions noblemen, knights and burgesses discussed the succession at great houses all down the Strand.

On Michaelmas Day Norfolk held the feast of the French Order at the Charterhouse with Leicester, and a great occasion it was, with both of them wearing their robes. Many English courtiers joined them for dinner at which the French ambassador was the guest of honour. Duke and earl were still at loggerheads, and although they each said it was because the other took a different stand on the perennial topic of the Archduke, those closest to them knew that the disputes arose 'on private affairs', the subject of the Queen's confidence.[27]

The Parliament that had been prorogued for the last three years re-assembled on 2nd October in a militant mood, determined to proceed with the question of the Queen's marriage and the settlement of the succession. In 1563 the Commons had gone home with a promise from Elizabeth that she would answer their petition for action under both these heads, yet she was determined that they should not meddle. To prepare her for the storm that might break out at any time, the almost forbidden topic was broached round the Council table, with the Queen herself present, on 12th October. As agreed with his colleagues, Norfolk began the discussion with a prepared piece: 'Madam, you know that I have taken an oath to Your Majesty as a Councillor, by which I am obliged to have regard to your well-being and that of your subjects. Pardon me, therefore, if I take the liberty of putting this matter before you.' He reminded her of the Commons petition, now three years old, which still awaited an answer, rehearsed the recent developments in England, Scotland and in Europe, and begged her to allow these weighty matters to be discussed openly in both houses. According to the French ambassador, who has left the only account of this meeting, Elizabeth replied angrily that she had governed her realm well. Who succeeded to her throne was her affair, not Parliament's, not even her Council's, and she had no wish by naming a successor to be 'buried alive'. As for her marriage, they knew full well the dealings with the Archduke and an alliance with him was not far off. A few words more and she had taken her leave of them.

This was an inauspicious start. The next week in the Commons, when the Subsidy Bill (the *ens entium* of the Sessions) was moved, debate on the succession began in earnest, with tempers raised and, it seems, members even coming to blows. Neither Cecil nor any other member of the government could give the House a satisfactory assurance, and as a result a message was sent to the Queen, via the Council, that the Commons' grievances must be redressed before taxation was approved. Utterly exasperated by this, Elizabeth poured out her heart to the Spanish ambassador. Two days later, on 22nd October, the Lords sent their own deputation to Whitehall Palace, led by old Winchester, who politely pointed out that Parliament was wasting its time; she should either declare her will or dissolve Parliament so they could all go home. Norfolk, still under half the Lord Treasurer's age, followed and then others, but Elizabeth was undaunted. The Commons were rebels, she said, and not a man there would have dared to have behaved like this in her father's time. 'My Lords, do whatever you wish. As for me, I shall do no otherwise than pleases me.' She would seek the advice of the best lawyers in her realm about the succession, but Parliament was too feeble-witted a body to deal with so important a matter.[28]

Next day the Commons sent a committee, led by Robert Bell, M.P. for King's Lynn, to discuss further with the Upper House, and in the end, over-riding Winchester's senile vacilation, the

Lords agreed to join with the Commons in a suit to Her Majesty, presenting a united front. Once again Norfolk was the spokesman. De Silva, in whom Elizabeth confided at this time, and with whom Sussex and the duke were quite open, pieced together an account of this stormy audience:

> *The Queen was so angry that she addressed hard words to the Duke of Norfolk, whom she called traitor or conspirator, or other words of similar flavour. He replied that he never thought to have to ask her pardon for having offended her thus. Subsequently they tell me the Queen asserted that she addressed no such words to the Duke. The Earls of Leicester and Pembroke, the Marquess of Northampton and the Lord Chamberlain spoke to her on the matter, and Pembroke remarked to her that it was not right to treat the Duke badly, since he and the others were only doing what was fitting for the good of the country, and advising her what was best for her, and if she did not think fit to adopt the advice, it was still their duty to offer it. She told him he talked like a swaggering soldier, and said to Leicester that she had thought if all the world abandoned her he would not have done so, to which he answered that he would die at her feet; and she said that had nothing to do with the matter. She said that Northampton was of no account, and he had better talk about the arguments used to enable him to get married again, when he had a wife living, instead of mincing words with her. With this she left them, and had resolved to order them to be considered under arrest in their houses. This she has not done, but she has commanded them [Leicester and Pembroke] not to appear before her.*

She later told the ambassador that being abandoned by all her Council, except Winchester, had so angered her that she had railed at them. But in the end, on 5th November, she decided to address a Committee of thirty members from each House, and her tongue lashed in turn Commons, temporal peers and the bishops for daring to discuss such matters. She would marry, she said, as soon as she conveniently could (hinting broadly at the Archduke Charles) and hoped to bear children. The succession in the interim was quite another thing, as experience of her sister's unhappy reign had convinced her of the unwisdom of naming a successor; once one was named he or she would become the focal point of every intrigue, thus uniting all her enemies at home and abroad, and would endanger her life. Fighting speech though it was, she concluded by grudgingly agreeing to settle the succession as soon as she could.[29]

In those stormy weeks in the Autumn of 1566 Norfolk, for the first time, displayed political leadership and courage. With his formidable speeches in the Upper House, the Council Chamber and the audience room his stature had grown enormously; he now towered above his fellow peers. It seemed that he had conquered his aloofness and had come to realise that routine opposition to Leicester was no substitute for resolute political action. In a succession of interviews he had persuaded Elizabeth to give way on what she regarded as a vital point, and in the weeks which followed she was actively pursuing plans he had recommended to her and she renewed the Hapsburg negotiations without apparent equivocation. When the duke went home for Christmas he must have felt he was at last acting the part for which he was fitted, the loyal, outspoken, vigorous councillor. He was also on the eve of his marriage to the widowed Lady Dacre, and this match with its detailed family compact between their children further increased the Howard family fortunes.

Chapter Seven

FAMILY FORTUNES

LAND was the fundamental wealth of Tudor England. English cloth may have been the staple of overseas trade, yet the goal of the clothier was to invest his profits in real property and found a family, while lack of ready money was of no significance provided an individual had land available to use as security for a loan. On the basis of his landed estates Thomas Howard was reckoned in his own day as the wealthiest man in England. By careful administration and his successive marriages to wealthy widows he substantially increased his inheritance. Mastering the laws of property and wardship as a modern financier would master the laws of taxation, he consolidated his estates and achieved a remarkable family settlement; he also arranged a series of dynastic marriages for his children, all but one of which came to pass, despite his own attainder.

The bastion of the Howard inheritance was the 'Norfolk Liberty'. In July 1559 the Queen had confirmed to him the very considerable privileges which successive dukes of Norfolk had enjoyed since 1468, when Edward IV had granted to John, the third Mowbray Duke, a private franchise. This liberty comprised the entire hundreds of Launditch, South Greenhoe, Earsham and Guilt-Cross (in which Kenninghall lay), with fourteen other manors in Norfolk, including Caister; nine parishes in Suffolk; the rapes of Lewes and Bramber, the hundred of Bosham and the village of Stoughton in Sussex; the manors of Reigate and Dorking in Surrey; and the lordships of Harwich and Dovercourt in Essex. This area of nearly 600 square miles lay outside the normal bounds of royal justice and administration, an *imperium in imperio*.

The detailed privileges are impressive. None of the royal officials, whether sheriff, escheator, coroner, clerk of the market,
steward or marshal of the Queen's household or (in maritime
areas) the lord admiral, could enter this extensive private franchise,
'so that the duke and his heirs may resist any of these ministers
wishing to exercise any jurisdiction there'. Instead, the duke
appointed his own coroner, clerk of the market and other officials.
To the duke's bailiffs belonged the right of returning and executing all writs and precepts, whether from the Crown or from
its judges and commissioners. The duke kept for himself all fines
imposed in any court in the kingdom on men residing in his
liberty, and also enjoyed the goods and chattels of all felons,
fugitives and outlaws. He had his own gaol at Lopham. His tenants
could not be summoned in the sheriff's court for debts under 40s
or for trespasses in which the damages were less than that sum,
nor could they be attached for appearance in court.

Such were wide privileges indeed for a subject. They were
analogous with the liberties enjoyed of old by the Dukes of Lancaster and of Cornwall in their Duchies and by the Bishop of
Durham in his Palatinate; it was not for nothing that Norfolk
styled himself 'a high and mighty prince'. What the profits of
justice were in his liberty is less certain, for he was to enjoy his
perquisites 'without rendering any account to the Queen', though
we do know that in one year fines and forfeitures from tenants of
his lands lying in Norfolk and Suffolk totalled about £100, made
up of the 6s 8d and 3s 4d fines imposed on hundred bailiffs, jurors
and others who had played truant from Assizes and Quarter
Sessions and the more substantial sums levied in the central courts
at Westminster Hall.

In 1567 when the Exchequer officials in Westminster were
auditing the sheriff of Norfolk's account, they queried the items
he had marked as illeviable on the grounds that these were due
from tenants of the ducal liberty. So Norfolk's steward was sent
for, to show good cause why this money should not be paid to
the Crown. The man came up from Kenninghall with Elizabeth's
charter of confirmation, which contained at the end the irrefutable
clause that the duke should have full allowance of these monies
in the royal courts 'on the simple production of these letters', and
at once the Attorney General stayed the process.[1]

The administration of the Norfolk Liberty accounted for the

large number of officials in the duke's service, and he paid out in annuities to servants £925 a year. He was too shrewd a man to tolerate sinecurists and his bailiffs had to work for their annuities. The standards of service were high, particularly with the surveyors. Men like Timperley, Holland and Cantrell followed their fathers and their grandfathers in the duke's household and expected their sons to follow them. This was a royal household in miniature, with its headquarters at Kenninghall, where decisions were taken, the audits made, and to which the estate records were in due course transferred. As some of the outlying properties were less easy to administer from the centre, local men of considerable standing were chosen to act as stewards. The duke appointed, for example, Sir Thomas Fanshawe, Queen's Remembrancer of the Exchequer, to be chief steward of a group of five Essex manors near his home. Fanshawe was an official of great power, for the post of Queen's Remembrancer was the equivalent in Elizabethan days of Permanent Secretary to the Treasury, yet he willingly accepted Norfolk's terms of acting as his steward for 20s a year. No doubt the post of 'master of the game' within these manors, which went with the stewardship, with full hunting and fishing rights, was what counted with Fanshawe; yet it was important for Norfolk to have the job done well, and useful for him to have as a retainer so important a man as the Queen's Remembrancer. Howard even had his own legal department, headed first by John Blennerhasset, later by Robert Buxton, who held the office of 'solicitor general for all the duke's causes'.[2]

The heir to a great estate suffered as much in the sixteenth century from the expenses of wardship as his modern counterpart suffers from death duties. Though Thomas Howard, as a noble minor, was granted his own wardship and was thus saved from having his inheritance exploited by a guardian, he was still required to pay very substantial sums into the Court of Wards and Liveries, which regulated succession to tenancies-in-chief. His liabilities in the Court of Wards continued to cast a heavy shadow over his affairs, for Norfolk spent more of his life since his father's death as a minor than he was to spend as a tenant-in-chief of full age. In June 1558 he found himself liable for £500 10s 2½d for 'mean rates' of his lands until his coming of age. Worse was in store for him when he became twenty-one and sued out livery of his estates. His fine for livery, with certain arrears, was fixed in

December 1559 at £2,334 18s 8¾d – an indication of the value of the Howard inheritance. To meet this sum he entered into a series of thirty bonds, to pay it off by six-monthly instalments over fifteen years; and he soon got behind with the payments. He also became liable for the fine of his second duchess, Margaret Audley, for the livery of her lands, that had been due on her earlier marriage as a minor, to Harry Dudley in 1555 – a modest sum of £250. It was not surprising that a few years later the duke should hope to turn the system of wardship to his own advantage over the matter of the Dacre inheritance.[3]

The duke's expenses in the first three years of Elizabeth's reign were exceptionally heavy. Quite apart from his dues in the Wards, there were his expenses as lieutenant-general in the North, and public service of this nature was a costly business. When he was appointed to his command at the end of 1559 the Exchequer advanced him £2,000 towards his expenses, but he was expected to repay this. As that sum was quite insufficient for his purposes, on Christmas Day he arranged a short term loan of £3,000 from Anthony Strynger, a London merchant, on the security of lands, which he undertook to repay by Lady Day.[4]

While he was at Berwick the Queen granted him in fee simple the manors of Bacton and Cotton in Suffolk, the advowsons of three churches there, and two fields near Clerkenwell for the sum of £2,654. To pay this in a lump sum necessitated extensive borrowing in the city, yet this proved a shrewd purchase and, five years later, he was able to sell the Clerkenwell fields, which in 1560 were estimated to have an annual value of £14 10s, to a London grocer for £1,600.[5]

In the summer of 1562 Norfolk took stock of his affairs to see how serious the situation was. First and foremost there were his debts to the Crown, which he calculated then stood at £5,252 18s 9½d, and he prepared a scheme for paying off this sum, which was by Tudor standards a staggering one. Of this total, £2,000 was not a personal debt, but the money advanced by the Exchequer towards his expenses as lieutenant-general in the North. He still owed £385 13s 2d in tenths on his own and his wife's lands under the sum voted by Parliament in 1559, and there was £166 10s outstanding for his purchase the following year of the manor of Axminster, with other Devonshire lands, £85 due for other grants from the Crown, and £234 6s 8d owing on various recognisances in the Exchequer. There was in addition some £2,584 owing in the Court of Wards and Liveries for fines and arrears on his and his wife's lands.

The duke offered to pay off these debts largely through the sale of timber; the remainder he would meet by instalments over ten years. This scheme, he said, was the only way in which he could satisfy the Crown without his 'utter undoing'. If his proposals were unacceptable then 'I shall be driven to break up my house and sell £300 or £400 land for answering of my debts to others, by which means never hereafter I should be able to live far off meaner degree than now I do, as also which much would grieve me never to be able in time of service to show myself according to my good will to Her Majesty and my country; and yet do I desire of Her Majesty but penny for penny and land for land'. The essence of Norfolk's scheme, as the last few words of his tearful preamble disclose, was that he and the Queen should exchange various lands of equivalent value. In return for certain outlying properties in Sussex, he hoped to acquire other lands in East Anglia which would help to concentrate his estates and thus simplify their administration. He offered to surrender to the Crown the manors and parks of Chesworth, in Horsham, and Sedgewick, in Nuthurst, the forest of St Leonard's with its iron mills, and other woodland in Crawley, Beeding and Horsham. The rent from these lands amounted, after deductions for repairs, to £300. In return he asked for a grant of St Leonard's house in Norwich, which had once belonged to his father, the rectory of North Wootton, Norfolk, a group of five Essex manors in Pitsea, and its neighbourhood, a smaller property in Lincolnshire and various granges in Axminster, near the manor he already owned, of practically the same value. The standing timber on the Sussex woodlands, which no tenant could fell, he thought might be worth some £5,000, as it was especially suitable for ship-building. Thus, he would be practically free of debt.

After full investigation by the Crown surveyors, Elizabeth accepted the duke's proposals with certain provisos. In the first place the surveyors' valuation suggested that the Sussex timber was worth £4,680 instead of Norfolk's figure of £5,000. Secondly although the surveyors agreed with the duke's figure of £300 as the annual value in rents from the Sussex properties he was surrendering, they estimated that the lands he was asking for were worth £301 11s 0¼d a year, and in the letters patent for exchanging lands he was required to pay an annual rent of 31s 0¼d to the Queen. Thirdly, the accountants found fault with the total of his debts in the Exchequer. The £234 6s 8d owing on recognisances was not a final figure; each year the sum would grow, unless he kept up with the instalments, and so they wrote in its place the accumulated sum of £1,282 13s 10d, making his debts to the Crown total £6,503 15s 5¾d. Subtracting the money to be realised through the sale of timber there was left a sum of £1,824 15s 5¾d, which the duke agreed to pay off over nine years by six-monthly payments of £100. The revised scheme was approved on August 20th and the following February took effect.[6]

Norfolk's officials were shrewd men who knew how to bargain with the Queen's surveyors, and the duke benefited in particular from this transaction by acquiring again the Howard property of St Leonard's, Norwich. By the exchange 'penny for penny and land for land', he had not diminished his personal property, merely redistributed it; such was the first rule of a landowner who regarded his inheritance as a trust for the next generation. What obviously upset Howard was the fact that the £2,000 expended in his service in the North was entirely forgotten, whereas Cecil, who had spent a third of the time in the north that Norfolk had been away, had been rewarded for his labours with a substantial grant of Crown lands and the extremely lucrative office of Master of the Wards, to whose fees the duke was now contributing heavily.[7]

Quite naturally Howard turned for advice about his affairs, if not at first for money, to the greatest financial expert of the day, Sir Thomas Gresham, whose services proved indispensable to successive Tudor sovereigns. Gresham had had private as well as official dealings with Lord Treasurer Norfolk and in 1540 had bought Old Norfolk House, at Broken Wharf, Thames Street, from him. His own estates lay in Norfolk and the duke must often have entertained him at Norwich and Kenninghall. But in December 1566 Sir Thomas was the host in London; he told a friend 'the Duke's grace hath invited himself to Gresham House upon Wednesday next at night and will dine with me upon Thursday'. They were clearly to discuss a matter of some importance if it were to take two successive days. Details of only one transaction between the two have survived, the duke's sale to

Gresham of a Suffolk manor and advowson over four years later.[8]

Retrenchment he dismissed as an impossible ideal. It was as unthinkable for Norfolk to make do with either Kenninghall or his Norwich mansion as it would have been for his Queen to surrender Greenwich or Hampton Court, for he was a prince indeed in his own country, and accepted the fact that maintaining six great houses would continue to swallow up a great deal of money. His grandfather had already found the charges of his palatial establishments a heavy burden when Thomas was born, but during the next thirty years the difficulties of a noble land-owner increased rapidly with the decline in the value of money caused by the 'Price revolution'. Spain had with a vengeance, called in the mineral wealth of the New World to upset the balance of the money markets of the Old; but other factors were at work and the first ten years of Elizabeth's reign experienced the worst of this inflation. The fourth duke was by any standards a very wealthy man and the dowries of his wives made him on paper the richest man in England, yet he found it impossible to live within his income. 'I have been a great turmoiler in worldly charges, sometimes purchasing, sometimes building, whereby I was enforced to be ever in debt and still in need of money', he confessed at the end. 'Keeping his state', as he felt bound to do, was more difficult than a generation before. He was probably less spendthrift than his grandfather, yet he had much fewer oppor-tunities of increasing his income than a Lord Treasurer. It was his inability to curb his expenditure and live on his current income that brought him so often to money-lenders. It was perhaps on Gresham's recommendation that he first went to Ridolfi in 1569 for the Florentine banker had recently provided letters of credit in Germany for an English envoy at Gresham's request. Other clients of Ridolfi at this time were Thomas Sackville and John Marsh, the Secretary of the Merchant Adventurers Company. In association with his kinsmen, Arundel and Lumley, he under-took to repay the Florentine £1,800 within the year at his house in Fenchurch Street, and to ensure payment the three peers entered into bonds for £3,000. Thereafter Ridolfi became a regular visitor at the Howard House.[9]

All landowners who were feeling the pinch of the rise in prices made the most of freeing the remaining bond tenants on their estates, by granting them copyholds on payment of suitable fines, but this did not amount to very much in the duke's case as, by 1560, there were few bondsmen left in East Anglia. A more remunerative practice was granting long leases and in the summer of 1567 Norfolk began to issue 1,000-year leases at peppercorn rents for substantial fines. This was done with restraint and most of the lessees were members of the duke's household, like William Dix at Wickmere and Humphrey Beddingfield at Banham.[10]

The duke obtained nearly all of his loans on the security of lands. In particular the manor of Axminster, one of his most outlying properties, served as an overcoat that was rarely out of pawn. In February 1562 he raised £1,000 on this property from Edmund Gilbert, a city goldsmith in Cheapside, to whom it was at once to be conveyed if the duke did not repay the sum by 1st May 1563. As further security for this transaction Norfolk entered into a recognisance for £2,000, undertaking to observe the terms of the agreement. He paid up with eleven days to spare and so both the recognisance and the prospective sale of the manor were cancelled. In a few weeks Axminster manor was again pledged for a further loan and in 1567 Gilbert was still lending £1,000 to the duke on its security, though the term of the loan was by now less than a year. The duke's Essex manors of Wigborough and Salcote were mortgaged for £1,000 in 1570, even though their annual value was as little as £5 5s.[11]

Not all the loans which Norfolk raised in this way were cancelled. In July 1569 there was a bargain and sale of Beding manor in Sussex to John God, merchant taylor, for £560 which would take effect if Norfolk failed to pay him £500 by the following June. The greater part of this sum was subsequently paid, but not all, and at the time of the duke's attainder, eighteen months later, it was found that he had mortgaged Beding to God for £130.[12]

There was nothing unusual about raising money in this way. Most of the Elizabethan peerage had part of their lands in mortgage most of the time. Among Norfolk's kinsmen Arundel, Oxford, Lord Howard of Bindon, Lumley, Scrope and Westmorland all sent their attornies into Chancery at least once a year to acknowledge a new debt; yet that did not mean that they were irretrievably set on a course for bankruptcy. A few peers, notably Arundel, were living extravagantly, but the majority who went to city merchants were merely raising money in order to invest it in landed property. Indeed, most of the so-called 'debts' of the

Elizabethan peers were notional, book-keeping entries. Provided they had their estates, ready cash counted for little. That the fourth duke could be able in 1570 to expend £8,000 in acquiring for his son an advance on his Arundel inheritance, shows that he was quite solvent.

In February 1566 he even offered to mortgage the Charterhouse for £2,800 to provide security for Edward Ward, a member of his household, in a complicated debt in which the man's mother and step-father were involved. The fact that the duke was prepared to put in pawn his finest jewel shows how little store he set by these fictitious transactions and well before the time specified in the document had run out, the matter had been settled and the Charterhouse 'saved'. He had not provided this security to his servant as an act of charity, for his terms were that Ward should sell to him extensive lands in Postwick, Great Plumpstead and Kirby Woodhouse, all a few miles from Norwich, at a favourable price. Thus by turning money-lender himself, he increased his estates.[13]

Because ready money was scarce, payments for land purchases were often spread over a number of years. When Howard acquired the Charterhouse for £2,200 he agreed to pay £500 by 1st May 1565, another £100 by 1st November following, £400 by 1st May 1566 and six instalments of £200 each by successive All Saints Days and May Days until 1st May 1569. For each of these payments he was allowed twenty-eight days' grace.[14]

In the critical days at the beginning of 1571, when Norfolk needed exceptional sums of ready money for his political designs, he went to the length of selling plate and jewellery. Over 3,600 ounces of silver plate from Howard House was sent to the Mint in the Tower to be melted down, and later he claimed to have sold 'all his jewels' at the same time. Characteristically kinsmen and members of his household were given first pick; Thomas Blennerhasset, for instance, bought 'one flower of gold with a saphire, set about with small garnets' for £13 6s 8d. Then private sales were made to courtiers – Leicester secured a valuable item for £335. The largest account was with a widow, Lady Champion, who spent £658 on Howard family jewels, ranging from a remarkable broach ('a flower of the History of Jacob with thirteen diamonds, four rubies and two little emeralds, with a cluster of diamonds pendant'), to sets of enamelled buttons. Few items were sold direct to goldsmiths, and the only substantial purchase was when William Denham bought 'two garters of gold and five georges'.[15]

Quite apart from the extensive properties which Norfolk's three marriages secured for the House of Howard, he succeeded in considerably enlarging the ducal estates by purchase and exchange in no more than a dozen years. The practice of mortgaging one property as security for a loan to finance another purchase proved remarkably successful. Little of these new estates came immediately from the Crown; most was ex-monastic property that had been granted out by Henry VIII a generation before. Throughout, the duke followed a deliberate policy of consolidating his estates in Norfolk.

He had begun this by exchanging lands with the Crown, as we have noticed, and in 1565 he exchanged properties with Lord Keeper Bacon. The duke acquired the manor of Brissingham and lands near Lopham, not many miles from Kenninghall, in exchange for 110 acres in the neighbourhood of Bungay in Suffolk. As Howard had the better of the bargain he undertook to pay the Lord Keeper £1,000 by instalments during the next twenty months. His surveyors had provided detailed information about the limits and values of the property with which he was parting; much less detail was available for Brissingham, and by mutual agreement a clause was added to the deed allowing for a reduction (or increase) in the money Norfolk was to pay if it appeared that the yearly values of either property had been wrongly assessed. Later the same year, despite other heavy commitments, the duke bought from Walter Norton of Gray's Inn the manor and advowson of Rendham Orville in Suffolk. No other peer was acquiring property at such a rate.[16]

In the management of his estates he commanded a team of expert surveyors and bailiffs, all of whom had grown up in his service, and his reputation as a just and popular landlord owed much to them. The Howards had an established tradition of estate management before so much of the English countryside was thrown topsy-turvy by the Dissolution of the Monasteries. The new landlords in general were after quick profits, whereas on the ducal estates the emphasis was on investing in careful husbandry. A striking example of the improvements which Howard's bailiffs made to properties is the manor of Chalvedon in Essex. In 1563, when Norfolk acquired it from the Crown, the manor-house and barns were in a tumble-down state. The duke at once spent money on putting things right and in five years its annual value had almost doubled. When he went to the block, fortunately for his under-tenants, life on the Liberty continued much as before, as the Crown leased the ducal lands in Norfolk jointly to his two chief surveyors, and they maintained the same high standards of estate management until Elizabeth eventually granted part of the lands to Philip Earl of Arundel.[17]

★   ★   ★

Towards the end of 1564 Norfolk opened negotiations with Edward, Lord North, for purchasing the Charterhouse, the finest mansion in private hands, and its private conduit put to shame the arrangements for fresh water supply in the royal residences. North, who had been Thomas Cromwell's successor as Chancellor of the Court of Augmentations, was by now an old man, long retired from public life. He had been granted the old Carthusian monastery, the greatest London property in the charge of the Augmentations, in 1545 but he had sold it under protest to the Duke of Northumberland in the summer of 1553 as a palace for his son, Guildford Dudley, until such time as his wife, Lady Jane Grey, should enter Whitehall as Queen of England. On North-umberland's fall the Charterhouse had reverted to the Crown but later in the year Queen Mary had again granted it to North. The duke agreed to buy the entire Charterhouse, which included the new mansion built within the monastic precincts, for £2,200. Edward North's death on New Year's Eve inevitably delayed the sale, which was to have taken place the following day, and it was not until the end of May that the deeds of sale were executed, though it seems that the duke made some use of the buildings in the interim. At the same time he purchased from Roger Lord North two neighbouring properties, that had not been included in the original transaction, for £320. These were Whitewellbeech, a garden of nine acres with a house in Clerkenwell, and Pardon Churchyard, adjoining the Carthusian site, which had once been a burial ground but was by now a walled garden and orchard.

For a London house the property was secluded. Even today Charterhouse Square, so close to Smithfield Market and busy thoroughfares, seems remote and peaceful. In the gardens of

Mary FitzAlan. Portrait in Arundel Castle

Mr Secretary, after my harty commendacions, I
have by your gentle lres, receyvid vnderstanding
of ye thyng, ye whyche, hathe so moche ben to my
grievte, as no thyng may be more. for had I
ben advertised of ye Quenes Maties Syrknes,
before the recoverie egayne of hyr Hyghnes,
yt must nedes have ben very great greif vnto
me. Now, at one tyme being assertained by yow,
ye hyr syrknes ys past, yt puttith away
ye kervnes y myght have growne of ye fyrst
part, and onlie Lebythe ye consolacion
yt ensewith of ye other, for ye whyche I can
not but give yow my most harty thankes,
having not elly to wright egaine to yow, but of
ye quieate state of or Contrie here, wch, at this
day, ys, in as good order and obedience, as at
any tyme, hertofor, yt hath ben. And so hopyng
yt I shall from tyme to tyme, receyve good newes
at your hand. I bid yow hartely well to fare from
my howse at Denninghall ye Last of August 1559
                    Your Lovyng frend
                         Tho. Norff

Norfolk to Cecil, 1559

Whitewellbeech grew a number of plum, willow and elm trees which, when Norfolk leased it, he forbade his tenants to fell. Other tenants of houses on the north-east end of the Charterhouse wall were not allowed to put in new windows that might over-look the gardens. The duke was, however, bound by the terms of the sale to allow Lord North and Sir James Dyer, as trustees of the North estate, to have a right of way to certain houses within the precincts; and all inhabitants on the Charterhousee state were to have the right to attend the duke's private chapel (burials excepted), provided they contributed towards the upkeep of the fabric.[18]

The Charterhouse took the name of its new owner. Howard House, or Howard Place by Smithfield as it was sometimes called, soon bore the unmistakable mark of the fourth duke. He embarked on a very extensive building programme, which was destined to transform the cluster of old monastic buildings round North's new house into the stateliest of homes: 'large and sumptuous buildings, both for lodging and pleasure', as John Stow put it, for besides magnificent residential quarters the duke laid out, as at Norwich, a tennis court and a bowling-alley. An indication of the improvements made by Norfolk is given by the later sale of Howard House to Thomas Sutton, founder of Charterhouse School, for £13,000.

The monks' refectory, which Lord North had adopted as a Great Hall, was considerably enlarged by Norfolk. An oriel window was inserted, the hall made loftier, a musicians' gallery installed and a great carved screen with frieze shields added to keep out the draught and hide the kitchen hatches from the diners' view. Howard also built a long gallery, running east and west, on the north side of the Hall, to make communications easier between his private suite in the west wing and the rooms in the east. Previously all the staircases had been external, but in 1569 he built a great staircase to the east of the Hall, which dignified the entire building. At the same time the great chamber was enriched with a splendid ceiling, painted with armorial bearings, and a new fireplace, while the erection of a terrace, with a brick arcade beneath it, gave covered access to the tennis court. Other im-provements were in progress during the duke's ownership of the house which taken together changed the old monastery beyond recognition and made Howard House the most comfortable mansion in London. The palaces at Kenninghall and Norwich have long perished, Cree Church Place and Howard House in the Strand have long since been demolished, but parts of the Elizabethan Charterhouse remain. It was until a generation ago the finest surviving example of Elizabethan domestic architecture in London, and though it suffered severe bomb damage, the restoration completed by the late Lord Mottistone has of late years given the buildings the appearance they must have had in 1572.[19]

Norfolk's dealings with the North family were not over, for in 1568, at the height of the enquiry into the conduct of Mary Queen of Scots, he sold some lands in Essex to the dowager Lady North for £500. Mindful of his happiness in acquiring the Charterhouse he treated her generously and did not ask for payment until New Year's Day 1575.[20]

*   *   *

Nothing illustrates the duke's concern for the Howard inheritance more vividly than the matter of the Dacre Wardships. In January 1567 he married as his third wife Elizabeth, the widow of Thomas Lord Dacre, who had died the previous July, leaving her a son and three daughters. The Dacre patrimony was a valuable one, with lands principally in Cumberland, Westmorland, Durham and Yorkshire bringing in, it was reckoned 8,000 crowns a year, and even before Dacre's death the duke was making enquiries about the wardship of the heir. It was not until November 1567, twelve weeks after his Dacre duchess's death, that he was formally granted the wardship and marriage of his stepson George, Lord Dacre, then a boy of five. He received an annual allowance of 200 marks out of the estate for applying to his education, and this was to be increased to £200 on his fourteenth birthday, to enable his guardian 'to educate him in a manner fitting his title'. Then, as now, education became progressively expensive.[21]

With wardship went the right of disposing of the ward's hand in marriage and Norfolk was carefully planning to marry his stepchildren to his own children. There was nothing of the fairy-tale wicked stepfather in his scheme; it was a prudent rather than an astute plan and there was more of current practice about it than sharp practice. The relationship of the prospective couples was not within the degrees prohibited by the Church, and the duke hoped they would all grow to love one another through being brought up in the same nursery. He intended Lord Dacre to marry his Megge – they were the same age; Nanne Dacre would make an excellent wife for Philip Earl of Surrey, his heir, even though she was a month or two his senior; and in due course his son Tom would marry Mall and Will would wed little Bess Dacre. Unlike other leading figures of the day, Norfolk had not hitherto interested himself in acquiring wardships, but now he devised what was the most remarkable family compact of the sixteenth century.

Though from the beginnings there were signs that Leonard Dacre, the children's uncle, would do all he could to challenge the validity of Norfolk's arrangements it was not until May 1569 that the scheme was in any way threatened. In that month little George Dacre died rather tragically. He was practising vaulting in a field at Thetford when the wooden horse collapsed on him and he was killed almost instantaneously. His death raised the whole question of the Dacre barony and inheritance, for although the escheator's inquisition named his three sisters as his next heirs, Leonard Dacre at once assumed the peerage title as the male heir on the grounds of a deed of entail which had been made by his father. The duke as guardian and stepfather of the three girls contested this claim, insisting that the barony should by right descend to the three co-heiresses, not for the sake of the title, but for the property: the great houses at Dacre and Naworth, thousands of acres in the Eskdale and Leath division of Cumberland, city properties in Carlisle, good sheep-grazing land in Blencow and Rockliffe and other estates at Appleby and Langdale in Westmorland, Eaton-Socon in Bedfordshire and elsewhere. Howard had heard about the possibility of an entail three years back and had taken the precaution of getting an opinion on the matter from Sir William Cordell, the Master of the Rolls, before he had applied for the Dacre wardship, so he felt in a strong position. But he made doubly sure of his position by obtaining a fresh grant of wardship from the Crown for the three step-daughters, which allowed him an annuity of 100 marks for each.[22]

The Duke was in some difficulty about proceeding as a case of this nature had to be heard in the Marshal's Court. Since he, the Earl Marshal, was a most interested party, he persuaded the Queen to appoint special commissioners to decide the controversy 'according to equity and right', thus avoiding suspicion of favour. These commissioners were the Marquess of Northampton and the Earls of Pembroke, Arundel and Leicester, who directed the parties to appear at Greenwich Palace on 12th June, barely a month after the tragedy at Thetford.

Justice required that Cecil, as Master of the Wards, should attend before the commissioners to state the case of the young wards. This was a ticklish matter, for at that moment (as will be described in a later chapter) Norfolk and Cecil were alienated; and yet Cecil could scarcely assign to a deputy his share in a suit which concerned the first peer of the realm. On the other hand he had no wish to befriend Leonard Dacre, who was the most headstrong and troublesome of the Catholic gentry in the north. In the end, as a typical piece of statecraft, Cecil appeared, and in so doing became reconciled with Norfolk and more openly hostile towards Dacre and his faction.

Although the commissioners were technically partisans of the duke the trial appears to have been quite fair. Dacre's counsel asked for time to make searches in the records, but the other side rejoined that this was only a plea for unnecessary delay; his counsel had, in fact, delved very deeply into the public records 'and had always been beforehand with his Grace'. Dacre's underhand ways did not make a good impression on the commissioners and they dismissed his plea for a postponement of the case. In fact, had much more detailed searches been made, Dacre's counsel might have found evidence, which certainly existed, to substantiate his claim. This was an award of King Edward IV that was also quite unknown to the duke's lawyers. The commissioners' decision in favour of Norfolk, though a wrong one in view of that neglected evidence, had been fairly arrived at. The Dacre inheritance was kept intact for the three wards and thus for Norfolk's own children. The whole business of the suit had proved worrying and costly, and the duke was not exaggerating when he talked of his great charges in defending his stepdaughters' inheritance 'against the unjust and underhand attempts of such of their kinsmen as sought to deprive them thereof'.[23]

As a further security, a fortnight after the case was decided, the duke conveyed his rights of wardship to trustees, composed of his treasurer, Sir John Blennerhasset and three other members of his household, all of whom were executors of his will.

Two years later, while Norfolk was still alive, Nanne, the eldest of the Dacre girls, married Philip Earl of Surrey. Mary, the second sister, who was just six years old when the case was heard at Greenwich, died before reaching the age of consent and so never married her child fiancé, Thomas. The youngest of the girls, Elizabeth, duly married Lord William Howard in 1577 when she was twelve and he thirteen. Their discredited uncle Leonard ('Dacre of the crooked back', as Mary Queen of Scots called him) was driven into rebellion and died in exile with a price on his head. Years afterwards another uncle, Francis Dacre, was to lay claim to the barony, but his intervention proved fruitless. It had passed into the Howard inheritance.[24]

Having settled the matter of the Dacre wardship the duke began to put his own estates in order, and in July 1569, at the height of his negotiations for marriage with Mary Queen of Scots, he executed a deed to ensure the succession of the Norfolk Liberty to his eldest son Philip and his heirs male. He created trustees to whom he undertook to assign before Michaelmas 'a good, sure, sufficient and lawful estate in fee simple' in the manor of Kenninghall and in the various other properties 'commonly called by the name of the Duke of Norfolk's Liberty' in Norfolk, Suffolk, Cambridgeshire, Essex, Sussex and Surrey. The deed was very similar to a settlement made by his kinsman, the Earl of Oxford, in 1562 in which Norfolk had himself been one of the trustees. His trustees were all senior officials in his household. Sir Thomas Cornwallis and Sir Nicholas L'Estrange, Thomas Timperley, his controller, William Barker and Robert Higford, his secretaries, and Edward Pecock, his clerk controller. They and their heirs were to hold the Liberty to the use of the duke during his lifetime, and afterwards to the use of Philip, his heir apparent, for his life and thereafter to his right heirs. The lands specified were of an annual value of £1,445. The duke reserved to himself for life the right of granting leases of lands within the Liberty and even the right of annulling or limiting the assignment to the trustees by a future deed.

The purpose of this 'marvel of conveyancing' was to keep the Howard inheritance intact. A man holding land in trust enjoyed very considerable benefits. Because the legal estate was vested in feoffees he was secure from forfeiture, he could evade his creditors and, most important of all, he was quit of feudal incidents – the dues in the Court of Wards and Liveries which had cost Howard so much. It was a way of taking advantage of a loophole in the law similar to the current practice whereby a landowner's gifts of real property, if made sufficiently in advance of his death, are free from death duties.[25]

Shortly afterwards, by a further deed Norfolk made the promised assignment of the Liberty to the trustees, who were to pay his death-bed debts and legacies, and hold the lands for Philip Earl of Surrey, with remainder to his heirs male, or, if that line failed, to the duke's sons Thomas and William, and in turn to any other branch of the Howard family descending from the second duke.

So much for careful planning. Though the Statute of Uses safeguarded trusts against forfeiture, there was no security against attainder, and when the duke was attainted for high treason the Liberty was seized by the Crown. The estates, however, remained as a separate entity and for a number of years were farmed by two of Howard's old surveyors, William Dix and William Cantrell. Most lands remained in the hands of the Crown until James I in 1604 revived the ducal Liberty by making a grant jointly to Lord Howard de Walden (Norfolk's second son), and Henry, Earl of Northampton (his brother).[26]

The next Summer, while still a captive in the Tower, the duke began to arrange for the settlement of the Arundel estates upon his son Philip. 'My son of Surrey' was due to marry Lady Nanne Dacre in the spring of 1571 and Norfolk had to provide his step-daughter with a dowry as well as to grant his son a competence. It was clear that in the fulness of time Philip Howard would become Earl of Arundel, in right of his mother, Mary FitzAlan. The widower Henry, Earl of Arundel, once spoken of as a possible husband for Queen Elizabeth, had never remarried. His only son, Henry Lord Mautravers, had died, as we have noticed, a year before Philip Howard's birth, while his daughter Jane FitzAlan, for twenty years the wife of John, Lord Lumley, was childless and there was no likelihood of her having a child. As both Philip's grandfather, Arundel and his uncle, Lumley, were in more than usual pecuniary difficulties, the duke suggested that a portion of the Arundel inheritance might be advanced to Philip on his marriage.

A letter of Norfolk's to his steward, Blennerhasset, written in

July 1570 from the Tower, reveals the hard bargaining that had been taking place with Arundel and Lumley. 'There wanteth nothing but money, whereof they be greediest, and I unablest to provide, as you know. Nevertheless, if this match take, I am determined to sell away those things that I never meant to depart withall; and therefore I pray you look over my revenue book and send me word of your opinion which things you think fitted to be sold and will best be bought.'27

His master having made up his mind, Blennerhasset made his calculations. It was no mean thing that a prisoner of state should be prepared to find £8,000 – for such was the sum below which Arundel refused to go – to finance his heir's marriage. At the end of September the Earl appointed a number of trustees, including the Lord Keeper, Cecil, Leicester and the Master of the Rolls, who were to oversee Philip's portion of his inheritance until he became twenty-five. During that period he was to have an income of £720 a year, but from 1582, if his grandfather and uncle were still alive, he would have absolute control of that (his late mother's) portion which comprised Arundel House in the Strand, where he had been born, and a dozen Sussex manors. At the same time the earl entailed certain lands on Lumley and his wife for the term of their lives, with remainder to any heirs of Joan and thence to the heirs of Philip Howard. If Philip had no issue the vast estates were to pass, like the Norfolk Liberty, to the duke's right heirs. This was a family settlement on the grand scale, which would have warmed the heart of old Lord Treasurer Norfolk, even at the price that was demanded.

In the deed by which these arrangements were effected Norfolk acknowledged that 'the earldom of Arundel is the most ancient earldom of this realm', and he promised that if it descended to his son then he and the heirs of his body 'shall in all manner of writings, wherein they shall write or set forth his or their names of honour or dignity, first [to] place and write . . . Earl of Arundel, before the writing and placing of the name Earl of Surrey'. A similar undertaking was given in the document about arms, since Arundel must take precedence over Warenne.

Lady Lumley died in 1574, as predicted without heirs. Six years later her father died, broken by political intrigue, financial troubles and gout. After some difficulty Philip succeeded in establishing his claim to be thirteenth Earl of Arundel. His uncle

Lumley eventually parted with his life interest in the remainder of the property, including the Lordship and Castle of Arundel, on the understanding that Philip and his successors paid him an annuity of £274 18s 4d. With Nonsuch as his country residence Lumley could not afford to keep Arundel going. This seemed a fair arrangement at the time, for no-one predicted that Lumley would live for another thirty years. Before then Arundel Castle had displaced Kenninghall Palace as the principal home of the Howards as fifty years back Kenninghall had displaced Framlingham Castle.[28]

To round off his family settlement the duke drew up a new will on 31st May 1571. He was particularly anxious to provide for his younger children, for Philip, Earl of Surrey, no longer a ward, now he was married to Anne Dacre, could stand on his own feet and be something of a guardian to his brothers and sisters. 'Weighing up how few I have of my own kin to whom I may commit the custody and bringing up of the rest of my children', wrote Norfolk, 'I have thought good that, by my executors, order be taken that there be a standing house kept by the name of my son of Surrey ... during his nonage, where he, with his wife, the rest of his brothers, sister, and sisters-in-law may live.' The executors were to do their best to persuade Elizabeth to allow Lord Thomas Howard, the second son, who would be the Queen's ward, to join the Surrey household and keep the children together as a generation earlier Norfolk and his brother and sisters had been together at Reigate.

In a schedule to his will the duke laid down rules for this household. London – plague-ridden and smoky – was no place for children, so Howard House was to be closed down. Instead, they were to make Framlingham their principal home, with visits to Lopham Lodge (on the edge of the Kenninghall estate) and Thetford House. Kenninghall Palace was too large a residence for them, and too expensive to run, but they could stay in part of it for hunting. He stated the exact number of servants in their establishment; they totalled sixty-five persons, ranging from Surrey's gentlemen attendants and page to a keeper of hounds and a carter. Special attention was paid to the scholastic staff. Apart from the chaplain, Surrey was to have his own tutor, with an assistant master to teach languages and another 'to teach the younger sort'. There was also to be 'a master of the nursery'.

Thanks to Norfolk's exertions and costs Philip was already provided with 'an honourable portion' of the Arundel inheritance. Howard's daughter, Lady Margaret, was to be granted 1,000 marks on marriage and her step-sisters, Mary and Elizabeth Dacre, were each to have the like sum if the marriages arranged with Thomas and William Howard respectively fell through.

All the servants in Norfolk's employ at the time of his death were to be kept on for a further six weeks and those who were then dismissed as redundant were to be given a year's wages in addition to the money due to them. Gifts totalling £115 were to be made to the poor of the parishes where the duke held property; most went to Kenninghall 'where they be poorest and have most need'. Finally, £20 was to be given to the churchwardens for the repair of Framlingham church. Because of the great trust he had always showed in his household officials, Norfolk thought it proper 'to trouble none of my honourable friends', but to appoint his treasurer, auditor and surveyors executors and he added the names of the Master of the Rolls and of the Attorney General purely as a matter of formality. The will was, of course, never proved, yet it was a characteristic document.[29]

* * *

Like every other Tudor magnate Norfolk frequently complained of his poverty. If it was in part a ruse to postpone payment of taxes, it was remarkably successful, for in 1571 he owed the Crown £660 for his assessments under the Subsidies voted by Parliament in 1559, 1563 and 1566 – he had not even made his first payment under the Act of 1559! In his last will and testament, however, when he was laying bare his mind he proudly admitted that he had been called in this life to great 'possessions and abundance of wealth and riches'. There was mention in the will of unsettled debts, but in the calm tone of a man who is able to settle his accounts the day they are presented.

What was his annual income? Despite the welter of documents no comprehensive figures survive for each year, and the total of a clear £1,600 from his estates (when all his officials had been paid their annuities) which was given by his household staff at the time of his attainder is undoubtedly far too low. In 1555 the lands which Howard inherited from the third duke were worth a clear annual value of £2,489. In addition, after his paternal grandmother's death in 1558, he received the £326 which had been her personal allowance. These figures did not, of course, remain constant, as he was forever selling and purchasing lands. His stipend from the Queen as Earl Marshal was £123 14s and his fees in the Heralds' College from pedigree-hunters and litigants probably were twice as much, yet were small in comparison with the perquisites of a lucrative office like Master of the Wards. Lesser amounts came his way from Crown and Duchy of Lancaster stewardships, fines from tenants within his own ducal Liberty, and gifts in cash or in kind from the towns of which he was high steward. If we place his own average income at £3,500 it will not be very wide of the mark. His share of the Audley lands which came to him on his second marriage produced a further £300 or £400 a year, and in his last years when the considerable Dacre estate came under his control some £700 was added to his income, making a total of something over £4,500.[30]

Though tax assessments are apt to be inaccurate guides to an individual's total wealth, they do provide certain information of interest, often the only information that is available for comparative purposes. In 1559 the assessors for the peerage estimated Norfolk's landed income at £1,200; as with the system for assessing the amount of subsidies to be paid by commoners it was known to be out-of-date, and we know the duke's landed income at that time was in fact £2,815. But what were the amounts for the other peers? The personal estate of Shrewsbury, Herfford, Huntingdon and Pembroke was reckoned to be £1,000, Arundel's assessment was fixed at £666, Lady Audley and Lord Howard of Effingham at £333 each. Only two peers exceeded Norfolk's figure in 1559: Derby was rated at £2,000 and Oxford at £1,600. Lord Treasurer Winchester assessed himself and the Earl of Rutland at £1,200, the same figure as the duke's. By 1566 Norfolk was still assessed at £1,200, though Derby's figure had nearly halved, Winchester's had declined to £800, while Oxford had dropped out of the picture entirely. That year the duke had been required to pay £160 as his first instalment of the subsidy, while Leicester's tax was as little as £20 and Cecil's £8 13s 4d. Such comparisons bear out the statement, oft repeated by ambassadors, that the duke was the richest man in England.[31]

Before his trial the duke's accountants took stock of his finances. They found he owed £3,959 to money-lenders, for which he had mortgaged three manors and the lordship of Clonne, the last to Sir Rowland Hayward, a former Lord Mayor of London, as security for a loan of £2,000. In addition there was a debt of £2,150 of Arundel's to Alderman Jackson's executors, which Norfolk had undertaken to discharge; some £300 was owing in the Exchequer and £1,200 in the Court of Wards for the short-lived wardship of George Dacre. Tradesmen's bills amounted to £239, and there were wages due to the workmen and other expenses at Howard House amounting to £200. This made a total debt of £8,000.

But there was another side to the story. At that time some £5,000 was owing to Howard from various sources – rents due from tenants, instalments due on property he had sold, £200 from Lord Leicester outstanding on his purchase of Paget House and £335 for the jewel he had bought in 1570. To balance the accounts the duke instructed his officials to negotiate for the sale of various lands in Essex and Suffolk – he was determined to keep the Liberty in his own county intact – and to approach tenants who might be prepared to buy their copyholds. This task was easily achieved by William Dix and his fellows. Despite the many moments when he had been hard-pressed for ready cash, despite complaints about his poverty and self reproaches about his extra-vagance, despite the mortgages and the sales of his plate and jewels, there is no doubt that at the time of his attainder Norfolk was still as exceptional in his wealth as in his rank.[32]

Chapter Eight

MARY QUEEN OF SCOTS

1567-8

NORFOLK had left London at the end of 1566 the acknowledged leader of the lords, in Parliament and in Council, in the design to bring Elizabeth to marry the Archduke Charles. For three months he had been in the very forefront of politics, yet in the eighteen months which followed he was to fall quite into the background. It was not a question of playing truant from court to avoid a fresh breech with Leicester or another misunderstanding with Cecil, for the policy of the Hapsburg match had been decided upon, and as the renewed negotiations were to be in the capable hands of Sussex the duke felt he had played his part and could withdraw. That same period while he concerned himself with his new marriage, his estates and, latterly, his health, was for Mary Queen of Scots turbulent and critical. For Norfolk one month followed another unperturbably at Kenninghall and Norwich, but for Mary events moved rapidly towards her abdication and imprisonment. For the first decade of Elizabeth's reign the main problems of politics related to the succession and the Queen's marriage, but when Mary sought refuge in England the political scene was changed dramatically. Henceforward the question of her future was to be the principal problem, and at each stage Norfolk was to be intimately involved.

After Christmas he returned to Court, as we have noticed, to marry Elizabeth Dacre. She was the daughter of Sir John Leyburne of Cunswick in Westmorland and twelve years before had married into one of the most important families of north-western

England, the Dacres of Gilsland and Graystoke. Her first husband, Thomas Lord Dacre, had died in July 1566 after some months of sickness, leaving her with four young children. Even before then, when it was clear that Dacre had not long to live, Norfolk was making enquiries about the wardship of George, the heir, and his sisters and in August he had discussed the matter with the Queen, who agreed in principle that he should become their guardian, though the matter was not to be settled for many months. 'They say his wardship will be worth 8,000 crowns a year', noted the Spanish Ambassador, for the Dacre estates in Cumberland, Westmorland and Bedfordshire were extensive; but before he committed himself Norfolk took expert legal advice about a supposed deed of entail 'on the most part of the inheritance' and was encouraged by what he was told by the Master of the Rolls. But at that time no-one dreamt of his marrying the Dacre widow.

Their courtship had been kept a close secret and the Queen knew nothing about it until three days before the wedding, when Norfolk told her himself. It was a quiet wedding, at Lady Leyburne's London house on 29th January 1567, 'without any rejoicing or demonstration'. After three years Kenninghall again had a mistress. The new duchess brought with her a Roman Catholic chaplain and her own set of altar cloths and copes, for she was, like her mother, a devout Catholic, 'hears Mass every day', and might soon convert her husband to the Old Religion, suggested the Spanish Ambassador. Lady Leyburne, her mother, was installed in a suite of rooms as well as her children.

There had been close friendship between the Howard and Dacre families of an earlier generation, for in 1558 the dowager Duchess Elizabeth had left substantial legacies to Elizabeth, Lady Dacre, and her daughters.

There were now nine children to be cared for, Norfolk's own five, and his four step-children, of whom he soon grew very fond. At the time of his mother's re-marriage George, the young Lord Dacre, was five, his elder sister Anne was almost ten, and his younger sisters, May three and Elizabeth two; the duke called the girls Nanne, Mall and Bess. He was anxious to settle the matter of their wardship, for two uncles, Leonard and George Dacre, were scheming to claim their inheritance. Since Norfolk was their stepfather, he could not tolerate an outsider being their guardian. It was not until November that he was formally granted their wardship, and even then his position was not absolutely secure for another two years.[1]

While Norfolk was immersed in family and domestic problems, for which he was granted leave of absence from court, events in Scotland took a spectacular turn. All the troubles stemmed from Rizzio's murder on 9th March 1566. Eleven months later Darnley was murdered in Kirk-o-field and Mary co-operated with Bothwell in ensuring that the trial of those responsible for this outrage was a fiasco. Soon she was 'carried off' to Dunbar by the earl, and kept there while he hurried through his divorce, and in May 1567 she married him in Edinburgh at a Protestant ceremony. Next month Bothwell's faction fought in vain at Carberry Hill, the 'Casket Letters' came into the hands of the Scottish lords, and before the end of July Mary was a prisoner in Lochleven, having abdicated the throne in favour of her infant son, with her half-brother James, Earl of Murray, as Regent. It was the most complete *bouleversement* imaginable.

At the time of Mary's marriage to Bothwell, Leicester was in Norwich, most probably staying as Norfolk's guest at the palace. Their relations were as good as at any time since the Queen's accession, largely because the duke was on leave from politics. Later that summer Howard became ill. The root of the trouble was some form of rheumatism, which had first troubled him at Berwick in 1560, but it now affected his general health quite seriously. He had to rest, yet he could not shake it off. This was the first real bout of illness he had endured, and as an active man it was hard for him to have to keep to his bed and he was doubtless a difficult patient. He looked forward anxiously to the safe arrival of the child which his duchess was carrying. Childbirth had caused the death of two wives and he would be relieved when the danger was passed for Duchess Elizabeth. In preparation for her lying in new 'cradle clothes of crimson satin, quilted' were purchased and 'a cover for a noble personage lying in childbed, bordered with gold and powdered ermine'. But once more Kenninghall Palace was plunged in despair, for on the evening of 4th September 1567 Elizabeth Howard died in childbed and her child died with her. Norfolk was beside himself with grief.

Depression hampered his physical recovery. He somehow forced himself to go to the funeral at Framlingham and then retired to Norwich, too low in spirits and sick of body to return to London at Michaelmas. Even writing tired him, so there are few letters for the latter half of 1567, and all of them touch on his illness. By mid-November he was 'far worse than ever', he told Cecil. 'Such a change hath my body made, who heretofore was able to brook any pain, though it were never so great, and now every little walk tires me.' He wanted to be at court to see that the Queen honoured her promises about the Hapsburg match, yet he had to keep his 'sickly carcass' in the warm at Norwich. He could not even face a visit to Kenninghall, but stayed in his palace, near the fire, testy, sorry for himself and full of pity for his nine bereaved children. Mistress Foster, the nurse who had been engaged for the baby, rose to the occasion, and the younger children must have taken to her mothering for she was still at Kenninghall in 1571. Christian patience and fortitude helped Norfolk to resign himself to his physical suffering: 'I must yield myself to God's will, whom it hath pleased to add this to other of my great griefs.' At the end of November he seemed to improve, but then came a relapse: 'I was prettily in the mending hand', he wrote with something of his old cheerfulness 'and now is shrunken again.' He did not properly recover until the spring of 1568.[2]

The previous summer Elizabeth had revived her interest in the Archduke Charles and after further delays the Earl of Sussex left for Germany in June, just as Mary Queen of Scots was being sent to Lochleven. Ostensibly he was to invest the Emperor with the Garter, so he was accompanied by Norfolk's henchman, Sir Gilbert Dethick, Garter King, but as the real object of his mission was to bring the matter of the marriage with Charles to a conclusion he took with him a portrait of the Queen. By his instructions Sussex was to explain that Elizabeth could not allow the exercise of any but the established religion, but since there was 'a general toleration therein used to divers subjects living otherwise quietly', he would be given a certain latitude for his private devotions. When the negotiations began in earnest in Vienna this assurance appeared to Charles far too vague. His terms were that Elizabeth should allow him his own private chapel for Mass while he would publicly accompany her to Anglican worship. It was a reasonable request, but Sussex, anxious as he was for the success of his mission, dare not proceed without seeking further instructions from Whitehall.

At the end of October the earl sent Henry Cobham home with

letters for Elizabeth, Cecil and Norfolk, asking for a clear lead. Leicester, anxious for the overthrow of his rivals' scheme, which would certainly bury any remaining hopes he had of becoming Elizabeth's consort, worked feverishly on Protestant passions, 'the like hath not been'. Under his influence Bishop Jewel of Salisbury harangued the multitude at Paul's Cross to abhor trafficking with idolatry and others drew a moral from Alva's militant Catholicism in the Netherlands. The Council were now equally divided on the question of the Archduke's religion and Elizabeth asked Leicester to write to the duke, hoping he might feel well enough to come to London to discuss this weighty matter or, if not, to send his advice in writing. A few hours before this letter reached Norwich, Norfolk had finished writing a lengthy memorial on the topic to Cecil, which had cost him a great deal of effort.[3]

To the Secretary, his great ally in the project, he said that his own fervour for the match had been increased by the Archduke's very reasonable demands. 'There is no prince of his calling, of his understanding, or that hath such plenty of natural, loving, sage or grave counsel . . . that would yield further upon uncertainty, than as I think by his offer he doth.' It was not only a reasonable request, but a diplomatic one: Charles would not have thrown away his principles if in the end the match fell through for other reasons. The duke reiterated that the danger to Church and State in Charles being allowed his private Roman Catholic chapel was small compared with the danger of the succession remaining unsettled. Not all 'earnest Protestants', he said, were like Leicester and his supporters, who were making 'religion a cloak for every shower . . . naming one thing and minding another, [who] will show reasons to save their own faces to overthrow so fortunate a marriage'. In short he encouraged Cecil to stand by the marriage and allow the terms demanded by Charles.

To Elizabeth he gave the same advice, though couched in much more cautious language. Being 'one of the youngest of your . . . Council, as also one that hath least experience', he was unhappy about committing himself to paper, and he argued the pros and cons more fully than in his letter to Cecil. The Archduke had said he wanted the right of private worship similar to that enjoyed by ambassadors; yet this was not a fair comparison, noted the duke, for 'an ambassador is but a man who neither cares for us nor we for him longer than the time of his negotiation'. With the Queen's

Margaret Audley. Portrait by Hans Eworth in Audley End

The quenes maiestye   The Scots quen

my lo. off leic.   my L Cobham

my

m. pelham

S. H. nevell

yours

R 101   A   R
                                  S. R. Sadler

B   φ
                              bangster

H.   M   C
   m Hatton
tc

K
cukbert   B   ≠
                                   Mr K. knolls   2
                                                    Sr W. Mildmay
                    N.   M
                 Sr H. nevell   L. Hun. Jrossen.

Mr Typole.   P   O
               Er. Arundell.   L. Lumley   Sr Nich. Throckmorton.

Mr Dyars.   2   3
               Sr Ni. 's Trong.   L. Lumley   Gordgiust.   books

189

Cipher found in Howard House, 1571

husband it was very different and there might be a risk of him proving 'an open maintainer of papistry' which would endanger both the Queen and her realm. 'Let your highness assure yourself' (counselled Norfolk 'the politique' in an aside) 'that England can bear no more changes in religion: it hath been bowed so oft that if it should be bent again it would break.' It was a pity the Archduke had made his request, yet it was a moderate one and Norfolk felt sure he made it on political grounds, not in deference to conscience, and he would be sorry to advise her to decline it. As in his letter to Cecil he discounted the risk of a Catholic chapel in the palace compared with the danger of the Queen remaining single. 'If this, then, should not take place, what present hope is there of any other, as delay of Your Majesty's marriage is almost an undoing to your realm ...' He could not write to Elizabeth on such a topic in the forceful language he used when writing about it to Sussex or Cecil, but there is no doubt about what was his final advice to her.

Howard then penned a postscript to Cecil's letter. As the journey to court was out of the question he begged the Secretary to see that his views were not misrepresented at the Council table or at large: 'I know how ready my enemies be to count me papist, which they shall never prove, by the Grace of God' – and such fears were justified. He was worn out by his letter writing, 'what with the Queen's letter and the copy (because I durst trust nobody withall)', and he prayed that Cecil might soon be able to tell him of Her Majesty's capitulation to the Archduke's terms.[4]

A letter from Cecil crossed with this and within a few days his own servants brought further news of Leicester's hot gospelling in London. The duke was extremely disturbed by these reports and wished he were not so out-of-touch. 'I like not the practices that now so fast work', he replied to the Secretary. You in London 'know much more than I can here, who neither heareth so certainly of their double proceedings, nor giveth any diligent ear thereunto, and yet my ears have glowed to hear [that] which I have heard within these two days concerning mythical devices which now begin to be sown abroad. First they mind to fight with their malicious tongues and afterwards, I warrant you, they will not spare weapon if they may. Some report that my own letter [to the Queen] shall be a witness against me ... but I assure you there is nothing therein written but that I will maintain to

TH K

be good for her and her realm, both unto my word and my deed.'
Absence from court had, indeed, made him an easy target for the
alarmists. His advice to Elizabeth had been 'scanned according to
every man's affection, and therefore', he told Sussex with disgust,
'I nearly am now counted a papist'. The feeling that Norfolk was
no longer a loyal Anglican but a befriender of recusants, which
was to bedevil him in 1569 and 1570, had its origins not in the
duke's indoctrination under Bishop White in his childhood, nor
in his marriage with a devout Catholic, Elizabeth Dacre, but in
the tales spread abroad by Leicester's party in November 1567.
He was weary of it all – in body and spirit he had become 'too
well mortified to care for slanderous reports'.[5]

In the event it was Norfolk's enforced absence from the Council
which made all the difference, particularly with Sussex anchored
in Vienna and Leicester rallying his supporters so effectively;
though the matrimonial misfortunes of Mary Queen of Scots
may well have been the deciding factor with Elizabeth. She professed to be keen still to invite the Archduke to visit England, and
during his stay for arranging a marriage treaty he would be
allowed the private exercise of his religion, though she hoped
that she personally could persuade him to give way. Two days
later she added a rider asking Sussex to make it quite clear to
Charles that there was not the slightest chance, if he came to
England, that he could persuade her to change her mind.

When Sussex had conveyed this message to Charles and his
brother, it was obvious that an *impasse* had been reached, so he
speedily invested the Emperor with the Garter and prepared for
home. He and Cecil were utterly dismayed that the door had been
finally closed. Though a newsletter from Germany in mid-
January announced in the plainest terms that 'the hot bruit of the
match is now cooled', the duke took a long time to grasp the fact
that his cherished design of a Hapsburg marriage had ended in
ruins. Perhaps Cecil, wishing to spare him unnecessary worry,
deliberately failed to tell him. As late as the following April he
still longed 'to understand some good success of the Archdukes',
but the scheme was as dead as last year's bracken on Thetford
Heath.

He was still unwell, but he implored Cecil to do all he could
to see that Sussex was rewarded as well as he deserved. Before he
went to Vienna he had been promised the post of President of the

Council of Wales and the Marches, but while he was away Leicester secured the presidency for his relative, Sir Henry Sidney. Sussex felt so put out at Elizabeth having gone back on her word that he even contemplated shaking the dust of England from his feet and settling in Italy. Norfolk, who had thought himself neglected and under-valued at the beginning of the reign, felt deeply for his friend and cursed Leicester for his intrigues. Thanks to the duke's intervention and Cecil's own prodding, Elizabeth appointed the earl in July to succeed Archbishop Young as Lord President of the Council in the North.[6]

       *   *   *

Howard spent Easter at Oxford in company with his learned brother Henry, and on the Monday both were created Masters of Arts. The duke's was an honorary degree, his brother's an M.A. by incorporation, as he was already a graduate of Cambridge. Norfolk had deliberately absented himself from the court when the Queen had visited Oxford in 1566 and was thus not among those nobles honoured at the special degree ceremony held in the Refectory at Christ Church, so he had escaped the tedium of a full round of Latin disputations and Greek plays and had avoided subservience to the Chancellor of the University – Leicester. Doubtless it had been agreed that when he came to Oxford this omission should be made good. The 1568 ceremony was, by contrast, very humble, being performed 'in a certain chamber in the house of Thomas Furse, commonly called the Bear Inn', at the corner of what is now Alfred Street, at which Norfolk was staying. The fact that it was university vacation had dictated a private ceremony, rather than a grand gathering of doctors, regents and masters, and the duke would certainly have wanted to avoid any function which would tax his health. On the same afternoon Norfolk's chaplain, William Hughes, a Caernarvonshire scholar who had graduated at Cambridge, was admitted as a Bachelor of Divinity. Five years later he was to be appointed Bishop of St Asaph.

During his brief stay in Oxford the duke visited St John's College and was introduced to Gregory Martin who was, after Campion, the most brilliant of the Fellows. Norfolk was so impressed with Martin that he engaged him as a tutor for his children.[7]

       *   *   *

After an absence in Norfolk of sixteen months the duke returned to court early in May. He was anxious now to see the progress that had been made at Howard House, on which he was lavishing so much money, and at last he was well enough to throw himself wholeheartedly into legal and financial problems connected with his estates and his wards, and was soon busying himself with reforms at the Heralds' College. Hard work was helping him to overcome his bereavement. But there was soon work of a different nature for him to do, for on 16th May Mary Queen of Scots, following her escape from Lochleven Castle and the final overthrow of her supporters at Langside, crossed the Solway and landed in England. Immediately the news reached Whitehall, Elizabeth summoned those of her Council in residence to decide how Mary was to be treated; for some reason Leicester, Norfolk and Arundel were all absent from this meeting at which most of the councillors opposed the Queen who spoke out for Mary. Another meeting was called, attended by the earlier absentees.[8]

Lord Scrope, Warden of the West March and Governor of Carlisle, who was in London at the time, was at once despatched to the north with Sir Francis Knollys, vice-chamberlain of the household, and Elizabeth ordered Lady Scrope, then at Bolton, to attend on the Scottish Queen 'and treat her with all honour'. Margaret Scrope, who was Norfolk's sister, waited on Mary first at Carlisle, and, from mid-July, at her own house, Bolton in Wensleydale, where she was to remain until she was removed to Tutbury. Bolton Castle, built at the end of the fourteenth century, was a strong, stately home in bleak country, with the highest walls of any residence in the realm. Escape was barely possible.

Tradition has it that Lady Scrope befriended Mary. As the mother of a young son herself she felt deeply for Mary's separation from her baby. Though no letter survives she must surely have written to Norfolk about her royal charge, described her person, and given him a sympathetic account of her problems. One source suggests that Mary knew from Lady Scrope before the York Conference opened in the autumn of 'the duke's goodwill toward her'. She may even have helped to foster the idea of a marriage between Mary and her brother.[9]

The crisis interfered with the established routine of the court. The Queen limited her summer progress to the home counties 'as she is careful to keep near at hand when troubles and disturbances

exist in adjacent countries', noted a foreigner. The duke himself
remained in London throughout July and August, an unheard of
arrangement, holding himself in readiness for discussions on the
Scottish problem instead of going into his county. Lord Fleming,
one of the envoys sent by Mary to gain Elizabeth's goodwill, was
confident he had won Norfolk's support – 'and I think he has',
wrote de Silva on 20th June. 'If it prove so, the Queen of Scots
will have a strong party in the country, for the Duke is much
beloved and has many friends.' If in fact Norfolk committed himself to Mary's envoy at this stage it was probably no more than a
general statement of sympathy; we do not even know the advice
he gave to Elizabeth, but it is unlikely that it differed from
Arundel's succinct remark 'one that has a crown can hardly persuade another to leave her crown because her subjects will not
obey. It may be a new doctrine in Scotland, but it is not good to
be taught in England.'

On 6th July when Elizabeth returned to London from Berk-
shire for a Council meeting, the duke entertained her to dinner
at Howard House. By the end of that month it was clear he was
to be one of the commissioners whom she was to appoint to
investigate the charges made against Mary, although it was not
until early September that the commission was issued.[10]

Norfolk, with Sussex, the newly-appointed Lord President of
the Council in the North, and Sir Ralph Sadler, stalwart of the
administration of the Border counties, were to meet at York the
following month and be joined by delegates appointed both by
Mary and by the Regent Murray. Mary herself would not appear;
indeed it was obvious that she would never acknowledge the
authority of a tribunal that sat in judgment on her affairs. Norfolk
and his fellows were first to hear the charges brought by Mary's
delegates against Murray; they were neither accusers nor judges,
but were investigating her case, which hinged on her complicity
in Darnley's murder. Her future would depend on their findings
and their instructions included advice on how she might return
to her throne 'without danger of relapse into misgovernment'.
With the arrival of the various delegates York became extremely
crowded that autumn and lodgings were scarce. The conference
was held in the building used by the Council in the North. On
Sunday 4th October the duke was met three miles outside the
city by the Bishop of Ross, Lord Herries and Mary's other

commissioners and next day the Regent Murray, the Earl of Morton and the remainder of the infant James's commissioners arrived.

John Leslie, Bishop of Ross, was to be closer to Mary than anyone during the next few years. As much the product of the University of Paris as of King's College, Aberdeen, Leslie saw himself as the Cardinal Pole of the Counter-Reformation in Scotland. A scholar of distinction, he had a brush with John Knox before he was commissioned by the Catholic lords on Francis II's death to travel to France and invite the widowed Mary to return to Scotland. Thereafter he was singled out for rapid preferment in church and state – Professor of Canon Law at Aberdeen, a Judge of the Court of Session, a member of the Privy Council in 1565 and elected Bishop of Ross the year following, though he was not consecrated until much later. He had been in attendance at Holyrood House on the night of Rizzio's murder and from that time onwards Mary found his services indispensable as a confidential secretary. While she was imprisoned at Lochleven he had withdrawn to his diocese and occupied himself with ecclesiastical affairs, but on her escape she commanded him to meet her at Hamilton; before he could obey, her army had been routed at Langside and she had crossed the border. Norfolk was much impressed by his ability at York, where the two met for the first time. Before very long they were to become deeply involved in each other's fortunes and it was Ross's confession, following the unmasking of the Ridolfi Conspiracy in 1571, which was primarily responsible for sending the Duke to the block.

From the start both the Scottish parties were ready, on the one hand to look for signs of the duke favouring their rivals, and on the other to take every opportunity to influence him in favouring them. As with so many conferences it was the unofficial talks which counted. On 6th October Norfolk reported to Elizabeth the preliminary discussions and difficulties which had arisen over the terms of the rival commissions. He did not underestimate the magnitude of the problem before him and was himself keen to delay 'the terrors of accusation' for as long as possible. 'The beginning is somewhat hard; Your Majesty may judge what is to be looked for in the sequel of the same.' Since he predicted a lengthy conference it was only tactful, at the end of his letter, to hope that Elizabeth might reign for 'the years of Nestor'.

The Regent was loath to produce his most telling evidence against the Queen of Scots until he was sure exactly what Elizabeth would do if Mary's guilt were established. According to Sir James Melville, who was present at York, Norfolk had a conversation with Murray in which, having sworn him to secrecy, he declared that he and other noblemen, 'as fathers of the country', were anxious to settle the question of the succession, so inevitably their eyes were turned to Mary and her infant son. 'He therefore wished', said Melville, 'that the Queen should not be accused, nor dishonoured for the King her son's cause and for the respect to the right they both had to succeed to the crown of England ... I am sent to hear your accusations; but neither will I, nor the Queen my mistress, give out any sentence upon your accusation.' He advised Murray that the next time that he asked him in conference to submit his accusations, he should require before so doing an undertaking in writing from Elizabeth that she would immediately 'give out sentence according to your protestation; otherwise, that you will not open your pack'. The Regent followed this advice and Norfolk passed on his request to Elizabeth for an assurance that she would 'aid and maintain them in this action if she found Mary guilty'. If, on the other hand, Elizabeth failed to support the Scottish lords and they proceeded to accuse Mary of Darnley's murder, they would be in danger of their lives. The Queen of England could do no more than say 'her promise would be abundantly sufficient', and so Murray held back the accusation.[11]

Meanwhile Norfolk had been privately shown five of the Casket Letters, the collection of letters and ballads from Mary to Bothwell which 'were closed in a little coffer of silver and gilt, heretofore given by her to Bothwell. The said letters and ballads', the duke wrote to Elizabeth with disgust on 11th October, 'do discover such inordinate love between her and Bothwell, her loathsomeness and abhorring of her husband that was murdered, in such sort as every good and godly man cannot but detest and abhor the same.' Murray and his supporters were prepared to swear that the letters were in Mary's own hand. Norfolk obviously thought they were genuine, 'the matter contained in them being such as could hardly be invented or devised by any other than herself', and he concluded that unless their forgery could be proved, Mary's guilt in Darnley's death was beyond question.

Information about the Casket Letters had first reached London soon after their discovery by the Scottish lords in June 1567 and copies of some of them had been sent by the Regent to Cecil a year later, so Norfolk's letter did not announce a major development. What is revealing is his own undisguised revulsion at the Casket Letters and his fears that they were most certainly genuine.

Three days later, on 16th October, Norfolk went hawking with Maitland of Lethington to Cawood, some eight miles south-east of the city, by the river Ouse. Of the Regent's commissioners Secretary Maitland was the one least inclined to press the charges against Mary, and he had his own reasons for not wanting a thorough enquiry into Darnley's murder. At the time of the siege of Leith he and Norfolk had got on very well together and now they renewed their friendship. On the ride to Cawood Maitland shrewdly suggested that the only way of cutting the Gordian Knot would be for Norfolk to marry Mary, who would be restored to her throne and in the fullness of time she and her issue would reign at Whitehall as well as Holyrood House. Such a match would save Mary from dishonour and carry the Anglo-Scottish alliance a stage further. This was the third occasion on which Norfolk had been suggested as a suitable husband for Mary, but the position was vastly different since Maitland had last mentioned his name in 1565; the duke had re-married and been widowed again, while Mary had married Darnley, seen him murdered, gone through a form of marriage with Bothwell and now exchanged her captivity at Lochleven for captivity in England. What were Norfolk's reactions to the proposal now he had seen the Casket Letters?

A year later Murray told Elizabeth that during the York Conference he 'partly smelt' Norfolk's intention. Later still the Bishop of Ross declared that the projected marriage had been discussed before the conference opened and that a servant of the duke's had mentioned the matter to Lady Scrope. What is quite clear is that on the hawking expedition the suggestion had come from Maitland. J. A. Froude thought it was 'certain that the Duke went down to York with the scheme already fixed in his mind', yet such evidence as there is points quite the other way. Froude would never have made that statement had he not been misled into placing the conversations with Maitland on the ride to Cawood on 9th October, a week before they actually occurred, and thus before, instead of after, the duke had been shown the Casket Letters. In view of his horror at the contents of the letters, he cannot have jumped at the idea of marrying as his fourth wife a woman he had never seen who appeared on the evidence he had just read to be a murderess and an adulteress. He certainly had not given any undertaking to Maitland, nor could he have done so had he wished. He was well aware of the clause in his instructions at York which stated that anyone with whom Mary Queen of Scots contracted a marriage, or anyone advising one, 'shall be *ipso facto* adjudged as traitorous and shall suffer death'.

The Bishop of Ross had come to Maitland's lodgings one night for a long discussion of tactics. He learnt that the duke 'had some intention to marry with the Queen' and as a result he called on him at seven in the morning, before the other commissioners were abroad. There was no mention of the marriage project, but in the gallery Norfolk assured the bishop of the goodwill he bore to Mary. He had seen the Casket Letters 'whereby there would such matter be proved against her that would dishonour her forever'; and he knew that once Elizabeth had her hands on them she would publish the fact of Mary's guilt and, as a result, all pressure from foreign courts for her delivery from captivity would fade away. Accordingly he advised Ross to confer with Maitland again to find means to stay the matter, and off the bishop rode to Bolton to report to his mistress.

The seed sown by Maitland would develop rapidly within a few months. Before the secret conversation on the road to Cawood, Knollys had suggested to Norfolk that one way of solving the problem of Mary would be for her to marry his cousin George Carey, son of Lord Hunsdon and a cousin of Elizabeth's. Knollys later mentioned this to Mary and gathered that she did 'not greatly mislike' the idea. Later that autumn Norfolk would come to ask himself, if George Carey, why not he himself. It is in fact impossible to say at exactly what date the duke began to take Maitland's suggestion seriously. Opposition from Elizabeth and Cecil was for once to provoke something of his father's strong-headedness and, as he allowed himself to be included in schemes devised by bolder spirits, he eventually reached the point at which he could not honourably withdraw.[12]

It was stalemate by the eleventh day of the conference. 'This cause', the duke wrote to Cecil on 16th October, 'is the doubtful-lest and dangeroust that ever I dealt in; if you saw and heard the constant affirming of both sides, not without great stoutness, you would wonder!' That same day Elizabeth sent word to York that she had decided to summon a full Privy Council to consider the points which Norfolk had raised, and so the sessions at York adjourned. Sadler was ordered to repair to court for discussions and would be joined by two of Murray's and two of Mary's delegates; Sussex was to busy himself with his duties as President of the Council in the North, while Norfolk was to inspect the defences on the Border. No-one doubted that later in the year the commissioners would reassemble at York.

It was no slight for the duke that Sadler should have been the commissioner recalled to Westminster, for from the beginning it had been intended that Norfolk should report on the state of the Berwick garrison and the Scottish Marches while he was in the north. He first visited Alnwick to confer with Sir John Forster, who had had trouble in the Middle March a fortnight before, through a typical Border skirmish in which six Englishmen had been killed. He found 'many wants in the Middle Marches' – almost every point mentioned in the articles of enquiry needed attention. Winter was setting in early that year and from Alnwick Norfolk wrote on 26th October that he had never seen 'worse weather for snow and frost in the south at Christmas and after', than he had met in his journey north from York. Conditions were even worse as he passed into Cumberland to inspect the West March. It was 'as ill a journey as ever he had in his life, with the unreasonablest weather that ever was seen in this country so early in the year'. The waters were so high in all the fords in Northumberland that some of his men were in danger of drowning. The West March, of which his brother-in-law Scrope was Warden, was in a better shape, and it needed to be, for the captive Queen was only fifty miles from the Border. Norfolk then returned to Berwick, his headquarters of eight years back, to review the fortifications and then to travel south, for his presence was now required at court. He was glad to be leaving the snowy north, but he was to regret the return to London.[13]

By then Elizabeth knew enough to suspect that Norfolk had shown undue partiality to Mary's cause, even though the York Conference had never properly got under way. She had chosen him as her chief commissioner because of his 'fidelity and circumspection' and he had taken an oath before the Dean of York to proceed 'sincerely and uprightly . . . not for affection, value or any other worldly respect to lean to the one party or the other'. That was the sole reason why the Conference was never resumed at York, and instead a greatly augmented English commission, which still included the duke, sat at Westminster and Hampton Court.

Rumours that Norfolk was contemplating marriage with Mary had also leaked to court and seriously discredited him. His absence from court always gave the gossips their opportunities, and Norfolk returned too late to stifle the whisperings about him. Fénélon, the new French ambassador, with his ears very much to the ground, had passed on a rumour to his sovereign before the end of the month.[14]

Back in Whitehall the duke found out how the land lay and at once denied the truth of the stories 'and did very well allow of his vehement misliking of such a marriage'. Elizabeth bided her time; it was probably not until the Conference had broken down that she asked him to his face about what she had heard. Though he now hated the idea of marrying Mary, perhaps in the future he could be persuaded to change his mind, if it were shown to be for the benefit of the realm and the safety of his Queen? Norfolk knew he was being tested and answered his mistress that 'no reason could move him to like of her that hath been a competitor to the Crown; and if Her Majesty would move him thereto he will rather be committed to the Tower, for he meant never to marry with such a person, where he could not be sure of his pillow' – an allusion to Darnley's fate. A politic answer, indeed, and not so hollow as some have made out, for by then the full horror of the Casket Letters had been brought home to him. Elizabeth herself was satisfied with this protestation; at any rate she had given Norfolk a broad hint. Ironically, it was hints such as this which played on his ambition and persuaded him to take the idea of the marriage seriously. It developed from a vague idea to a serious project.[15]

The Conference had opened in the Star Chamber on Thursday 25th November. The English Commissioners, who had been appointed the previous day, were Lord Keeper Bacon, Norfolk, Arundel, Sussex, Leicester, Clinton, Cecil and Sadler, though Arundel was absent sick for the first week. As at York the oath-taking and other preliminaries took up a great deal of time. When

Ross had read his commission, apologising for the fact that it was sealed only with Mary's signet, as she had no Great Seal since leaving Scotland, he insisted on making his Protestation: Mary was not to be treated judicially 'in respect she is a free princess with an imperial crown given her of God'. This done, he and his fellows withdrew and Murray, Morton, the Bishop of Orkney and the rest of King James's commissioners entered the room. The Regent for his part presented the English commissioners with four articles, to which he required answers, about their authority to pronounce on Mary's guilt. They told him they would report to Elizabeth what they found to be true; if she were found guilty of Darnley's murder, 'which were much to be lamented', she would either be delivered to Murray or continue to be kept in England, and Elizabeth would then acknowledge Mary's dimission of the crown to her son and respect Murray's authority as Regent.

Next day, after much hesitation, the accusation against Mary was delivered; that as Bothwell was the chief executor of Darnley's horrible and unworthy murder, 'so she was of the foreknowledge', and a maintainer of the evil-doers. The official Journal of the Commissioners gives no hint of the dramatic scene in the Star Chamber which Sir James Melville relates in his memoirs. Cecil had asked if the Regent's party had the accusation with them, and John Wood, Murray's secretary, plucked it out of his bosom, but said he would not deliver it until the Regent was given Elizabeth's assurance in writing for which (on Norfolk's advice) they had asked at York. But in the heat of the moment the Bishop of Orkney snatched the document from Wood's hands and passed it to Cecil. 'Well done, bishop, thou art the frankest fellow among them all', cried out one of the English lords. Norfolk, we are told, had much ado to keep his countenance while Wood and Cecil smiled and winked at each other. The fat was now in the fire. Murray tried to undo the damage by asking for the accusation to be returned to him, saying he had more to add to it, but was told he could submit supplementary matters later. He left the conference in tears and went home to his lodgings in Kingston-on-Thames utterly shaken.[16]

Though the Westminster Conference dragged on for another fortnight the rest is soon told. Bacon, prompted by Elizabeth, roundly rebuked Murray and his fellows from daring to accuse their sovereign in this way, and on 7th December James's commissioners, with a show of mock reluctance, offered to produce the Casket Letters and other incriminating documents, sworn to by Morton as authentic, to support their accusation. While they were being perused Ross and Lord Boyd arrived to present a further Protestation which they had already privately communicated to Elizabeth at Hampton Court. Ross dug his heels in firmly and said it was quite impossible for them to attempt any answer to the accusation; they had no authority to act in this way and it was imperative for Mary to be allowed to come in person to Elizabeth's presence and answer for herself. In short Mary's commissioners would take no further part in the proceedings and stalemate had again been reached. Elizabeth called her commissioners before her at Hampton Court on 14th and 15th December to go over the ground once more and subsequently wrote to Mary herself, congratulating her on so faithful and skilled a servant as Ross, but advising her most earnestly to answer the charges against her in writing so she could be delivered by the justification of her innocency. In fact now that the Casket Letters had been produced Elizabeth was in a very strong position for she had ample evidence to justify her treatment of Mary to the courts of Europe. She would in truth never agree to meet Mary, but at least she would not rule out the possibility of her restoration, which might still be the best solution to the Scottish problem, for she made it quite clear that she despised the Regent.

Outside the conference room Norfolk discussed the problem of Mary with Murray, Maitland and others. Exactly what took place and what was said is conjectural, for the evidence of these conversations, most of it set down two or three years later is conflicting, but the following is the most likely reconstruction. Morton, out to embarrass the Regent still further, had sent a servant to divulge to Huntingdon details of the agreement reached at York between Murray and Norfolk, and as he had hoped Huntingdon told Leicester, who told the Queen, though Elizabeth had long suspected this. Norfolk by all accounts was exasperated and we are told that to get his revenge on the Scottish commissioners he asked the Earl of Westmorland to intercept them on their way home to Edinburgh; how far he intended to go is conjectural and in the event he changed his plans and wrote to his brother-in-law to cancel the *coup*. The idea may have been no more than to give Murray a scare and if this were so it served its purpose, for catching wind of the rumour that his throat might be cut on the way to the Border, he decided to go in penitence to the duke to patch things up. A rendez-vous was arranged in Hampton Court Park and Sir Nicholas Throgmorton brought them together. Murray asked for Norfolk's pardon, blaming the intrigues of his associates for the way the conference had developed. Howard replied that 'he knew his gentle nature was abused by the craft and concurrence of some of the Council of England, who had joined with some about him' to overthrow the agreed plan of campaign. They agreed for the future to keep closely in touch and swore themselves to secrecy. The duke again reminded Murray that he was resolved to marry Mary and hinted at the possibility of a match between the young King James and his own daughter: 'Earl of Murray', he said, 'thou knowest that thing whereunto I will make none in England nor in Scotland privy, and thou hast Norfolk's life in thy hands.' The duke even undertook to persuade Elizabeth to grant the Regent £2,000, for he was in desperate need of money.

Norfolk was delighted at his new concordat with Murray, but Mary must have been alarmed when she had a letter from him announcing this resumed friendship, for she knew her brother could not be trusted for one moment. Before he left London he had related to Elizabeth the tenor of his secret conversations with the duke: he did not in the least feel bound by his promises to Norfolk, for he had made them 'for fear of life'. Elizabeth agreed to support him as regent and provide him with £5,000 to maintain his ascendancy in Scotland on condition that the infant James should be educated in England and that English troops should garrison Edinburgh, Stirling and Dumbarton; though there was such an outcry in Scotland that this plan had to be abandoned. To justify himself he issued a proclamation declaring that he and his party having been charged with treason against Mary had proved to Elizabeth their entire innocence, but in so doing had been compelled to make manifest the complicity of Mary in her husband's murder. There were other discussions in which Lumley and Arundel took part. Norfolk sent Lumley to Ross begging him to open official discussions with Elizabeth to win her over to the idea of his marriage, and almost at once sent his man Liggons to tell the bishop that the Queen had heard the rumours of his fresh dealings with Mary, 'but he had satisfied her well enough'.[17]

It is impossible to make these developments to the Norfolk-Mary marriage project in the aftermath of the Westminster Conference appear tidy, logical or systematic, for the stages of back-stairs diplomacy are never orderly; and here their very nature was one of confusion. Moreover most of the actors in this drama were playing a double game, and it was to be Norfolk's fate that he accepted Murray's assurances at their face value. One thing is certain. By the opening of 1569 he had determined, when opportunity served and she was a free woman, to marry Mary; who was now to be removed to the safer custody of the Earl of Shrewsbury at Tutbury; and for all his protestations to the contrary he would never give up this ambition so long as he lived. It was for him a dynastic alliance that would at one stroke solve the difficult Scottish problem and settle for good the uncertainties of the English succession. This was no love match, for he still had not set eyes on Mary, and he could not forget she was an adulteress. What mattered to him was that she was a Queen and marriage with her would provide him with a throne, and because of this the temptation to marry Mary was irresistible.

The monarchy had been elevated by the break with Rome and had now been given a new mystique by a young and masterful Queen. As the Crown grew in splendour people's pre-occupation with the succession became obsessive; it was this which would later in the reign make Shakespeare's cycle of historical plays, centred on the Crown, so certain of popular success, and it was this which spelt the Duke's downfall. By birth a thane of Cawdor, he saw in marriage with Mary the opportunity to be 'King hereafter', for he had not the will to resist his impulses and hold back from the realisation of so glittering an ambition. The proposal that he should marry the Queen of Scots was the turning-point in his career, for lured by chance of a Crown he went to pieces. For this cause he would be prepared to sink differences with his enemy Leicester and break his friendship with Cecil; for this he would dally with conspiracy and break his oath to his sovereign. He would refuse to heed warnings, refuse to learn any lessons from imprisonment and dishonour, for nothing would distract him from the prize he had set his heart upon, and in the end he would be trapped into committing treason and compromising his religion.

Chapter Nine

PRIVY CONSPIRACY

1569

THE new year began with Norfolk under a cloud for his suspected dealings with the Queen of Scots, yet in a matter of weeks he and Leicester were to head a powerful alliance of malcontents that would challenge the dominant position which Cecil had held since the beginning of the reign. In Tudor England it was the duty of the opposition to intrigue, and thus the year 1569 passed in a succession of plots, some involving foreign powers, which culminated in the Northern Rebellion, and during this, the most critical year of the whole of Elizabeth's reign, the duke became the central figure in politics.

The seizure of four Spanish treasure ships, bound for the Netherlands, which had taken shelter in Plymouth Sound the previous November, had provoked a commercial crisis and brought England to the brink of war. For the sake of £85,000 of Spanish loot Cecil had overthrown the traditional pattern of English foreign trade and, when English property in the Netherlands was confiscated and an embargo imposed, he was the most unpopular man in London. Such was the genesis of the movement for his dismissal, and this was the first real chance he had given his opponents, on whatever grounds they based their hostility. 'Many did also rise against his fortune, who were more hot in envying him than able to follow him, detracting his praises, disgracing his services and plotting his danger' – so runs a biographical sketch written while Cecil was still alive.[1] His opponents were strange bedfellows. There was Leicester, convinced that it was

Cecil who had prevented him from winning Elizabeth's hand; Norfolk, who saw Cecil as the arch-enemy of Mary Queen of Scots whom he was now committed to marry; Pembroke and Northampton who disliked the policy that Cecil's Protestantism had led him to pursue, especially aiding the rebels in the Netherlands and France, and supporting the Suffolk claim to the succession; Arundel, Lumley, Northumberland and Westmorland, who as Roman Catholics saw the Secretary's dismissal as the essential preliminary to a re-establishment of their religion; and even old Winchester, still in his dotage swaying with the wind. Many of them regarded Cecil, as Norfolk had once done, as the 'new man' bent on overthrowing the old nobility in the power of the state. There were others, too, who viewed with alarm the growing estrangement from Spain, not solely on grounds of commercial prudence but also because they feared England would be thrown into alliance with France, her traditional enemy, and anti-Gallic prejudice died hard in 1569. In the City and the ports Cecil's name was cursed as trade slowed down to a standstill and in the country as a whole he forfeited the goodwill of ordinary folk by his mishandling of the public lottery. To him was ascribed the severity with which the laws against recusants were now being enforced. In short there was a wave of protest about his presumption 'to reign in the Commonwealth'. No minister of later days could have remained in office in the face of such unpopularity, but a Tudor minister, who retained his sovereign's confidence could only be removed by intrigue.

Norfolk and Arundel made it their business at the end of February to contact the Spanish ambassador. Guerau de Spes, who was confined to his house and under guard. They sent along the Florentine banker, Ridolfi, with whom each had had dealings in the past, and provided 'a safe cipher'. They assured de Spes that the treasure would eventually be returned to Spain, but that as yet they were not strong enough to resist Cecil; they were (as the ambassador managed to report to Alva), 'gathering friends, and were letting the public know what was going on, in the hope and belief that they will be able to turn out the present accursed government and raise another ... Although Cecil thinks he has them all under his heel, he will find few or none of them stand by him.' Leicester seemed slow to declare himself. De Spes wrote again a fortnight later in much the same vein: the duke and his friends dared not resist Cecil, he said, or even point out his failings to the Queen 'until they have felt their way with the other nobles and with the people. This they have now done and have many sure pledges'. Unknown to the ambassador they had already moved.[2]

They intended that Cecil, like Thomas Cromwell before him, should be charged at the Council table with being an evil adviser, in the Queen's absence, arrested and sent to the Tower. Once he were imprisoned 'means to undo him would not be far to seek'. Queen and Secretary caught wind of the design just in time. She immediately summoned a Privy Council meeting, to quash the affair, but everyone who counted – even Leicester – made excuses. She had a further opportunity a day or so later, on Ash Wednesday. Cecil, Norfolk and Northampton were in her chamber before supper when in came Leicester, whom she rebuked for the unbusinesslike behaviour of the Council. The earl thereupon burst into an attack on Cecil whom in the eyes of so many people was ruining the State. She flew to the Secretary's defence, castigating Leicester, while the duke at the other end of the room said to Northampton (not as an aside, but loud enough for Elizabeth to hear): 'You see, my Lord, how the Earl of Leicester is favoured so long as he supports the Secretary, but now that for good reasons he takes an opposed position, she frowns upon him and wants to send him to the Tower.' 'No, no, he will not go alone,' Northampton replied. 'I praise God that you, the first subject of the realm, are willing at last to show your quality. I am prepared to follow you and to support you in every way I can, for I have come to complain.' The Queen's comment is not recorded. This interview should have shown them all quite plainly that Cecil was not to be sacrificed by his mistress and that if they wanted a change of policy that would mean a change of sovereign.[3]

The conspiracy against Cecil still went on, but it had lost its force. De Spes reported that on three occasions in April, when the others had steeled themselves to act, Leicester 'softened and said he would tell the Queen'. Delays gave Cecil the chance of uncovering the design and he begged his fellow councillors 'not to do anything scandalous', offering to come over to their wishes, but saying quite firmly they must present a united front to Spain. One of their schemes, apparently, was a plot to accuse Cecil of having caused a book to be written attacking the nobility. Finding that they could not secure his removal a number of the mal-contents rallied round Norfolk, to promote his marriage with Mary.

Towards a settlement of the commercial dispute, the occasion of the crisis, there was talk of sending both Norfolk and Arundel to Spain, though this came to nothing. Norfolk did, however, firmly advise Cecil to abandon his hostile policy towards Philip II that had so estranged the Council. By the end of May they again became drawn closer together – a reconciliation in which Cecil's share in obtaining for the duke a satisfactory judgment in the matter of the Dacre estates played its part.

When he had first heard of the estrangement between the two men, on 15th May, Sussex had thought it the 'worst thing' possible and, although he knew not its cause, he implored Cecil to 'rip up this matter from the bottom with the Duke himself', offering to ride to London – 'yea to Jerusalem' – to act as media-tor, if one were needed. A fortnight later, when news arrived of their resumed friendliness, Sussex was delighted, for he had always pinned high hopes on Norfolk as a statesman 'whom the world hath always judged to be void of private inclines'. Yet it is most unlikely that the duke at this time took Cecil into his confidence by mentioning, even in the most general terms, his hopes of marrying Mary and, tactics apart, it was not a matter which he was as yet in a position to reveal. Cecil may even have suggested in good faith that Norfolk should marry his younger sister-in-law, recently widowed, the third of the remarkable daughters of Sir Anthony Cooke of Gidea Hall. She certainly had a suitable dowry, but as de Spes put it 'the duke would not listen to it, for he has his thoughts high, having fixed his eyes upon the Queen of Scotland'.[4]

Following the crisis on Ash Wednesday at least three distinct, yet simultaneous, designs can be traced. There was in the first place the scheme, probably initiated by Maitland, for Mary to marry the duke, which was now put forward by Leicester as the sure remedy for the body politique both in England and in Scotland. Throgmorton was the earl's go-between with Norfolk and later with Pembroke. They discussed the matter with the Bishop of Ross and opened negotiations with the Regent Murray. The terms suggested were that Mary's abdication should be cancelled, Darnley's murder forgotten and a divorce from Bothwell obtained, so that she would be free to marry Norfolk. Once restored to her throne, Mary was to ratify the Treaty of Edinburgh and the Parliament at Westminster would then pronounce her heir presumptive to the throne of England. She was on no account to conduct an independent foreign policy though she was to grant freedom of worship in Scotland.

Leicester later admitted that 'he would not have' Mary 'if he might' and that the duke was only persuaded to contemplate the match to benefit Elizabeth – 'if it was for her commodity he would sacrifice himself'. Ever since Mary had returned from France to Scotland there had been the question of a suitable husband for her. The suggestion now made at one stroke solved the problem of Mary and her kingdom and also of the English succession, for Mary already had a son. The attraction of the scheme for Leicester was just that. It would no longer be of prime importance whom Elizabeth married. The diplomatic manoeuvres with imperial archdukes and French princes would at last cease, to everyone's intense relief, and Dudley could himself marry the Queen and wear the crown matrimonial.

Norfolk hesitated out of discreet convention, but he had already made up his mind before Throgmorton approached him. Personal ambition and studied resentment at Elizabeth's treatment of him, and alarm at her treatment of Mary, at last began to have full play once he had persuaded himself that it was his plain duty to fall in with Leicester's design. Whatever the fate of the earl's own courtship, Norfolk would be assured of being King Consort in Scotland with a fair chance of seeing his wife succeed Elizabeth. There were but two obstacles: Cecil's known preference for the Suffolk line of succession, and Elizabeth's aversion to Mary. Leicester aimed at carrying the Council with him and of then forcing the issue with the Queen, in the face of Cecil's opposition, if necessary. As far as the duke was concerned his allegiance to Elizabeth was not at stake; as he understood Leicester, he would undertake the affair with his own Queen's permission, encouragement, even.[5]

There was, secondly, a more desperate design, directed by Arundel and Lumley, which was supported by Northumberland, Westmorland, Leonard Dacre and the northern Catholics. This had as its objects the liberation and enthronement of Mary in Elizabeth's place, and the restoration of Roman Catholicism, with

Spanish aid. Mary was to marry Norfolk as a means to this end. At the outset Northumberland, who had all the militancy of a recent convert, and others were suspicious of Norfolk's religious leanings; the best that could be said of him was that he had Catholic connexions, for while he most certainly did not appear as a champion of Protestantism, like Leicester or Huntingdon, he nonetheless seemed to them indifferent, undeclared, and as such would be an unsuitable husband for Mary, to whose cause they were attempting to attract the full support of the powers of the Counter Reformation. Besides this dissatisfaction on religious grounds there was the personal enmity which the Dacres and others felt for Norfolk as a result of the wardship. But eventually Arundel persuaded them, through Christopher Lascelles, that no better candidate could be found for Mary among the English nobility; the duke was popular, and the fact he was a *politique* had its advantages, though they had little doubt that between them they would soon convert him to the faith. If Alva would send over an army the northerners would muster 15,000 'selected' troops, quite apart from considerable support in the West Country, Wales and East Anglia.

While this scheme was taking shape in the minds of Arundel and Dacres, the Spanish ambassador was still confined to his residence, so he heard of the proposal only through such intermediaries as Ridolfi and Ross and, as a result, was either misinformed, or himself misunderstood various particulars. Always over-optimistic, in his despatches to Spain and the Netherlands de Spes exaggerated the chances of Arundel's schemings succeeding. Every hot-headed Catholic whom de Spes heard about became on paper 'a powerful ally' in his master's cause, yet both Alva and Philip II were too cautious to take his hopes literally.

Norfolk was only on the fringe of these negotiations, for neither Arundel nor the northern earls took him into their confidence until it was too late. While Leicester's scheme to persaude the Queen of the suitability of the Norfolk-Mary marriage was still gaining support in the Council, it is most unlikely that the duke would have sanctioned a plot fraught with so many dangers. Could he have changed his views so drastically about England being unable to bear any more changes in religion? He only heard of the details in the summer and then he tried, too late, to stop its execution, and it went off, at half-cock, as the Northern

Rebellion. When de Spes wrote to Philip II on 15th June that Ross had told him the duke had said he wished to serve Spain either bishop or ambassador was not telling the truth. The secret negotiations of de Spes with Arundel are bedevilled by the fact that simultaneously Arundel and Norfolk were acting as official agents over the vexed question of the restitution of the Spanish treasure. The 6,000 Spanish crowns sent over by Alva to Arundel, Lumley and Norfolk were to be used as bribes in those commercial negotiations, for 'these people are very fond of money'.[6]

There were, thirdly, Mary's own negotiations, with both sets of English conspirators and also with the Scots, which she conducted chiefly through the Bishop of Ross, and though she grasped at straws for her release and restoration, she was shrewd enough to beware of dissipating her efforts. To her the cardinal feature of any plan was marriage with Norfolk, and she sought to work upon his ambition, his vanity, his sense of honour and his very real sympathy to bring him to collaborate in her designs. Directed from her successive houses of captivity, her letters in cipher and her messages in hushed whispers passed to her potential protagonists in five kingdoms and the Papacy, but her detailed plans can never be properly unravelled; such evidence as survives is in the confessions and examinations of those who became involved in her cause, in the frenzied outbursts of men put on the rack and the accusations of those trying to save themselves. Finally, there were the independent intrigues of Ross and Ridolfi which were not to take shape into coherent plans until after the other designs had failed. All hinged on a marriage between Norfolk and Mary, and by mid-May the two of them had exchanged tokens.

That summer the storm gathered. Elizabeth watched her nobles uneasily, conscious of the undercurrent of dissatisfaction which might at any time flare up into open revolt, especially in the north. She ordered systematic musters of the militia to be taken in each county. In Durham a return was made by the Bishop, the Earl of Westmorland and Sir George Bowes on 28th June in which Brancepeth, the bastion of the earl's territory, provided twenty-nine light horsemen, led by the constable of the lordship – all of whom would fight for him in the autumn – and this was the highest figure for any area in the county. Most of the able men were noted in the list as 'naked', signifying they were foot soldiers without any arms. A muster made at York the following day revealed the unpreparedness of the county largely on account of its poverty; there were too few calivers, and many men refused to bring their armour or bows and arrows to the musters, 'the people having been greatly charged heretofore, and mistrusting some present charge, did of purpose forbear to bring them'. Even the clergy of the diocese of York were mustered.[7]

About the time that these musters were being taken Norfolk and a group of friends met at Tattershall in Lincolnshire for a day's hawking on the Clinton estate. Henry Fiennes, the Admiral's son, was host and the duke's brothers-in-law, Lord Scrope of Bolton and Lord Berkeley, were in the party; their wives were probably also staying at Tattershall. The day's sport ended, they all went to a tree and each pulled off a bough and, hand in hand, swore a solemn oath that they would again meet in the self-same spot a year later. As it happened none was able to keep his vow. A generation later Henry Clinton, by then Earl of Lincoln, was cross-examined about the Tattershall meeting. In the aftermath of Essex's Revolt, informers were hard at work and, grasping at old hearsay, they tried to implicate Clinton in the conspiracy of 1569 and of underhand dealings with the duke. He easily cleared himself by assuring his accusers that there had been nothing sinister about the day's hawking or the vow under the greenwood tree: 'they did like the place of their hawking near my house so well that they all vowed to meet that day twelvemonth there'. Indeed, the presence in the party of so loyal a servant of the Crown as Lord Scrope, Warden of the West March, ensured that everything was above board. What is interesting about the case is that apart from Clinton's examination thirty-three years later we would never have heard of the affair. Nothing in Cecil's voluminous correspondence indicates that the Secretary knew about the Tattershall meeting; no amabssador with his ears to the ground noted it in his despatches home. This lack of contemporary evidence for so distinguished a gathering suggests that all kinds of meetings were taking place in those disturbed months, particularly in the north country, of which we know nothing.[8]

Murray remained an enigma. Back in Scotland after the Hampton Court Conference he paid no more than lip service to the marriage scheme, but set about quelling his opponents, largely with the aid of Elizabeth's money. But in the spring he changed his tune, for Elizabeth was having second thoughts about Mary and talked quite openly of returning her to Scotland on condition that she would leave Murray as the effective ruler and support the English alliance. This change of front so alarmed the Regent that he agreed to give his assent to the Norfolk marriage as the only feasible alternative. For a while, until this danger had passed, his promises were in earnest, but by July he had again come down against the scheme though he continued to keep in with Norfolk and Ross in order to discover all he could about his sister's intrigues in Scotland.

Mary moved cautiously. On 3rd June she received from Ross the heads of the proposals made as a result of conferring with 'some of the nobility of England' regarding her restoration. In these she was 'wholly to refer' to Elizabeth the question of her marriage with Norfolk, moved to her by Murray and Maitland.

To this Mary made a diplomatic reply. She affected not to leap at the idea of the marriage, but weighed the advantages and disadvantages, and ended by accepting the proposals more or less as they stood, including the suggestion that she should abide by Elizabeth's advice over the match. 'My fortune hath been so evil in the progress of my life and specially in my marriages, as hardly can I be brought to have any mind to take of a husband, but rather by a simple and solitary life to give testimony to my continent behaviour to all them which might put doubt therein.' Her vicissitudes had so affected her health that she could not look far into the future; she certainly looked for no felicity in marriage, and was sure she would squander her prospective husband's fortune. 'Nevertheless, being resolved of certain doubts which occurs [sic] to me, for trust I have in the Queen my good sister and her nobility's good friendship towards me, as also for the goodwill I perceive my lord of Northfolk bears towards me, hearing him so well reputed abroad' Mary agreed to abide by Elizabeth's advice; she asked – and it was no more than an academic question – how her sister's assent could be obtained. This was the very question which worried the duke.

At the end of June Mary, in poor health, had 'remitted all my causes' to him 'to do as for yourself'. He had asked her to be cautious over sending letters from Wingfield, but she refused to listen and, signing herself 'your assured Mary', warmed to the task of courting him by proxy. 'God preserve you from all traitors and make your friends as true and constant', she wrote, sending him a cushion she had herself embroidered depicting her arms and a hand with a pruning knife cutting down a green vine. Norfolk knew that the vine symbolised Elizabeth.[9]

That summer he stayed unwillingly at court. At this juncture he could not risk being out of touch with events and he was too troubled to go home to Kenninghall until the air had been cleared by securing Elizabeth's permission for the marriage. He feared she might hear of the plan by a side wind, and after a merry evening with Leicester and Arundel at Bletchingley he returned to Howard House to learn that the Queen 'had been out of quiet'. Cecil, who was now told in confidence what he had long suspected, urged Norfolk more than once to make a clean breast of the affair, but the duke was reluctant to act against Leicester's advice. The earl had insisted that the proposal should come from Scotland, preferably at the hands of Maitland, who was daily expected in London. They waited in vain, for Maitland had staked all on getting the Convention at Perth to pronounce in favour of Mary's divorce from Bothwell in July, and when Murray secured the defeat of his motion he saw the writing on the wall; five weeks later he was arrested and imprisoned by Murray in Edinburgh Castle on the charge of being an accomplice in Darnley's murder. The duke then implored Leicester to give a lead himself; he eventually agreed, but said he must wait for the right moment or the result would be disastrous. And so July was giving way to August with nothing decided, the future as uncertain as ever.

Wishing to test his strength in the Council, Norfolk had raised the matter from a new angle at a meeting in Pembroke's rooms at Greenwich Palace while Cecil was away. He proposed that Mary should be set at liberty on condition that she married an Englishman, and this motion was passed by an overwhelming majority. Indeed 'the greatest in the land agreed in writing to stand by the duke to carry this resolution into effect'.[10] At last he and Leicester could confront Elizabeth with the fact that most of the Council were in favour of the match, and the French ambassador was convinced that she dare not oppose it. Yet still they tarried.[11]

In those critical days Norfolk missed the guidance of his closest friend, Sussex, and he had no-one else to turn to for advice. His alliance with Leicester was first to last an uneasy one, a marriage

of convenience in which the vows were taken in order to be
broken. Pembroke lacked strength of purpose and was then under
Leicester's domination. The duke's relations with Cecil could
never be the same after the intrigues of the past spring, and the
wily Secretary characteristically refused to commit himself until
the Queen had made up her mind.[12] Only Sussex could have
steeled Norfolk's irresolution and made him stand up for himself
against Leicester, only from Sussex would he have taken to heart
a warning to stop playing with fire. A visit to York to talk things
over with the earl was impossible, but he sent up Cantrell with
a message, that Arundel, Pembroke and Leicester had 'earnestly
moved him' to the marriage, and asked Sussex's advice as a friend
whom he trusted. But Sussex felt it was both too late in the day
(if Leicester and Pembroke had already moved the duke) and too
early, as he knew not how the Queen liked the scheme; he rued
the day he had been sent to York as Lord President and was thus
denied the opportunity of stopping Norfolk's folly.[13]

At the end of July the court had moved to Richmond and
Norfolk followed a day or so later, even more anxious to have
the matter settled. He came across Leicester fishing in the Thames
near his house at Kew, who told him affairs had reached a critical
stage: some women at court had babbled to the Queen who
became convinced that they were going to proceed with their
plans for the marriage without consulting her – indeed, 'that the
matter was already concluded'. Leicester had satisfied her, so he
said, that such tales were false, but made it clear to Norfolk that
they must walk warily and pick their time most carefully for
speaking with Elizabeth on the topic.[14]

The Queen gave Norfolk a chance of speaking out himself a
day or so before the court left Richmond on progress. He had
just returned from a visit to Howard House and was talking in
the garden to Sir William Drury, Marshal of the Berwick garrison, about the state of the Scottish border, when Elizabeth noticed
him and called him to her side. What news had her cousin to
tell her? The duke replied that he knew of nothing. 'No!' She
exclaimed, 'You come from London and can tell no news of a
marriage?' It was a dramatic moment. Just then Lady Clinton
came up to Her Majesty with some flowers and Norfolk, rather
than wait and say his piece when the lady withdrew, took the
opportunity of slinking off to Leicester's rooms dumbfounded,

yet determined after the Queen's broad hint to persuade the earl
to let him tell her himself. As luck would have it Leicester was
out stag-hunting near Kingston, but Howard waited patiently in
his rooms talking with Throgmorton until he returned. Dudley
again insisted on secrecy until he had spoken with Elizabeth. As
a result no steps had been taken to obtain the Queen's permission
when she left Richmond on 5th August for her summer progress.

Norfolk was an unwilling member of the royal entourage, for
a royal progress was for him the worst aspect of a courtier's life,
which he had hitherto avoided by spending the summer on his
estates, but in August 1569 he had to accompany the Queen to
keep Leicester up to his promises. After a few days at the royal
manor of Oatlands near Weybridge Elizabeth journeyed to
Guildford and then spent two days at Loseley, the fine house in
Guildford Park which Sir William More had finished building
the previous year. The duke again spoke earnestly with Leicester
and the next morning (probably 12th August), as he was going
into the room that was being used as the privy chamber he found
one of Sir William's children 'playing upon a lute and singing,
Her Majesty sitting upon the threshold of the door, my Lord of
Leicester kneeling by Her Highness'. Months afterwards the duke
vividly recalled that charming scene: 'Her Majesty commanded
me to come by, into her chamber. Not long after my Lord of
Leicester rises and came to me, leaving Her Highness hearing the
child, and told me that as I was coming, he was dealing with Her
Majesty in my behalf; to which I answered, if I had known so
much I would not have come up; but I desired to know how he
found Her Majesty, when he told me, indifferent well, and that
Her Highness had promised to speak with me at Thornham',
Arundel's house in Kent, much later in the progress.

Before then, in fact, Elizabeth had put out another feeler. At
Farnham on 15th August she requested the duke to dine alone at
her table, but he still found himself unable to speak about the
affair, partly out of timidity, partly for fear of upsetting Leicester's
plans, and at the end of the meal she gave him a nip, saying 'that
she would wish me to take good heed to my pillow', an allusion
to their interview nine months back. 'I was abashed at Her
Majesty's speech', Norfolk confessed, 'but I thought it not fit time
nor place there to trouble her.' He had been given three opportunities of speaking in ten days and he had let all three slip by. There

was no excuse for his remaining tongue-tied and he had given Elizabeth every reason for feeling he had forfeited her confidence. Later on he tried to excuse his silence at Farnham by saying he understood that she had appointed Thornham as the occasion for their private talk on the subject, but this betrays how muddled he had become in according Leicester's message greater authority than the Queen's own command; and in the next few weeks his constant pre-occupation with the Scottish match would blind him to all else.[15]

They continued on progress, reaching Southampton by leisurely stages, but after a day or so there Norfolk returned to London, both Leicester and, apparently Cecil, having promised to speak with the Queen in his absence. While at Southampton he told Richard Cavendish that 'before he lost that marriage he would lose his life' and boasted about his ability to handle the affair, yet by now he was desperate, and on top of everything else came disastrous news from Scotland.

Six weeks earlier he had written in cipher to Murray, as 'a natural brother' to obtain his assurance before they finalised their plans. With regard to the marriage he had 'proceeded so far therein as I with conscience can neither revoke that that I have done, nor never do mean, while I live, to go back from that is done, nor with honour proceed further until such time as you' in Scotland, 'remove all such stumbling blocks' to our design. Murray had delayed replying until after the Perth Convention and now informed Norfolk that he had decided against supporting the marriage. 'Take heed', the duke cryptically told the Regent 'in time that your friends here may continue as they have done, which I assure you by this your dealing they neither can nor will do.'

In London he approved a plan for Northumberland and Leonard Dacres to descend on Wingfield to rescue Mary Queen of Scots from Shrewsbury's custody once the duke should give the signal, and Northumberland proudly claimed that 'the whole of the north' was at his devotion. After a fortnight away from court Howard was more at ease, and Pembroke wrote to him from the Lord Treasurer's house at Basing that Elizabeth dare not refuse her permission to the marriage as there was not a person about her who dared to give her contrary advice. And then Cecil wrote a day or so later from the Vine, near Basingstoke, telling him to hasten to court as the Queen had asked for him; Cecil's views about the marriage had hardened after a letter from Hunsdon who spoke out against it most strongly, despite his affection for Norfolk.[16]

Howard reluctantly rode south, but instead of seeking an audience straightway he bided his time, awaiting a summons to the presence. Leicester in the meanwhile had taken to his bed at Titchfield, the Earl of Southampton's mansion – a tactical sickness. He begged Elizabeth to visit him and when she came to his bedside on 6th September, anxious and full of sympathy, he for the first time revealed the full details of the plan for the marriage with Mary. Though his own loyalty was never at issue, he swore, he craved her pardon. That same day in the gallery at Titchfield she rated Norfolk, and in a temper, deciding that the time of friendly warnings was past, she charged him on his allegiance 'to deal no further with the Scottish cause'. To escape her wrath he promised to give over his pretensions and told her he had 'a very slight regard' for Mary. Her position and fortunes if she were to be restored, were, he said, no attraction for him; indeed his own 'revenues in England were not much less than those of the Kingdom of Scotland . . . and that when he was in his Tennis Court at Norwich he thought himself in a manner equal with some kings'.[17] He could not put away his pride even in the act of penitence, but at last he knew where he stood. Elizabeth was as stubborn as he and had determined that in the light of the widespread political unrest the projected marriage would spell disaster for her – within four months of it taking place, she said, she would be in the Tower. De Spes in London was completely out of touch with these developments and told Alva, 'All is arranged in the Scottish Queen's favour.'

Had Norfolk and Leicester moved quickly in July, following the Council meeting at Greenwich, there might have been some chance of forcing the marriage scheme on Elizabeth; had Leicester even told her on 6th August what he had blurted out to her when he feigned sickness on 6th September, Howard's life would have taken a very different turn. But these delays had strengthened her position and made Leicester and his group look like whispering conspirators who would never come into the open. During those six tense weeks the duke had constantly pressed Leicester to act as he had promised, yet he had shirked it and forbidden Norfolk to speak to the Queen on his own behalf. Howard was slow to realise the way things had been going and he was slower still to grasp that Leicester had been deceiving him.

He did not at once escape from court, for such would have aroused the worst suspicions, but remained with the progress, uncertain of his plans. Courtiers began to shun him. 'I am right sorry', he told Cecil, 'that no man can keep me company without offence. I never deserved to be so ill thought of. I hope time will bring her Majesty to like of them which wish best to herself and till then I must bear all overwarts with patience.' He still hoped his mistress would change her mind, but the hope became daily much fainter. Each day he grew more uneasy. No other peer joined him at table, everyone was whispering about him and, worst of all, Leicester treated him with cold disdain. At last he could stand it no longer and left on 16th September, without seeking formal leave to depart from court, but instead he let it be known that he needed to be in London for some days to prepare for some law suits that were coming up in Michaelmas term. A servant of Arundel's, named Hugh Owen, met him as he left Titchfield and suggested in all seriousness that they should take the Tower, but the duke thought it a monstrous idea. On the way he called in at Wilton to talk matters over with Pembroke who hoped he could still influence the Queen, but Howard reckoned that persuasions were now useless. In London he found no peace of mind, for there were too many rumours concerning his own safety.[18]

Elizabeth was no less anxious. She feared the duke's withdrawal might be the prologue to a general rising, which would bring under one banner all the opponents of her regime, rescue Mary from Wingfield and advance on London. Already her two most formidable enemies, the religious malcontents in the north under Northumberland, and the political malcontents among the ranks of the Privy Council were in alliance and the slightest pressure might plunge England in civil war. The duke's great popularity and his hold over East Anglia made up for his lack of courage. The report of the musters taken that month in Suffolk by the duke's step-father, Thomas Steynings, and others, made dismal reading for Cecil, for the whole of Loes hundred, in which Framlingham lay, mustered as few as five horsemen to serve the Queen in an emergency. The government's intelligence service was rudimentary in the extreme despite the close watch on Mary, Cecil as yet knew nothing about possible aid to Mary's cause from Philip II or Alva, but feared the worst. To surmount the crisis, the most dangerous moment since her accession, Elizabeth swiftly made her dispositions. Huntingdon was sent to Wingfield to supersede Shrewsbury, who was ill, as Mary's gaoler, with orders to remove her for greater safety to Tutbury. The ports were closed and the militia alerted. She would shut herself in Windsor Castle, prepared to stand a siege if need be. But there was still the chance of calling Norfolk's bluff and she instructed Leicester and Cecil to write to him jointly, ordering him to repair to Windsor and submit.

Norfolk pleaded an ague. He told Cecil that he did not wish to risk going about until the attack was quite over, but he hoped to be at Windsor by 26th September. Mary wrote from Tutbury to Fénélon, asking the ambassador to warn the duke of the dangers of the Tower and advising him of new precautions to be taken over her correspondence, though the message may never have been delivered. A further letter from Leicester that came to Howard House on the afternoon of the 22nd shattered his confidence, by warning him of the likelihood of his being sent to the Tower; that night Lumley and Ross called in turn to offer advice, the latter bringing Norfolk a ring, as a token from Mary, but it gave him little comfort. His courage failed him and rather than face the Queen and his accusers he rode off on the night of 23rd September to Kenninghall.

His escape was not made in the spirit of throwing down a gauntlet, but out of fear. Safe at home he wrote to Elizabeth: 'My enemies found such comfort of Your Highness's heavy displeasure that they began to make of me a common table talk; my friends were afraid of my company.' Overnight he realised that he had become 'a suspected person' and he saw the shadow of the Tower 'which is too great a terror for a true man'. He wrote telling friends that he had withdrawn himself 'to procure a remedy against indignant rumours which are always entertained at Court'.[19]

When Elizabeth heard on Saturday 26th of his leaving London she did not realise it was a retreat, but imagined it as the signal for rebellion, and everyone at court assumed he had ridden north, not to Kenninghall. Arundel and Pembroke were to keep their lodgings under house arrest and Lumley was summoned to court. Camden, who later enjoyed Cecil's confidence, wrote that 'all the whole court hung in suspense and fear lest he [Norfolk] should break forth into rebellion; and it was determined (so the report went) if he did so, forthwith to put the Queen of Scots to death'. Letters were sent to all lords lieutenants to scotch rumours that Elizabeth intended to deal harshly with the duke, 'Her Majesty being loath to have such a noble man abused with untrue reports', and Cecil anxiously awaited letters from Sussex on the state of the north. For eleven years there had been peace within the realm. It was almost unprecedented: Mary Tudor had had to face the supporters of Lady Jane Grey and of Wyatt; her brother's reign had seen the Prayer Book Rising in the West and Ket's Rebellion; even her father's position had been seriously challenged by the Pilgrimage of Grace. Twice in the last hundred years the crown had been seized by claimants with far fewer influential supporters than Norfolk could command, far fewer troops than Northumberland could muster. Yet instead of emulating Edward of York or Henry Tudor, Norfolk now astounded his countrymen by doing nothing.[20]

In the crisis his nerve failed him. There were not wanting men who would have flocked to the Howard Banner from East Anglia, the Midlands and the North as their fathers had been drawn irresistibly to the Banner of the Five Wounds of Christ under Robert Aske. Then it had been the Howards who had saved the day for Henry VIII by vigorously suppressing the Pilgrimage of Grace, but in the autumn of 1569 a Howard stood as champion in the opposite camp and had behind him the bulk of the nobility. Norfolk was expected to lead a movement which would put back the clock in religion and politics, a rising not so much against the Crown as against its 'evil advisers' – the traditional formula favoured by English rebels. The Earls of Northumberland and Westmorland had promised him that if he could not achieve his purpose with Elizabeth's goodwill he could count on their assistance 'to the uttermost of their powers'. This was no idle promise. Throughout that summer they had been holding meetings in Yorkshire and Durham 'to allure the gentlemen' and prepare for war. Even in mid-September, right under Sussex's nose, 'all the principal gentlemen and their wives' gathered together for country sports, to be ready for action. Christopher Norton, reckless and gallant, planned to ride off into the night, as soon as word was given, to liberate Mary Queen of Scots, 'under the colour of another of her ladies whom he feigned to be in love withall'. They plotted to kill Sir Francis Knollys, Sir John Forster of the Middle March and even the Regent Murray. All were fearless, prepared, waiting on the duke, who could have drawn the people to him by his own popularity, the apparent justice of his cause, and the overwhelming sympathy which was felt for Mary, and the movement at the least would have achieved the rehabilitation of the Queen of Scots and the dismissal of Cecil and might well in the end have transformed the Tudor monarchy. But instead of taking the field proudly as Surrey's son, Norfolk lay paralysed by fear for his own safety at Kenninghall. De Spes, who had strongly advised him to stay at his palace and rally his supporters, thought he would only be ruined by 'his own pusillanimity', and ruined he was.[21]

Thomas Howard was his own worst enemy; at the critical moment he had no plan of campaign. He had withdrawn from the court on progress furious that his immediate hopes of marrying Mary had been dashed, and he had left London frightened of being sent to the Tower. At Kenninghall his temper cooled and he began to master his fears. That he was ill with an ague is not to be doubted, though modern medical opinion would possibly ascribe the return of his old trouble to the worry and uncertainty of the previous ten weeks. Word of his return went quickly round, for Sir Thomas Cornwallis, out hunting on the Friday afternoon, met the duke as he was nearing home. As always when he arrived at Kenninghall the leaders of the county came within a day or so to pay court, ignorant of the fact that on progress men had been shunning him. His sudden return surprised them even more than his long absence had done. Were men like Sir Christopher Heydon and Edward Clere (the deputy lieutenants of the county) or Paston, Gawdy, Woodhouse and the other Norfolk gentry rallying to his cause? There had certainly been general unrest in East Anglia that summer, as the closure of the traditional markets for English cloth on the continent, through Alva's advance in the Netherlands, had caused a crisis in the clothing industry, and there was much bitterness in Norwich about the presence of so many Huguenot settlers who were responsible for flooding the market with manufactures. Moreover, a vigorous attempt to enforce the Acts of Supremacy and Uniformity was for the first time seriously embarrassing those Catholics who had hitherto been permitted to wink at the law.

Any remaining hopes Howard may have had about taking advantage of the government's unpopularity and rallying the country to his cause were gone when he talked to Edward Clere on Tuesday 28th September, and told him three courses lay open: for him to go to Windsor and submit to the Queen, to depart the realm and live privately, or thirdly to 'stand upon his guard'. Clere advised him most strongly to take the only honourable course and go to court. Norfolk could never have lived as an expatriate, but if it needed courage to stand at the head of an army of insurgents, it also required courage to take his life in his hands and submit to Her Majesty. Tortured by having to chose between the two, he lay abed, feeling desperately ill.

Elizabeth's letter of 25th September, written as soon as she had heard of his going home, commanded him on his allegiance to repair to Windsor without delay in the company of the bearer, Edward Fitzgarret, a gentleman pensioner. The sting was in the tail for, she wrote, she never intended 'to minister anything to you but as you should in truth deserve'. Howard still delayed, and made his excuses, and when Fitzgarrett went back to court without him he was roundly reprimanded. On the night of 28th September she sent Fitzgarrett with a more peremptory letter: sickness was no valid excuse, and regardless of his health he was to set out for Windsor, if necessary in a litter and making the journey by easy stages. His case, she warned him, was notorious – first his unauthorised departure from court and then his disobedience to her commands to return; he must now come to her and demonstrate that loyalty and humility which his letters had professed. Cecil wrote, too, advising him that Elizabeth's counsel was 'very earnest and straight', and trusted that he would endure nothing more harmful than words – at the most be forbidden to come to her presence, as in the cases of Arundel and Pembroke.[22]

Another letter counted far more with him. John Foxe, in London, was astounded at the rumour 'in every man's mouth almost' and implored the duke to be circumspect. If he hoped to marry Mary he would ruin both himself and his country. 'There is no greater cunning in these days than to know whom a man may trust; examples you have enough within the compass of your own days, whereby you may know what noblemen have been cast away by them whom they seemed most to trust. Remember, I pray you, the example of Mephibosheth, whereof I told you being young . . .' Lord Wentworth, the Lord Lieutenant, charged to 'stay all sinister practices', kept an eye on the comings and goings at Kenninghall Palace and found none, except a few papists, prepared to stand by Norfolk. At last he sent a messenger (Havers) to Topcliffe to the northern earls to call off their projected rising, 'for if they did, it should cost him his head, for that he was going to court'. He pleaded with his brother-in-law of Westmorland to remain at home even if Northumberland should rise. (When the message was delivered, Lady Westmorland commented on her brother: 'what a simple man the Duke is to begin a matter and not to go through with it.') Norfolk had decided to swallow his pride and throw himself on Elizabeth's mercy, and he persuaded himself that if he submitted with a good grace he might yet obtain her permission to marry Mary. Crumpled and bowed he set out for Newmarket, on the first stage of his journey to Windsor on 1st October, with Fitzgarrett, accompanied by some thirty of his own retainers. He was never to set eyes on Kenninghall again.[23]

Fitzgarrett sent Cecil daily reports of their progress. From St Albans on 2nd October the duke sent word of his impending arrival at court and asked his usual lodging to be prepared. That evening Lawrence Bannister brought a message from Throgmorton warning him that, instead of going to Windsor, he was to be taken to Paul Wentworth's house at Burnham, and urging him to devise a scheme for passing letters. Instructions awaited Fitzgarrett at St Albans which he was to reveal to Howard when they reached Uxbridge, and in the afternoon of 3rd October he entered Wentworth's house to all intents a close prisoner. That afternoon Sir Henry Neville was appointed his keeper; he was to remove various of the duke's servants, to deny him visitors and to see that no letters passed – he soon rumbled Norfolk's plans for passing messages inside bottles. After eight nights at Burnham, Howard was taken to the Tower by Sir Francis Knollys, though Neville was to have special charge of him. Here he was to remain for ten months, uncertain of his fate, in the very same room in the Constable's lodging which his grandfather had occupied for six years. He was to be permitted no more than two personal servants, and as pens and paper were denied him he required

Neville to write to Cecil asking for leave to put in writing his humble submission to the Queen or, failing that to write to the Lords of the Council. Cecil refused to be moved.[24]

Meanwhile the lesser fry were being rounded up. The Sheriff of Norfolk was ordered to arrest some twenty retainers and other servants of the duke and send them to Windsor for cross questioning; in particular Sir Nicholas L'Estrange, Robert Higford, William Barker and Lawrence Bannister were put through their paces. A week earlier Pembroke, Arundel and Lumley had been first examined and during October they and Throgmorton were again questioned most searchingly, principally by Lord Keeper Bacon, Admiral Clinton, Bedford, Sadler and Knollys. Interminable questions were asked of the Bishop of Ross, Mary Stuart had her papers ransacked, and slowly the ramifications of the conspiracy were pieced together. Leicester had gone on his knees, told all he knew and received absolution, although Elizabeth had been 'grievously offended', and for anyone else it would have been the Tower. Even Cecil received some censure for being privy to part of Norfolk's plans, though he excused himself by claiming that he had kept a foot in his camp solely to keep himself informed of the designs. The Earl of Southampton was also charged. Elizabeth pressed Murray by special messenger to 'procure as many proofs ... to make it appear' that it was the duke who first suggested the marriage scheme to him, and not *vice versa*, and she hinted broadly that if he found such proofs her favour would follow. The Regent could not in fact oblige in the way she wanted, though he wrote a long account by way of a self-justification, laying the blame on Maitland, and sent down his Secretary, John Wood, with 'all the letters' from Norfolk 'which would lend to undo him'.[25]

Sussex, as the duke's particular friend, was under suspicion. When he heard from Cecil of Howard's withdrawal from court he was 'greatly appalled and marvellously perplexed'. He loved Norfolk dearly – 'above all others' – yet this affection did not blind him to his duty towards the Queen. The Secretary had taxed him with approval of the marriage plans, which he firmly denied. 'When I think I might do some good by imparting of my mind to you, I find myself so ignorant of the whole of the duke's doings in this camp [at York] as I wot not where or how to begin', and he implored Cecil to do what he could to persuade Elizabeth that Norfolk was an innocent conspirator. Neither Queen nor Secretary were satisfied, for they were not at all sure that Sussex was acting as vigorously in preserving public order as was expected of a militant Lord President of the Council in the North, so they pressed him again for explanation; if he were to side with Northumberland, then the north was lost indeed. Much later on it came out that the northern earls 'first had some hope of friendship of my lord of Sussex, but he had failed their expectations', but at Michaelmas 1569 it seemed, rather, that he had failed Elizabeth's expectation. Regretting his distance from court, he wished he could speak rather than write, as his letter might be capable of various interpretations. He claimed, and there is no reason to doubt his word, that he had only heard of the affair through the duke's messenger, Cantrell, and that he had replied that his assent to the marriage hinged on Elizabeth giving her approval. Once more he professed that his loyalty to his sovereign counted far more with him than his personal regard for Howard – and he had always 'hitched his staff at her door'. Sussex was still under a cloud when the Rebellion in the North made it imperative for Elizabeth to put her confidence in him, for by then it was too late to recall him from his command for examination.[26]

Roberto Ridolfi, the Florentine banker, was for a season placed under surveillance in Walsingham's House. His visits to the Spanish embassy and to Howard House had not gone unnoticed and it was known that he had been in touch with the northern earls, with Arundel, Lumley and Ross. Ridolfi was, indeed, so obvious a suspect that it would have been sheer incompetence on the part of the government had he not been questioned. Even so the Italian was able to satisfy his examiners that all his alleged intrigues were negotiations 'in the ordinary way of banking'. Cecil failed to discover that he had distributed 12,000 papal crowns to the northern earls, and could find nothing incriminating among the papers in his house.[27]

About this time Walsingham wrote a forceful political pamphlet which aimed at closing the ranks of the nobility behind the government. 'A Discourse touching the pretended matche betwene the D. of Norfolk and the Queene of Scotts' in essentials states what was Cecil's own position. The fact that Mary was a Guise – 'a race that is both enemy to God and the common quiet of Europe' – an ardent papist and a competitor with Elizabeth for the throne of England, spelt danger and discord. Walsingham did not pretend to know the duke's conscience in matters of religion, but thought it abundantly clear that he was unsettled, as was indicated by his marriage with Lady Dacre, the education his son was receiving, the numbers of Catholics in his household and his trust in 'the chief Papists of this realm'. 'Touching his credit with the nobility and commons it is well known to be great, with the one in respect of his alliance, with the other in respect of a kind of familiarity used towards them in public sport, as in shootings and cock-fightings, a thing not to be discommended if it savoured not of an ambitious and aspiring intent.'[28]

This could not be a love match, for Norfolk and Mary had never set eyes upon each other, and was it likely that a man of religious principals, who respected worldly honour and regarded his own safety would want to marry the Scottish Idolatress? It was nothing but a political match, for furthering their respective ambitions, which would plunge England into Civil War, 'for the thirst of a kingdom can never be quenched until it hath hazarded the uttermost trial'. Walsingham said he left to the lawyers whether Norfolk's presumption in seeking to marry a claimant to the throne without his sovereign's permission could be construed as high treason, but in effect his whole essay was a direction to the lawyers that it was so.

Mildmay, too, drew up a long memorandum about Mary in which he came down in favour of keeping her in captivity for a year or more until conditions in Scotland and elsewhere had become more settled; but he advised Elizabeth to let it be known that the reason for her confinement was 'her late practice with the Duke of Norfolk'.[29] A vast mass of evidence was being collected and sifted from which Elizabeth felt sure she would be able to charge the duke with high treason, though it was not until the following January that a list of charges was made against him. The cause of this delay was that on 16th November the peace of the realm was broken by the northern earls, who, disregarding Norfolk's warnings, had raised the standard of revolt.

Chapter Ten

REBELLION
1569-70

THE north had been in ferment all summer, with 'a great bruit in Yorkshire' and beyond, and when Norfolk departed from court the earls of Northumberland and Westmorland were ready to strike to preserve the Old Religion and maintain Mary's right to the succession. When the duke had left Kenninghall to make his submission he despatched a messenger, urging the earls to call off the proposed rising, yet a rumour went round the north country that Norfolk's tenants had done their best to dissuade him from going meekly to Windsor and had hung upon his horse's tail and legs, exclaiming that the whole county would live and die with him. It was on just such blind devotion from a near feudal tenantry in the Palatinate and the North Riding that the rebel earls counted when the day of decision came. This was the north, with its patriarchal society Howard had discovered as lieutenant-general in the Scottish War, which he had wooed when he had won Lady Dacre and won when he had wooed Mary. 'He is a rare bird', wrote Sussex from York when the Northern Rebellion was a week old, that 'hath not some of his [family] with the two earls, or in his heart wisheth not well to the cause they pretend.' The response to the earls' summons was truly remarkable: 'if the father came to us with ten men', said Sadler, 'his son goes to the rebels with twenty.'[1]

There were six weeks of uncertainty before the standard was raised. Sussex, the Lord President of the Council in the North, was not the man to panic and believe the thousand rumours that were afoot of intended risings. Much more in command of the situation than Cecil imagined, he felt he could handle the earls in his own way. He summoned both of them to York on Sunday 9th October, when he required their assistance in scotching the rumours and sent them to their homes to be ready to deal with any hotheads. 'I trust the fire is spent with the smoke', he reported to Cecil on 10th October – 'a great bruit of an intended rebellion, the cause of which is yet unknown, and which I think is now at an end' – and he placed his faith in extemporising to avoid open action until the restlessness should die, like foliage, with the coming of winter.

Elizabeth was not satisfied with this policy. Sussex's close friendship with Norfolk had placed him under suspicion and she was not only convinced that he underestimated the gravity of the situation but also feared he must abuse the trust placed in him, at best to treat the earls with more sympathy than they deserved, at worst to come down openly on their side. She intended to deal with Northumberland and Westmorland as she had dealt with the duke and on 24th October ordered Sussex to send for them without delay and in her name summon them to court. He was also to report to her all that he knew about the proposed rising, including the authors of the rumours, and at the same time the other members of his Council were to write individually to Cecil about the disturbing recent events – an indication of the Queen's lack of confidence in the Lord President. Sussex told her that all his Council agreed with him that it were best, for the sake of keeping the country quiet, to postpone an examination of the causes of the recent troubles and to delay sending for the earls until dead of winter, but seeing her pleasure was otherwise he had now summoned the earls to York once more and would command them to go to Windsor. His intelligence about who had been conferring with the earls and the nature of their discussions was remarkably accurate, judging from Northumberland's later confession: 'the motives of their counsels seem of divers natures – some specially respect the Duke of Norfolk, some the Scottish Queen, some religion and some, perhaps, all three yet use my Lord of Norfolk for a cover to the rest.'[2]

Sir George Bowes, Sir Thomas Gargrave and Sir Henry Gates all reported to Cecil in like strain. 'Upon the first bruit of a marriage between the Duke of Norfolk and the Scottish Queen, the Papists much rejoiced and imagined that religion would be altered, and thereby took encouragement to speak liberally against the Protestants ... In the nick thereof, news came that the Duke had left the court and gone into Norfolk, and that thereupon the earls of Northumberland and Westmorland had caused their servants to take up their horses and be in readiness, whereupon the people imagined that they would assist the Duke ... When the Duke returned to Court it was bruited that the confederants in their assembly asked that religion should be the cause of their stir, upon which point it was said they disagreed, and so departed.' Such appears to be a shrewd interpretation of the events leading to the abandonment of the rising planned for 6th October. By the beginning of November all the Council in the North agreed both that the danger was over and that Sussex's policy of avoiding further disturbances by not enquiring too closely into past troubles was the best.[3]

The earls feared for their safety as Norfolk had feared for his when he had withdrawn to Kenninghall, and his subsequent fate made it impossible for them to believe that submission would not mean the Tower. When they requested to be excused from attending on Sussex at York, pleading urgent business, the President sent a pursuivant to them on 4th November, demanding their immediate appearance. Northumberland temporised; he would come in a few days when his business was settled; but Westmorland sent a blank refusal: 'I dare not come where my enemies are without bringing such a force to protect me as might be misliked; therefore I think it better to stay at home and use myself as an obedient subject.' It was his wife (Norfolk's sister Jane) who had stiffened him, to avoid putting his head in a noose. Sussex was thus driven to write again, setting down what he had intended to say to them both by word of mouth, namely to repair to court on their allegiance. He exhorted them to obey, 'to follow the good counsel I have oftentimes given you, and take heed of the counsel of such as would show you honey and deliver you poison, and stand, as nobleman upon your honour and truth, for it will stand by you'. They were not to be frightened of their own shadows, but to submit with humility to the Queen's clemency, otherwise a show of wilful disobedience might provoke her into acting with extremity. It was still touch and go.[4]

While Sussex's messenger was still at Topcliffe, towards mid-night on 9th November, he heard the bells of the town ring backwards, as the signal to raise the county, for Northumberland had believed a rumour that a force was being sent to seize him. After a night in a keeper's house, the earl rode north to Brancepeth to join Westmorland and found him at a council of war with Richard Norton, the sheriff of Yorkshire, and his seven sons, Thomas Markenfeld, the Tempests, John Swinburne and West-morland's uncles who had assembled there with great numbers of armed retainers. They were still uncertain whether to flee, to fight or submit. In a forceful letter Sussex gave them a final chance before proclaiming them as outlaws, but at Brancepeth Lady Westmorland swayed the waverers, when it seemed they might once more depart to their houses, and in tears harangued them: 'We and our country were shamed for ever, that now in the end we should seek holes to creep into.' This goaded her husband into taking up arms, but Northumberland was much more hesitant. To show their hands the earls rode off to Durham next morning and stormed the cathedral, throwing down the communion table, tearing up the Prayer Book and the English Bible, and read Mass. The people of the Palatinate flocked to them in their thousands for they had risen for their faith.

Six weeks earlier at Topcliffe, when Norfolk's messenger had arrived, Westmorland had asked his confederates what was the cause for which they were taking up arms. Markenfeld and Old Norton had answered 'For religion', but the earl disagreed: 'No, those that seem to take that quarrel in other countries are accounted as rebels, and therefore I will never blot my house which hath been this long preserved without staining.' By now, however, he had been persuaded that the religious was the only ground that could command widespread support and he could hide his own disobedience to his sovereign under the cloak of religion; yet in all their edicts the earls stated they were acting as true and faithful subjects of the Queen. Who could doubt the aims of the rebels when a few days later they went in procession to Ripon Cathedral for a solemn Mass? Behind the cross, borne by Richard Norton, with the banner of the Five Wounds of Christ and the words *In hoc signo vinces* trooped the rank and file of the earl's supporters, each bearing on his back the red crusaders' cross to show he had taken up arms for a holy war.[5]

What of Mary Queen of Scots and the Duke? In their first proclamation the earls stated that the object of Norfolk, Arundel, Pembroke, themselves and others of 'the ancient nobility' was to determine 'to whom of mere right the true succession of the crown appertaineth', yet the recognition of Mary's right was for them secondary to the restoration of Roman Catholicism. Their proclamation of Ripon, which they addressed to all members of 'the old Catholic religion' on 16th November, made this quite clear. 'Forasmuch as divers evil-disposed persons about the Queen's Majesty have, by their subtle and crafty dealing to advance themselves, overcome in this our realm the true and Catholic religion towards God and by the same abused the Queen, disordered the realm and now lastly seek and procure the destruction of the nobility, we therefore have gathered ourselves together to resist by force, and the rather by the help of God and you good people, to see redress of those things amiss, with restoring of all ancient customs and liberties to God's church and this whole realm...' Though Norfolk's fate was recognised in 'the destruction of the nobility', Mary's claims did not feature at all; nevertheless their plan of campaign hinged on her release.[6]

By-passing York they rode on south, from Ripon to Wetherby, Knaresborough and Cawood, to reach Selby on 24th November, where they were within striking distance of Tutbury. Sussex, with only the skeleton of local levies at his disposition, did not try to halt them. But on 25th November, when Mary was hastily removed to Coventry, the rebels were checked abruptly in their plans; to proceed further south was out of the question owing to the threat of Hunsdon's army, and as they withdrew north, intending to give battle to Hunsdon on their own ground, the heart was taken out of the rebellion. As the pace of the retreat quickened, their numbers melted away in the face of deteriorating weather and internal dissension until they reached Brancepeth again on 30th November. To Sir George Bowes's dismay Westmorland took Barnard Castle, largely through the treachery of the garrison, but this was of small moment in the general retreat. The foreign aid promised by Alva to Northumberland never materialised, even though the rebels had captured Hartlepool as a suitable port for him to disembark troops. At Durham on 15th December the earls decided to flee before it was too late, and with a few horsemen rode from Hexham and across the Pennines to Naworth Castle, the Dacre stronghold, and thence across the Border into Scotland.

Leonard Dacre, one of the most militant of the northern Catholics, had hitherto played an equivocal part. At the outbreak of the rebellion he was in London, seeking the means to undo the unfavourable verdict of the previous summer in his claim to the Dacre lordship. Embittered by the duke's success in retaining the lordship for his stepdaughters, he looked on Norfolk's imprisonment, not as a blow against the cause, but as a golden opportunity, and to the chagrin of the earls he had obtained an audience with Elizabeth at Windsor at the very time when his presence had been so badly needed in the urgent discussions at Topcliff and Brancepeth. Dacre had professed himself a faithful subject and returned to his home to render lukewarm assistance to Scrope in the West March in rounding up rebels; even Sussex commended him for his diligent service against his kinsmen. But after the flight of the earls, Dacre seized Greystoke Castle and the other houses of the Dacre inheritance from Norfolk's officials, fortified Naworth Castle under the pretence of protecting his interests in that lawless region, and assembled a private army of some 3,000 rank-riders of the Borders. When it was obvious that he was bent on playing a dangerous game Scrope tried to induce him to go to Carlisle, but Dacre was too wary and invited him to come and dine at Naworth instead. Not until mid-February did Hunsdon receive Elizabeth's order to seize him, and on 20th February he and Sir John Forster brought their troops to Naworth, but finding the castle too strongly defended decided to move on to Carlisle. Leonard Dacre followed them to fight a valiant action by the banks of the Cleth; he gave 'the proudest charge upon my shot that ever I saw', wrote Hunsdon, but it had been of no avail. When Dacre fled into Scotland, leaving three hundred dead and as many prisoners, the rebellion was over.[7]

The north was never the same. Destruction of life and property – including the Dacre inheritance in Norfolk's hands – was intensified by the wholesale looting which the 'southern' army under Clinton and Warwick extended to areas some distance from the seats of revolt. Some seven hundred and fifty rebels were executed according to martial law, others awaited the special sessions of justices at York, Durham and Carlisle; and in the aftermath of the Revolt the church courts in each diocese and the Court of

High Commission of the Province of York were as active as the lay tribunals in seeking out offenders and inflicting punishments. Over two thousand of the lesser fry who had marched with the earls were pardoned on condition that they took the oath of allegiance and paid a fine according to their means. The City of Durham's list of pardoned rebels opens proudly with the name of Christopher Surtees, who was assessed at £1 – surely the ancestor of the historian of Durham and creator of 'Jorrocks'?[8] Yet a quarter of those pardoned were considered to be too poor to pay anything, then or later. This poverty was to persist and the north did not recover from the effects of the rebellion for perhaps two centuries. The surveyors who took stock of the earl's properties, now forfeited to the Crown, remarked on the impoverishment of the land. The tenants of Westmorland at Brancepeth had been men of substance before the rebellion, but the place 'will soon decay if no nobleman live there'. His tenants on the Raby estates had risen as a man to their utter subversion, so 'the country is left void and barren of governors and guides and very much impoverished'. Scores of clergy were deprived of their livings. With no Earl of Northumberland at Alnwick Castle to defend the neighbourhood from Scots raiders and the thieves of Tynedale the countrymen became poor 'because they are able to keep no greater number of cattle of any kind than may live in the house at night'.[9]

Gradually the estates of the earls and their principal followers were distributed among fervent supporters of the Elizabethan regime, few of whom had any previous links with the north. Some properties, such as Raby, were kept in Crown hands for a number of years for strategic reasons, but most were parcelled out to the men who had sided with Hunsdon, Clinton and Sussex, and this redistribution of lands, much more extensive than the granting out of abbey estates a generation earlier, helped to break down the particularism of the north. The close ties binding tenant to feudal overlord for those who had known no prince but a Percy, a Neville, or a Dacre, were cut once and for all in 1570.

★   ★   ★

Norfolk must bear his share of guilt for the tragedy of the north. The plotting had been the work of others, but he had allowed himself to be drawn into their schemes as a result of his attempt to marry Mary. The Bishop of Ross was to attribute the rebellion to the 'continual communications' kept up between Mary and the Duke and the Northern Earls. Howard knew enough about the state of the north to realise that the earls' offer to come to his aid with an army was no idle boast; he knew that considerable preparations for a rising were being made in the summer while he followed the court on progress, yet instead of giving his brother-in-law a forceful warning to stop playing with fire he left it until it was too late before asking them to call off their revolt. His withdrawal to Kenninghall had in fact been for his friends in the north the signal for which they had waited, an overt action which the secret messages of a fortnight later could not in their eyes effectively cancel. Their plan to rise on 6th October was abandoned, but the partisan hopes and fears of their supporters, which they had brought to fever-heat, could not easily be cooled. Sussex alone could have prevented trouble by adroit handling of the difficult situation had he not been forced by Elizabeth into employing tactics he knew to be fundamentally wrong. Norfolk was sympathetic to the earls' general political designs, and their attitudes to Mary, and to Cecil, were largely his own, yet he could never have been happy about the rebels' religious aims which dominated their plans.

The rebellion lengthened the duke's captivity and increased the Queen's mistrust of him, for the events in the north had changed the whole political atmosphere so that Norfolk appeared as too dangerous a man to be given his liberty. It also prevented any rational reconsideration of Mary's position. The initial success of the earls had encouraged Pope Pius V to publish the bull *Regnans in Excelsis* in which he deposed Elizabeth and absolved her subjects from their oaths of allegiance; but the fateful bull arrived long after Hunsdon's victory and provoked a spate of penal legislation against Roman Catholics which was to be rigorously enforced. The rebellion was of a truth a watershed in the relations between church and state in England.

*   *   *

There had been general unrest in East Anglia in the summer of 1569, which a bolder man than Howard could have turned to good advantage, yet he had dithered and drifted into submission instead of putting in the field an army of tenants and well-wishers.[10] When the news arrived that the duke had been sent to the Tower, uneasiness and suspicion increased up and down the county of Norfolk, even among some of the gentry. Preoccupied with the problem of the north the government had left Norfolk to the care of the local Justices, reminding them on more than one occasion during those critical weeks that their first task was to maintain public order. On 1st December the new sheriff, Sir Christopher Heydon, and the local Justices assured the Privy Council that all was well in their shire. They had caused 'a universal privy search to be made with the straightest order they could for the due punishment of seditious attempts. And we find hereunto all things in good order.' Yet before this letter reached Whitehall the first rising began. On 6th December the men of Kenninghall, all trusty tenants of the duke, were encouraged by news of successful rebellion in the north by the Earls of Northumberland and Westmorland to show their hands.[11]

On that Tuesday a group of villagers led by John Welles, a sawyer, John Barnarde, a linen-weaver, and Thomas Alexander a yeoman farmer, levied public war against the Crown by declaring themselves adherents of the northern earls. By their proclamation at Ripon the earls had called on all of the 'old Catholic religion' to come to their aid in rescuing the Queen from evil advisers, who had disordered church and state 'and now lastly seek and procure the destruction of the nobility'; this last seemed to the men of Kenninghall to have especial reference to the duke. Welles was the hothead, the orator of the group. He harangued his fellows: 'There are two earls amongst other in the north who been in great business and trouble, and except they be holpen they be but undone. But if all men would do as I would, they should have help.' The crowd around him grew, but the passive mutters of agreement which greeted his words disappointed the ringleader; so Welles now did his utmost to spur the men to rise in force. 'It is a pity you live and that one hundred of you were not hanged one against another for that you have not stirred all this while; for those that dwelled three hundred miles of us have done more for his Grace (the Duke of Norfolk) than you. But if you will do as I will we should rise for the delivery of the Duke out of the Tower; and if I had but two others I would go ring out to assemble the people, for I know where to have the key of the church door. And the longer to tarry the worse it will be, for the key will be taken away; but I care not if it be, for I will go in at the window or set the door on fire. My Lord's council have set open Kenninghall gates to the intent that every man that would might have arms and armour there; and you shall not need to doubt the want of a head or captain, for I can govern five or six hundred men; for it is my fortune to be captain of so many.'

Welles's capacity to lead an army was clearly doubted by the majority of his hearers, who saw him for what he was – a mob orator, all words and no action. Later that day Welles and Barnarde pledged themselves to raise a host of followers and place themselves under Henry Howard, the Duke's brother, who was then at Tambridge, and go with him to aid the men of the north. They needed a drum to call men to their colours, and Barnarde going off to borrow one that he had brought 'out of Scotland, which was sold to a town nearby', disappears from the scene. The crowd dispersed and Welles walked down the village to the house of Thomas Heylocke and persuaded him to join. Two men from Bunwell, John Symson, labourer, and Henry Sporle, a sawyer, were also active in Kenninghall and the neighbouring villages exhorting men to rise during the next few days. But the whole affair fizzled out. We hear nothing more of Welles, the leader, between 8th December when he was still at Kenninghall and 16th May when he appeared in custody at the Shirehouse, Norwich, with some of his fellow conspirators to be tried for treason by the Justices sitting in special sessions.[12]

The Kenninghall rising was indeed premature, ill-organised and lacking in leadership. It had been all too easy for the authorities to arrest the principal troublemakers. News of the affair had reached Sir Christopher Heydon, the sheriff, at Bunwell, not ten miles away, all too soon, and he sent a posse to deal with the rebels: his official expenses in 'apprehending the conspirators dwelling in and about Kenninghall' amounted to £13 6s. 8d. Before Christmas they were all safely locked up in Norwich gaol. On 9th January the Spanish ambassador, reporting the incident to Philip II, commented: 'if they had been able to join with the northern people they might have succeeded. All these enterprises are lost by bad guidance, and although they are undertaken with impetus, they are not carried through with constancy.' To succeed, the malcontents must wait for the better weather in the spring, and, more important, must find a leader of very much greater weight and experience than the sawyer of Kenninghall.[13]

Yet by the spring of 1570 conditions were very different. With Lord Hunsdon's victory over Dacre the fate of the Northern Rebellion was sealed. Although the rescue of the Duke from the Tower was one of the various objectives of the insurgents who troubled the government in Norfolk in 1570, so far as is known the men of Kenninghall remained entirely aloof. Sir William Buttes, Thomas Gawdy, serjeant at law, and their fellow justices sentenced Welles and the other chief conspirators to imprisonment to await Her Majesty's pleasure. Four and a half years later, with the duke executed and the country quiet and prosperous, they were all pardoned and released at the petition of Buttes and Sir Christopher Heydon. But Kenninghall's connexion with the Northern Rebellion did not end there. Some years later Jane, Countess of Westmorland came to live in Norfolk. Her husband, the last of the Nevilles, had fled to the Spanish Netherlands to spend the rest of his life in exile. His vast estates were confiscated and Queen Elizabeth was moved to grant the Countess an annuity of £300. She died in 1593 and was buried in Kenninghall church.[14]

*   *   *

With the duke still a prisoner the county was understandably backward in subscribing towards the costs of suppressing the Northern Rebellion. Elizabeth's system of voluntary loans did not meet with the ready response she had counted on and she chided her deputy lieutenants in April, who drew up a list of the defaulters with their various excuses. The letter to William Dix, Norfolk's surveyor, had been returned to them as he was not at home; Knyvet and Paston, Blenerhasset and Gawdy, Bedingfield and Jerningham – all Howard retainers or supporters – 'asked for respite'. Still the spring of 1570 had passed without apparent incident in Norfolk, and in the second week of May the sheriff was able to assure the Privy Council that the justices had been active in rounding up suspect and idle persons, committing some to gaol and binding others over to appear at the next sessions of the peace. He hoped that through such diligence 'this whole country shall grow to better state and quietness'. Yet, as in the previous December, the sheriff's words were scarcely dry when trouble began again. On 16th May the standard of revolt was raised at Norwich and for the next six weeks, until the fateful Midsummer Day, a succession of risings threatened the established order of church and state in Norfolk. On 16th May the citizens of Norwich heard for the first time a battle cry of the insurgents that was to become only too familiar to them and to many others throughout Norfolk. 'We will raise up the commons and levy a power and beat the strangers out of the City of Norwich; and also take Sir Christopher Heydon and Sir William Buttes and put them in the Guildhall in Norwich and there keep them; for Norfolk had never the like cause to rise. And after we have levied out power, we will hang up all such as will not take our parts.'[15]

The leaders were of a very different stamp from Welles and Barnarde of Kenninghall, or indeed from Robert Ket of famous memory. Chief among them was John Appleyard, a man of some substance in the county. He was the son of Roger and Elizabeth Appleyard of Standfield. After her husband's death Elizabeth married Sir John Robsart of Siderstern and bore him a daughter – the tragic Amy Robsart. With his half-sister's marriage to Robert Dudley, John Appleyard began to become prominent in local affairs. Thanks to Dudley's patronage, as we have seen, he was appointed sheriff of Norfolk and Suffolk in 1559 and enjoyed the issues of the portership of Berwick. His connexions with Leicester and his supporters did not end with the mysterious death of his sister at Cumnor. More recently he had been involved in somewhat underhand political intrigues, concerning which he was examined at Court in 1567. About John Throgmorton of Norwich we know much less, though he came from a well-known Norfolk family. Two other ringleaders, George Redman of Cringleford and Thomas Brooke of Rollesby, each bore the quality of 'gentleman'; Redman was possibly related to the future bishop of Norwich, at this time a fellow of Trinity College, Cambridge. Of the remaining conspirators Brian Holland of Redenhall had been escheator of Norfolk in 1556-7; the Holland family administered much of the Duke of Norfolk's property in the county. Both John Jernegan of Somerleytown in Suffolk and James Hobart of Hales Hall came from important families, as we can see from the heralds' visitation of 1564; a Hobart had been sheriff in 1546. These conspirators, then, were men of some standing in their county. Although out of office at this time – and for good reason – they had all had some administrative experience;

and they naturally expected that a successful rising would place the government of the shire in their hands. Even Thomas Cecil, a cousin of the Secretary of State, was involved in the plotting.[16]

There was no sudden mass movement for which these men had hoped, as there had been in 1549. The commons to whom the proposed expulsion of the Huguenot weavers might have appeared attractive, sat tight. The mayor for his part let the incident of 16th May pass; Appleyard and his fellows went unmolested, the authorities perhaps thinking it would be as well to give them as long a rope as possible. Ten days later Appleyard publicly announced in Norwich that if he could get 'but four faithful gentlemen in Norfolk' to take his part he would himself drive the foreigners out of the city. The idea of appealing to the commons for aid had been shelved, though on 6th June the original battle cry was again in favour. On that day the ringleaders, together with Anthony Nolloth of Yarmouth, Clement Haywarde of Norwich and Brian Holland treasonably assembled a little force in the city, armed with hand guns, daggs and pistolets and clad in armour ('coats of defence' as they were called). Their band of supporters was again mustered in Norwich on 10th June and at Trowse, on the outskirts of the city, on 16th June, with the numbers growing on each occasion. But still the authorities failed to take any action. Day by day the leaders plotted amongst themselves. The inclusion of Brian Holland in their councils on 6th June is significant. He hailed from Redenhall; and it was at Harleston in the parish of Redenhall, right on the Suffolk border, that the main rising was planned to take place.

The chapelry of Harleston was a liberty of the Duke of Norfolk. The chapel itself, dedicated to St John Baptist, had been dissolved under Edward VI, but the annual fair continued to be held on the patronal festival, though shorn of much of the pageantry which the religious processions had provided. Midsummer Day was, indeed, Harleston's great day. From far and wide people came to the fair; and it seemed to Appleyard and Throgmorton an ideal place at which they could recruit followers, with sound of trumpet and drum. Smaller gatherings were to be made on the same day nearer Norwich. The troops raised at Harleston, gathering reinforcements at Bungay and Beccles, were to march on Norwich. There they were to have surprised the mayor and principal citizens at a banquet, to have taken charge of the city and used the civic plate to finance further operations. The Flemish immigrants were to be hustled out of town and a proclamation was to be made against the Queen's 'evil advisers' in much the same form as the northern earls' proclamation at Ripon. The port of Yarmouth was then to be betrayed to the Duke of Alva and a force of Spanish troops; and it was hoped that this great soldier would soon make himself the master of East Anglia and march on London. The imagination of the conspirators knew no bounds.[17]

During the previous weeks the word had been passed round the county to all sympathisers with the cause to be at Harleston Fair on 24th June with arms and horses. Edward Smith, who farmed a small holding at Oxnead, was one of the many who failed to reach Harleston. He got no further than Aylesham, where he attempted to raise rebellion more or less single-handed. 'If all things had fallen out right', he proclaimed, 'I should not have been here this day, but I should have been at Harleston Fair with my fellows and horse and armour; and if we had been there we should have been good enough for a good many to have rapped them down.'[18]

Although the conspirators did muster a small force at Cringleford on 24th June, which on the following day appeared at Trowse just outside the city, armed with guns, daggs and pistols, the grand design at Harleston simply petered out. The rebels' plans had been betrayed to the authorities with disastrous results. Some said it was a Ket (a Thomas and a William Ket are both mentioned) that discovered the conspiracy to Drew Drury, J.P.; others that William Holmes confessed his own and practically everybody else's share in the affair to the deputy lieutenants and the mayor of Norwich. Even Appleyard was not, it seems, to be trusted by his fellows, for at his trial he maintained to the end that he had intended 'to have had them to a banquet, and to have betrayed them all, and to have won credit thereby with the Queen'. At any rate the whole affair failed miserably. The justices and civic officers pounced swiftly and soon had all the ringleaders and many of the lesser fry in gaol. Only a very few managed to escape, such as a servant of the Duke of Norfolk who was safely sent over to France by the Bishop of Ross. Norwich gaol had never been so crowded; indeed, the sheriff had to take over a number of other buildings as additional prisons and provide suitable warders for them at a further cost of £5 a week. Rounding up the traitors had cost the Crown £26 13s 4d.[19]

News of the Norfolk conspiracy soon reached London. A Spanish merchant there, already knew the main facts on 1st July, when he sent home a brief account of it. But the matter was not officially reported to the Court for some days. Cecil wrote to the deputy lieutenants:

> *We greet you well. Although we have heard much more by common report of the Conspiracy there intended at Norwich than we could hitherto by any of your letters, and did hear thereof a good space before any knowledge came to our Council from you, yet do not think but your care hath been as much as the case hath required, and so are we persuaded and by some your late letters with examinations of some of the authors, we do well perceive that you have begun well and will proceed further to the apprehension of the rest. And considering such attempts cannot at the first be wholly discovered, but that wisdom willeth to suspect of more, we will that you shall have special regard of the state of the City of Norwich, where the conspiracy, as it seemeth, had its beginning; and for maintenance and comfort of the citizens who generally are faithful – and yet consisting of a great multitude of people of mean and base sort cannot be void of fear – we would have you so order the matter betwixt you as one of you might be there by turns, to tarry there, or at least to be frequently there, where by your presence, with the company of Edward Clere and Drew Drury, our faithful servants, and such others the heads and governors of the City may be boldened to retain the multitude in quietness and obedience.*

Cecil went on to require them to order all loyal gentlemen to muster their tenants, to find arms for them and to arrange for inspections of these voluntary bands up and down the shire. They were to make a full return to him of all available men, horses and weapons. They were to see that warning beacons were in readiness, and to make special orders for suppressing vagrants, for seeing the Queen's peace was kept in fairs and markets, to prohibit unlawful assemblies and punish all rumour-mongers. In the next few weeks the sheriff, the two deputy lieutenants and the justices made amends for their earlier silence and spent over £20 in sending letters to the Court.[20]

The government was extremely anxious to discover any ramifications the Norfolk plots might have, especially since the bull *Regnans in Excelsis* had been published. The international situation loomed dark and uncertain. In the middle of July the five principal conspirators were sent under an escort of the Queen's guard from Norwich to Chenies in Buckinghamshire, the seat of Francis Russell, Earl of Bedford, where Her Majesty was staying. With them went forty-five witnesses. For their cross examination Cecil and the other ministers had by them an elaborate table, drawn up by Clere and Drury, the deputy lieutenants. This table showed which of the seventeen main charges referred to which prisoners, and gave the names of the various witnesses in each case: the charges ranged from imagination of the Queen's violent death and rescuing the duke from the Tower, to firing beacons and 'foreknowledging the hurly burly'. It was a summary of all the available evidence on the rising which the Secretary of State needed by him in connexion with investigations into other conspiracies in those tangled weeks of plot and counter-plot.[21]

Prisoners and witnesses were escorted back to Norwich ready for the Assizes, which began on 17th July before Sir Robert Catlin, Chief Justice of Queen's Bench (very much on his home ground as a Norfolk man) and Gilbert Gerrard, the Attorney-General. The smaller fry were summarily dealt with, thus easing the shortage of accommodation in the gaol. After formal indictments for high treason had been preferred, the trial of the others was adjourned until the arrival of a special tribunal.

On 28th July Cecil ordered the Lord Keeper to make out two commissions of over and terminer. One was for the trial in London of John Felton, in the Tower for high treason for fixing the Papal Bull to the door of the Bishop of London's palace in Paul's Churchyard; and the other commission was for the 'seditious and rebellious persons . . . of late indicted of treason in our counties of Norfolk and Suffolk and in our City of Norwich, who we mean to have arraigned and tried according to the course of our law'. The commission for Norfolk was a powerful one. It was headed by Thomas, Lord Wentworth, the lord lieutenant of the county, who had himself been in the Tower during the first year of the Queen's reign but was acquitted of high treason. In 1572 he was to be one of the peers who tried the duke. With him sat the Chief Justice of Queen's Bench and the Attorney General, fresh from the Norwich Summer Assizes. There were also

Thomas Bromley, solicitor general, the principal justices of the peace in the county, including Thomas Gawdy, a future Justice of Queen's Bench, Edward Flowerdue, a future Baron of the Exchequer, and the mayor of Norwich. The chief counsel for the Crown on whom the weighty task of the prosecution lay was Robert Bell, serjeant at law, acting in place of the Attorney General who was sitting on this occasion with the judges. Bell considerably enhanced his reputation by his handling of the prosecution. He had served as a member for King's Lynn in the last Parliament, and on his re-election in May 1572 was to be appointed Speaker of the House. In 1577 he was knighted and appointed to the important judicial office of Chief Baron of the Exchequer.[22]

The Chief Justice and his retinue arrived at Norwich on Saturday 19th August to find a suite of rooms prepared for them at the Crown Inn. The bill for the judges' lodging and entertainment during their five day stay is happily extant. Although they did not enjoy sturgeon, as did the Justices of Assize in July, they did themselves well.

In primis paid for the hire of the Inn called the Crowne at Norwich aforesaid, in which the said Justices lay during the said sessions, with the furniture of household stuff, wood, coal and hay, £20.
Item paid for 2 hogsheads of wine, £6.
Item paid for one little vessel of sack, 11s 4d.
Item paid for spices and sugar, £8 6s 8d.
Item paid for bread and beer, £16 19s 4d.
Item paid for 4 steers, £10 18s.
Item paid for 24 muttons, £8 12s.
Item paid for 7 veals, £3 10s.
Item paid for geese, swans, capons, rabbits, pigeons and chickens, £10 4s.
Item paid for all kind of wild fowl, £9 5s.
Item paid for butter and eggs, £5 12s 7d.
Item paid for fruit: apples, pears, cherries, quinces and strawberries, 52s.
Item paid for candles, 25s.
Item paid for horsebread and oats, £6 9s.[23]

On the Monday the great trial opened. Many witnesses were

present in court; others had sworn to depositions. Among those to give evidence was the Reverend John Gascoyne, rector of Howe and parson of Portingland, who knew about a design to proclaim the Duke of Norfolk as king, once he was out of the Tower; and Gascoyne 'vehemently suspected' William Cantrell, the vicar of Hingham for his 'continual conversation with the chief traitors'. Dr Martin Alcumbe (or Holcombe) a physician, gave evidence with others of the 'sowing of sedition, slander and boiling treasons' of Throgmorton, Heyward and Thomas Cecil. Ten of the accused had also made statements, some, like William Holmes, hoping to save their necks by implicating others in the plots. Of the nineteen chief conspirators only three were found guilty on the principal counts – namely, the destruction of the Queen's person, the imprisonment of Cecil, Leicester and other ministers, the release of the Duke and the banishment of the alien settlers. Appleyard succeeded in saving himself, but Throgmorton, Brooke and Redman were sent to the gallows: all three were hung, drawn and quartered.

Brooke whiled away the days in prison between his sentence and execution by writing verses in which he prepared to take leave of this world. They form neither a recantation nor an apologia in the strict sense; and he can hardly have expected that his eleventh-hour 'vivats' for the Queen would procure him a pardon. His lines seem merely to embody his own happy resignation to his fate, and they are interesting chiefly as being the first of the long series of literary compositions that have been penned in English gaols. The verses were duly licensed by the authorities and were issued as a broadsheet on 30th August, the eve of Brooke's execution, by Anthony de Solempne, the Brabant printer who had settled in Norwich.

> All languishing I lie,
> And death doth make me thrall,
> To cares which death shall sone cut off
> And sett me quyt of all.
>
> Yett feble fleshe would faynt
> To feale so sharpe a fyght,
> Save fayth in Christ doth comfort me,
> And fliethe such fancy quyght.

For fyndyng forth howe frayle
    Each worldly state doth stande,
I hould hym blyst that, fearing God,
    Is redd of such a band.

For he that longest lyves,
    And Nestor's yeares doth gayne,
Hath so much more accompte to make,
    And fyndyth Lyfe but vayne.

What cawse ys ther to quayle?
    I callèd am before
To tast the Joyes, which Christ'is bloode
    Hath bowght and layde in store.

No, no! no greter Joye
    Can eny hart posses,
Then throwgth the death to gayne a lyfe
    Wyth hym is blyssednesse:

Who sende the Quene long lyfe,
    Much Joye and countries peace,
Her Cowncell health, hyr fryndes good lucke,
    To all ther Joye's increase.

Thus puttyng uppe my greives,
    I grownde my lyfe on God,
And thanke hym with most humble hart
    And mekely kysse his rodde.

            Finis, quod Thomas Brooke.[24]

On his arraignment Throgmorton had stood mute, but at the gallows he confessed that he was the arch conspirator. A number of hotheads paid for their rash words by imprisonment or fine, whether they were guilty of expressing a vague hope to see the duke as King of England before Michaelmas, or a vow to wash their hands in Protestant blood when Alva should land at Yarmouth. One individual who had been bold enough to suggest that the Earl of Leicester had had two children by the Queen was to lose both his ears if he could not find the £100 for his fine. Justice was however tempered with mercy. Throgmorton's widow, Margaret, was in 1571 granted certain of her husband's property, including land in Suffolk which he had jointly owned with Thomas Gawdy, for the relief and education of her six children. James Hobart of Hales Hall had pleaded not guilty to participating in the conspiracy; he was convicted and sentenced to life imprisonment with forfeiture of his goods. Some three years later, at the special pleading of the Earl of Leicester, he was pardoned and released. Edward Smith of Oxnead, the supporter of Appleyard who had failed to reach Harleston Fair on Midsummer Day, and Robert Fludd of Norwich were also released from their life imprisonment by the Queen's graciousness in November 1574. Brian Holland, a close prisoner for some years, was deprived of his stewardships, but the duke replaced him by his son John.[25]

Thus ended the fiasco of Harleston Fair. Already, before the special sessions began, the duke had been moved from the Tower to his own residence in the Charterhouse; the county of Norfolk was again quiet. The news of the rising had temporarily frightened the central government, but the leaders had shown themselves to be no more able to achieve their wild schemes than the leaders at Kenninghall in the previous December.

While Brooke was awaiting execution a report was prepared of known papists in Norfolk. The list was headed by Mr Dirricke, lately chaplain to the Archbishop of Canterbury and now well beneficed – 'a rank and arrant papist'. There was Christopher Plater, a substantial Norwich merchant and a brother-in-law of Throgmorton, who had travelled to Rome the year before, returning home through Flanders where he had met Woller, a Suffolk man who had served for a time in Alva's army; and this Woller was by now home again and suspected of causing much trouble. Even John Paston featured in the list, being noted as indulging in 'too broad talk for religion'. Yet so long as the duke was confined to Howard House none of these men would stir.[26]

Chapter Eleven

HOWARD HOUSE

1570-1

THE rebellion had delayed a full investigation of Norfolk's case, for the Queen and her Council had more urgent matters on hand than to examine a suspect already safely in the Tower. On 12th December Sir Henry Neville asked him orally a number of questions about his dealings with Mary, and he answered, he said, as far as his ill memory allowed him. The duke straightway wrote to the Queen promising never to deal further with Mary and offering to subscribe to any assurance which Elizabeth might demand of him. Neville was hauled over the coals for trusting to his memory over the questions he put to his prisoner, instead of asking for them in writing, and was thought to have misrepresented them. In fact, when they came in writing, Norfolk found he had already answered all except one, where the form of words had been changed: he meant by entering into the marriage negotiations to prevent a papist prince from marrying Mary, 'which I judged to be the greatest peril'. At length on 20th January Cecil drew up a list of ten charges, ranging from the days when the duke had sat as a commissioner at York in October 1568 to his last letter to Murray on 1st July 1569. 'All these things he did without making Her Majesty privy thereto', yet they did not add up to high treason, however frequently Elizabeth called him 'traitor', and Cecil even sent her an abstract of the Treasons Statute of Edward III's reign to show that Norfolk was innocent of such a charge. Nevertheless, in the existing state of politics he was considered too dangerous a man to be set at liberty.

His health deteriorated in confinement, for he missed his exercise and there was a swelling in his stomach. He had been in poor
shape physically at the time of his arrest, and the Tower was not
the ideal place for making a recovery, but no-one on the Council
was convinced that Norfolk was as ill as he made out. After a
month, however, the Lieutenant was granted leave to remove
him to any rooms (other than the Queen's Lodging) adjoining
the Long Gallery, in which he was now allowed to walk in the
company of Henry Knollys, who was to take over Neville's
duties as gaoler for the moment.[1]

But Norfolk was still able to keep in touch with his friends. A
cipher had been prepared and detailed arrangements made for
passing messages in leathern bottles; Higford, his confidential
secretary, was with him from the first to decipher letters. In time
the duke succeeded in increasing his establishment of personal
servants from two to six and each one of them was absolutely
dependable. Some were allowed to go outside the Tower to buy
provisions and thus had many opportunities for acting as post-
men, or, when things were difficult, of memorising oral messages.
One of his men, brought into his chamber under guard, made a
practice of throwing letters wrapped in black paper into a dark
privy from which they were later collected. There was 'Nell',
soon to become a housemaid at Howard House, who carried
letters beyond the walls; and there was the seven-year-old daughter of one of the gaolers who came every morning to his room
with a nosegay and received gold for her pains. In his later months
of captivity Norfolk had 'so much favour and liberty that his
men had recourse to him freely'.

In time there came letters even from Mary, for Higford to
decipher, professing her love, anxious to keep Howard constant.
She told him she wore his diamond about her neck until she could
'give it again to the owner of it and me both', for neither weale
nor woe should make her desert him; a strange love affair this,
in which neither had beheld the other, and the *billets* were always
in cipher! But despite the codes, Mary 'dare not write' as she
would. She warned him of the malice of Huntingdon, her keeper,
who said oft 'it were a pity you should live'. The earl had rightly
prophesied that Norfolk would never leave the Tower unless he
refused her hand, but she answered that he was not worth a wart
if he did. Murray's assassination in January made her bolder, as

the hopes of her restoration seemed to her brighter, and though she was a perpetual prisoner for his sake she was planning a new enterprise and implored him to follow her example in caring not for danger, 'for if you and I could escape both we should find friends enough. Being free and honourably bound together, you might make such good offers for the countries and the Queen of England as they should not refuse. Our fault were not shameful; you have promised to be mine and I yours.' There were plans devised by Hugh Owen for removing Mary from Tutbury to Arundel where she should take ship for France with the Earl of Arundel's cook, and the Scottish Queen said she would be prepared to adventure it if the duke, Arundel or Pembroke would appoint a knight to make the attempt, but nothing came to pass.

Throughout that spring she had little news from him and although she appreciated it was difficult for him to write she worried about his health and even more about his constancy. She was 'Your own Mary', 'Your faithful to death, Queen of Scots, my Norfolk', but he seemed distant, offended with her for her over-optimism and fondness, broken and too timid to want to try and follow her lead. In the event he shrank from committing himself, for while he was in the Tower he centred his hopes on the reigning Queen in Whitehall not on the captive Queen at Tutbury. Unknown to Mary he suggested to Cecil in February that he should be allowed to go home to Howard House to take a course of physic, which would make him fit enough to serve Elizabeth in the north in the coming summer, and that 'the Queen of Scots should take his place in the Tower'. The weeks slipped by and he no more than pondered Mary's suggestions, almost disinterestedly, and not for a full year would Norfolk find himself swept by the current across the Rubicon.[2]

It was as well that he had other problems to occupy him. With the north in revolt, the Dacres' faction had taken forcible possession of various estates that in the summer of 1569 had been declared by the Courts to be the rightful inheritance of Norfolk's step-daughters. Edward Dacre had led a party to scale the walls of Greystoke Castle, the Bells and Milburnes of Gilsland had occupied Naworth Castle, the Borderers entered Rockliffe and Christopher Elwood had come in the night to Kirk Oswald Castle and starved the duke's servants before throwing them out of doors. 'The taking of the said castles was, as it were, all in one instant, in the name of Leonard Dacre to the Queen's use, for that his grace was beheaded, as the report was, with the day and place of his execution.' This letter from his auditor in the north must have made him shudder. Muniment chests had been plundered and beacons lit to call men to the standard for preventing the entry of the Lord Warden. Norfolk reckoned he had lost £2,000 as a result of this intrusion. Another worry was the settlement of the Arundel inheritance as Philip's marriage portion, which was still being negotiated when the duke was released.*

At the end of February rumours were going round town that he was being secretly put to death. One such story, passed round the Fleet among the prisoners for debt, was that Bacon and Cecil had consulted together and thought it well to have Norfolk executed within the Tower, and his head would already have been off had not Leicester intervened. The Catholic Sir Francis Englefield, who was well informed, wrote in April that Norfolk was no longer so closely guarded as before and was well looked after by his servants, 'but of his delivery there is little hope'. The same month an anonymous reply was penned to Walsingham's pamphlet of the previous autumn. Each point in the 'Discourse touching the pretended match' was answered in turn and the treatise ended with a lengthy attack on the political group with which the author identified it and a warning to the rumour-mongers who fabricated plots and counterplots. This pamphlet circulated in manuscript but owing to the government's close control of the press was never printed and its composition, if anything, delayed the duke's release. In April and May he managed to send several letters to Mary, and in a less despondent tone, which cheered her after a bout of sickness at Chatsworth – 'comfortable writings which are to me as welcome as ever thing was'.[3]

News of Christopher Norton's execution at the end of May brought Howard to plead more strongly for his liberty, until at length on 23rd June he was granted permission to make his own voluntary submission in writing. He 'most humbly and with all reverence and duty' submitted himself, 'acknowledging my offence and by my voluntary offering to make amends for the same with a determinate mind never to offend Your Majesty either in the same or in any like'. He offered to serve in any way she might direct to make the world see his loyalty and sense of repentance.

* Above, pp. 120-2.

'And where I did unhappily give ear to certain motions made to me in a cause of marriage to be prosecuted for me with the Queen of Scots, I most humbly beseech Your Majesty permit me to declare such part of the truth that maketh in some part my excuse, as I will also willingly confess the rest wherein I did err.'

'Surely I never consented to accord thereto in any respect, but whatsoever reasons were propounded to me to induce me thereto for Your Highness's benefit and surety, yet I humbly thank God that I always referred the allowance and disallowance to Your Majesty's own judgment, as it might appear to be agreeable or disagreeable ... And on the other part I do confess that now sithence I have further considered thereof (notwithstanding any appearance of the reasons made to Your Highness's benefit to follow upon that marriage), I did err very much in that I did not cause the same to be known to Your Majesty upon the first motion made to me.' He craved forgiveness from the bottom of his heart and since Elizabeth did not like the proposed match he solemnly, yet voluntarily, 'bound himself' by his bond of allegiance 'never to offend Your Highness in the same, but do utterly renounce and revoke all that which on my part anywise hath passed, with a full intention never to deal in that cause of marriage of the Queen of Scots, nor in any other cause belonging to her, but as Your Majesty shall command me'. Finally, he hoped that now Elizabeth would release him 'out of the dungeon of your displeasure', give him some relief for his ill-health and allow him to recover her favour by putting his life and wealth at her service.[4]

It reads as full a confession as it was fulsome, yet Norfolk's submission was neither as comprehensive nor as wisely worded as some would have wished. Only one or two of Norfolk's most trusted intimates knew about his sending a draft of his submission to Mary for her approval before he had the document laid before Elizabeth. It was probably Sir Francis Walsingham who drew up a detailed memorandum on the subject early in August.[5] 'Those to whom it may come, seeing so great submission and deep repentance for only forgetting or neglecting to tell a matter supposed for Her Majesty's benefit – and that in so great a personage – will surely conclude in him small error and great lowliness, and in the Queen small indulgence and much hardness, to the peril of augmentation of his popularity and of the people's grudge against her, or her good counsellors, or both.' And if Norfolk was treated thus for lending his ear to the designs of others, people could not help wondering how the architects of the design were going to fare. The duke, moreover, had written nothing to show that he now misliked Mary, her title, or her claim to the throne of England. He was free to reason that such a marriage would still be for Elizabeth's benefit, still free to persuade her to sanction it – and the marriage might well be for her benefit though she might not think so.

The duke could hold that his renunciation of Mary was void if there were a prior contract between them, and, given the opportunity, he could cancel his submission on the grounds that it was made under duress, even though he had said it was made voluntarily; 'an honourable mean to obtain performance of the former faith of the marriage ... which excuse would be well liked in such a case of conscience of marriage, or of weighty commodity as a crown' – shrewd words indeed. Howard may mean well, concluded the writer, 'but he has not said well enough' and it would be far safer to keep him in the Tower.

Rather surprisingly Cecil thought otherwise. He knew, of course, that it was out of the question to charge Norfolk with high treason, but he could not afford to prejudice the security of the realm by releasing him and as a compromise he allowed him to return to Howard House under strict supervision. The duke's health has been seriously undermined by the 'noisome airs' of captivity, as the doctors admitted, and the plague was rampant in the Tower hamlets that hot summer; at all events if Norfolk died in the Tower he would provide Mary's cause with a martyr. Among the prisoners of state who died of the plague at this time were the brothers Arthur and Edmund Poole, confined in the Beauchamp Tower, as a result of their madcap traitorous designs of eight years back for which they had been sentenced to death but reprieved. Howard had followed up his submission with a series of letters to Cecil and to the Council, challenging them to substantiate the charges against him and imploring them to move the Queen to permit him continue his imprisonment in his own house, free from the dangers of infection. Neville wrote to the Secretary saying that the duke feared he was to remain in close custody 'for how long God he knoweth', and the story that Leicester had put about 'that he had the Queen in very good tune, till you [Cecil] took her aside and dealt with her secretly' had

convinced Norfolk that Leicester was determined to keep him
locked up for months to come. That factor counted a good deal
with Cecil who for his own reasons would welcome Howard's
return to the council table as his supporter against the enigmatic
Leicester. It was not, however, until he had read the memorandum
which we have ascribed to Walsingham that the Secretary made
his decision on 3rd August and persuaded the Queen to transfer
her prisoner to Howard House, with Neville as his resident keeper.
Home at last after ten months of the Tower, Norfolk penned 'a
few ragged lines' to Elizabeth, laying himself prostrate before
her, and at the same time thanked Cecil for his share in saving
him from 'yonder pestilent infectious house'. He was not free,
but he was in his own castle.[6]

This new chapter in his life began inauspiciously for the very
next day John Felton went to his trial for high treason and later
in the week was hanged in St Paul's Churchyard, just in front of
the Bishop of London's Palace where he had published the Papal
Bull in May. The same week, too, Ridolfi paid an ominous visit
to Howard House, which seriously disturbed Norfolk. He had
written to the Italian to cancel a recognisance for debt for £1,800
which he had entered on behalf of Arundel and Lumley as part
of the price of the settlement of the Arundel inheritance; but
Ridolfi had replied that he wanted to talk with the duke himself
and so it was arranged that Barker should bring him in secretly
one evening to avoid Neville's suspicion. Howard was understandably ill at ease. The financier refused his entreaties to cancel
the bond and spurned the offer of twenty yards of velvet, yet he
agreed that he would not prosecute the debt. He went on to
relate his affairs from the time he had been imprisoned in Walsingham's house the previous autumn and talked of his schemes
for liberating Mary and for sending money to relieve the Earl of
Westmorland, the Countess of Northumberland and other exiles
in the Netherlands. The object of his present visit was in fact to
ask Norfolk to write to the Duke of Alva, Governor of the Spanish Netherlands, for money for the Scottish Queen, 'to her own
use and for necessaries', but he declined to undertake such a commission however much Ridolfi pressed him. 'I began to mislike
him' and 'sought ways to shift me from him.' He was thankful
to get Ridolfi off the premises undiscovered and did not see him
again for six months.

TH O

The duke spent his enforced residence in Howard House in improving the mansion and the very month in which he left the Tower workmen began building the brick-covered arcade and terrace which led to the new tennis court. For the next year the various embellishments to the house were at their height and the splendid screen in the Great Hall bears Howard's initials and the year '1571'. The coming and going of an army of workmen made it very difficult for Neville to keep a close watch on Norfolk's visitors and his correspondence. At first it seemed almost like old times, with Cecil writing for his views on the negotiations that were now in train for Elizabeth to marry the Duke of Anjou, which would put a stop to French intervention on behalf of Mary, and by mid-September he was again 'Your ever most beholding Norfolk' in his letters to Cecil. He still longed for some positive assurance from Elizabeth that he had been forgiven: 'I have omitted nothing that lay in me to do to recover Her Highness's favour', he wrote, hoping Cecil would help him to obtain it, 'without the which I wish no life.' But Elizabeth would not forgive or forget, for Norfolk had forfeited her confidence; and it was because he found it impossible to recover her favour that he was led into renewing his intrigues for the hand of Mary Queen of Scots. He had been lukewarm about the match for the previous two months, but by mid-October, when it was clear he was to remain a prisoner in Howard House, he began to grow more fervent, for it seemed the only chance of real liberty.[7]

The events of the autumn of 1569 had convinced Ridolfi that the English Catholics were too inexperienced as revolutionaries to be allowed to make plans for themselves. The Florentine was an inveterate plotter; all through 1570 he had been thick with the Bishop of Ross, the Spanish Ambassador, Lord Lumely and others in scheme after scheme, and it had been from his hands that Felton had obtained his copies of the Bull. He was shrewd enough to predict that the latest attempts to restore Mary to Scotland by negotiation would founder and concluded that her salvation lay in a concerted rising of her English friends, strongly supported by money and arms from the Catholic Powers. The first draft for a grand design to liberate Mary appears in a long letter which Ridolfi wrote to Pius V on 1st September 1570. Mary's party in England, he wrote, were again prepared to take the field, but they wanted Alva to provide munitions and money, and if he were forthcoming they 'will undertake with the help of all the Catholics to deliver the Queen of Scotland safe out of the hand of this Queen and to re-establish religion in this realm'. If at the same time the French supported the Marians in Scotland 'there is no reason to doubt the speedy accomplishment of the desired end'. Such a plan, he added, had the full support of the Spanish Ambassador. Ever the optimist, Ridolfi, believed that every second Englishman most fervently desired to spring to arms in obedience to the Papal Bull and confidently listed various peers who promised to raise between them 39,000 men. An analysis of the English nobility he made with the help of Arundel and Lumley six months later put thirty-three peers as Catholics, sixteen as Heretics and fifteen as 'Doubtful' or 'Neutral' – the last group including Leicester and Sussex! Thus as a militant crusader of the Counter Reformation Ridolfi began to weave the threads of the conspiracy that bears his name, which was destined to bring about Norfolk's final downfall.

Since Ridolfi and the duke had parted on far from friendly terms in August, the Italian made sure that his scheme had the entire support of Mary and Ross before Norfolk was again approached. In January 1571 Mary wrote to Ross, then confined to his London House, commending the design in general, suggesting that she refer the details to Norfolk's direction and proposing that Ridolfi was himself 'the fittest messenger' for entreating foreign aid. The bishop forwarded this ciphered letter to Howard House, with another from Mary to the duke and also a copy of the new cipher. Norfolk's first reaction, after Higford had done his deciphering, was 'The Bishop of Ross will never be quiet', and his reluctance to approve the scheme sorely tried the patience of both the principal conspirators. Later he ordered the letters to be burnt, but they were not. Early in March Ridolfi was again smuggled into Howard House at 8 p.m. to talk with Norfolk in the Long Gallery; Barker brought him from behind the workhouse at the further end of Lavendry Court, up the new staircase to the Old Wardrobe, and through the dining-room used by Lady l'Estrange. Norfolk still refused to write or sign any document, but agreed that Barker should go on his behalf to the Bishop of Ross for further discussions. The Italian left with the duke a paper summarising his scheme with a list of peers and others who were supporters of Mary, each name in the list being

given a number for use in ciphers; Norfolk's own number was
40. Shortly afterwards Barker went to Ross's town residence to
vow his master's general assent to the scheme in the presence of
the Spanish ambassador. There he saw three Latin letters of
credence for Ridolfi, all drawn up in Norfolk's name; one was
for accrediting the Italian to the Pope, another for Alva and the
third was addressed to Philip of Spain. Ross said that after he had
had them put in cipher he would subscribe the duke's name to
them – 'and that the duke might deny it when he list'. Back at
Howard House Barker told Norfolk what Ross had said, and
although 'he seemed not to like well thereof, he did not send to
stay the Bishop from doing as he had said'. The duke, while
wishing success to the enterprise, shrank from committing himself too deeply in the plotting and convinced himself that so long
as he did not actually sign any document he was not committing
treason. Ross much later admitted that after much persuasion
'he heard the Duke so precisely affirm his contentation and agreement' to the letters, that it was as binding as if he had signed them.
It suited Ridolfi and Ross for Norfolk to leave the arrangements
entirely to them, but they could have wished he had made less
play with his lingering scruples. The Tower had not in fact taught
him sufficient caution and he failed to realise there could be no
half-measures where Mary Queen of Scots was concerned; as he
had remarked himself the previous spring: 'I hold a wolf by the
ears; I can neither let go without danger, nor hold without peril.'
Thomas Howard was not of the stuff of which successful conspirators are made. In his heart he knew that 'England can bear
no more changes in religion', and that to bend it again would
inevitably break it, yet the prize of Mary's hand once more egged
him on.[8]

That Howard had in fact committed himself is clear from the
sales of plate and jewellery which he ordered to be sold that
spring. In a matter of ten days 3,650 ounces of silver goblets,
ewers, platters and bowls were delivered to William Denham for
melting down in the Mint in the Tower, and the duke began his
private sales of family jewels; he even went to the length of disposing of his grandfather's Garter jewels. He did not need this
money for the improvements at Howard House nor for his family
settlement; instead he wanted to lay his hands on every penny he
could for buying horses and arms to equip an army and to bribe

wavering supporters in England and Scotland. Ridolfi, his normal broker, was out of the country, and in view of his close confinement his credit with goldsmiths and other financiers was at its lowest ebb, indeed he told Ross he could get no credit upon land and thus desperate means were needed.[9]

The letter to the Pope to which Norfolk's name was set ran (in translation) as follows:

> *Pondering the deplorable plight of the Christian world and especially of this island of Britain, in which misery and anxiety prevail on all hands by reason of the enfeeblement of religion and by consequence of the civil power, I, by the advice of the nobles of this realm, send to your Holiness this envoy, Robert Ridolfi, a worthy man well known to your Holiness, with instructions to confer with your Holiness touching matters that concern the common weal, whom I most humbly beseech you to trust and speed upon his errand, and send back to us with the prompt despatch which the circumstances and the importance of the business require; and that the whole enterprise may be brought to the desired end, I most faithfully promise not only to do all my endeavour so far as my powers may extend, but also to hazard my life for the glory of God. The other matters which the envoy will fully and perspicuously discuss with your Holiness, as also whatever concerns me, I beg leave to submit to the pious sagacity of your Holiness to decide. Our Lord Jesus Christ preserve you to utmost length of days to govern His Church.*

With this there was a long letter in Italian, also in the duke's name, addressed to Ridolfi, which set out the plans in detail and concluded with a list of friends, foes and neutrals among the peerage. Though addressed to Ridolfi, the text of the letter was also written by him and at no time did Norfolk see it. 'By reason of the trust which the Queen of Scotland and I, and other nobles of this realm, our friends repose in you, we by common counsel have resolved to commit to your diligence and integrity the negotiation of a treaty of the utmost importance.' He was to proceed to Rome for an audience with the Pope, and thence to Philip II, to describe to them the woeful plight of England and inform them of the sure measures which existed for saving the country from disaster and Christendom from untoward consequences. Ridolfi was to ask Pius V and Philip II for their aid in a just enterprise 'which has the promise of assured success, if they would but grant the succour that is craved for the furtherance of the Queen of Scotland's title, the re-establishment of the Catholic religion and the suppression of those that are of the opposite side'. Ridolfi was also to explain 'how well disposed and ready to act are the Catholics, who preponderate in numbers and power in this realm'.

Since Pope and King may be somewhat suspicious of Norfolk not having declared himself, 'but rather having worn the appearance of a Huguenot', Ridolfi was to explain that this 'has not been due to any ill-will towards the Holy See, but in order that, when in due time the occasion should present itself, such as that which now offers, I might be able to do such signal service to all this island and Christendom at large as the result will show'. Many English Catholics could tell the Pope how stout Norfolk has been in their defence; how his chief officials, friends and the tutors of his children are all Catholics; yet at present many Protestants follow his lead in attempting to further Mary's title. He was not actuated so much by the desire to advance himself through marrying Mary as by the hope of uniting all this island under a lawful sovereign and re-establishing true religion, and he pledged himself 'ever to observe all that by the Pope and the Catholic King and the Queen of Scotland shall be ordained in this matter'.

Ridolfi was to remind Philip II of the duke's great affection for him, dating from the days when he was a member of his household in England, and to assure him that his inclination had always been towards the Spanish interest, even though at times, for reasons of state, it may have seemed that he had sided with the French. All his followers hoped Philip would agree to his continuing to conclude the match with Mary. The scheme was for Spain to provide an experienced general, commanding 6,000 arquebusiers and bringing with him twenty-five pieces of field artillery and other arms for the English force which the duke would raise – estimated at 20,000 foot and 3,000 horse. The invading army should land preferably at Harwich ('in Norfolk'),[*] 'where I, with many of the nobles resident in those parts will promptly be on the spot', though Portsmouth ('in Sussex') was

---

[*] This reveals the limitations of Ridolfi's knowledge of England. Harwich was, however, part of the liberty of Norfolk.

mentioned as an alternative. It was suggested that smaller Spanish armies might mount side-shows in Scotland and Ireland. The army under Norfolk was to rescue Mary and endeavour to capture Elizabeth and hold the capital. Action was urgent, and in the face of the negotiations for Elizabeth to wed the Duke of Anjou, it seemed to the conspirators imperative to put the enterprise into operation before the end of the summer.

Mary had already written her own letters of credence for Ridolfi, to enable the Pope 'to trust him even as you would Ourself', and now Ross provided her letters of introduction for Ridolfi to state her case at Brussels, Rome and Madrid. In this she reiterated Norfolk's loyalty, for he 'has been one of those that covertly have counselled and admonished me to stand firm and constant', and had always declared her to be the true successor to the throne. For this he has won the confidence of all the Catholics, who do not doubt his sincerity in the matter of the re-establishment of the ancient faith, yet he still retains the support of not a few Protestant nobles who favour her title against the pretender, but who would desert her cause if the duke announced a change of religion. There is no word in Mary's letter about a marriage with Norfolk, though she did ask Ridolfi to sue for a divorce from Bothwell at the Papal Court on the ground that he had seized her, kept her in captivity at Dunbar while he had procured a pretended divorce from his lawful wife and then forced her to go through a heretic form of marriage with him.

With amazing cheek Ridolfi had an audience of Elizabeth at Greenwich before he left, telling her he had to go to Italy on private business and she obliged by providing him with a 'very favourable' passport under her own hand. On Lady Day Ridolfi left for Brussels with his sheaf of documents to broach the matter with Alva, on whom he made a very poor impression. The Spanish general thought the plans unrealistic and their author a 'great babbler'. An invasion of England did not at all suit his own plans in the Netherlands, for he had neither the men nor the money to spare, and he was then straining himself to secure at all costs the restitution of the three treasure ships by deft diplomacy. An intervention in English affairs at this juncture would drive England into a French alliance, with disastrous consequences for the safety of the Spanish Netherlands. The difficulties of sending an army across the channel were legion and the chances of a successful campaign so slight that it would be foolhardy for him to make the attempt. Failure would assuredly increase the plight of the English Catholics and would almost certainly provoke Elizabeth into executing Mary Queen of Scots. Knowing that Norfolk was still confined to Howard House Alva doubted whether, as Ridolfi maintained, he could escape whenever he liked to take the field. Alva would recommend aid only if the English rebels would initially stand on their own feet; as he wrote off to Philip II: 'The Queen being dead (naturally or otherwise), dead, or else a prisoner there will be an opportunity which we must not allow to escape. The first steps must not be taken by us . . . but we may tell the duke that those conditions being fulfilled he shall have what he wants.'

Little knowing how much cold water Alva was pouring on his cherished plans, Ridolfi deemed it important to report straightway to Norfolk, Ross, the Spanish ambassador and Lumley, before journeying on to Rome. In Brussels he fell in with Charles Bailly, a Fleming in the service of the Bishop of Ross, who had been sent over to obtain copies of his pamphlet *The Defence of Queen Mary's Honour* that was being reprinted at Liège. Bailly agreed to put Ridolfi's letters into cipher, using an alphabet he had with him, 'never before used'. When he had finished the task Ridolfi put the numbers '30' and '40' on the outside of two of the sealed letters and gave instructions for their delivery, with the rest in the packet, which he was to take with him to England. But when the messenger reached Dover it was found that he had no passport for landing and his belongings and person were searched; the letters were found 'hid behind his back secretly'. As a result he was handed over to Lord Cobham, the Lord Warden of the Cinque Ports, who had him brought to his house at Blackfriars. Won over by his brother, Thomas Cobham and Francis Bartie, who were friends of Norfolk's, the Lord Warden merely took the portmanteau of seditious pamphlets to Burghley.* Cobham himself sealed the packet of letters and had it taken to Ross, on the understanding that the bishop should only open it in the Lord Warden's presence. So next day he and Ross came to Bartie's house and the seal was broken. When he saw Ridolfi's letter the bishop withdrew aside, saying 'These I cannot decipher' and the others assumed they must be for the Duke. Meanwhile

* Cecil had been raised to the peerage in February.

Burghley had been sent a report from Dover about letters being found on the Fleming and asked Cobham for them, 'whereupon it was devised that another packet was counterfeited by the Bishop of Ross and so by Lord Cobham sent to Burghley, containing letters of no moment'. Bailly was put in the Marshalsea Prison where, for the moment, we will leave him. Six months later Lord Cobham was himself to be a prisoner for his share in aiding the conspirators in this way; it would have been the Tower, but for Burghley's influence with the Queen, who permitted him to be confined to Cecil House.[11]

Ridolfi moved on to Rome, satisfied that his plans would be speedily brought to fruition, and following his audience with Pius V, Cardinal Alessandrino wrote on 8th May to assure Norfolk of the Pope's zeal for the affair and of his conviction that Philip of Spain would do his part most willingly. Within the week Pius himself wrote to both Mary and the duke. It was unnecessary, he said, to be prolix; he had commended the scheme to Philip and would rely on his judgment, since he was 'better versed in these matters than Ourself', but he was careful to add that if it proved impossible to act decisively during the coming summer they must not lose heart and wait patiently for the right opportunity.

In grand style Ridolfi had presented the Pope with a manifesto summarising the far-reaching political results which his design would achieve. The blow it would strike for Holy Church would be felt far outside the British Isles – in La Rochelle, the Netherlands and even in the remoter corners of Germany. He went so far as to predict that James VI would be brought up at Philip's court and be affianced to one of the infantas. But above all the operation was a service to God and the honour it would bring to the King of Spain 'to succour an oppressed ill-treated Queen, to chastise her that has made so little account of the obligation under which she lies to his Majesty and of his friendship and to have a second time reclaimed' England to religion. Such a document readily secured Papal blessing, but it made Alva wince.[12]

In a further memorial the Italian elaborated his earlier plans. The expedition of 2,000 men that Alva should equip for Scotland must be joined by the Earl of Westmorland, Leonard Dacre and other leading fugitives from the Northern Rebellion at present in Flanders, for the power of their names in the north would rally a considerable army of old retainers and associates 'and in better array than when they rose the last time'. A sum of 50,000 crowns would be needed for mustering a goodly army from Mary's Scottish supporters. By now Ridolfi was confident that the Earl of Derby would hold the West Midlands and the Welsh Border, 'where the people are all Catholics'. He still thought that Norfolk should throw down the challenge by rescuing Mary and then advance on the court. The main Spanish expedition of 6,000 men, with their heavy artillery, having landed at Harwich was to 'march forthwith upon London or wherever Queen Elizabeth and her counsellors may be, to the aid of those [i.e. Norfolk] in whose power they should by that time already be'. Converging armies from Scotland and the north, the West Midlands and East Anglia would effectively prevent any reinforcements from reaching Elizabeth. Ridolfi was absolutely sure his master plan could not fail, providing Spain did her duty, but he was prepared to make such changes as Alva thought necessary and accordingly asked Philip II to give his general a liberal commission to reach agreement with Norfolk and Ross. It was ironic that he should add to his paper, the ominous words: 'enterprises so important as this, in which many people are concerned cannot but by dalliance come to be discovered or interrupted.' The whole trouble with Ridolfi's plotting was that too many people were involved and he learnt too late that the cipher was not a foolproof weapon. Worse, on his way from Rome to Madrid, the babbler made it his business to stay with the Grand Duke of Tuscany and confidently told him of his plans which the duke obligingly passed on to Elizabeth.

In July Ridolfi hastened to report to Norfolk from Madrid what he considered a most favourable reception from Philip, who said he hoped through his aid soon to see the duke 'reinstated in freedom and the peaceful tenor of his life, and the Queen of Scots safeguarded in her right' and he did not doubt that Norfolk would secure the re-establishment of the true faith. In a day or so he would send a special courier to his ambassador in London with detailed instructions. Meanwhile the duke was to arrange all things 'secretly and wisely', and however desperate the situation might seem at home – even if Elizabeth should announce her betrothal to Anjou – he was to prevent any premature attempt. In fact, before Ridolfi had his audience with Philip, the latter not only had Alva's unfavourable report on him but also knew of Bailly's confession. No-one in Madrid could guess exactly how much of the plot had been unravelled by Burghley's spies, or how closely Norfolk was now being guarded, yet the King could not but give Ridolfi a hearing 'as the conspirators are so great and powerful'. Philip feared that discovery of the details would be 'the death blow' for both Mary and Howard, as Elizabeth 'will make it an excuse to wreak her ill-feeling on them, and with ample cause'. Still trusting the rumours were false yet moving very cautiously on 17th July he decided to send his special agent to London to encourage Mary and Norfolk, intimating that Alva would only send across an army once their supporters in England had successfully raised the standard of revolt and had captured Elizabeth; and Ridolfi's grand design began to lose its core. At the end of the month, undismayed by reports of the discovery of the plot, Pius V delegated to the Archbishop of St Andrews and others the task of investigating the whole case of Mary's marriage to Bothwell, yet by the time the brief reached Scotland at the end of August, the situation had radically changed.[13]

★   ★   ★

When Ross was given the packet of ciphered letters found on Bailly he decided to substitute others of a quite harmless nature which should then be forwarded to Burghley. To concoct such letters was a far easier matter than deciphering the original letters, for although he had the cipher, Bailly had 'mingled it in making up the packet' and it proved a laborious business to make head or tail of what Ridolfi had written. The bishop entrusted the task to John Cuthbert, his secretary, who had some experience of ciphers, but Ridolfi's letter to Norfolk was particularly hard to make sense of and it took Cuthbert ten days to translate, when it was sent straightway to Howard House. In it Ridolfi said that Alva had taken favourably to the scheme and would do his best to further it, but could do nothing without his master's authority. Meanwhile Norfolk was to 'keep the matter very close' and hold his friends in readiness 'for he had good hope that the matter should have good success'. An unneccessary letter that can have given the duke little satisfaction. Soon afterwards Burghley ordered a general search for the decipherer, Cuthbert, who was secreted in the French ambassador's house, but a passport was procured for him from Lord Cobham, who also sent his sister-in-law to Norfolk to arrange for the man's disappearance. Lumley, too, received his letter, but became wary and asked Ross to tell Ridolfi not to write again.

Charles Bailly grew despondent in the Marshalsea. 'One day seemeth eight days to me', he wrote to Ross, 'and to be shut up without any air almost'; and to make the time drag less heavily he asked his master to send him some good book, such as *The Golden Epistles* that was in his trunk. Bailly could not understand why he had not been brought at once before the Privy Council and feared the authorities were making full enquiries about him among English agents in Flanders, yet he resolved he would reveal nothing 'though they should pluck me in a hundred pieces'. He was relieved to learn from Ross that the incriminating letters and 'alphabet' had reached him safely, and offered to help translate them if Cuthbert became stuck. But on 21st April he was examined by Burghley about the copies of the seized pamphlet, and wrote to Ross in cipher, telling him how little he had revealed. The bishop had bribed Bailly's jailer in the Marshalsea to help convey these letters and he also tried to persuade William Herle (or Erle), another prisoner, to act as a go-between. He was a cousin of Lady Northumberland and had been arrested after the Northern Rebellion, but by now, as it happened, he was a spy of Burghley's; one letter which the Fleming sent to Ross never arrived and something Herle said convinced Bailly that he was betrayed. He was more closely questioned by Burghley who now threatened to cut off his ears, if not his head, and had him sent to the Tower where he was to be racked if he would not confess all he knew. But Bailly still held his tongue. Ross for his part required Burghley and Leicester to treat him more leniently, maintaining in high tone that it was 'a cruel and terrible practice to take ambassadors' servants and to lay them on the rack to confess their master's secrets'. He now assured Bailly that life would be a lot easier for him and exhorted him to remain steadfast. The bishop took comfort in the fact that Elizabeth's intelligence system could not break the cipher and, in any case, the letters on which they were working were the substituted ones. 'Burghley has had a secretary at work upon it for days', chuckled de Spes, 'and has sent copies to France and Italy, but without effect, for there is nothing in it.'[14]

In the stonework of his cell in the Tower Bailly carved the following inscription: 'Wise men ought to see what they do; to examine before they take in hand; to beware whose company they use, and above all things to whom they trust.' Unfortunately for the conspirators the Fleming did not practise what he preached. The racking, the thumbscrews and threats of worse to come frightened him out of his wits. Another of Burghley's spies, by pretending he was Dr Storey, the civil lawyer, who had taken refuge in Flanders for his faith and had been kidnapped the previous August to be taken home to the Tower for plotting with Alva, managed to worm his way into Bailly's confidence and advised him that the safest way of saving his life would be to reveal all he knew and offer to decode the letters. After much heart-searching Bailly gave in and early in May wrote to Burghley, telling him the broad features of Ridolfi's plans and giving general intelligence about the Countess of Northumberland, Sir Francis Englefield and other exiles. Much more important from Burghley's point of view was Bailly's statement that two of the letters he had brought over were addressed to 'two lords of the realm', under the ciphers '30' and '40'. These letters, he said, were nearly the same, except that one of them mentioned that the Duke of Norfolk was thought by the English exiles in Flanders to be 'not half a sound Catholic'. Could not the other letter, Burghley wondered, have been intended for the duke himself? A day or so later Bailly tried to ingratiate himself even further by admitting that he had helped Ridolfi with writing the letters, but he still kept quiet about Ross's counterfeit letters. He craved Burghley's aid to release him that he might then return to service with the bishop and spy on his master. The offer was not accepted and Bailly was held as a prisoner, for Burghley was convinced he had not revealed all he knew.[15]

It was inopportune that Norfolk should choose this moment to write to the Council asking for greater freedom, as his physicians had told him that exercise and a change of air was absolutely necessary, or 'my poor body is not like to endure'. He had not, as some said, set foot outside Howard House, nor had large numbers of visitors come to him; but quite apart from questions of health his personal affairs now required him to be less confined. The duke was aware of rumours that the Queen was in fact contemplating a much stricter regimen for him. 'Marry, it may be that by the sinister reports of my enemies such bruits are brought to Her Highness's ears as do cause Her Majesty to withdraw her further favour from me.' He even offered to enter into bonds for his good behaviour, but it was not the slightest use.

The first Parliament to meet since 1566, when Norfolk had spoken with such force about Elizabeth's marriage, was now in session and tempers were raised over a treasons bill. Private members' amendments to it would have barred the succession to anyone who in the Queen's lifetime had put forward a claim to the throne – a pistol aimed at the heart of Mary's pretensions – and would have made traitors of her supporters. Norfolk's henchmen in the Commons fought the amendments tooth and nail, particularly Henry Goodere, who was to be imprisoned in the autumn for carrying coded messages between Mary, Ross and the duke; but Elizabeth was equally anxious that these should not be incorporated in the Act and they were dropped. Bills making the bringing of Bulls from Rome a treasonable offence and for depriving fugitives over the water from their revenues in England received the royal assent as Burghley tried to unravel Ridolfi's skein. The Bishop of Ross had devised a madcap scheme to which the duke was privy, for 'breaking-up' that Parliament, but he had to abandon it as during the session he was removed out of London to the country where he could do no harm.[16]

At last the government decided it was time to question Ross; he pleaded illness though four of the Council who called on him found him well enough to answer them about the instructions taken abroad by Ridolfi and about the identity of '30' and '40'. The bishop admitted he had received letters sent by Ridolfi from Flanders, but that he had burnt them, and said that the Florentine had taken with him letters from Mary to Alva, the Pope and Philip II, and also a letter he had written to Alva, begging for aid 'to come into Scotland, to land at Dumbarton or Leith'. Ridolfi's commission was to solicit money from the Pope and Philip to support Mary's schemes in Scotland. 'After some long pause' Ross mentioned that '40' was the Queen, his mistress; pressed further he told Sussex that '30' was the Spanish ambassador. There for the moment the matter rested. Burghley knew Ross must be lying, for Bailly had stated categorically that each of the numbers signified an English peer; and this made him suspicious of the bishop's other answers. When he was sufficiently recovered from his illness he was moved to the Bishop of Ely's house in Holborn. Meanwhile intelligence reports came in from the continent confirming a widespread plot, assisted by foreign invasion, that had as its object Elizabeth's deposition and Mary's enthronement in her place. As for the duke, much was suspected but nothing could as yet be proved. If he were involved it would be merely a matter of time before the facts were ferreted out. At all costs Burghley had to identify the two noblemen. Other intelligence systems were also active for on 10th May the Spanish ambassador in London wrote off to Philip II and Pius V giving Bailly's own account of his confession: 'I have not confessed so much, but that Milord Burghley gave me to understand that he knew much more of Ridolfi's journey.'[17]

There were other plots in the wind, for rescuing Mary. Since the beginning of 1570 there had been at least half-a-dozen schemes and in each case Norfolk had been asked for his views on them and on those who were to put them into effect. Ross at one time had thought that a few Spanish troops despatched to Scotland might easily overthrow the Regent Lennox and establish a new government favourable to Mary. The Queen herself favoured a *coup de main* to free her and whisk her out of the kingdom to Spain. Hugh Owen, Arundel's servant, had his head full of ideas, and when Mary lay at Chatsworth came to Ross with 'a great map of England' to show him how easy it would be for her to escape to the west. Later they brooded over other plans: one was for her removal to East Anglia, where Sir Nicholas L'Estrange would see her safely embarked at King's Lynn. Ross himself measured the windows at Chatsworth and was satisfied Mary could climb through them into the park and into freedom if horses and riders were organised. He asked Norfolk for his opinion and he replied that Sir Henry Percy was 'the fittest man in England for the task'. Once again, however, the plans petered out. Nothing daunted Sir Thomas Stanley, second son of the Earl of Derby, and Sir Thomas Gerrard said they were prepared to try and rescue her, and the duke through Barker gave his assent. It was too difficult to leave Chatsworth at night as all Mary's servants were locked in their rooms, so instead they decided to make the attempt when the Queen 'walked to the height of the moors'. Horses were to take her to the Lancashire coast where a vessel would be waiting to bring her to the Isle of

Man, the Earl of Derby's private *imperium*, and 'thence whither she liked'. In the event John Beton, Mary's personal retainer, persuaded her that the risks were too great, though Ross had for weeks been confident.

As part of that scheme John Hall of Tynedale, who had once been in Shrewsbury's service, had been won over by the bishop, to have 'a melling' and intelligence, because of his good standing in the earl's household, and when the scheme was abandoned he acted as a messenger, riding between London, Chatsworth and further afield. In the spring of 1571 he was given letters from Ross to take to Mary's staunch suporters Lords Herries and Fleming and he made his way through Lancashire and took a boat to the Isle of Man, the route intended for Mary, and eventually sailed on to Whitehaven in Scotland. Hall delivered the letter to Lord Herries and went on to Dumbarton Castle where Lord Fleming was, riding in the company of the Abbot of Arbroath for greater security. Unfortunately he tarried too long at Dumbarton for on the night of 2nd-3rd April the castle fell to the Regent Lennox, as a result of a gallant action by Captain Crawford; Hall was arrested and Ross's letter, giving details of Mary's relations with Alva, was found. Lennox examined him and sent him down to London where he disclosed to Sir Thomas Smith and Dr Wilson, Burghley's henchmen, a great many facts. Still hoping for the identity of '30' and '40' to be revealed, Burghley cross-questioned Sir Thomas Stanley, Sir Thomas Gerrard and Francis Rolleston in July and sent them to the Tower, but without success. The vital clue was to be presented to him six weeks later from other letters bound for Scotland, and within a matter of days he had all the threads of the conspiracy in his hands.[18]

One night in August 'a great arch of fire appeared in the heavens' for two hours and then broke up into many parts. The superstitious Londoners who saw it were greatly disturbed, not knowing what terrible event it might portend, and if Howard was told about it next morning perhaps he was reminded of the horoscope the Italian astrologer had drawn up for him the day he was born. Before the end of the month he and his servants had taken a fatal step. Meanwhile a close watch was being kept on Howard House and on Burghley's instructions lists of the household and of all visitors were prepared so that all could be examined.[19]

A neighbour of the duke's in Charterhouse Square was the French ambassador, de La Mothe Fénélon and in August he received three hundred French gold crowns and three hundred English angels which had been subscribed by Mary's supporters in France. For some months, indeed, the hopes of her party in Scotland had been kept alive by money coming from abroad. The ambassador at first planned to send the gold by one of Ross's servants, but then he had second thoughts, as the man being a Scot might be searched by his compatriots. Staying with Fénélon was M. de Foix, who was in England to conduct the negotiations for Elizabeth's projected marriage with the Duke of Anjou, and William Barker, Norfolk's confidential secretary, called on him to renew a friendship they had struck up when his master had been created a Knight of the French Order of St Michael. As a result Barker agreed to arrange with the duke for the delivery of the bag of money and accompanying letters. From time to time he had sent secret correspondence from Howard House into Scotland through Lawrence Bannister, the duke's 'officer general in the north' and at the end of July Barker had sent him a packet of ciphered letters from Norfolk and Ross. Barker and Higford were on the best of terms with Bannister, who earlier in his career had been with them at Kenninghall, and with the July packet Higford had sent Mrs Bannister a pair of harvest gloves. On Sunday 26th August the ambassador's servant crossed the Square to Howard House and delivered the bag of money and letters to Barker in the chapel.

On the Wednesday following a ciphered letter to Bannister was added to the bag, which was then sealed with the duke's great seal. Bannister was told that the money 'must be presently sent to Lowther', another of Norfolk's officials in the north, who was Goodere's brother-in-law, 'to be conveyed to Scotland to the Lord Herries, to be sent by him forthwith to Leddington and Grange, according to a letter which is among the money'. The bag was then given to Higford who later in the day entrusted it to Thomas Browne, a Shrewsbury draper then in London on business, who knew Bannister well, as he bought butter from him. Browne was told the bag contained £50 in silver, which was Bannister's own money, and he agreed to arrange for its safe delivery to him. By the same hands Robert Higford sent Bannister his usual chatty letter – not in cipher – with details of goods he had bought for him, news of the Anjou marriage negotiations, of Elizabeth's impending visit to Audley End and that all the household at Kenninghall were now on hunting progress at Flitcham. Higford was not feeling as well as he might and sighed for 'a quiet life'. Ominous words indeed![20]

The Shrewsbury draper knew enough about the weight of coins to realise that the bag was far too heavy if it contained only £50 in silver, but like everyone else in London he knew that everything connected with Howard House was at that time under grave suspicion, so he decided to break the seal and see what was inside. When Browne saw the gold coins and the ciphered letters he realised it was time to report it to the authorities and as a result Higford and Barker were both examined by Sir Thomas Smith and Dr Wilson on Sunday 2nd September and the dénouement of the Ridolfi plot began.

Under pressure Higford agreed to decipher the letters as far as he could from memory and said he would reveal everything he knew; but his translation was not word perfect. Sir Thomas Smith wrote to Burghley: 'in my mind the matter being now so manifestly opened and the duke taken as it were ἐπ αὐτοφώρῳ* it were very fit he were more safely kept.' He then asked Higford if there were not a key to the cipher at Howard House. Higford at first either would not, or could not, recall where it was, but frightened of being racked he suddenly thought he remembered it 'was left under the mat, hard by the window side in the entry towards my Lord's bed-chamber, where the Map of England doth hang'. When Neville went in haste to turn up the mat he found the key to the cipher 'gotten away', but in its place was a much more incriminating document – a ciphered letter, that was later found to be from Mary Queen of Scots. It was by itself enough to hang a man. This was the break for which Burghley had being praying for weeks, and the good news reached him the same night at Audley End. He straightway instructed Sadler to repair to Howard House and prepare to examine the duke and by eight next morning Sadler was there.[21]

As soon as Higford and Barker had been taken off, Norfolk in desperation tried to concoct a satisfactory explanation for the bag of gold, for he knew he was bound to be questioned about it. What he thought out was a not very convincing story about £200

* i.e. caught in the act.

being due to his vintner and so forth, but the least he could do
was to try and ensure that all the culprits told the same tale and
he managed somehow to get in touch with his secretaries and to
get word back from them, whereupon he wrote off to Bannister
in Shropshire. It was not the slightest use, for Higford under
threat of torture had broken down. Later in the month Bannister's
house was searched and the letters with others were discovered in
his study 'nailed under a mat'. Mats had a fatal fascination for
our conspirators.

In Madrid Philip II, ignorant of the turn of events, was writing
to de Spes to encourage Norfolk to carry out his 'laudable and
Christian purpose'; in London Lord Buckhurst trusted the duke
would be able to clear himself, 'otherwise he must lose many
friends that are now abused with a quite contrary opinion of him'.
In the Tower that afternoon Higford and Barker revealed further
details about ciphered letters and as a result Sir Henry Neville
confined Howard to his chamber at Howard House and secluded
all but two of his servants from him. Burghley instructed Smith,
Wilson and Sadler, the duke's old friend from his days at Berwick
and colleague at the York commission, to examine him, but
Norfolk denied all, unaware that the confessions of Higford and
Barker had cut the ground from under his feet. If, remarked
Sadler, all that Higford said were true 'then is the duke a devil and
no Christian man'. On Friday, the 7th September, when a warrant
arrived from the Queen for conveying him to the Tower, he was
questioned again and at last became more submissive, admitting
some part of his share in the arrangements for sending letters and
money to Mary's supporters in Scotland.[22]

A horse was got ready, caparisoned with foot cloth, to take the
duke with some vestiges of dignity to the Tower; it was eleven
months since he had ridden. On one side of him rode Sadler, on
the other was Sir Thomas Smith, while Dr Wilson came behind.
None of Norfolk's servants was allowed to accompany him.
The little procession arrived at the Tower about 5 p.m. 'without
any trouble save a number of idle rascal people – women, men,
boys and girls – running about him, as the manner is gazing at
him'. A servant of the Spanish ambassador was among the crowd
of sightseers and told his master that as there was no regular guard
for the noble prisoner and since the shouts of the populace were
so much in his favour, 'a very little more and he would have been

liberated'; he added, rather oddly, that Norfolk seemed 'very gay'. He was only to leave the Tower for his trial.[23]

The same day that the bag of French gold had been brought to Howard House Norfolk had written to Leicester and Burghley lamenting the fact that Elizabeth, on her summer progress, had decided to stay at Audley End, the house of Thomas, the duke's second son, who had been born there. He felt sure that the boy's tender years and lack of experience in courtly matters should exempt him from the highly expensive honour of having to entertain the Queen and her entourage for five days. Such pleading had been of no avail, for Elizabeth had made up her mind. When she arrived at Audley 'great means were used to Her Majesty to put [Norfolk] in full liberty ... whereunto Her Majesty seemed to give favourable ear, specially upon asseverations that it was thought that he would become a good subject and that he had foresaken the matter of the Queen of Scots and that he was not suspected of Her Majesty to be any of the two lords ciphered with 40 or 30' (wrote Burghley long afterwards). By a touch of irony she was still in residence there when the fateful news came from London of the overwhelming evidence against the duke. The Privy Council, sitting at Audley, approved orders for Sir Thomas Wrothe to repair to Howard House, summon the duke's officers and make a complete inventory of his goods. Similar instructions were sent to Sir Christopher Heydon to survey all his properties in Norfolk and by 26th September he and his fellows had finished their long task. It was 1547 all over again.[24]

Heydon, who had been sheriff the year before, was assisted by Sir William Buttes, Sir Edward Clere, the deputy lieutenants, and Thomas Sydney. They made an interesting quartet. Earlier in the reign Clere had been a protégé of Norfolk's and had sat as M.P. for Thetford, but before 1569 he had parted company with his former patron. Thomas Sydney was the customer of King's Lynn and had been included owing to the difficulty of finding in the county another knight who was not a supporter of the duke; he had married Barbara, the sister of Sir Francis Walsingham. All four were men who had their eyes on inheriting the remnants of the duke's power in the county. Before long Heydon and Sydney were to fall out, as a result of a complaint to the former of the widespread corruption among the customs staff at Lynn, which was to bring the port under close scrutiny, though thanks to his brother-in-law's growing influence at court Sydney managed to cling to office despite the revelation of a series of most shady transactions.[25]

The visitors found the servants at Kenninghall and elsewhere 'very sorrowful for the duke his trouble', but they co-operated in the disheartening task of making a grand inventory of his possessions. They patiently listed the furniture, pictures and other belongings in every room of each residence. Each item of the extensive wardrobe of the late duchess at Kenninghall was described – French gowns of pink taffeta, of crimson velvet with wide sleeves of cloth of tissue, fifty other dresses and her fine set of altar cloths and copes. They inspected a number of items parcelled up ready for sending to Audley End, they even noted the presence of holy water sprinklers in the armoury at Norwich and noticed the edition of the Bible in Thetford chapel. They reckoned that the duke's flocks totalled some 16,800 sheep, but reported that most of them were 'in lease and cannot be had till the leases fall in'. Heydon was surprised to find so little plate and passed on to Burghley the explanation given by the staff, that nearly a year before Howard had sent most of his plate and jewels to London to be sold. 'We have not left to our knowledge any closet or coffer of the duke unsearched', he reported, 'but only his Grace's evidence house at Kenninghall.' Mr Hassett, the custodian of the only key, was out of the county, so Heydon put a new lock on the door, sealed it up and left the key with Edward Pecocke, the clerk controller.[26]

Philip, Earl of Arundel, aged fourteen, had been greatly perturbed by the arrival of the commissioners, which 'doth make me greatly afraid that the Queen is very much displeased with my lord my father' and he wrote to Burghley beseeching him to remember his old friendship with the duke and help to mitigate the Queen's anger. Early in October Heydon and Buttes received orders from the Privy Council for closing down Kenninghall Palace and for establishing a separate household for Norfolk's children at Audley End on lines very similar to those proposed by the duke himself in his will; but the Council were taking no chances and listed the sixty-five persons who were to accompany the seven young Howards and Dacres. Sir Nicholas and Lady

L'Estrange were to supervise the domestic arrangements of the household while the scholastic side was to be in the charge of George Laughton, a Fellow of King's College, Cambridge and a sound Protestant, who had replaced Gregory Martin, the friend of Campion. Nurse Foster was to remain to look after the youngest children and Jane Goodman – the same who as a girl had been left a legacy by the third duke – was still a member of the household, in an honoured position as a kind of unofficial aunt. Four gentlemen in waiting, a page, three yeomen in waiting, three grooms of the chamber, kitchen staff, laundry maids, grooms of the stable, a porter, a slaughterman and a woodcutter were all ordered to prepare for their removal. Some sixty servants were left and those that had no houses of their own on the estate were required by the Council to make a home with friends. All but three or four aged retainers, whom nobody wanted to look after, were suitably settled; to relieve the old folk the commissioners decided off their own bat to give them a pension, a charitable gesture which would have warmed the duke's heart. In the end all was ready and on 12th October Arundel's party set out for Audley End. The gates of Kenninghall Palace were closed and would not re-open during Norfolk's lifetime.[27]

Chapter Twelve

WESTMINSTER HALL

1571-2

'MY LORD of Norfolk's causes filleth out daily more and more to the offence of Her Majesty', wrote Burghley to Shrewsbury on 18th September, 'whereof in respect of the honour and love I bear him I am right sorry.' The long series of examinations of witnesses, accomplices and of the duke himself was only at a beginning, for it lasted into December. William Barker was examined on no fewer than twenty-one occasions, Robert Higford on twelve and Lawrence Bannister on ten. Sir Thomas Smith and Dr Thomas Wilson, on whom the brunt of the questioning fell, soon craved to be relieved from their 'unpleasant and painful' toil, which sometimes involved the torture of prisoners, because the Queen insisted on it. They told Burghley they would not want to be Minos, Aeacus or Rhadamanthus, the dread judges from the Homeric underworld, but rather play the part of the least of the shades in the Elysian Fields. Never before had investigations into a case of high treason been conducted with such thoroughness or given rise to such mounds of paper. From all the evidence they accumulated, every fact that added to Norfolk's guilt was extracted, for this time the duke had over-reached himself, and, when the indictment was ready, would assuredly go for trial before his peers in Westminster Hall.[1]

When Mary heard of the duke's re-arrest she burst out in self-defence that all she had tried to do was to regain her own throne; 'those who said that she had done more were false villains and lied in their throats.' As for Norfolk, she added, he was the Queen of England's subject 'and for him she had nothing to say'.

On his knees Norfolk now told the truth about the bag of gold and letters sent to Bannister and admitted he had again been corresponding with Mary, though he insisted that none of their letters had 'tended to renew or continue the matter of marriage'. As for the letter of February, found under the mat at Howard House where the cipher should have been, he denied ever having seen it. Next day he wrote a most humble submission to Elizabeth, praying for pardon 'with an overwhelmed heart and watery cheek', as he now realised how serious the situation was. 'Woeworth the day', he lamented, when he had first contemplated the Scottish marriage which had brought him into such intolerable troubles, whereas all his days he had 'coveted nothing but a quiet life'.

This time the Tower was to be kept 'very strait' and every precaution was taken to prevent messages passing. Sir Owen Hopton, the Lieutenant, intercepted one anonymous letter to the duke: 'We received from you, though not at that length that was desired. Your friends at court dare not deal. There are two ways to receive intelligence and both, I hope, trusty. You shall hear this day of some things that stand you upon to be very circumspect how you do confess, for in confessing there may be much peril. Your case, for anything we can learn, groweth very hard, therefore standeth you in hand to comfort yourself as you may and God comfort you. We hear not whether you have well looked on the covering of your book.' This obvious clue was followed up and inside the binding of his copy of *Flores Historiarum*, which Norfolk had sent for, were found various documents. On another occasion the duke's Bible was taken from him and found to contain three ciphers. The books in the library at Howard House were also searched and the most recent edition of *Grafton's Chronicle* revealed a cipher and a letter. Despite the close watch kept on him, Norfolk still managed to send and receive a few letters, for Elizabeth Massey, the wife of the Chaplain in the Tower, had been persuaded by the duke's laundress to co-operate with her. The laundress had told Mrs Massey in no uncertain terms that Elizabeth would not be Queen for much longer, 'being a bastard', nor could she take Norfolk's life from him, 'for he hath too many sparks abroad'.[2]

In his cell in the Beauchamp Tower Higford had been put to

deciphering letters from memory, but he could not make a satisfactory progress without the key, so the duke was charged with having it. He thought it had once been kept for security under the tiles and might still be in the roof of Howard House. The unfortunate Higford was again questioned by Smith and recalled that it had indeed been put under the tiles in the days before the workmen had finished. Next day the confidential secretary was convinced the paper was still in the roof and offered to show where he thought it might be, so Smith and Dr Wilson accompanied him to Howard House, where Higford found the cipher 'betwixt two tiles in the roof, so hid as it had not been possible to have found it otherwise than by unripping all the tiles, except one had been well acquainted with the place'. The discovery of this cipher enabled further damning evidence against Norfolk to be brought to light.[3]

Robert Higford had begun by lying, but in successive examinations he steadily lost ground to his accusers and on 28th September, to try and save himself, wrote out a full confession. He admitted he had 'done many things in the Scottish affairs against my professed allegiance' and was privy to many matters which he should have revealed to the Queen or her Council. In particular he had written and translated many ciphered letters to or from Mary and Ross, and had arranged for the duke to receive and send letters when he was first in the Tower by passing them in leather bottles and then, when the regimen was relaxed, by messenger. Though the duke's confidential secretary, Higford said he was 'a man of simple wit . . . not worthy to bear the name of Secretary'; he knew most of his master's secrets but was never asked for his opinion about the designs that were afoot. Over and over again he claimed he knew of no practice which would imperil the Queen's person or bring civil strife. When asked if he had heard that there were astrologers and others in England who were attempting to divine the Scottish Queen's future, he remembered the duke once saying to him 'Higford thou shalt hear see a foolish prophecy' and passing him a paper. This prophecy, in Latin, was that when the moon shall rise (meaning the rising of the Earl of Northumberland), then a lion (Her Majesty) shall be overthrown, and a lion and lioness shall be conjoined (Norfolk and Mary, each having lions in their arms, shall marry), and their whelps shall reign. In due course this prophecy was made public at the duke's trial and fully expounded. For sharing his master's secrets, Higford the cipher expert was to be tried for high treason himself in February, found guilty and sentenced to death.[4]

William Barker, the other secretary, was Higford's junior. A Cambridge man, he had travelled in Italy, where he had hob-nobbed with Sir Thomas Hobby, the translator of *Il Cortigiana*, which became the standard work on the education of a gentle-man. It was Norfolk's fate to have entrusted him with matters which put him under a constant strain; as Barker put it, he was never of much account in the household except in times of adver-sity, when he was 'put to do that I detest'. Fear of the rack made him confess and, as Sir Thomas Smith well knew, once he had decided to open his mouth the confidences of three summers flowed in ceaseless torrent – anything, Barker thought, that would rid him of the clog that encumbered his conscience.

He told of 'the grand resort' to Norfolk throughout the omin-ous summer of '69 and of the money passing from Howard House to Ross, for Mary's use, beginning with £1,000 which the duke had received from Ridolfi in September of that year. Barker was able to give graphic accounts of the whole series of plots to liberate Mary and proved himself a key witness for the duke's assent to Ridolfi's conspiracy, for he told his questioners of the two visits the Italian paid Norfolk in the spring of 1571, of the list of noblemen friendly to Mary's cause, which the duke liked 'well enough', and of his acting as intermediary at Ross's house when de Spes was present. 'When the duke refused to subscribe the letters which should have gone to the Duke of Alva, and other, yet to satisfy the Spanish ambassador, the Bishop of Ross . . . this examinate [Barker] went to the Spanish ambassador, bidden by the duke, and told him that the duke was content and glad to relieve the Scottish Queen; and that she had appointed Ridolfi to go to the Duke of Alva, the Pope, the King of Spain, about that matter; and that the duke was content that those letters in his commendations should be written and sent, and that he was privy to that journey and liked it well. And further he saith, all this message he did at the duke's commandment, given this examinate in Howard House in the gallery . . .' De Spes was satisfied of the duke's good intention and would certify that the letters of credence were as well from him as from Mary . . . Damning evidence indeed.

From his 'dull memory' Barker recalled the contents of Ridolfi's letter to Norfolk from Flanders, and that '40' stood for his master and '30' for Lumley. Indeed he revealed a great deal about ciphers, the gist of many letters passing between Mary and Norfolk and the words of the Pope's missive to the latter. Barker also mentioned a bag of the duke's writings, including letters from Mary, which had been left for safety with a tailor in Aldersgate Street, who buried it in the ground. As an M.P. he had kept Ross informed of what went on in the Commons during the late Parliament and of the outspoken attacks on his mistress. The bishop had told him: 'In Scotland five or six lords could disturb the whole Parliament . . . Will my lord duke do nothing for her?'; and though Barker had told him that such a proceeding was out of the question, his conscience would not allow him to forget about it all. And the same was true of his versifying. Before a visit to Chatsworth, Ross was compiling a book of songs and ballads and he asked Barker for a contribution in an English metre, and now the secretary felt it was necessary to quote the first stanza to his examiners:

Whan thow hast felt what Fortune ys,
   And fownd hyr firme to sew,
Thy Trade in Truth and Fayth parformyd,
   Shall clere all clowdy shew.

('Some more verses there were, which I do not remember.') Ross showed Mary the poem 'and told her more of me, wherefore she wrote a letter of thanks to me'.

Barker knew too much and trotted it all out. Next to Ross no man's testimony did so much to bring Norfolk to the block. Though tried in King's Bench on 31st January and sentenced to death for high treason, he was reprieved and in 1574 pardoned. That Higford should have suffered and Barker escaped was scant justice.[5]

Norfolk made a poor showing in his cross-examination on the additional evidence provided by Barker, though he insisted that only once had Ridolfi visited him at Howard House in the early spring. He had written again to the Privy Council, in all humility praying them to use their influence with Elizabeth to pardon him, though in this letter he foolishly went out of his way to maintain that he had never, by plain writing or cipher, assented to any scheme which might prejudice the Queen or the safety of her realm. It was unconvincing as it went against all the evidence so formidably assembled and still being augmented. Accordingly, on 13th October the Privy Council called the Lord Mayor and aldermen of London together and informed them of the duke's complicity in a plot to dethrone Elizabeth with Spanish and Papal aid, and soon his guilt was common talk.[6]

Of Lawrence Bannister much was suspected. Not only was the bag of French gold with the cipher letters addressed to him, but he had long ago been in Lord Herries' service. It was Bannister with whom Norfolk had talked at St Albans when on his way to Windsor to submit to Elizabeth and Bannister who had been among the few trusted servants to be allowed to visit his master in the Tower in 1570. As soon as he was arrested, the papers in his study at his house at Wem in Shropshire were impounded, and in the Tower he was 'threatened to the rack and tasted the smart thereof'. The commissioners went the whole gamut of Norfolk's affairs with him and although he could tell them no new, startling facts he provided some nice touches of detail. There was the conversation in the lovely garden at Howard House in March 1569 in which the duke had told him he was being pressed by many friends to marry Mary, but liked it not and thought his brother Henry would make a more suitable husband for her. Later, when Norfolk had made up his mind, Bannister had warned him of the danger of pursuing the affair; and he was sorry 'his lordship's hap was to fix his mind of no other person, for I partly knew by former experience that when he is entered into matter of love he will hardly be removed from the same'. When Howard was in the Tower Bannister had provided the money for Barker to buy two rings, each set with diamonds, which were sent to Mary as love tokens, and in August when he returned to Howard House the duke had asked him to keep safely various tokens Mary had sent him – seven handkerchiefs, a pair of writing-tables 'and a little tablet of gold wherein was set the Queen of Scots' picture'. Bannister also told of his bringing to Norfolk from Ross the letters of credence for Ridolfi, and how the duke had exclaimed, as he read them, 'God's blood, would the Bishop have me to do this? If I should set my hand to this I shall commit treason'. Bannister, a Justice of the Peace for his county, was a straightforward witness, conscious of his master's failings, yet unwilling to be disloyal. Not for nothing that Norfolk said at his trial, 'I would sooner have trusted one Bannister than fifteen Barkers'. There was nothing to incriminate him personally in Norfolk's tragedy and twenty years on he was still living in a house in Charterhouse Square.[7]

The staff at Howard House were then grilled. There was Lyggons who had often let in Ross by the back door; there was Chaplain Sewell who had bribed Sir Henry Neville's footman to take the duke's letters; and there was John Sinclair, the gardener, who was regarded with some suspicion as he was a Scot – perhaps he was the first of the long line of Scots that have beautified the gardens of English noblemen. At any rate in the Tower all the information Sinclair could give was classed by his interrogators as 'alehouse babbling, such as is common with such rascals'. Sir Nicholas L'Estrange, Norfolk's chamberlain, and the hardworking Cantrell and Dix were all able to vindicate themselves completely, though for a few months Cantrell was kept in custody.

Henry Goodere, the M.P., was among those called in for questioning and admitted not only taking letters between Mary, Ross and Norfolk, but also writing to the duke in cipher about his projected marriage. In the cipher which he had devised for this correspondence two different forms of the letter W stood for Mary and for Norfolk respectively, as if to signify they would soon be one.

The one individual who escaped examination was the arch conspirator himself. When he was in Paris at Michaelmas Ridolfi had learnt that every facet of his grandiose scheme had been brought to light and knew he could never again set foot in England. After a short stay in Flanders, where he found himself despised as heartily by the English exiles as by the Spanish, he returned to Rome where Pius V shortly before he died created him a papal senator. By dint of abandoning a life of international intrigue Ridolfi survived for another forty years in his native Florence, where he lived the life of a leisured senator, making a comfortable income from his financial dealings.[8]

Ross was brought up to London to the Lord Mayor's house from his enforced retreat in Cambridgeshire for further examinations. On the way he received a message from Fénélon that Norfolk had not made a detailed confession and that it would be safe for him to deny all; but the bishop was soon to grasp that

such a course was utterly impossible. To clear the air Burghley
had already put to the civil lawyers the question whether an
ambassador who endeavoured to bring about a rebellion against
the sovereign to whom he was accredited, was entitled to enjoy
diplomatic privileges. The doctors answered that in international
law such a man was indeed liable to punishment and they added
that Ross was not even a proper ambassador, but 'the solicitor of a
lawfully deposed queen'.

The bishop who had been so confident when questioned in
May was prepared to brazen it out again. After being kept in
suspense for five days, Burghley, three other councillors and the
soilcitor and attorney general called on him, and when he hedged
they told him of the civilians' opinion and warned him of severe
punishment unless he made a full confession. Ross now became
thoroughly scared and feared his life, for he was sent to the Tower
and his servants were given three days to leave the country. He
concluded that too much telling evidence had already been
amassed for him to attempt to save Norfolk and that he must, as
his accusers advised, save his own skin, even at the expense of his
mistress's position. In the course of a week he made a clean breast
of the conversations with the duke at the York Conference and
of the relations between him and Mary since that autumn. He
told of the various attempts to rescue Mary from her first days at
Bolton and revealed a number of fresh facts in the chain of events
leading to the Rebellion of the Earls. He related the inner history
of the Ridolfi Plot with as much detail as if he were dictating his
memoirs, and at last Burghley had from an impeccable source the
full story of the substituted letters, confirmation of the identity
of '30' and '40' and of the rest of the secrets wrung only partially
from Bailly. Ross spoke of his visits to Howard House where,
despite Neville's precautions, the back door was left unbarred and
told of the letters, messages and tokens that had passed between
Mary and the duke, including the affair of the embroidered cushion. Norfolk's guilt was proved up to the hilt, and not only
Norfolk, for in his eagerness to save himself Ross incriminated
Lord Cobham and his brother, Lumley, Arundel, Southampton,
Sir Thomas Stanley and a host of others, including the Spanish
ambassador. He felt relieved at having confessed so fully; relieved,
even, that the match between his mistress and the duke had not
succeeded, for he let out that Mary was not fit to have a husband,

would never have kept faith with Norfolk for long and he 'should not have had the best days with her'. She had, he said, poisoned her first husband, Francis II, consented to Darnley's murder, married the murderer and then led him out to the battlefield that he in turn might be murdered. This frank betrayal was too much for Dr Wilson: 'Lord what people are these' he wrote off to Burghley, 'what a Queen, and what an ambassador!' The prince among witnesses, his examiners would not leave him alone even after Norfolk's trial, but retraced the ground again and again in order to prepare an equally cast-iron case against the Queen of Scots.[9]

By permission the bishop wrote to Mary telling her it had been necessary to reveal all and regretting they had 'ever meddled with such things' as Ridolfi's design. So sure was Mary of his loyalty that when she heard he had made a full confession she assumed it must have been extracted from him under torture, and burst out to Shrewsbury, her keeper, that he was 'a flayed and fearful priest'. A letter in his hand was no guarantee, she decided; 'the hand was Esau's hand, but the voice was Jacob's; the bishop held the pen, but someone else had guided it'.

*   *   *

The duke had been questioned again about the fresh evidence provided by Ross and now begged Burghley once more to intercede with Elizabeth, for he 'cannot excuse' his continued prosecution of the marriage with Mary and threw himself absolutely on his sovereign's mercy. As a result Elizabeth commanded him to write out a confession; but his 'brief declaration' of 10th November contains not a word about Ridolfi, although it runs to 6,000 words, and claimed to deal with his affairs down to the day on which he was writing. It is largely his version of the events of the summer of 1569 and he attempted to show that he had the Council and peerage behind him when he took up in earnest the marriage scheme with Mary as a service to Elizabeth. Burghley, who was suffering from gout, asked in reply if he had anything further to confess, which reduced Norfolk to tears. He says, reported his gaoler, Skipwith, 'he can write nothing more concerning the great matters, or anything else that concerns Her Majesty or the State. I have used as many ways as I can to persuade him, but other answer than this I cannot get. He concludeth

in great lamenting manner for Her Majesty's indignation and
saith he knoweth not how to redress it.'[10]

In essence Norfolk's treachery lay in the fact that under colour
of restoring Mary Queen of Scots to liberty he had conspired to
place her on the throne of England. An unwilling, and at times
unconscious, traitor but a traitor for all that; and however much
Burghley's colleagues on the Council might feel that the duke
had been the victim of Ridolfi's scheming they knew they could
not draw back from putting him on trial, with the verdict a
foregone conclusion; as Hunsdon put it, 'Her Majesty and he
cannot continue in one realm'.

In mid-November from the mass of documents Burghley made
a summary under thirteen heads of the principal offences with
which Norfolk was to be charged, 'partly by his own confession,
partly by others, and by writings and letters in cipher and otherwise'. Six of the charges related to the year beginning September
1568, the others to events between then and September 1571, and
it will be convenient to give this document in its entirety.[11]

1. The disclosing of the Queen Majesty's counsel when he
   was in commission at York in favour of the Queen of
   Scots, both to cover her faults and to further of her
   marriage.
2. The labouring to marry with the Queen of Scots, without
   Her Majesty's knowledge, whom he himself had known
   to have attempted the depriving of Her Majesty from her
   crown and had not made satisfaction to Her Majesty.
3. The aiding of her and her ministers with sundry sums of
   money and the recovering into his custody sundry great
   sums of money sent from the Duke of Alva to her use.
4. The knowledge of the intentions of the Northern
   Rebellion.
5. The knowledge of the intentions of certain lords to have
   taken the Tower of London with all the treasure and
   munition in it, thereby to have commanded the Queen
   Majesty etc.
6. The continual writing and conference by ciphered letters
   betwixt the Queen of Scots and him.

All these premises preceded the time of his first committing to
the Tower.

7. Notwithstanding his committing to the Tower for dealing with the Queen of Scots (and notwithstanding the Queen's Majesty's indignation declared for that attempt), yet he did secretly continue his former practice with the Queen of Scots by letters, messengers and others.

8. He made a submission to the Queen Majesty and acknowledged his offence, and promised by writing never to deal in that matter; and yet he dealt with the Scots Queen for her directions therein and immediately continued his former practices with her. He also gave consent by the Bishop of Ross in the matter of the treaty.

9. He also aided the Queen of Scots and her ministers with money to maintain the Queen Majesty's enemies in Scotland that received and maintained her rebels, and did also help by his advice how money that was sent from the Pope for the relief of the rebels should be distributed amongst them.

10. He also was maintainer of a great number of practices to have had the Scots Queen taken away, part by force, part by fraud.

11. He was principal counsellor and director of Ridolfi to persuade to the Duke of Alva, the Pope and the King of Spain to have foreign force to invade this realm and Ireland, and to have maintained the Scots Queen in this realm by force.

12. He continued the practice of Ridolfi and received letters both from him in cipher and from the Pope two several times, and helped to convey away the Scot John Cuthbert that deciphered the letters.

13. He was made privy to an attempt of a violent breaking up of the last Parliament and a taking of the Queen Majesty's person with others of the court.

All these things above-mentioned he is charged with all to have been done before he was committed now last to the Tower.

Undoubtedly the most serious item was the eleventh, which related to foreign invasion, and although Norfolk was guilty of giving his assent to the scheme it was a gross over-statement to term him Ridolfi's 'principal counsellor and director'. What

TH Q

Elizabeth still regarded as the worst offence was the first, his betrayal of the trust she had placed in him at the York Conference, which had led inexorably to the rest; and after that his breaking his solemn word about never again dealing with Mary (number 8). The fifth and thirteenth charges about the duke's knowledge of designs to take the Tower and break up the Parliament were technically true, though of little significance in the light of the other charges on which Norfolk's guilt was now unquestioned; and for Norfolk to maintain that he never acted to the Queen's prejudice either 'by plain writing or by cipher' damaged him even more seriously.[12]

In further preparation for the trial Burghley set a lawyer to the task of jotting down useful maxims to adorn the speeches of the prosecutors, though most were platitudes. 'It is reason that accessory follow the nature of the principal ... The ignorance of the deed excuseth, but not ignorance of the law.' But one dictum on the list did not appeal to the Secretary: 'In all penal cases the gentlest interpretation is to be made for all judgments.' Meanwhile Gerrard, the Attorney General, wrote out in his crabbed hand page upon page of extracts from the depositions and examinations of the witnesses. The duke did what he could to prepare a defence and, despite what he said at his trial, he must have had a few law books by him or he would never have quoted Bracton or known about Stafford's case, on which he was basing his claim to be represented by counsel, a claim which he felt certain would be allowed. Meanwhile since he was denied access to his lawyers he must have regretted he had not taken his days at Gray's Inn more seriously.[13]

While Elizabeth was thankful that at last the conspiracy had been laid bare, she took cold comfort in the fact that various of her nobles had to a greater or lesser degree been involved in Norfolk's schemings. Whom beside Burghley could she trust? By mid-October Lumley had been sent to the Marshalsea Prison, Southampton, another zealous papist, was again in the Tower, while Cobham was under arrest in Cecil House and Arundel placed under guard in Arundel House. As yet she knew nothing of Oxford's intrigues but, as usual, Leicester's position was not at all clear and he it was who had proposed the match with Mary in 1569. Since the duke was connected by marriage to all the peers, Elizabeth could not but feel there might be others sympathetic to

his cause, and if tried by his peers what would their verdict be? At
least one of Derby's sons and a stepson of Shrewsbury were deep
in the plot and over the water and north of the border were
others intriguing for all they were worth. Among courtiers even
Sir Christopher Hatton was uncertain in his loyalties. Burghley
apart she could rely only upon Bacon, Knollys, Sadler and her
cousin Hunsdon among the inner circle of her Council; but none
of these was popular, while Burghley, her greatest supporter, had
earned almost as much enmity up and down the land as Thomas
Cromwell.

Despite the treacherous role he had played, there was still much
sympathy in the country for the duke for the people loved him
dearly. In the north and in his own East Anglia men could not
believe that the Queen would not pardon him. A friend of
Browne, the Shrewsbury draper, told Burghley how outspoken
many of the Shropshire gentry were of the way Norfolk was
being treated – these 'double-faced gentlemen who will be Protestants in the court and in the country secret Papists'. Country
folk in the parts which Bannister used regularly to visit were loud
in their condemnation of the government for daring to clip the
wings and singe the feathers of so proud an eagle. Fifteen months
after Norfolk had gone to the block his name still exerted a
powerful influence in different parts of England and the men of
Sawston in Cambridgeshire staged their own protest by rising
in revolt under the Howard Banner, held high by Edmund
Ormes, while a demogogue named John Wilkes made his proclamation. Already some people looked back on him as 'the good
duke', a veritable martyr. Indeed in the autumn of 1571 as Dr
Wilson and Sir Thomas Smith went about their business Elizabeth
had known she had no alternative but to sacrifice Norfolk to save
her throne; *salus reipublicae suprema lex*.[14]

When it was obvious that he could not possibly escape arraignment, could not possibly be acquitted, courtiers began to cast
envious eyes on his lands and offices. Some had coveted his possessions as early as his first disgrace at Titchfield two and a half
years before, but now the crows prepared to swoop in earnest.
A week before Christmas Hunsdon openly told Burghley he was
hoping to be made Keeper of Howard House: 'I dare not ask it
as a gift of the Queen', he added, as it was too princely a mansion
and he knew his sovereign too well. Other courtiers who felt they

had not been granted as much as their services had deserved from the lands of the Northern rebels looked on the vast tracts of the Norfolk Liberty as a promised land.[15]

On 22nd November there was a preliminary hearing of the case against Norfolk at the Middlesex Sessions, where the jury, led by no less a man than Sir Thomas Gresham, found a true bill. A fortnight later the law officers of the crown were at last ready, and Burghley was over his attack of gout, but Elizabeth procrastinated. She had already moved into Whitehall Palace for Christmas and felt that a state trial in Westminster Hall, so near at hand, would cast a gloom over the traditional festivities. Burghley, too, now favoured a postponement, for his daughter Anne was marrying his ward, Edward Earl of Oxford, just before Christmas, and he had planned this to be the great social event of the winter, with a banquet in Whitehall.[16]

Norfolk had been disappointed in his young cousin of Oxford. A year before he had committed himself to a madcap plot to take the duke away from Howard House to a ship lying in the Thames, which was to sail at once for Spain; but although de Vere had hired the *Grace of God* for the expedition he failed to make other arrangements and the scheme was abandoned. In November 1571 he had apparently hatched a plan to rescue Norfolk from the Tower but once more lost interest or realised his foolishness. It was with some bitterness that the duke told his children that Oxford was 'too negligent of friends' causes, or he might do you more good than any kinsman you have'. But Norfolk's trial had a great effect on him and in the following March he pressed his father-in-law to obtain a reprieve for Howard, and later still, when the execution had been carried out, blamed Burghley for failing to prevent it, making his attack the occasion for an unseemly family row. Eventually an old woman came forward with the information about Oxford's plans to rescue Norfolk in 1570 and 1571 and he deemed it politic to leave England for a spell.[17]

Advantage was taken of the delay in bringing Norfolk to trial to expel the Spanish ambassador whom the examinations of all the conspirators had revealed as an incorrigible plotter. De Spes, who in the summer had boasted to Philip II that he could easily throw Burghley 'still further off the scent' of the Ridolfi plot and claimed he would 'bring due punishment on the heads of these people for their insolence', was summoned to appear before the

Council on 13th December when a long document in Spanish was read to him, accusing him of advising the King of Spain to declare war on England and of encouraging the Northern rebels, Norfolk, Mary and Ridolfi. To appeal was useless. There is no doubt, as Burghley put it, that he had 'used himself very crookedly perniciously and maliciously'. De Spes pleaded for time to pay his bills and settle his affairs and it was not until Christmas Eve that he left London. After a miserable Christmas at Greenwich with Knollys, who had been ordered to attend him until he was out of the country, he moved on to Gravesend and took the Dover Road. To add insult to injury Sir John Hawkins, the hero of the seizure of the Spanish treasure ships, had been appointed to take him across the Channel. But when the party reached Canterbury, Borghese, the ambassador's steward, was arrested on suspicion for his share in a plot to murder Burghley and was sent back to London for interrogations, so de Spes' final leave-taking was a pitiful affair.[18]

Edmund Mather and Kenelm Berney, who were to have made the attempt on Burghley's life, were both sons of well-to-do Norwich families. Each of them had spent a number of years abroad: Berney, who had run a man through with his sword in a brawl in Norwich, to escape from the law, and Mather, more respectably, as secretary at Paris in turn to Sir Henry Norris and Sir Nicholas Throgmorton. Mather was already in touch with some of Norfolk's household, for in July 1569 he told a colleague at the embassy in Paris that he was 'sure of a general hurly-burly in England, as the duke would marry the Queen of Scots, either by fair means or foul, and he would be well appointed to serve them'. Both he and Berney came to London *via* Flanders in the summer of 1571 to take part in the coming rebellion which they felt certain would place Mary on the throne of England. When they met in London they lamented that their liege lord, Norfolk, was a man of straw; indeed, Mather called him 'a beast and a coward, that when he was in his country' in the ciritical days of September 1569 he did not take arms .'Then he might have saved the Scotch Queen, and have altered the state.' Mather had no strong religious convictions, but was 'inclined to defend Popery for faction's sake'.

The discovery of the Ridolfi Plot convinced Mather that desperate action was needed and he fancied himself as the means by which the fortunes of Mary and Norfolk could be miraculously restored; and 'if he could devise any way to do the duke good, it would deserve double recompence, and so [he] made reckoning to have had some great preferment by the duke'. A hothead, described by a contemporary as the kind of man who would 'content himself with nothing less than the shaking a kingdom', Mather offered his services during November at the Spanish Embassy and they were eagerly accepted by Borghese. He arranged for Mather to meet de Spes who apparently ranted against Burghley and cried out for 'some man of spirit who will kill that wretch and cut him in pieces'. He talked over with Berney how good it would be 'to have a name and die famous' and, as a result, suggested to the ambassador's steward that they should assassinate Elizabeth, but Borghesi insisted that their victim was to be Burghley.

The would-be assassins made the fatal mistake of blabbing out their plans to Burghley's spy Herle, whom they met over supper at the *Three Tuns* in Newgate Street, and Herle at once warned his master, on the very day of the Oxford wedding. Hence Borghesi was stopped from leaving the country and held for questioning. Mather and Berney were given sufficient rope to incriminate themselves. They prowled round the gardens of Cecil House, observing Burghley's movements, and had ample opportunity of making the attempt, but their courage failed them. Then one, or both, of them sent their victim an anonymous letter, and Burghley decided it was time they were arrested. They were examined on the eve of Norfolk's trial in case they could provide any further information to incriminate him, but there was not the slightest suggestion that he was aware of their plans. Subsequently both were executed on February 11th, the day originally fixed for the duke's own execution.[19]

*   *   *

All was prepared for the duke's trial before his peers in Westminster Hall on 16th January. Elizabeth had appointed George, Earl of Shrewsbury, Mary's custodian, to be Lord High Steward and he had summoned the lords to appear in the Great Hall of Pleas 'between 7 and 8 in the morning'. Norfolk did not leave the Tower by water as the state of the tide made the passage of London Bridge impossible; instead he was taken by Sir Owen

Hopton and Sir Peter Carew through the City to the *Three Cranes* at Vintry Wharf where he boarded a barge that took him to Westminster Bridge. Six score of halberdiers escorted him from the river stairs to Westminster Palace, where he was taken through the Star Chamber and into the Lord Treasurer's room to wait until it was time for him to be brought to the bar, soon after eight o'clock.

A high scaffold, six foot wide, had been built in the Hall in the middle of which was placed a raised chair, with a cloth of estate, for the Lord High Steward. On either side of him sat the twenty-six peers who had assembled to sit in judgment on the duke – men he had known intimately, such as Sussex, others with whom he was closely related; nonentities like Burgh, and the two men who in their different ways had effectively barred his way to power, Burghley and Leicester. Beneath them, on a lower platform, sat the judges; to the right were Sir Robert Catlin, Chief Justice of Queen's Bench, Sir James Dyer, Chief Justice of the Common Pleas, and Sir Edward Saunders, Chief Baron of the Exchequer; and to their left the remaining judges in order of seniority. Flanking the judges were Knollys and other members of the royal household and Privy Council, Mildmay, Chancellor of the Exchequer, Dr Thomas Wilson and other notabilities. To the north of the scaffold, near the bar, were the law officers of the crown who would conduct the prosecution – Gerrard, the Attorney General, Bromley, the Solicitor General, Nicholas Barham, the Queen's Serjeant, and Thomas Wilbraham, the Attorney of the Court of Wards. Not far away were Garter King of Arms, gentlemen ushers and serjeants at arms. In the body of the Hall stood a great crowd which had come to witness the first state trial of a lord by his peers since the beginning of the reign; order was preserved by the Warden of the Fleet Prison and his tipstaves.

The Lord High Steward stood up in his place and bared his head, while the serjeant at arms held before him the white staff; and after calling for silence the Clerk of the Crown recited the Queen's commission. Shrewsbury then sat down and had delivered to him his staff, the symbol of authority, which as of custom he would break in half at the end of the proceedings. The roll of peers was called over: 'All earls, viscounts and barons', proclaimed the serjeant at arms, 'summoned to appear this day, every one answer to your names upon pain of future peril.' Beginning with the senior earl present, Reynold Earl of Kent, each answered in turn by standing in his place. After further preliminaries, including the reading of writs and precepts, the Lieutenant of the Tower was ordered to bring forth the prisoner, and he left the Hall to return with the duke. At the bar Hopton stood on one side of Norfolk, Carew on the other, each holding him by the arms, and a little apart stood the Chamberlain of the Tower with the axe. A murmur went round the Hall as Norfolk appeared. One who was present reckoned that he looked as proud as ever, as he surveyed the lords on each side of him, 'oft biting his lip'. The Clerk of the Crown addressed him: 'Thomas, duke of Norfolk, late of Kenninghall in the county of Norfolk, hold up thy hand', which he did so 'very lustily', and apparently continued to hold high during the reading of the long indictment.[20]

Words, words, words. He can have caught no more than snatches of what was being read out in the Latin of the lawyers, with its stately pleonasms. 'A false traitor against the most illustrious and Christian Princess Elizabeth, Queen of England – seduced by the instigation of the devil, contrary to all cordial affection and bounden duty that true and faithful subjects do, and of right ought to, bear – on 22nd September 1569 at the Charterhouse in the county of Middlesex (was it an intentional slight not to call it Howard House?) and at divers other times both falsely, maliciously and traitorously conspired, imagined and gone about not only to deprive, depose and cast out the said Queen from her royal dignity, title, power and government of her kingdom, but also to bring about and compass her death – to spread a miserable civil war – to subvert and destroy the whole constitution of the said state – to endeavour to change the sincere worship of God – seeking to be joined in matrimony with the aforesaid Mary, late Queen of Scots – traitorously aided and assisted the said enemies of our Sovereign Lady – Wicked and traitorous messages in unusual characters called ciphers – most pernicious example to all other delinquents – contrary to the form of the several statutes in this case made and provided . . .'

When the Clerk of the Crown asked him to plead to this indictment, Norfolk, instead of pleading, asked very humbly for leave to be represented by counsel. 'I had had very short warning to provide to answer so great a matter. I have not had fourteen hours in all, both day and night . . . yet I am put at once to the whole head of the laws, and not knowing which particularly to answer unto.' As for law books he had not so much as a breviate of the Statutes and was being brought out to fight without a weapon. Thereupon there was a legal wrangle and the case of Humphrey Stafford, which the duke had cited as a precedent for allowing a prisoner charged with high treason legal representation, was ruled as irrelevant. 'All our books do forbid allowing of counsel in the point of treason', said Dyer, 'but only it is to be answered Guilty or Not Guilty.' This meant that in the course of the proceedings Norfolk would frequently intervene, as his counsel would have done had he had one. Next he asked if the Indictment was sufficient in law and was told by Catlin that if the matters expressed in it were indeed true in fact, the Indictment was wholly and in every point sufficient. 'Be all the points treason?' asked Howard. 'All be treasons if the truth of the case be so in fact', came the answer. He was again asked to plead: 'How sayest thou, Thomas, duke of Norfolk, are thou guilty of the treasons which thou stand here indicted in manner and form as thou art indicted, Yea or No?' 'Not Guilty.' 'By whom wilt thou be tried?' 'By God and my peers.'

The task of prosecuting was shared between Serjeant Barham, who concentrated on Norfolk's attempts to marry Mary, Gerrard, the Attorney General, who pressed home the charges of conspiring to make rebellion, and Wilbraham, who was mainly concerned with Norfolk's part in relieving the rebels with papal money and sending money to Mary's supporters in Scotland. A number of documents were read in their entirety and from others long extracts were quoted, thus adding to the length of the trial. There was Murray's letter to Elizabeth relating his dealings with the duke from their very first meeting at York in October 1568, a letter from Norfolk to the Regent about the marriage, and letters passing between Mary and Ross. Long extracts were read from the examinations and confessions of Ross, Bannister, Barker, Bailly and of the duke himself. There was only one witness present in person in Westminster Hall – Richard Cavendish, Leicester's agent and a stepson of Shrewsbury, the High Steward. Cavendish, who had been with Norfolk at Southampton in August 1569 and had accompanied him to Kenninghall the following month, repeated on oath treasonable words which the duke had spoken touching his suit with the Scottish Queen.

Norfolk, scowling, retorted that Cavendish was lying – 'You an honest man indeed!' Much was made of the tokens sent by Mary, especially the embroidered cushion depicting the hand with a pruning-knife cutting down the green vine, and the 'foolish prophecy' about the lions, related by Higford, was expounded.

Throughout the long day Norfolk spoke out calmly, if ineffectively, trying to convince his judges that he was being accused by false testimony; 'None accuse me but three, one absent [Ridolfi], a stranger [Ross] and a traitor' [Barker]. Only three times, perhaps, was there a burst of anger or it may have been no more than an edge to his voice; when he spoke out against Cavendish to his face, against Barker, and against Ross. Serjeant Barham had reminded him that the Bishop had accused him of his own speeches 'without any compulsion'. 'He is a Scot', answered the duke. 'A Scot is a Christian man', countered the serjeant. Norfolk had pleaded not guilty to the gravest charge on the grounds that it was Barker and Ross who had conspired with Ridolfi, not he himself. For the rest he took his stand on his own interpretation of the Treasons Statute of Edward III. 'That Statute standeth upon three points', he said, towards the end of the trial; 'conspiring the death of the prince's person, levying of war against the prince, and aiding of the prince's enemies.' Of such crimes he claimed he was guiltless and to the end he seriously thought he could convince his judges of this.

It was a quarter to seven in the evening when the lords withdrew to a room prepared for them in the Chancery Court to consult together, having sat, apparently without interruption; and it had already passed eight when they re-assembled on the platform. Beginning with the youngest baron, De la Warr, the Lord High Steward asked each of the peers in turn his verdict. All pronounced him Guilty. Norfolk was then brought back to the bar for judgment, and Shrewsbury addressed him thus: 'The Lords, thy peers, have found thee Guilty. What hast thou to say why I may not proceed to judgment?' The duke replied, 'The Lord's will be done; God be judge between me and my false accusers'. The edge of the axe from the Tower was turned against him as Shrewsbury pronounced the inevitable sentence: 'Thou shalt be had from hence to the Tower of London from thence thou shalt be drawn through the midst of the streets of London to Tyburn, the place of execution. There thou shalt be hanged, and being alive, thou shalt be cut down quick; thy bowels shall be taken forth of thy body and burnt before thy face; thy head shall be smitten off; thy body shall be divided into four parts or quarters; thy head and thy quarters to be set up where it shall please the Queen's Majesty to appoint; and the Lord have mercy upon thee.' It was the very same words his father had heard twenty-five years before.

Norfolk was allowed to speak. 'This is the judgment of a traitor, and I shall die as a true man to the Queen as any liveth.' Seeing the lords had pronounced him unfit for their company, 'I trust shortly to be in a better'. He would not ask them to petition the Queen for his life, but to beseech her to look favourably upon his children and servants. Next day Burghley set on paper some notes about the trial. His final words, he noted, he spoke 'with some passion, otherwise truly he did use himself all the day long very modestly and wisely, as far forth as his cause would serve him'. His speech ended, Shrewsbury broke in two his white staff, to dissolve the commission; the people made their response, 'God Save the Queen', and the duke was returned to the Tower, exhausted and utterly broken.[21]

Chapter Thirteen

THE TOWER

1572

SPECIAL arrangements were made for the security of so important a prisoner. An escape was out of the question, but Hopton, the Lieutenant of the Tower, was determined that there should be no opportunities for letters passing through the small, barred windows. One window looked on to a little yard and the gate leading into it was nailed up; the other looked on to Hopton's own garden, and the door in the fence was locked: 'in the night the march goeth continually hard by that garden and in the daytime the warders and their wives that dwell near have a common course that way, so it is very unlikely for any to receive letters there.' The other state prisoners of the Ridolfi Plot were also guarded with extreme vigilance. Cobham, Lowther and Lascelles were in the Beauchamp Tower, Bailly, Cantrell, Hussey and others in Cold Harbour, Powell and Bartie in Salt Tower and Bannister, Higford and Barker in other parts of the Tower. Not since the middle of Henry VIII's reign had the Tower been so full.[1]

No visitor was allowed without Burghley's express permission. Norfolk first asked for Alexander Nowell, Dean of St Paul's and 'longeth much for Mr Foxe, his old schoolmaster', wrote his gaoler, Sir Henry Skipwith, 'to whom he most desires to perform that faith which he first grounded him in; and sure I find him little altered, but liveth now in such order as he before did, determined and very well settled towards God as ever I saw any'. Skipwith had been told to send Burghley reports of all the pri-

soner's doings and sayings, but the under-lieutenant was clumsy
with a pen and preferred to dictate his messages to a clerk, until
his master told him that for greater security these reports must
be in his own hand. On 19th January the Dean and Foxe both
came, and after they had left Skipwith passed on Norfolk's request
for two other divines to visit him: 'the more good men that
shall talk with him in this time (in my humble opinion) is the
better'. None imagined he was more than a few days from his
end.[2]

Next day he bade farewell to his children by writing them a
testament which he hoped might reach them. This long letter,
written by a fond father in so gentle and calm a way, is full of
pathos, yet is bereft of self-pity. It is both a simple lesson in
Christian conduct, written in terms which the elder children
could readily understand, and a practical guide on what they
should do when he has gone. Lengthy though it is, we must print
it in its entirety, as the children read it, for it is the most revealing
of all Norfolk's letters.

Dear Children,[3]
    *This is the last letter that ever I think to write to you, and
therefore if you loved me, or that you will seem grateful to me for
the special love that I have ever born unto you, then remember and
follow these my last lessons. O Philip, serve and fear God above
all things; I find the fault in myself that I have, God forgive me,
been negligent in this point. Love and make much of your wife,
and therein, considering the great adversity you are now in, by
reason of my fall, is your greatest present comfort and relief, besides
your happiness in having a wife which is endued with so great
towardness in resolve and good qualities and in person comparable
with the best sort. Follow these two lessons, and God will bless
you, and without these, as you may see by divers examples out of
the Scripture, and also by ordinary worldly proof, where God is
not feared all goeth to wrack, and where love is not between the
husband and the wife, there God doth not prosper.*
    *My third lesson is that you shew yourself loving and natural to
your brothers and sisters and sisters-in-law. Though you be very
young in years, yet you must strive with consideration to become a
man, for it is your own presence and good government of yourself
that must get friends. And if you take that course, then have I been*

so careful a father unto you, as I have taken such order as you, by God's grace, shall be well able, besides your wife's lands, to maintain yourself like a gentleman. Marry, the world is greedy and covetous, and if the show of the well government of yourself do not fear and restrain their greedy appetite, it is like that by indirect means they will either put you from that which law layeth upon you, or else drive you to much trouble in trying and holding your right. When my grandfather died I was not much above a year older than you are now, and yet I thank God I took such order with myself, as you shall reap the commodity of my so long passed travail, if you do now imitate the like. Help to strengthen your young and raw years with good counsell. I send you herewith a brief schedule whom I wish you to make account of as friends, and whom as servants. And I charge you as a father may do, to follow my direction therein: my experience can better tell what is fit for you, than yet your young years can judge.

I would wish for you the present to make your chief abode at Cambridge, which is the place fittest for you to prosecute your learning in, and besides is not very far hence,* whereby you may within a day's warning be here to follow your own causes, as occasion serveth. If after a year or two you spend your time in some house of the law, there is nothing that will prove more to your commodity, considering how for the time you shall have continued business about your own law affairs; and thereby also, if you spend your time well, you shall be ever better able to judge in your own causes. I too late repent that I followed not this course that now I wish to you, for if I had, then my case perchance had not been in so ill state as now is.

When God shall send you to those years as that it shall be fit for you to company with your wife, (which I had rather were sooner, then that by ill company you should fall into any ill rule), than I would wish you to withdraw yourself into some private dwelling of your own. And if your happ may be so good, as you may so live without being called to higher degree, O Philip! Philip! then shall you enjoy that blessed life, which your woeful father would fain ha' done and never could be so happy. Beware of high degrees! To a vainglorious proud stomach it seemeth at the first sweet. Look into all chronicles and you shall find that in the end it brings heaps of cares, toils in the state, and most commonly in the end

* i.e. from Audley End.

utter overthrow. Look into the whole state of the nobility in times past, and into their state now, and then judge whether my lesson be true or not.

Assure yourself, as you may see by the books of my accounts, and you shall find that my living did hardly maintain my expenses, for all the help that I had by Tom's lands, and somewhat by your wife's and sisters'-in-law, but that I was never a beggar. You shall, by the grace of God, be a great deal richer and quieter in your low degree, wherein once again I wish you to continue. They may, that shall wish you the contrary, have a good meaning, but believe your father, who of love wishes you best, and with the mind that he is at present fully armed to God, who sees both states, high and low, as it were even before his eyes.

Beware of the court, except it be to do your prince service, and that as near as you can in the meanest degree; for place hath no certainty, either a man by following thereof hath too much to worldly pomp, which in the end throws him down headlong, or else he lieth there unsatisfied, either that he cannot attain to himself that he would, or else that he cannot do for his friends as his heart desireth.

Remember these notes and follow them, and then you, by God's help, shall reap the commodity of them in your old years; when you, if it be his will, may give the like advice to your own. If your brothers may be suffered to remain in your company, still I would be most glad thereof, because continuing still together should still increase love between you. But the world is so catching of everything that falls, as I believe Tom being after my death the Queen Majesty's ward, shall be begged by one or another. But yet you are sure to have your brother William left still with you, because poor boy he hath nothing to feed the cormorants withal, to whom you will as well be a father as a brother, for, upon my blessing, I commit him to your charge, to provide for, if that which I have assured him by law shall not be so sufficient as I meant it. If law may take place, your sisters-in-law be surely enough conveyed to the behoof of your brothers, and then I would wish them to be brought up with some friend of mine, as for the present I allow best of Sir Christopher Heydon, if he will so much friend you as to receive them to sojourn with him, if not, then in some other place as your friends shall best allow of.

And touching the bestowing of your wife and Meggy, whom I

would be loth should be out of your wife's company, (for as she should be a good companion for Nan, so I commit Megg of special trust to her), I think good till you lie together, if my Lady of Sussex might be entreated to take them to her as sojourners, there were no place left so fit considering his kindred unto you, and the assured friend that I hope you shall find of him; besides she is a good Lady. If it will not be so brought to pass, then, by the advice of your friends, take some other order, but in no case would I wish you to keep any house till you and your wife lie together.

Thus I have advised you, as my troubled memory can presently suffer me. Beware of pride, stubbornness, lechery, taunting, and sullenness, (which vices nature doth some what kindle in you), and therefore you must with reason and discretion make a new nature in yourself; to give your mind too much and greedily to gaming make a pastime of it and no toil. And lastly, delight to spend some time in reading of the Scriptures, for therein is the whole comfort of man's life, and all other things are vain and transitory, and if you be diligent of reading of them they will remain with you continually to your profit and commodity in this world, and to your comfort and salvation in the world to come, whither in grace of God I am now with joy and consolation preparing myself. And upon my blessing beware of blind papistry, which brings nothing but bondage to men's consciences. Mix your prayers with fasting, not thinking thereby to merit, for there is nothing that we of ourselves can do that is good, we are but unprofitable servants: but fast, I say, thereby to take the wicked affections of the mind, and trust only to be saved by Christ's precious blood, for without your perfect faith therein there is no salvation. Let works follow your faith thereby to show to the world that you do not only say you have faith, but that you give testimony thereof to the full satisfaction of the godly. I write somewhat the more herein, because perchance you may heretofore heard, or perchance hereafter shall hear, false bruits that I was a papist. But trust unto it, I never since I knew what religion meant, I thank God, was of other mind than now you shall hear that I die in, although I cry God mercy I have not given fruits and testimony of my faith as I ha' ought to have done, the which is the thing that I do now chiefest repent.

When I am gone, forget my condemning, and forgive, I charge you, my false accusers, as I protest to God I do, but have nothing to do with them if they live. Surely Bannister dealt no way but

*honestly and truly; Hickford did not hurt me in my conscience
willingly, nor did not charge me with any great matter that was of
weight otherwise than truly. But the Bishop of Ross, and especially
Barker, did falsely accuse me, and laid their own treasons upon
my back. God forgive them as I do, and once again I will you to do;
bear no malice in your mind. And now dear Philip, farewell. Read
this my letter sometimes over, it may chance make you remember
yourself the better, and by the same, when your father is dead and
rotten, you may see what counsel I would give you if I were alive.
If you follow these admonitions, there is no doubt but God will
bless you, and I your earthly father do give you God's blessing and
mine, with my humble prayers to Almighty God, that it will please
him to bless you and your good Nann, that you may both, if it be
his will, see your children's children to the comfort of you both, and
afterwards you may be partakers of the heavenly Kingdom Amen,
Amen.*

*Tom, out of this that I have written to your brother, you may
learn such lessons as are fit for you and therefore I will not repeat
them again; that I write to one I write to all except it be particular
notes which particularly touch any one of you. To fear and serve
God is generally to you all, and of my blessing take greatest care
thereof, for it is the foundation of all goodness. You have even from
your infancy been given to be stubborn, beware of that vice, Tom,
and bridle nature with wisdom, for all ills commonly depends of
that vice. Though you be her Majesty's ward, yet if you use
yourself well to my Lord Burghley, he will, I hope, get you to
buy your own wardship, and then I should have liking to my
daughter-in-law, Mary Dacres; I hope you shall have it in your
own choice. I will not advise you otherways than yourself when
you are of fit years shall think good, but this assure yourself it will
be good augmentation to your small living, considering how charge-
able the world groweth to be. Follow your elder brother's advice,
who, I hope, will take such a course as may be to all your comforts.
God send him grace to do so, and you too. If you follow these my
advices, then I gave you God's blessing and mine, and I hope the
Lord will prosper you.*

*Well-beloved Nann, that hath been as dear to me as if you had
been mine own daughter, although considering this ill happ that is
now chanced, you might have had a greater marriage than now
your husband shall be; yet I hope you will remember that when*

TH R

*you were married the case was far otherwise, and therefore I hope
your dutiful dealings shall be so to your husband and your sisterly
love to your brothers-in-law and sisters-in-law, as my friends that
shall see it, may think that my great affection to you was well
bestowed. Thanks be to God, you have hitherto taken a good course,
whereby all that wishes you well take great hope rather of your
going forwards theirin than backwards, which God forbid. I will
request no more at your hands, now that I am gone, in recompense
of my former love of you, but that you will observe my three
lessons, to fear and serve God, flying idleness, to love faithfully
your husband, and to be kind to your brothers and sisters, specially
committing to your care mine own only daughter Megg, hoping
that you will not be a sister-in-law to her, but rather a natural
sister, yea, even a very mother, and that as I took care for the
well-bestowing of you, so you will, when her years shall be fit for
marriage, take care for the well-bestowing of her, and be a continual
caller on to your husband for the same. If this mishap had not
chanced, you and your husband might have been awhile still young,
and I would, by God's help, have supplied your wants. But now
the case is changed, for you must to your years of fifteen attain to
the consideration and discretion of twenty, or else if God send you
to live, in your age you shall have causes to repent your folly in
youth, besides the endangering and casting away of them that do
wholly depend upon your two well doings. I do not mistrust, but
that you will be mindful of my last natural requests, and so doing,
God bless you, and the issue that I hope will spring of your two
bodies, and send you to be old parents to virtuous children, which is
likeliest to be if yourselves give them good example. Farewell,
for this is the last that ever you shall receive from your loving
father. Farewell, my dear Nann.*

*Megg, I have as you may see, committed you to your loving
sister, I charge you, therefore, upon my blessing, that you obey in
all things, as you would do me, or your own mother if she were
living, and then I doubt not by her good means you shall be in fit
time bestowed to your own comfort and contentation. Be chaste, no
babbler, and ever be busied in doing somewhat, and give mind to
reading in the Bible and such other good books, whereby you may
learn to fear God, and so you shall prove, by God's help, hereafter,
the better wife, and a good and virtuous woman in all other respects.
If you follow these my lessons, then God's blessing and mine I give*

you, and pray to God that you may both live and die his servant.
Amen.

Will, though you be now young, yet I hope if it shall please
God to send you life, that you will then consider of the precepts here
before written to your brethren, which I gave as well to you as to
them. Be obedient to your elder brothers. I have committed the
charge of your bringing up to your elder brother, and therefore I
charge you to be as obedient to him as you would ha' been to me,
if I had been living. I do assure myself that his dealing to you will
be like a brother of the whole blood, and not half blood.

If you follow these my precepts, then God shall bless you, if
otherwise, think not that God scourgeth lightly children that be dis-
obedient to their father's godly lessons. As you are the youngest, so
the more you ought to be obedient to your elders. God send you
good younger brother's fortune in this world, and his grace, that you
may ever be his, both in this world and the world to come. Amen.

I may not forget my two pretty daughters-in-law, Mall and
little Bess. I pray God send all things so prosperous, as, if it be his
will, you may be double daughters-in-law, as well by your own
marriages as you were before by my marrying of your good and
virtuous mother. These lessons that I have given to your sisters
without repetition I give unto you. Though I were not your natural
father, yet my deserts have been deserved so well at your hands, as
few of mine own I have done so much for, you and those that shall
come of you shall fare the better for my cost and travail. I hope
you will be mindful hereof when your years and occasion shall
desire proof. God send you both, my loving daughters-in-law, as
well to do, as I wish to those that are come of mine own body. Now
to bid you all farewell together, I desire you for Christ his sake to
be mindful of my short lessons, which are proceeded from as natural
father and father-in-law as ever children had, and in so doing God
will bless you, and I send you my blessing, which I pray God may
prove to you, my sons, as well as Isaac did to Jacob; and to you my
daughters, as well as [Jacob] did to Rebecca. Amen.

And now, my dear and loving children, farewell. God I hope
will be your comfort and guide, and I hope ere it be long to be rid
out of this wretched world, to follow my dear wives and your mother
in the heavenly joys, whither pray God send me, and you afterwards, when it shall be his will and pleasure to take you out of this
vale of misery. Amen. Once again, lastly, and for ever I charge

*you all to remember my honest requests, in following whereof in the
end yourselves shall reap the commodity.*

*The 20 of January, 1572 God be all your comfort,
Amen, and send me to die his servant.*

*Tom, I had forgotten to request one thing at your hands, which
I hope you will hereafter, when time cometh, perform. It is this:
I promised Bowles a lease of a farm of yours, in your lands called
St Taylots, which, if I had lived, I would have performed, and now
I hope you will, if God send you to come to years, perform as much
as I meant to have done. He hath been as honest and true a servant
to your father as any that he hath had, and therefore I hope at this
my request, he shall have the lease at your hand. God bless you
and you in his fear! Amen.*

*Written by the hand of your loving father, and father-in-law,
now being ready and willing to part out of this world, I hope unto
life everlasting.*

T. N.

In an enclosure, addressed to Philip, he counselled him to trust
implicitly Burghley, Oxford, Sir Christopher Hatton and others
and named various servants on whom he could rely. In the past
few weeks Hatton had been trying to persuade Elizabeth to issue
a pardon, and Oxford, filled with remorse, was at last attempting
to influence his father-in-law. Norfolk's letter duly reached his
children at Audley End, but it was not to be the last they received
from him. Next week he wrote at even greater length almost
entirely on religious matters, and the tone of it was markedly
anti-papistical. A further note on 28th January touched on money
matters and Philip was advised how he could clear outstanding
debts.

Unknown to Norfolk, a solemn, yet wretched ceremony had
been performed at St George's, Windsor on 26th January. Before
morning service began, when all the canons, poor knights and
choir were ready in their stalls, Sir Gilbert Dethick, Garter King
of Arms, officiated at the duke's degradation from the Order of
the Garter. All the officers of arms were present: Robert Cooke
(Clarencieux), William Flower (Norroy), with Lancaster, Windsor, Richmond, York and Somerset heralds, and Rouge Dragon
and Portcullis pursuivants. The Earl Marshal's men had come to
degrade their master.

Garter stood over the duke's stall in the choir and read out the
Queen's letter of 22nd January commanding the ceremony to
take place. As a knight of the most noble order Norfolk had been
required to be 'strong in the faith of Holy Church' and to love
the Queen and defend her and her rights. As a traitor he had
broken his vows and could no longer remain a member of the
order, but must be expelled, 'and not worthy that his arms etc.
shall remain amongst the ensigns of other noble, virtuous knights'.
'Then Windsor Herald of Arms threw down first his banner of
arms, and Garter spurned the same out of the north door and all
the other kings and heralds followed him.' In turn Norfolk's
sword, mantles, helmet and crest were trampled underfoot, kicked
out of the chapel door 'and from thence clean out of the Castle
Gate into the ditch', to be an example for evermore. Finally
Garter removed the duke's plate of arms, and then morning prayer
began. The verses of the appointed psalm made their comment:
'Thou hast trodden down all them that depart from thy statutes,
for they imagine but deceit. Thou puttest away all the ungodly
of the earth like dross; therefore I love thy testimonies.'[4]

For the prisoner one day dragged on into another. Norfolk
wrote to the Queen, abjectly repenting and thankful for her
mercy, but without thought of his sentence being stayed. He was
a 'castaway', 'prostrate at her feet', 'overwhelmed with sorrow';
he was anxious that he should receive forgiveness and a token that
she would look with tenderness over his children. Next day,
Elizabeth sent him a message, agreeing that Burghley should
become the children's guardian, as he had wished; and this care
for 'my poor unfortunate brats' overwhelmed him. He wrote
again, thanking her, and even more abjectly as 'a dead fly',
craving forgiveness. Mary became 'the shameless Scot' and the
slippery Ridolfi 'the Italianised Englishman'. Some have doubted
the authenticity of these letters and of other memorials of the
Ridolfi conspiracy which Norfolk wrote at this time, and imagined that whole sentences of cringing repentance were dictated
to him. But there is no doubt that all are genuine. Norfolk's fall
had utterly cowed him and the uncertainty of whether his execution would take place in a matter of days or weeks all but
unhinged him.[5]

Early in February, surprised to find himself still alive, he wrote
out a final defence, intended for Philip's eyes, which was in sub-

stance the same as his speech at his trial. He was worried about his mother, Lady Steyning, and hoped she would be sent into the country, for he feared that if she were still in London on the day he was executed the shock would kill her. He also wrote to Dr Thomas Wilson who had cross-questioned him so often in the Tower, asking him to see that keepsakes were given to certain friends after his execution. Lord Keeper Bacon was to have the jewelled crystal cup; his close friend Sussex 'my best George, chain and garter', and Leicester a ship of crystal glass. Sir Walter Mildmay was to be given some fine glass and the gold spoons with pearl on the handles, and Burghley a piece of cloth of gold and a ruby ring. Lastly, '£20 a year to be allowed to Mr Foxe'.[6]

His execution now seemed certain; for the Queen signed the warrant on Saturday, 9th February and 'all preparations were made, with the expectation of all London and a concourse of many thousands' on the Monday morning when Norfolk was due to mount the scaffold; but the Queen had had second thoughts on the Sunday and professed 'a great misliking that the duke should die next day'. The government deemed it advisable that the crowds should not be entirely cheated of a spectacle, and so it was arranged that Mather and Berney, who had plotted to kill Burghley, should be executed on the Monday.[7]

Norfolk was now given permission to write to some of his old servants and he sent William Dix a New Testament with a touching letter written inside, thanking him for his years of faithful service, and sure that he would continue steadfast in looking after the estates for the children and advising Philip's and Nanne's inexperienced years. He also managed to write once more to Philip; he was convinced the end was nigh and he still did not know whether his earlier testaments had reached his children, but there was still time for a short letter. He wrote it on a blank sheet of his Bible at the end of the Book of Job; for he felt sure the Bible would reach his son, but feared an ordinary letter might not. The earlier precepts were briefly repeated. Philip was to fear God, honour the Queen, 'to make some satisfaction for your father's disobedience', and obey his guardian, Burghley – 'so friendly and vigilant a nobleman'. Norfolk had chosen this particular blank leaf by design: 'I write this much unto you in this place of the book because by godly Job you may learn to be prudent in this adversity that my deserts hath now laid upon you, and say with good Job, the 21st verse of his first chapter,* and on the other side of the Psalms of good King David you may choose some selected sentences . . . Philip, is not this a worthy book, that if you ply it thoroughly will keep you in awe from deadly sinning?' Such sinning included becoming involved with factions.

He gave his final blessing to all his children and prayed they might have a joyful meeting in heaven. 'The 11th of February, which within four hours might be written with my heart's blood. Remember my lessons and forget me. Written between 4 and 5 of the clock, by me your earthly woeful father, but joyful. I most humbly thank the Lord that I hope my time draweth so near that my soul shall enjoy bliss and leave this crooked lump of sinful flesh.

Sometime NORFOLK

now

Thomas HOWARD.'

This was Norfolk's last letter. The vigilant Skipwith saw him writing in the Bible and had a copy made which the Duke checked and marked 'examined by myself'. The Bible itself certainly came to Philip at Audley End.[8]

Once again the duke's life was spared. The Queen, making a virtue of indecision, cancelled the warrant at the last minute, and other warrants were to be issued and countermanded the following month. Howard was immediately thankful for the Queen's mercy, but soon heavy and ill at ease again. His own cook, Blower, could not tempt him with dainty dishes, though the cost of diet for the duke and his men in the Tower was as high as £100 a month.[9]

Dean Nowell who came regularly to the cell noticed how the duke's health was deteriorating. He refused to have a doctor, he even refused a purgative, though he was used to taking one in the spring; he thought care of the body a sin in one so near to his end, yet he did not want illness to hinder his spiritual preparation for death. His linen and clothes became tatty. The Dean often heard him say that he had only one pair of hose left; he had other pairs with velvet on them which he refused to wear as they were too sumptuous for a condemned person, so he was often driven

---

* 'Naked I came out of my mother's womb, and naked I shall return thither. The Lord gave and the Lord hath taken away. Blessed be the name of the Lord.'

to patching the one wearable pair. Norfolk would not hear of new ones being bought as 'it would be misconstrued by some as a sign of his hope and desire of a long life', as was an earlier request to eat meat during Lent. Truly a difficult prisoner, and Skipwith hearing the Dean was at a nearby church would sometimes slip out from the Tower for the chance of a talk with him about the duke's state of mind, the problems of his food, his health and his clothes. There was, too, much gossip throughout the Tower about its principal inhabitant. Rumours about impending execution or sudden release started easily and passed to the duke *via* his servants. Even a chaplain's wife, perhaps the same Mistress Massey, who had been in league with the laundress for carrying messages, began to fabricate discreditable stories as a means of ingratiating herself with the Queen.[10]

The Dean of St Paul's brought Norfolk his Easter Communion and worried Burghley for a back-dated warrant to give him access to the prisoner, 'for else I have nothing to show for me the doing of the same, in case I should be called unto any account'. Understandably, everyone who had dealings with so eminent a prisoner of state was on edge. On the Wednesday after Easter there were fresh rumours that execution was nigh and Skipwith wrote to Burghley for information, since Hopton, his chief, was 'very secret, so will not let me know of any such occasion or warrant that hath come'. Dean Nowell was equally in the dark and wondered whether the Friday would be 'the late Duke's great day'. Burghley had no definite news, but the Dean still visited the prisoner, exhorting him to Bible reading, meditation and prayer. The Duke feared a sudden execution, without time for preparation, more than death itself.

In the middle of April he was certainly ill. His stomach was tormenting him and some sunny days made close confinement in an airless cell intolerable. Both Skipwith and Nowell thought he might die a natural death at any time. He seemed to his gaoler 'more dolorous and sad than yet ever he hath been. Sure, I marvell that any man can hold so long without extremity of sickness'. Still no news of a warrant by May Day when Norfolk was very ill, and when the fever left him he repeated again and again how thankful he was to Elizabeth for sparing his life for so long. In a flush of loyalty he offered to write a piece that might be of value as propaganda for the government in the aftermath of plots and 'might tend to her Highness's safety', but he was too weak to put pen to paper.[11]

Norfolk passed five long months as a prisoner of state under sentence of death, yet his father had had to endure no more than six days between sentence and execution. This weary waiting was a torture worse than the rack. After the shock of the first stay of execution he lived from day to day, not knowing whether the morrow would bring a fresh warrant, another reprieve, or nothing. At times he certainly hoped he might die in his bed in the Tower and be spared the ordeal on Tower Hill. In less despondent moments he must have thought about his grandfather, the old Lord Treasurer, who had escaped the axe by a hair's-breadth and then, after six and a half years of captivity, had been restored to liberty and honours upon a new accession. Yet before long Thomas Howard was so utterly weary of life itself that he had not the will for anything but death.

Elizabeth could not make up her mind whether or not to allow the law to take its course. She drafted orders, then hastily cancelled them. One day, as Burghley told Walsingham with feeling, when she thought of her own danger, she was determined that justice should be done; the next, when she considered Norfolk's 'nearness of blood, of his superiority of honour, etc., she stayeth'. Perhaps she, too, hoped that death might come to her cousin naturally. For a time there had been good reason for keeping the prisoner alive, for the government had still needed to question him about other individuals caught in the web of Ridolfi's spinning. These lesser traitors received their sentences, yet Norfolk remained. Every ounce of evidence that he could supply about Mary Queen of Scots had been squeezed from him and as a witness of state he had outlived his usefulness long before Easter. At one time there were fears that his execution might provoke riots in the capital as well as in East Anglia, but they soon dwindled. 'God's will be fulfilled and aid Her Majesty to do herself good', muttered Burghley, his patience almost at an end, as his mistress delayed yet again. When Parliament had met at the beginning of May, the demands for Norfolk's head on a charger first made by Thomas Norton had grown from a murmur to a deafening shout, but Elizabeth had steadily resisted, and by the end of the month even Leicester could see 'no likelihood of her surrendering to the clamour'.[12]

Then at last Burghley persuaded his mistress that the sentence could be delayed no more. The Secretary, once his 'most loving friend', had never doubted that Norfolk must pay the penalty for high treason. Justice apart, he would not be sorry to see the duke removed from the political arena. Ever since those critical days early in 1569 when Norfolk had tried to unseat him from power, and so nearly succeeded in depriving him of the Queen's confidence, Burghley had feared him. There had been a *rapprochement*, but relations between the two men were never the same again. Thereafter Howard and he had underlined their disagreements, whether it was foreign policy, the religious settlement, or the problem of the succession. Norfolk remained, for Burghley, the leader of a shadow cabinet composed of the principal peers and wealthiest landowners in the realm who were united only in their dislike of the pushing Secretary. Burghley saw the Ridolfi Conspiracy as a godsend and he intended exploiting it to the full to consolidate his position. 'The adverse party must needs increase when they see justice forbear against the principal, and him spared to set up the mark', Burghley had written early in April. For reasons of state traitors must go to the block and that right soon; and he knew that unless he got his way over Norfolk there would be no hope of persuading the Queen to bring Mary Queen of Scots to justice. Elizabeth could not indefinitely hold out against the logic of statecraft. She finally agreed to sign the warrant and not retract, but for years to come Norfolk's death would gnaw at her conscience and she would lay the blame for it on Burghley.[13]

On Saturday, 31st May 1572 Hopton and Skipwith were each warned that the execution would take place on Tower Hill on the Monday morning. The sheriffs of London and Middlesex were sent the warrant, workmen erected the scaffold on the Saturday afternoon, and the executioner was told to prepare. The news travelled throughout the Tower, along the little streets of London and Westminster and across the Thames. Sir Henry Skipwith warned his prisoner to make his final preparations, but found that death was 'now more stranger to him than ever it was'. The duke asked for Dean Nowell to attend him both in his cell and on the scaffold. He came round that same evening and again the next day, and about nine o'clock on the Sunday night Hopton, the lieutenant of the Tower, visited Norfolk in person to tell him that the next morning would be his last – a sure sign that this was no false alarm, for the lieutenant had contrived to keep out of the prisoner's way as much as he could. Norfolk replied calmly 'God's will and Her Majesty's be done'. Even later that evening, when it was almost dark, Elizabeth herself came by water to the Tower, a melancholy visitor, to make sure all was in readiness for the morrow. The Tower had cast its shadow over the House of Tudor no less than the House of Norfolk, and as a result the Queen and the Duke had much in common. Her mother had gone through Traitor's Gate when Elizabeth was three years old and later, for a season, she had been a captive in the Bell Tower herself, not knowing whether her sister would spare her life. In the end Elizabeth could not bring herself to see her cousin.[14]

A little before eight o'clock on 2nd June the duke stepped on to the scaffold at Tower Hill, with Dean Nowell and John Foxe at his side, and when the crowd that had gathered to watch had been silenced, Norfolk began his final speech. 'For men to suffer death in this place is no new thing, though since the beginning of our most gracious Queen's reign I am the first, and God grant I may be the last.' Before he had got much further one of the officers of the guard interrupted: 'We are come to see you put to execution, and we must not delay while these speeches pass from you, for in these we hazard our lives.' The Duke continued: 'I acknowledge that my peers have justly judged me worthy of death; neither is it my meaning to excuse myself. That I have treated with the Queen of Scots I freely confess, and that in matters of great moment, without acquainting my sovereign, which I ought not to have done.' He then stated his innocence in the graver charges of rebellion, castigated Ridolfi, and assured his hearers that he was not a Catholic. 'I have not been popish from the time that I had any taste in religion, but have always been averse from the popish doctrine and embraced the true religion of Jesus Christ and have put my whole trust in the blood of Christ my Redeemer and Blessed Saviour.' He did not deny that some of his friends and his servants were Catholics and asked forgiveness if he had offended Protestants by maintaining them. A few more words and he was finished.

The sheriff bade him be brief with his final leave-taking. In turn he embraced Sir Henry Lee and Dean Nowell and shook hands with Foxe and others on the scaffold. As of custom the executioner knelt to ask the prisoner's forgiveness and Norfolk gave him a little purse with four gold sovereigns and some odd shillings in silver. He then knelt beside Nowell for prayers, and read the 51st Psalm, but at verse 18 paused, and instead of saying 'Build up the walls of Jerusalem' said 'Build up the walls of England, good Lord'. In the middle of another psalm he remembered he had not asked the world forgiveness. This done he spoke very quietly the familiar words, *In manus tuas, Domine, commendo spiritus meum.*

He pulled off his cloak, cap and black satin doublet, which he gave to the executioner, revealing the white satin clothes in which, four months before, he had intended to die. Someone offered a handkerchief to cover his eyes, but he refused it, saying 'I fear not death'. He re-arranged some of the straw and knelt for a last prayer with the Dean who then turned to the crowd, asking them to pray with one voice for God's mercy and then stay silent lest they trouble the prisoner. 'Lord Jesus preserve thy soul' came the murmur of a hundred voices as Thomas Howard stretched forward his neck upon the block. The executioner cut off the head with one stroke and held it up 'to the sorrowing and weeping people'.

Howard was spared the indignity of quartering or having his severed head put on a spike of London Bridge. His corpse was put in a coffin and taken into the chapel of St Peter ad Vincula, where it was buried in the chancel the same day by Alexander Nowell, in the presence of three or four people.[15]

EPILOGUE

THOMAS HOWARD was doomed by the tragedy of his high birth, and the shadow of the Tower lay over him from an early age. Too mighty for a subject, he was motivated by an over-riding ambition and his aspirations proved the stumbling-block. He was piqued at Elizabeth for undervaluing his qualities and for her consequent refusal to take him into her confidence, while men like Cecil and Dudley were favoured with positions of power and trust. For long he nursed the grievance that he, the first peer of the realm, should be no more than stage manager of pageantry on state occasions, while men of lowly birth were promoted to high office and had their advice heeded; and it was Elizabeth's treatment of him which first made him seriously consider the proposals to marry Mary Queen of Scots. Howard gradually became hypnotised by the idea of the Scottish match, for such would automatically lead him to real power. Characteristically it was Elizabeth's opposition to the marriage which hardened his own resolve, yet his very stubbornness blunted his chances of opportunism. The idea of wearing a consort's crown, first in Scotland, then in England, was sufficient to make him woo a woman he had never seen whom he knew to be both a murderess and an adulteress, for the thought of power had corrupted him and his behaviour from the last days of 1568 until his trial three years later can only be explained by his being blinded by ambition, as his father Surrey had been in 1546.

Events had cast Thomas Howard for a role which he was totally incapable of filling, for he had inherited Surrey's hot-tempered pride but none of his strength of character and at the critical moments of his life he was paralysed by indecision, so that with his 'soft and dastardly spirit' he behaved with utter foolishness, drifting into treason without realising the significance of what he was doing. By some curious blindspot he failed to see that his

loyalty either to his Queen or his loyalty to his faith was in question, and he made the grave mistake of playing a dangerous game
without first learning what were the rules. His upbringing had
left him with scars that never healed. His father's execution for
high treason, the fact that his most impressionable years were the
reigns of Edward VI and Mary Tudor, when religion and politics
see-sawed from one extreme to the other, the cruel shock of losing
his young wife so soon (and the blows were to be even harsher
with the second and the third bereavements) were experiences
that made for instability. He never thought seriously about religion until he was condemned to die and his reflections then
mocked not only his intrigues at the hands of Ridolfi, but also
his marriage to Lady Dacre and the appointment of a Roman
Catholic tutor for his children. Indeed, between the boyhood
years with John Foxe at Reigate and the visits of Foxe and Dean
Nowell to his cell, he was a 'politique', observing the formalities,
without apparent conviction.

High position, stubborn pride and natural aloofness cut Howard
off from his fellow men so that he made few friends and his
relations with his brother were never close. Understandably he
was a reluctant courtier, never really happy unless he was in his
own country where he alone was monarch. As a widower for the
third time, he was the loneliest man in England and when the
crisis came, under the strain of the negotiations for Mary's hand,
he found he had no-one to turn to for advice.

It seems incredible that the man who had shown himself such
a sound judge of men over his household officials and in his days
on the Border should have failed to see through the machinations
of Ridolfi; incredible that one who had earlier singled out
Leicester as his greatest political enemy should have suddenly
agreed to entrust him with the trickiest negotiations affecting his
future. Yet under the spell of Mary, Norfolk threw all caution
to the winds and behaved as one possessed. Once he had swallowed
their bait his weakness was exploited by Ross and Ridolfi and his
sense of honour by Mary; he allowed himself to be twisted by
Leicester and misunderstood by Burghley. By his conduct he
alienated his friends Pembroke and Sussex as he had earlier forfeited Burghley's genuine affection, and he lost the respect of those
who had applauded his lead over the affair of the Archduke Charles
and his outspokenness in the Parliament of 1566. Isolated in his

high dignity he had perforce to rely on his own sense of judgment and it failed him miserably.

The gravest mistake was his failure to appreciate the strength of Elizabeth's position and the force of her own obstinacy. She never forgave him for his behaviour at the York Conference at which she was convinced he had shown partiality to Mary's cause and after that betrayal his sovereign would never feel able to trust him again, least of all would she agree to his marrying Mary. Foolishly he moved ahead with his plans, confident that Elizabeth would give in, and when after sundry warnings he continued to pursue his intrigues behind her back, assuring himself that they were in her best interests, she had no alternative but to regard him as a public enemy. In a similar way the duke had seriously under-estimated Mary Queen of Scots. His execution foreshadowed her own and it was at Fotheringay fourteen years later that she spoke his epitaph: 'Alas, what has the House of Howard suffered for my sake.'

Only when Howard returned to the Tower after his trial did the full seriousness of his offence come home to him, and he was filled with remorse. For three years he had been following a will-o'-the-wisp, curiously unaware that it was anything but the most honourable path, but now he was jolted into seeing himself face to face. There is no need to question the sincerity of his letters to his children from the Tower or the depth of his penitence, and he took leave of this world with dignity. Notwithstanding all the abysmal confessions and examinations, the abject submissions and the pitiful pleas for mercy it is impossible not to be impressed by the man and to realise the impact which he made on his contemporaries, whether they respected or feared him. 'Incredible it is', wrote William Camden, 'how dearly the people loved him; which he had purchased through his bounty and singular courtesy, not unbeseeming so great a Prince. The wiser sort were diversely affected. Some were terrified with the greatness of the danger which while he lived seemed to threaten, by means of him and his faction. Others were moved with pity toward him as a man of high nobility, singular goodness of nature, goodly personage and manly countenance, who might have been both a great strength and ornament to his country, had not the cunning practices of his malicious adversaries and slippery hopes under colour of the public good diverted him from his first course of life.'[1]

It was because he was the last of the dukes of medieval creation
that so many ordinary folk thought Howard hedged about with
a near divinity; because of his exceptional rank and his nearness in
blood to the throne that Elizabeth hesitated so long over signing
his death warrant. It is a commonplace that the Wars of the Roses
depleted the peerage and that after Clarence had been drowned
in a butt of malmsey there were few dukes left in England. In
turn the royal dukedoms of Gloucester, York and Cornwall
merged with the Crown and, with the lack of male heirs after
1547, the Tudor lines of royal dukes came to an end. There were
only three new creations, all of them short-lived: for Richmond,
King Henry's natural son, died in 1536 and the successive Lords
Protectors, Somerset and Northumberland went to the block on
Tower Hill, where earlier Buckingham had perished. With the
execution of Suffolk in 1554 Norfolk became England's sole duke
and after he had gone there was no successor for over thirty years,
when Prince Henry, James I's eldest son, became Duke of Cornwall.

The first two Stuart Kings greatly augmented the peerage,
which at Elizabeth's death numbered no more than fifty-nine
titles; yet, with the exception of the favourite Buckingham, the
dignity of a duke was reserved for princes of the blood. Even with
the lavish grants made by Charles II when he came into his own
there were only two new dukedoms, those created for Albemarle,
the architect of the Restoration, and for Norfolk. Thomas
Howard, Earl of Arundel and Surrey, the fourth duke's grandson,
had been created Earl of Norfolk in 1644, and now his grandson,
another Thomas, was advanced to the dukedom, as the fifth of
the Howard line. He died unmarried and when his brother succeeded him the earldom of Arundel descended with the dukedom
of Norfolk. Since that day the succession has been unbroken,
though no duke has taken part in political life, for all have professed the faith taken by Philip Earl of Arundel from his step-
mother, Lady Dacre.

Though the dukedom was revived, the territorial entity of a
Duchy of Norfolk ceased with Thomas Howard's execution.
Under his son Philip, Arundel Castle succeeded Kenninghall
Palace as the principal Howard residence and the close connexions
between the family and East Anglia began to be severed. At
Arundel the visitor may still see the rings which Mary Queen of

Scots gave to the fourth duke as earnest of the marriage which would shake the throne of England; but at Kenninghall not a stone remains of the great palace which symbolised the power of the house of Howard under the Tudors and was Thomas's most prized possession until, under Mary's influence, he lost all through making a bid for power that had no chance of success. He never appreciated the fact that England, as she emerged in the hostile Europe of the Counter Reformation, could not afford to be divided against itself, and that the future lay with the moderates, not with those who sought to put back the clock in religion and politics.

KEY TO PUBLIC RECORD OFFICE REFERENCES

C.54	Chancery, Close Rolls.
C.56	Chancery, Confirmation Rolls.
C.65	Chancery, Parliament Rolls.
C.66	Chancery, Patent Rolls.
C.82	Chancery, Warrants for the Great Seal, series II.
C.142	Chancery, Inquisitions Post Mortem, series II.
C.P.25(2)	Common Pleas, Feet of Fines.
E.101	Exchequer, King's (or Queen's) Remembrancer, Various Accounts.
E.122	Exchequer, K.R. Customs Accounts.
E.137	Exchequer, K.R. Estreats.
E.163	Exchequer, K.R. Miscellanea.
E.164	Exchequer, K.R. Miscellaneous Books, series I.
E.178	Exchequer, K.R. Special Commissions of Enquiry.
E.179	Exchequer, K.R. Subsidy Rolls etc.
E.190	Exchequer, K.R. Port Books.
E.315	Exchequer, Augmentation Office, Miscellaneous Books.
E.351	Exchequer, Pipe Office, Declared Accounts.
E.368	Exchequer, Lord Treasurer's Remembrancer, Memoranda Rolls.
E.372	Exchequer, L.T.R., Pipe Rolls.
H.C.A. 24	High Court of Admiralty, Libels etc.
K.B.9	King's (or Queen's) Bench, Ancient Indictments.
L.C.4	Lord Chamberlain's Department, Recognizances.
L.R.1	Auditors of the Land Revenue, Enrolment Books of Grants, Leases etc.
L.R.2	Auditors of the Land Revenue, Miscellaneous Books.
L.R.8	Auditors of the Land Revenue, Views of Account.
S.P.1	State Papers, Henry VIII, General series.
S.P.10	State Papers Domestic, Edward VI.
S.P.12	State Papers Domestic, Elizabeth I.
S.P.15	State Papers Domestic, Addenda Edward VI-James I.
S.P.46	State Papers Supplementary.
S.P.52	State Papers Scotland, Elizabeth I.
S.P.53	State Papers Mary Queen of Scots.
S.P.70	State Papers Foreign, General series, Elizabeth I.
Wards 9	Court of Wards and Liveries, Miscellaneous Books.

OTHER COMMON ABBREVIATIONS IN THE NOTES

B.M.	British Museum.
Cal.	Calendar.
For.	Foreign.
H.M.C.	Historical Manuscripts Commission Reports.
L. & P.	Letters and Papers, Foreign and Domestic Henry VIII.
Pat.	Patent Rolls.
P.C.C.	Prerogative Court of Canterbury, Registers of Wills.
S.P.	State Papers.
ser.	Series.
Soc.	Society publications.

NOTES

CHAPTER ONE

1. Bodleian, Ashmole mss. 394, *fo.* 93. G. F. Nott, who printed part of this in *The Works of Henry Howard* (1815), I, p. xxxi, wrongly corrected the year given in this manuscript to 1536. That it was properly 1538 appears from the letter of 14th March 1538, cited in note 2 below. Nott relied on the third duke's inquisition post mortem in 1554 which states the age of his grandson and heir as 'eighteen years and upwards', but ages given in these inquisitions are now known to be notoriously inaccurate. In the licence, 1st July 1557, for Thomas Howard to succeed to his grandfather's estates the year is correct, but the birth-day wrong, making it appear that he was born 12th March 1538 (*Cal. Patent Rolls, 1557-8*, p. 323). Thomas Howard himself provides a further check. In January 1572, he reminded his eldest son, Philip (b. June 1557) that at the time of the third duke's death (in August 1554), 'I was not much above a year older than you are now'. (T. Wright, *Queen Elizabeth and Her Times* (1838), I, 403.)

2. S.P.1/130, *fo.* 43.

3. *ms.* 'unto'.

4. This son of Lord Thomas Howard (later Viscount Bindon) died in infancy; his name is not known.

5. E.101/519/30; S.P.1/130, *fo.* 43.

6. L.R.2/115, 117 *passim*; *Norfolk Archaeology*, VII, 294-5, XV, 22-38.

7. *H.M.C. Rutland*, IV, 272; Nott, *Howard's Works*, pp. xxii-iv. For Jane's birth see *L. and P. Henry VIII*, XII pt. 2 no. 973 (mention of a gift of girdles to 'the Lady of Surrey at the christening of a child'). The dates of the births of the three youngest children are given in *Complete Peerage s.v.* Berkeley, Northumberland and Scrope.

8. L.R.2/115, *fo.* 47d.

9. *Norfolk Archaeology*, XII, 194-5, XV, 195-6; Blomefield and Parkin, *Norfolk* III, 268, IV, 168, 427.

10. Quoted in *Complete Peerage s.v.* Berkeley p. 138n.

11. Nott, *Howard's Works*, I, lxi, lxii, cix, 420. Thomas Howard in a letter to Foxe, 5th March 1560, wrote '*Pudet me meam dissuetudinem in literis tibi his scriptis*'; see also *Cal. State Papers For. 1563*, p. 26, and *D.N.B. s.v.* Churchyard.

12. Nott, *Howard's Works*, I, appendix xviii.

13. J. A. Froude, *History of England* (1858), IV, 105; *Archaeologia*, XXII, 62.

14. Nott, *op. cit.*, I, pp. l, li; *L. and P. Hen. VIII*, XVIII, i no. 542.

15. *Ibid.*, nos. 327, 251. Froude, *op. cit.*, 252-3 quotes a slightly different version of the affair.

16. *Acts of Privy Council, 1542-7*, 104; Nott, *op. cit.*, lii, liii, 53-55.

17. *L. and P. Hen. VIII*, XXI, i no. 356.

18. *Ibid.*, nos. 146, 394.

19. Erna Auerbach, *Tudor Artists* (1953), 71, 73.

20. *L. and P. Hen. VIII*, xxi, ii, no. 554.

21. *Ibid.*, no. 347.

22. *Ibid.*, nos. 547, 605; Roper, *Life of More*, 71.

23. S.P.1/227/26; S.P.1/245, *fo.* 145; L.R.1/42, *fo.* 281.

24. The original depositions of the Duchess of Richmond and of Elizabeth Holland have not survived, but the version of them quoted here from Lord Herbert's *History of Henry VIII* is probably trustworthy. Froude in his *History*, IV, 514, 515, incorrectly cites a State Paper Office volume, but these are not with the other depositions, which he partially quotes, in S.P.1/227, *fos.* 97-129, nor could they have been contained in the letter of 15th December 1546 (*fo.* 88) now torn. The passages which Froude quoted are in fact taken from Lord Herbert.

25. *ms.* 'destraction'.

26. S.P.1/227, *fos.* 97-115; *L. and P.* xxi, ii, pp. xli-xliii.

27. *Ibid.*, i, no. 1426; ii, pp. xxxix, no. 697.

28. S.P.1/227, *fo.* 123.

29. *A Chronicle of Henry VIII* (ed. Martin Hume, 1889), pp. 145-6; *L. and P.* xxi, ii, no. 697.

30. *Baga de Secretis* printed in 3rd *D.K. Report* (1842), app. II, 267-8; *Chronicle of Henry VIII*, c, lxiv; *Wriothesley's Chronicle*, 177.

31. *L. and P.* xxi, ii, pp. xxxix, xlviii.

32. *Ibid.*, no. 554.

33. *Ibid.*, no. 696.

34. *Ibid.*, no. 770 (86); *Lords Journals*, I, 284-5.

35. *State Papers* (S. P. Commission), xi, 387, 391.

36. *L. and P.* xxi, ii, nos. 646, 671.

37. Nott, *op. cit.*, I, cviii-cxxiii.

38. *L. and P.* xxi, ii, no. 548, 14th Dec. 1546, the Duchess 'looks to lie in at Candlemas next'.

CHAPTER TWO

1. E.101/625/2; E.315/503/41; S.P.46/1, *fo.* 19; Arundel Castle mss., Inventory of Plate, etc., *fo.* 104.

2. *Acts of Privy Council, 1548*, 183.

3. J. Pratt, *Acts and Monuments of John Foxe* (1870), I, i, 9-10.

4. J. A. Froude, *History of England*, IV, 106.

5. *Acts and Monuments*, I, i, 10; H. F. N. Prescott, *Spanish Tudor* (1940) 142.

6. See my *Captains Outrageous* (1961), 54-55.

7. The best account of the rebellion is the Historical Association pamphlet by S. T. Bindoff (1949). Much valuable information about 'spoilers of church lands' in Norfolk is given by Sir Henry Spelman in *History and Fate of Sacrilege* (1698).

8. *Cal. Pat. Rolls, 1551-2*, 237; S.P.10/14/45; S.P.46/1, *fo.* 154; S.P.46/2/80; *Acts of Privy Council, 1552-4*, 13.

9. *Cal. S.P. Spain*, 1553-4, 70, 87, 103, 107; *Machyn's Diary* (Camden Soc., Original Series XLII), 38; *Acts of Privy Council*, 1552-4, 315, 334.

10. *Machyn's Diary*, 45-46, 118-19; Strype, *Ecclesiastical Memorials*, III, i, 57; C. V. Malfatti, *The Accession, Coronation and Marriage of Mary Tudor* (Barcelona, 1956).

11. C.65/162, nos. 22, 34; Arundel Castle mss., G.1/7; Principal Probate Registry, P.C.C. 14 More.

12. *Acts and Monuments*, I, i, 12-13; J. A. Muller, *Stephen Gardiner and the Tudor Reaction* (1926), 340, 379.

13. *Complete Peerage*, IX, 621; *H.M.C. Gawdy*, 13; E. Harris Harbison, *Rival Ambassadors at the Court of Queen Mary* (Princeton, 1940), 193 *n.* 53; L.R.1/42, fo. 269d; S.P.14/55/11, p. 1 (from internal evidence the funeral was that of Mary Fitzroy, Duchess of Richmond, in 1557, not that of Elizabeth, Duchess of Norfolk, in 1558. *Cf.* Bodleian Library, Ashmole mss., 836, 185-6); *H.M.C. Various Collections*, II, 231-4.

14. *Cal. S.P. Spain*, 1553, 197; *Ibid.*, 1554-5, 217. The Spanish ambassador may have confused Howard with the Bishop of Norwich, who was sent to Germany at this time, Arundel Castle mss., Autograph Letters, no. 19.

15. He retained the title Earl of Surrey until his son was born. He was also accounted in his day, though the entitlement is inaccurate, Earl of Warrenne, Lord Mowbray, Segrave and Brewes.

16. C.142/103/56; Principal Probate Registry, P.C.C. 14 More; *H.M.C. Gawdy*, 13.

17. *Cal. S.P. Spain*, 1554-5, 258; Renard, the imperial ambassador, already called Howard 'Arundel's son-in-law' in Sept. 1554, showing that a marriage was being arranged. *Ibid.*, 46; Arundel Castle mss., G.1/7; *Cal. S.P. Venetian*, 1555-6, no. 308; C.65/164/23; B.M. Royal mss., 12A, i-iv.

18. *Cal. S.P. For.*, 1553-8, 242.

19. *Cal. Pat. Rolls*, 1557-8, 362-3; *Machyn's Diary*, 139.

20. *Ibid.*, 141; Duke of Norfolk, *Life of Philip Howard, Earl of Arundel* (1857), 5.

21. *Machyn's Diary*, 149; Strype, *Memorials*, III, 385; Strype, *Annals*, I, ii, 45.

22. *Cal. S.P. For.*, 1553-8, 370, 374, 384, 389; *Cal. S.P. Venetian*, 1557-8, 1569.

23. The actual date and place of the marriage are uncertain. It was most probably 28th or 29th November, for when the Dowager Duchess of Norfolk revised her will on 30th November, Norfolk had already married again, (P.C.C., 31 Welles).

24. *Lords' Journal*, I, 557; Stow, *Survey of London* (ed. Kingsford), I, 142.

CHAPTER THREE

1. *Machyn's Diary*, 178-9; *Acts of Privy Council*, 1558-70, 4.
2. *Machyn's Diary*, 181-2.
3. *Ibid.*, 186.
4. *Cal. S.P. Venetian*, 1558-80, 16-17.

5. See my article 'The Coronation of Queen Elizabeth I' in *Quarterly Review* (1953), 397-410.

6. *Cal. S.P. Venetian, 1558-80,* 17-18.

7. *Ibid.,* 11, 19, 27.

8. *Ibid.,* 91-2; *Machyn's Diary,* 196, 200; Nicholls, *Progresses,* I, 67-8.

9. G. D. Squibb, *High Court of Chivalry* (1959), 32; A. R. Wagner, *Records and Collections of the College of Arms* (1952), 9-12, 56-7, 68-70, 79-80.

10. Bodleian, Ashmole mss., 846, 102-16. This version is dated 1568, no doubt a final codification, for he had made earlier decrees (see *Machyn's Diary,* 309).

11. P.C.C., 31 Welles; S.P.12/81, *fos.* 61*d.,* 69*d.,* 73*d.,* 75; E.190/471/7; Arundel Castle mss., Inventory of Plate, etc., *fos.* 77-103; Blomefield, I, 224.

12. S.P.12/81, *fos.* 77-78*d.*; Fuller's *Worthies,* II, 154; The dimensions of the bowling-alley are given in L.R.1/43, *fo.* 309*d.*

13. J. T. Murray, *English Dramatic Companies, 1558-1642,* II, 59-61, 364-5; S.P.12/81, *fo.* 73*d.* Arundel Castle mss., Inventory of Plate, etc., *fo.* 103*d.*

14. Cooper, *Annals of Cambridge,* II, 92-3, 99-100, 203-6.

15. S.P.12/6, *fo.* 67. For posts see *L. and P. Hen. VIII,* xx, i, no. 1041.

16. *Church Historians of England,* I, i, 31, 34-7; R. Green, *Framlingham and Saxtead* (1834), 93.

17. *Cal. Pat. Rolls, 1563-66,* no. 1694; *Cal. S.P. Spain, 1558-67,* 418; *Machyn's Diary,* 294.

18. *Harleian Miscellany,* IV (1809), 478; *Norfolk Archaeology,* XXXII (1959), 76.

19. E.179/69/78.

20. *Cal. S.P. Spain, 1558-67,* 107.

21. *Ibid.,* 113-14, 117.

CHAPTER FOUR

1. Bodleian, Ashmole mss., 858, 54; *Cal. S.P. Foreign, 1558-9,* nos. 845, 868, 902. A coloured drawing of the arms sent from France is in B.M. Cotton mss., Caligula, Bx. 17.

2. *Sadler Papers* (ed. Clifford) II, 115, 173, 178, 221-2; *Burghley State Papers* (ed. Haynes, 1740) 261. For Norfolk's attitude to the command see Froude, *History* VII, 165-6, based on De Quadra's letter to the Duchess of Parma, 18th Dec. 1559, in the Simancas Archives, which is not noted in the *Spanish Calendar.*

3. *Burghley State Papers,* 210, 229.

4. *Ibid.,* 222; *Cal. Pat. Rolls, 1560-63,* 62.

5. E.351/226.

6. *Burghley State Papers,* 238, 253-5, 276.

7. *Ibid.,* 283-7, 303, 306; *Cal. S.P. Venice, 1558-80,* 234; Conyers Read, *Mr Secretary Cecil* (1955), 164.

8. *Burghley State Papers,* 239, 241, 274, 300, 312, 320-1; *H.M.C. Cecil,* I, 218.

9. *Ibid.,* 227; *Burghley State Papers,* 230, 235, 242, 244, 247.

10. *Ibid.,* 237, 275, 299, 303, 311.

11. *Ibid.,* 261, 264, 322; *Cal. S.P. Spain, 1558-67,* 133, 137, 141.

12. *Burghley State Papers,* 322; Read, *Cecil,* 171-80.

13. Rymer, *Foedera*, xv, 593-6.
14. H.C.A.24/31/28-9; *Burghley State Papers*, 357.
15. Bodleian, Ashmole mss., 840, 153.
16. Clinton to Sussex, 8th Aug. 1560; *Burghley State Papers*, 360. He was paid as lieutenant-general up to 23rd Aug. (E.351/226).
17. S.P.70/17, *fo. 128d*.

CHAPTER FIVE

1. Murdin, *Burghley State Papers*, 180; *The Chorography of Norfolk* (ed. C. M. Hood, 1932), 7.
2. R. H. Tawney, *Agrarian Problem in the Sixteenth Century* (1912) contains a mass of information about conditions in Norfolk. Professor Bindoff's pamphlet on Ket's Rebellion (above II, *n.* 7), adds important details.
3. William Camden, *Brittannia* (ed. R. Gough, 1806), II, 269-70. For the area served by Lynn see the Common Staith Accounts, 1580-1, and the Water Bailiff's Accounts, 1586-7, among the municipal records.
4. Camden, *op. cit.*, 213; Cooper, *Annals of Cambridge* (1843), II, 55-8, 357-9, 366. Star Chamber Proceedings Edw. VI, 2/68; E.190/427/7 *s.v.* 16th Dec. for virginals; E.122/155/22 *s.v.* 10th July for books.
5. E.178/1528; Bodleian Lib., Tanner mss., 241, *fo.* 57. Fuller, *Church History* (ed. Brewer, 1845), IV, 42; J. Speed, *Theatre . . . of Great Britaine* (1611), *fo.* 35. For details of trade on these rivers see entries in the Yarmouth Water Bailiff's Accounts, which are enrolled on the Borough Court Rolls.
6. W. Harrison, *Description of England* (1877 ed.), pt. II, 109-15; F. M. Stenton in *Economic History Review*, VIII (1936-7), 1-21; J. Ogilby, *Britannia* (1675), 151; Bodleian, Tanner mss., 241, *fo. 12d*.
7. E.164/46, *fos.* 175-9; S.P.12/81, *fos.* 77-79d.; P. Millican, *Freemen of Norwich* (1934), 150.
8. Blomefield, *Norfolk*, IV, 298; L.R.1/43, *fo. 309d*.
9. C.66/1054, *mm.* 14-15; *Records of City of Norwich* (ed. W. Hudson and J. C. Tingey, 1910), II, lxiii, 332-3, *Tudor Economic Documents* (ed. R. H. Tawney and E. E. Power, 1924), 299-300; M. R. James, *Catalogue of Corpus Christi College, Cambridge Mss.* (1912), I, 254.
10. See my 'Two Documents Concerning the New Draperies' in *Economic History Review* 2nd series IV (1952); S.P.12/106/47; *Norfolk Archaeology* XXI (1923), 248; *Norwich Records*, II, lxxx, 184-5; W. J. C. Moens, *Walloon Church at Norwich* (Huguenot Society of London, 1887-8).
11. *Norfolk Archaeology*, V (1859), 75; J. S. Burn, *History of Foreign Protestant Refugees* (1840), 62-66.
12. A translation of the Latin couplet by the Scot, Arthur Johnson (see Camden's *Britannia*, ed. R. Gough, 1806, II, 177).
13. *Cal. Pat. Rolls, 1558-60*, 31; E.159, 7 Eliz. I. Hil. Communia *rot.* 337; Great Yarmouth Corporation Records, Assembly Books, II, 15, 36, 40d., 183d. Henry Manship, *Booke of the Foundacion and Antiquitye of . . . Greate Yarmouthe* (ed. C. J. Palmer, 1847), 26-45, and his son's *History of . . . Yarmouth* (ed. Palmer, 1854), 84-97.

14. S.P.12/81, *fos.* 81*d.,* 82.

15. *E.H.R.* XXIII (1908), 470; J. E. Neale, *Elizabethan House of Commons* (1949), 160-1.

16. *Ibid.,* 193; W. Alberry, *Parliamentary History of Horsham* (1927), 7, 16.

17. Blomefield, *Norfolk,* I, 133, 141; II, 57, 70-77; Neale, *op. cit.,* 195.

18. *Ibid.,* 196; S.P.15/13/52; Thomas Gawdy, son of the Norfolk serjeant at law, was appointed to the Marshalsea, 25th Nov. 1561, Arundel Castle mss., G.1/7.

19. *Cal. S.P. Dom.,* 1547-80, 98; *Acts of Privy Council,* 1558-70, 116, 121; H. le Strange, *Norfolk Official Lists.*

20. *Cal. Pat. Rolls,* 1558-60, 353; 1560-3, 439-42; 1563-6, nos. 151, 220, 222; 1566-9, no. 2386.

21. E.g. *Acts of Privy Council,* 1558-70, 116, 121.

22. C.66/1116, *m.* 18; Blomefield, *Norfolk,* IV, 268.

CHAPTER SIX

1. *Cal. S.P. Spain,* 1558-67, 183.

2. *Cal. Pat. Rolls,* 1560-3, 305.

3. *Register of Admissions to Gray's Inn* (ed. J. Foster, 1889), col. 30; Arundel Castle mss., G.1/7.

4. *Cal. S.P. Spain,* 1558-67, 229, 235. In the first of these letters De Quadra wrongly noted that the meeting was to be in 'Lancaster'; in the second he corrected this. Lady Lennox was sent to the Tower at the end of March 1562. (*Cal. S.P. For.,* 1561-2, no. 980 (5)), not in Nov. 1561 as stated in *D.N.B.,* LIV, 288.

5. *Cal. S.P. Spain,* 1558-67, 261-3; *Machyn's Diary,* 294; S.P.12/31/15. The sole source for this crisis is De Quadra's correspondence. The pages of the Privy Council Register between Sept. 1562 and Jan. 1563 are missing. It is quite possible that the Queen herself later tore out the offending pages for the days on which the Council discussed the delicate topic of the succession while she lay unconscious.

6. *Cal. S.P. Spain,* 1558-67, 272-3.

7. *Ibid.,* xliii-iv, xlix, 280 *et seq.*; *Cal. S.P. For.,* 1563, 25. The importance and, in general, accuracy of De Quadra's intelligence reports are now recognised by historians.

8. S.P.70/62/1037; S.P.12/31/15.

9. She had died before 31st May 1571 when the duke made his will (Arundel Castle mss., T.4).

10. C. Read, *Cecil,* 326-32.

11. Cooper, *Annals of Cambridge,* II, 181-208; F. Peck, *Desiderata Curiosa,* VII, 25-46; J. B. Mullinger, *History of Cambridge University,* II, 189-92.

12. *Cal. S.P. For.,* 1564-5, 1118, 1135; Teulet, *Relations,* II, 196; *Cal. S.P. Spain,* 1558-67, 399.

13. *Cal. S.P. For.,* 1564-5, 1129; S.P.12/46, *fos.* 105-6.

14. S.P.52/10, *fo.* 68. Only a portion of Randolph's letter has survived.

15. *Harleian Miscellany,* IV (1809), 478.

16. Wright, *Queen Elizabeth and Her Times*, I, 209.

17. *Cal. S.P. Spain*, *1558-67*, 449-50, 479-81; *Cal. S.P. For.*, *1564-6*, no. 1224.

18. Wright, *op. cit.*, I, 210-11; Nicholls, *Progresses*, I, 198.

19. S.P.12/44/42; *Cal. S.P. For.*, *1564-5*, nos. 1657 (3), 1658; *Cal. S.P., Spain*, *1558-67*, 504, 518.

20. There was a general prohibition on the export of wool. Norfolk's licence was finally granted him on 15th Dec. 1565, allowing him to export 30 sarplers of wool from his own sheep, providing he paid customs duties, in exchange for commodities for his household (*Cal. Pat. Rolls*, *1563-6*, no. 2860).

21. Haynes, *Cecil Papers*, 442.

22. *Cal. S.P. Spain*, *1558-67*, 511; *H.M.C. Cecil*, I, 350.

23. *Cal. S.P. For.*, *1564-5*, 536; Aitkin, I, 397; *Cal. S.P. Spain*, *1558-67*, 511-12.

24. Bodleian Library, Ashmole mss., 840, 267.

25. *Cal. S.P. Spain*, *1558-67*, 518-19, 524, 544, 549, 571; Wright, *Queen Elizabeth and Her Times*, I, 225.

26. *Cal. S.P. For.*, *1566-8*, 99, 111.

27. Froude, *History*, VIII, 281, 289; *Cal. S.P. Spain*, *1558-67*, 586-9.

28. J. E. Neale, *Elizabethan Parliaments*, *1559-81*, 136, 141-3.

29. *Cal. S.P. Spain*, *1558-67*, 591-2.

CHAPTER SEVEN

1. *Cal. Charter Rolls*, VI, 223-5; C.56/78, no. 17; E.368/346, Mich. Communia 1 Eliz., *rot.* 136; E.368/367 Hil. 9 Eliz. de Processu tangenti T. Ducem Norfolk.

2. L.R.1/42, *fo.* 360; L.R.1/43, *fos.* 156d., 174d.

3. Wards 9/264, *fos.* 34d., 38d., 73.

4. S.P.12/24/10; L.C.4/188, *fo.* 525d.

5. *Cal. Pat. Rolls*, *1558-60*, p. 393; C.54/677, no. 60.

6. S.P.15/11/56 and 57; S.P.12/24/10; C.54/641; *Cal. Pat. Rolls*, *1560-3*, 564-6; Wards 9/264, *fo.* 34d.

7. Read, *Cecil*, 192.

8. *Lords Journal*, I, 149; Burgon, *Life of Gresham*, II, 184; C.66/1075, *m.*44.

9. *Catholic Rec. Soc.*, XXI, 7; C.54/800 m. 10d., C.54/734, nos. 20, 23; *Cal. S.P. Spain*, *1568-79*, p. 85. Economic historians are still far from decided about the relative weight to be given to the different factors which caused the Price Revolution. *See* Y. S. Brenner, 'The Inflation of Prices in Early Sixteenth Century England' in *Econ.H.R.*, 2nd ser., XIV (1961), 218-39.

10. L.R.1/43, *fos.* 261-4, 281-2d.

11. C.54/606, nos. 25-6; C.54/734, no. 14; C.54/830; S.P.15/11/57.

12. C.54/807, *m.* 10; *H.M.C. Cecil*, I, 525.

13. C.54/715, nos. 12, 15, 16.

14. C.54/673, no. 51.

15. Arundel Castle mss., Inventory of Plate etc., *fos.* 73-6.

16. C.54/701, no. 1; C.54/684, no. 29; C.54/703, no. 16.

17. *Cal. Pat. Rolls*, *1560-3*, 564; C.54/806, *m.* 15; L.R.8/158/15, 22.

18. G. S. Davies, *The Charterhouse in London* (1922) is incorrect in stating the house became Norfolk's on 1st January 1565 (*See* C.54/673, no. 51; C.54/679, no. 74); L.R.1/42, *fo.* 362*d.*

19. Stow, *Survey* (ed. Kingsford), II, 83; Davies, *op. cit.*, 161-7.

20. C.54/806, *m.* 15.

21. C.66/1033 *m.* 16; Wards 9/264, *fo.* 88.

22. C.142/151/2; C.66/1060 *m.* 20; Wards 9/264, *fo.* 88*d.*; *Lives of Philip Howard etc.* (ed. Norfolk, 1857), 172-3; *Collectanea Topographia et Genealogica,* V (1838), 322-8.

23. Arundel Castle mss., T.4, 5; *Collectanea Topographia loc. cit.*

24. Arundel Castle mss., Inventory of Deeds, etc., *fos.* 19*d.*-20.

25. L.R.1/42, *fos.* 400-3; Arundel Castle mss., G.1/7; for the Earl of Oxford's settlement *see* C.54/626, no. 45. The best description of feoffees to uses is R. B. Pugh, *Antrobus Deeds* (Wiltshire Records Branch, III, 1947), xlii-iv.

26. L.R.8/158/22; Blomefield's *Norfolk,* I, 237-9.

27. Arundel Castle mss., Autograph Letters, no. 42.

28. C.54/830, no. 2; C.P. 25 (2), 229 Mich. 12 and 13 Eliz.; M. A. Tierney, *History of Arundel* (1834), II, 360.

29. Arundel Castle mss., T.4, 5.

30. E.372/ 15 Eliz., *rot.* Item Norfolk; Arundel Castle mss., G.1/7 and T.4, 5; *H.M.C. Cecil,* I, 370.

31. E.179/681/78, 79, and 83.

32. Arundel Castle mss., G.1/7; E.163/16/4, *fo.* 1; *H.M.C. Cecil,* I, 527, 570.

CHAPTER EIGHT

1. S.P.12/40/86; S.P.12/81, *fo.* 75; *Cal. S.P. Spain, 1558-67,* 524-5, 571, 616-17; P.C.C. 31 Welles.

2. S.P.12/44, *fo.* 90; *H.M.C. Cecil,* I, 348; Arundel Castle mss., G.1/7 and Inventory of Plate etc.; *H.M.C. Bath,* II, 17, S.P.12/81, *fo.* 111.

3. *Cal. S.P. For., 1566-8,* nos. 1296, 1327.

4. S.P.12/44/42; *H.M.C. Bath,* II, 17-18.

5. S.P.12/44/46; B.M., Lansdowne mss., 9, 64. I have treated the last stages of the Hapsburg suit rather fully, as they are passed over in most works.

6. *Cal. S.P. For., 1566-8,* nos. 1857-8, 1947; Haynes, 464; *D.N.B. s.v.* Radcliffe, T.

7. Anthony Wood, *Athenae Oxonienses* (ed. P. Bliss, 1815), I, 487, II, 844, and *Fasti,* 183.

8. *Cal. S.P. Spain, 1568-79,* 36.

9. *Cal. S.P. Scotland, 1563-9,* 457; Murdin, *Burghley State Papers,* 52.

10. *Cal. S.P. Spain, 1568-79,* 50, 52; *Cal. S.P. Scotland, 1563-9,* nos. 469, 476.

11. Anderson, *Collections Relating to the History of Mary Queen of Scotland* (1728), IV, ii, 3-32; J. Melville, *Memoirs* (ed. W. Mackay Mackenzie), 104-6.

12. *Cal. S.P. Scotland, 1563-9,* 530-5, 693-4; Murdin, 52; Anderson, *op. cit.,* 17; Froude, *History,* IX, 280; *State Trials* I, 976-7, 983.

13. *Cal. S.P. For., 1566-8,* nos. 2571, 2608, 2619-20.

14. *Dépêches de Fénélon* (ed. C. P. Cooper, 1838), I, 17-18; Froude, *History*, IX, 297n. cites a Spanish despatch containing the rumour.

15. *Haynes*, 574.

16. Anderson, *op. cit.*, 97-163; Melville, *Memoirs*, 107.

17. *State Trials*, I, 981-3, 989.

CHAPTER NINE

1. F. Peck, *Desiderata Curiosa* (1732), Book I, 15-16.

2. *Cal. S.P. Spain, 1568-75*, III, 136.

3. Read, *Cecil*, 442-3, quoting the French ambassador, the only contemporary account of the dramatic meeting.

4. Peck, *loc. cit.*; Lodge, *Illustrations of British History*, I, 475-9; *Cal. S.P. Spain, 1568-79*, 166-7.

5. *Haynes*, 541-3.

6. *Cal. S.P. Spain, 1568-79*, 158, 166-7; *Cal. S.P. Scotland, 1571-4*, 343.

7. S.P.12/51/14, 16; S.P.12/54/5.

8. S.P.12/284, fos. 173, 206.

9. S.P.53/3, fos. 205-6; Labanoff, *Lettres*, II, 368-70, 24 [June] 1569.

10. J. A. Froude (*History*, IX, 471-2) places this meeting on 27th August, relying on the Spanish despatch. From the itinerary of the court it must have been 27 July (*cf.* C.82/1206-8). The Council Register is, unfortunately, missing for this crucial period.

11. *Fénélon*, II, 127-8.

12. There is no foundation for Miss R. R. Reid's statement that Cecil was urging Murray 'to further Mary's marriage with Norfolk' during that summer ('The Political Influence of the North Parts under the later Tudors' in *Tudor Studies Presented to A. F. Pollard*, ed. R. W. Seton Watson, p. 222). Neither of the documents which she cites supports this rather strange interpretation of Cecil's role at that time.

13. Read, *Cecil*, 448; *Cal. S.P. Scotland*, III, 674.

14. The chronology of the events described in this and the following paragraphs has never previously been properly established. The itinerary of the court reconstructed from the Chancery Warrants, (C.82/1206-8) does make it plain that matters came to a head during August, and not, as generally thought, three or four weeks later.

15. *Cal. S.P. Scotland*, IV, 32 *seq.*

16. *H.M.C. Cecil*, I, 414; *Cal. S.P. Scotland*, III, 669; *State Trials*, I, 997; Froude, *History*, IV, 470.

17. W. Camden, *History*, 130.

18. *Haynes*, 522; *State Trials*, I, 994-5.

19. S.P.12/58/24; *Haynes*, 527-8; Camden, *History*, 130; Labanoff, *op. cit.*, II, 381.

20. Camden, *op. cit.*, 131; *Haynes*, 531.

21. S.P.12/67, fo. 140; S.P.12/85/33; S.P.15/14, fo. 220.

22. *H.M.C. Cecil*, I, 438, 440; *Haynes*, 529-33; Read, *Cecil*, 450-1.

23. Wright, *Queen Elizabeth and Her Times*, I, 324-6; *Haynes*, 538; S.P.12/81/57.

24. *H.M.C. Cecil*, I, 429, 433; S.P.12/59, *fos.* 7, 9, 13.

25. Read, *Cecil*, 451; *Cal. S.P. Scotland*, III, 687, 693; Melville, *Memoirs*, 110.

26. S.P.15/14/89, 97, 102; S.P.12/67, *fo.* 140.

27. Read, *Walsingham*, I, 65-7; S.P.12/59/5.

28. Read, *Walsingham*, I, 68-74. Another copy of this pamphlet is in the library at Arundel Castle.

29. *H.M.C. Pepys*, 166-70.

CHAPTER TEN

1. *Cal. S.P. Addenda 1566-79*, 362; Sir Cuthbert Sharp, *Memorials of the Rebellion* (1840), 56; S.P.15/15/54.

2. S.P.15/14/94, 99, 100, 104.

3. S.P.15/15/4, Gargrave's enclosure.

4. *Ibid.*, 12, 14, 18 1; *Memorials*, 13.

5. *Cal. S.P. Add.*, 108-9; *Memorials*, 199.

6. *Ibid.*, 52; R. R. Reid in *Trans. Royal Hist. Soc.* new ser., Vol. xx (1906), 197.

7. *Op. cit.*; and R. R. Reid in *Tudor Studies Presented to A. F. Pollard* (1924).

8. E.137/133/1. The writer is editing this roll of Fines for the Surtees Society.

9. Humberston's Survey in E.164/37, 38.

10. Much of the following paragraphs appeared in *Norfolk Archaeology*, Vol. xxii (1959).

11. *Cal. S.P. Venetian, 1558-80*, 437; *Cal. S.P. Spanish, 1568-79*, 179, 181; S.P.12/60 *fo.* 2.

12. C.66/1112 *mm.* 1, 2.

13. E.368/383, Hil. 13 Eliz. I, status et visus compotorum, Norfolk membrane (Sheriff Heydon's cravings for his expenses); *Cal. S.P. Spanish, 1568-79*, 225.

14. C.66/1112 *m.* 1; *D.N.B. s.v.* Neville, Charles.

15. S.P.12/57, *fos.* 111-12; S.P.12/68 *fo.* 57. Details of the incidents in Norwich and elsewhere have been taken from K.B.9/627[i], no. 109.

16. *Lincolnshire Pedigrees*, Harleian Soc. L (1902), 32-3; *H.M.C. Cecil*, I, 344-51; Blomefield's *Norfolk* I, 344.

17. *Ibid.*, III, 284; K.B. 9/627 (i), no. 109. *H.M.C. Cecil*, I, 557.

18. C.66/1112, *m.* 1.

19. K.B. 9/627 (i), no. 109; Stow, *Annales* (1631), 666; E. Lodge, *Illustrations of British History* (1838), I, 513; *H.M.C. Cecil*, I, 557; Heydon's cravings in E.368/383.

20. *Cal. S.P. Spain, 1568-79*, 258; S.P.12/71, *fo.* 155, undated but probably 11th July 1570 (portions of this were printed by R. Hindry Mason, *History of Norfolk* (1884), 158 with various inaccuracies).

21. S.P.12/71 no. 61, dated in *Cal. S.P. Dom.*, *1547-80* '? July 28', but it must have been written a fortnight earlier. This is the document printed *in extenso* by Mason, *op. cit.*, 158-9, but it is not a document of the trial itself.

22. K.B.9/627 (i), no. 109; S.P.12/71, *fos.* 151-2.
23. Heydon's cravings in E.368/383.
24. *Norfolk Archaeology*, Vol. v (1859), 78-9.
25. Stow, *Annales*, 666; Lodge, *Illustrations*, I, 512-14; C.66/1077 *mm.* 14-15; C.66/1111 *mm.* 18-19; C.66/1112 *mm.* 1-3; L.R.1/42, *fo.* 344.
26. S.P.12/73, *fo.* 27.

CHAPTER ELEVEN

1. Haynes, 572; H.M.C. *Cecil*, I, 436-7, 443, 458, 461.
2. Labanoff, *Lettres de Marie Stuart*, III, 4-6, 11-12; 19-20, 31-2, 35; Murdin, 20.
3. H.M.C. *Cecil*, I, 455-6, 459, 472-3; S.P.12/67, *fos.* 7-12; S.P.15/18/38; Read, *Walsingham*, I, 74-9; Labanoff, *op. cit.*, 36-7, 47-8.
4. Haynes, 592-8.
5. S.P.15/19, *fo.* 1. Walsingham was at this time on a mission to France. The writing of this unsigned document is similar to that of the clerk who wrote his letter from Paris on 21st August, (S.P.70/113, *fo.* 180).
6. S.P.12/71/19 and 36; S.P.12/73, *fos.* 9-10; H.M.C. *Cecil*, I, 474-6, 479.
7. S.P.12/73, *fos.* 152, 164; S.P.12/74, *fo.* 71; *Cal. S.P. Spain, 1568-79*, 282.
8. *Cal. S.P. Rome, 1558-71*, 346-8, 412; H.M.C. *Cecil*, I, 536; Murdin, *Burghley State Papers*, 25-6; *State Trials*, I, 1008, 1043.
9. See above p. 112-13; Arundel Castle mss., Inventory of Plate etc., *fos.* 71-6; Murdin, 28.
10. *Cal. S.P. Rome, 1558-71*, 393-405.
11. Murdin, 15-17; Froude, *History*, X, 205-8; S.P.12/81, *fos.* 117-18; Read, *Burghley*, 39.
12. *Cal. S.P. Rome, 1558-71*, 407-8, 411-13.
13. *Ibid.*, 413-14, 433-6, 442-3, 445; *Cal. S.P. Spain, 1568-79*, 319, 336-7.
14. S.P.12/81, *fos.* 117-18; Murdin, 4-9, 23-5; *Cal. S.P. Spain, 1568-79*, 322. Much fresh material has come to light on the unravelling of the Ridolfi Plot since Froude made his masterly reconstruction (*History*, X, 202-23), e.g. S.P.12/85/11.
15. *Cal. S.P. Spain, 1568-79*, 272, 288, 312, 326; Murdin, 9-12; *D.N.B.* s.v. Bailly, Charles.
16. S.P.12/77, *fo.* 133; J. E. Neale, *Elizabeth I and Her Parliaments, 1559-81*, 225-34; S.P.12/81, *fos.* 138-9d.; S.P.12/83, *fo.* 57d.
17. Murdin, 13-14; *Cal. S.P. Rome, 1558-71*, 408-10.
18. H.M.C. *Cecil*, I, 503-18; *Cal. S.P. Spain, 1568-79*, 274, 335.
19. *Ibid.*, 327; S.P.12/80, *fo.* 21.
20. S.P.12/81, *fo.* 1; H.M.C. *Cecil*, I, 512, 516; Murdin, 67-70.
21. *Ibid.*, 67-9, 87, 91; S.P.12/81, *fo.* 1.
22. S.P.12/83, *fo.* 58; *Cal. S.P. Spain, 1568-79*, 333; S.P.12/81, *fos.* 12-16; H.M.C. *Cecil*, I, 520, 522; Read, *Burghley*, 41.
23. Murdin, 149; *Cal. S.P. Spain, 1568-79*, 335.
24. S.P.12/80, *fo.* 117; Read, *Burghley*, 40; *Acts of Privy Council, 1571-5*, 43.
25. S.P.12/81/28; Sir Henry Spelman, *History and Fate of Sacrilege* (1698), 260; my article in *English Historical Review*, Vol. 64 (1951), 387-95.

26. S.P.12/81, *fos.* 67-82.
27. *Ibid., fos.* 61, 109, 111.

CHAPTER TWELVE

1. Arundel Castle mss., Vol. of Autograph Letters, no. 49; *Murdin*, 95.
2. Froude, *History*, x, 296; *Murdin*, 151-3; *H.M.C. Cecil*, I, 529, 525, 532, 561; S.P.15/20/81.
3. *Murdin*, 89.
4. *Ibid.*, 69-86; *State Trials*, I, 1041-50.
5. *Murdin*, 94, 97, 99, 101-7, 110-111, 116. Barker was pardoned 17th May 1574 at the suit of Leicester, C.66/1108, *m.* 24.
6. *Murdin*, 157, 162; *Cal. S.P. Scot.*, 1571-4, 14; Read, *Burghley*, 42.
7. *Murdin*, 130-6, 138, 144.
8. S.P.12/81, *fos.* 138-9d.; *D.N.B.*, *s.v.* Ridolfi, Roberto.
9. Froude, *History*, x, 279; *Murdin*, 18-61.
10. Froude, *op. cit.*, 300; B.M. Cotton, Caligula, C.III, 198. There are many copies of this confession and it is printed *in extenso* in *Cal. S.P. Scot.*, 1571-4, 32-40; *H.M.C. Cecil*, I, 564, 568-9.
11. S.P.12/83, *fo.* 57.
12. *Murdin*, 157.
13. S.P.12/83, *fos.* 152-3; S.P.12/85, *fos.* 19-34. See below p. 235.
14. S.P.12/81, *fo.* 129. The Sawston rising was on 26th Sept. 1573, C.66/1116, *m.* 18.
15. *Cal. S.P. For.*, 1569-71, no. 2182.
16. *Cal. S.P. Spain*, 1568-79, 355, 358.
17. S.P.12/95, *fo.* 202; *Catholic Rec. Soc.*, xxi, 6; B. M. Ward, *The Seventeenth Earl of Oxford* (1928), 68.
18. *Cal. S.P. Spain*, 1568-79, xxv, 322, 356; Read, *Burghley*, 44. De Spes had also hampered all attempts to settle the vexed question of the compensations for goods arrested during the embargo with Spain, beginning in December 1568, and London merchants were now as anxious as Spanish for an end to the affair. Once de Spes had left England, Elizabeth appointed an international panel of experts to settle the matter swiftly, C.66/1083, *mm.* 1d., 5d.
19. S.P.15/21/14; *Murdin*, 202-8; Read, *Burghley*, 45-6. Froude, *History*, x, 310-16, assigns de Spes a larger part in the assassination plot than the evidence warrants.
20. The following paragraphs are based on *State Trials*, I (1816), 958-1032, which is reprinted *verbatim*, including such printer's errors as 'Reminghall' for 'Kenninghall' from *The Tryal of Thomas Duke of Norfolk by His Peers* (1709), 1-136.
21. S.P.12/85/12. See also *Sadler Papers*, III, 98-100.

CHAPTER THIRTEEN

1. S.P.12/85, *fo.* 6.
2. S.P.12/85/13, 14.

3. B.M. Harleian mss. 787 no. 112, printed in T. Birch, *Queen Elizabeth and Her Times* (1838), I, 402-15.

4. Ashmole mss., 1109, *fo.* 10; *cf.* Ashmole mss., 846, *fo.* 109; Arundel Castle mss., Autograph Letters no. 51B.

5. *Murdin*, 166-74; S.P.12/85/25.

6. *Cath. Rec. Soc.*, XXIII, 9-10; S.P.12/85/36; *Murdin*, 171.

7. This death warrant, among the Arundel Castle mss., G.1/22, had been ready for some days and the date was filled in only as the Queen at last added her signature. *Court and Society* (1864), being excerpts from the Duke of Manchester's papers at Kimbolton, I, 236-7.

8. S.P.12/85/42 is the copy examined by the duke; another copy S.P.12/85/43 has certain differences; *Murdin*, 172. For a discussion of the Bible see *Cath. Rec. Soc.*, XXIII, 10-13. The 'Dix' New Testament is at Arundel Castle.

9. S.P.12/85/54; Ashmole mss., 1729, *fo.* 13; *Murdin*, 176, 177.

10. S.P.12/85/73; *Murdin*, 177.

11. S.P.12/86/3, 6, 11, 12, 31.

12. *Court and Society*, I, 236-7; Neale, *Elizabeth and her Parliaments, 1559-81*, 247, 311.

13. *H.M.C. Cecil*, II, 15; *Cal. S.P. Scotland*, IX, 298.

14. S.P.12/86, *fo.* 228. Skipwith in his letter to Burghley from the Tower on the night of 1st June adds a postscript: 'When I had written this much the Queen came', (S.P.12/88, *fo.* 2).

15. S.P.15/21/46; W. Camden, *Historie of Elizabeth* (1630 edn.), 40, 41; *State Trials*, I, 1032-4; Fénélon, *Dépêches*, V, 7; J. A. Froude transcripts from Simancas archives in B.M. Add. mss., 2b, 056 B; S.P.12/86/55; S.P.12/88/2.

EPILOGUE

1. W. Camden, *Historie of Elizabeth* (1630 edn.), 41.

INDEX

INDEX

Alessandrino, Michael, cardinal, papal secretary of state, 203

Alnwick, co. Northumb., 61, 140, 175

Alva, duke of, captain-general in Netherlands, 75, 130, 147, 151-2, 161, 163, 173, 182, 187-8, 195-6, 198, 201-5, 208, 220, 226-7

Anjou, duke of. *See* Henry Valois

Appleyard, John, 49, 95, 180-2

Arundel, co. Sussex, 191; castle, 122, 258; earldom, 121. *See also* FitzAlan *and* Howard Philip

astrologies and prophecies, 1, 37, 210, 219

Audley: Elizabeth, lady Audley, 46, 87, 124; Margaret. *See* Howard, Margaret

Audley End, co. Essex, 46, 87-8, 212, 215-16, 246

Axminster, co. Devon, manor, 107, 111

Bacon, Nicholas, lord keeper, 80, 87, 113, 121, 141-2, 166, 184, 192, 229, 248

Bacton, co. Suffolk, 107

Bailly, Charles, 202, 206-7, 209, 235, 238

Bannister: Edward, 76; Lawrence, 76, 166, 211, 217, 222-3, 229, 235, 242; Peter, 55

Barham, Nicholas, queen's serjeant at law, 235-6

Barker, William, Norfolk's secretary, 76, 119, 166, 197-8, 211-13, 217, 220-1, 235-6

Barnard Castle, Durham, 173

Bartie, Francis, 202, 238

Basing house, co. Southampton, 158

Beccles, co. Suffolk, 26

Bell, Robert, 75-6, 101, 185

Berkeley: Henry, lord Berkeley (1534-1616), 32, 153; Katherine, wife of Henry, (daughter of Henry, earl of Surrey, 1539-96), 4, 6, 32

Berney, Kenelm, 231-2, 248

Berwick upon Tweed, 54-7, 63, 180; garrison at, 58, 62, 79, 140; herald of, 59; treaty with Scottish lords (1560) at, 56

Beton, John, 210

Blagge, Sir George, 16, 18

Blennerhasset: Sir John, 76, 106, 118, 120-1; Thomas, 112

Boleyn: Queen Anne, 8; Sir James, 18

Bolton in Wensleydale, co. York, 134

Bonner, Edmund, bishop of London, 38

Borghese, Sr., steward of Spanish ambassador, 231-2
Bothwell: Adam, bishop of Orkney, 142; earl of. *See* Hepburn
Bowes, Sir George, 63, 152, 170, 173
Boyd, Robert, lord Boyd of Kilmarnock (d. 1590), 143
Bramber, co. Sussex, 76
Brancepeth, co. Durham, 172-3, 175
Brissingham, co. Norfolk, 113
Bromley, Thomas, solicitor general, 185, 233
Brooke: George, lord Cobham, lord warden, 202, 206; Thomas, of Rollesby, 180, 186-8
Browne, Thomas, of Shrewsbury, 211-12, 229
Buckenham, co. Norfolk, manor, 37
Buckhurst, lord. *See* Sackville
Bungay, co. Suffolk, 2
Bunwell, co. Norfolk, 178
Burghley, lord. *See* Cecil
Bury St Edmund's, co. Suffolk, 78
Buttes, Sir William, 55, 179, 180
Buxton, Robert, 76, 106

Caister, co. Norfolk, castle, 67
Calais, France, 62-3
Cambridge, co. Camb., 45-6, 66, 88-90; University, 10, 46, 88-90, 240
Camden, William, 66, 162, 257
Campion, Edmund, 133
Cantrell: William, Norfolk's surveyor, 55, 106, 120, 156, 167, 238; William, vicar of Hingham, 186
Carafa, Alfonso, cardinal archbishop of Naples, 35
Carew: Sir Gawen, 16; Sir Peter, 61, 233; Wymond, 14
Carey: George, 139; Henry, lord Hunsdon (d. 1596), 83, 92, 173-6, 179, 226 229
Carlisle, co. Cumb., 117, 134
Casket Letters, 128, 137-9, 143
Castle Acre, co. Norfolk, 18, 32
Castle Rising, co. Norfolk, 2, 5, 26, 70, 75-6
Catlin, Sir Robert, chief justice of the Common Pleas, 184, 233
Cavendish, Richard, 158, 235-6
Cawood, co. York, the ride to, 138-9
Cecil: Thomas, 181, 186; Sir William, lord Burghley, 21, 47, 49, 53-6, 58, 60-2, 74-5, 77, 80-3, 85-9, 91, 109, 118, 121, 139, 141-2, 145, 155-62, 164-7, 169, 183, 186, 189, 192, 194, 196, 202-3, 205-7, 208-10, 212-14, 217, 224-6, 228-30, 232-3, 238, 243, 246, 250-2, 256; early friendship with Norfolk, 61, 63-4; supports the Hapsburg match, 88, 92, 94, 130-3; Norfolk's opposition to, 146-9; on Norfolk's trial, 237
Cecilia, Princess of Sweden, 93
Charles IX of France, 95-6
Charles, archduke of Austria, 50, 54, 86, 88, 92-3, 98-100, 126, 129-32, 257
Chatsworth, co. Derby, 192, 209-10
Chenies, co. Buckingham, 184

Churchyard, Thomas, 7
ciphers, 190, 197-8, 202-3, 205, 207, 211-12, 218-19, 221, 223, 226
Clere, Edward, 163-4, 183-4, 214
Clerk, John, 27
Clinton, lord. *See* Fiennes
Cobham: lord. *See* Brooke; Henry, 129; Thomas, 202-3, 238
Cooke, Robert, clarenceux, 42, 81, 246
Cordell, Sir William, master of the rolls, 117, 121, 123, 127
Cornwallis, Sir Thomas, 119, 163
Cotton, co. Suffolk, 107
Crofts, Sir James, 58-60
Cromwell, Thomas, earl of Essex (d. 1540), 1-2, 8, 10
Cumberland, county, properties in, 17
Cuthbert, John., 205-6

Dacre (or Dacres): Anne (or Nanne). *See* Howard, Anne; Edward, 191;
    Elizabeth, widow of Thomas, lord Dacre. *See* Howard, Elizabeth, duchess of
    Norfolk; Elizabeth (Bess), daughter of Thomas, lord Dacre. *See* Howard,
    Elizabeth; Francis, 119; George, lord Dacre (d. 1569), 116-17, 125, 127;
    Leonard, 60, 99, 117, 119, 127, 150-1, 158, 174, 192, 203; Mary (Mall), 116-17,
    123, 127, 216, 243, 245; Thomas, lord Dacre (d. 1566), 127
Dacre inheritance, 98, 103, 116-19, 127, 191-2
Dannett, Thomas, 98-9
Darnley, lord. *See* Stewart
Denham, William, 113, 198
de Quadra, Alvarez, bishop of Aquila, Spanish ambassador, 50-1, 61, 82-3, 85-6
de Silva, Spanish ambassador, 92-3, 95, 97-8, 100-101, 127, 135
de Spes, Guerau, Spanish ambassador, 147-8, 151, 163, 197, 202, 206, 213, 220,
    230-1
Dethick, Sir Gilbert, Garter King, 96, 129, 233, 246-7
Diss, co. Norfolk, 76
Dix, William, 120, 125, 179, 248
Dorking, co. Surrey, 104
Dorset, earl of. *See* Sackville
Douglas: James, earl of Morton (d. 1581), 142; Lady Margaret, countess of
    Lennox, 37, 82-3, 85
Dover, co. Kent, 202
Dovercourt, co. Essex, 104
dramatic companies, 45
Drury: Sir Drew, 183-4; Sir William, 55, 156
Dudley: Ambrose, earl of Warwick (d. 1590), 83, 86, 89, 174; Lord Henry, 34,
    107; John, viscount Lisle, earl of Warwick, duke of Northumberland, Pro-
    tector (d. 1553), 13, 26-7, 49, 114; Lord Robert, earl of Leicester (d. 1588),
    38-40, 48-51, 60-1, 80-2, 84-100, 102, 118, 124-5, 128, 130-1, 134, 141, 145,
    148-51, 155-7, 159-61, 166, 180, 186-8, 195, 197, 206, 214, 228, 233, 248, 256
Dumbarton, 144, 208, 210
Dunwich, co. Suffolk, 77
Durham, 55, 59, 152, 172-5

Dyer, Sir James, chief justice of the common pleas, 115, 233

Edinburgh, 57, 61, 91, 99, 128, 143-4; treaty of, 62-3, 150
Edward VI, 14, 21, 27
Elizabeth I, 36-40, 47-51, 54, 58, 60-4, 74, 88-9, 133, 135, 137, 140, 174, 179,
    184, 187, 214; illness, 84; problems of marriage and succession, 84-6, 88, 90,
    93, 97-103, 129-32, 150, 196, 204, 211; relations with Norfolk, 81, 91, 93,
    100-1, 108, 127, 136, 140-1, 144, 150, 159, 164, 166, 189, 196, 225-9, 247, 251;
    loses confidence in Norfolk, 140-1, 157-9; relations with Mary Queen of
    Scots, 122, 134-5, 140-4, 154-5; fears for her safety, 159, 161-2, 170; signs
    Norfolk's death warrant, 252; visits the Tower on the eve of Norfolk's
    execution, 253, 274n.
Englefield, Sir Francis, 192, 207
Essex, county, Howard properties in, 111, 113-14, 116
Essex, earl of. *See* Cromwell, Thomas

Fanshawe, Sir Thomas, queen's remembrancer, 106
Farnham, co. Surrey, 157-8
Felton, John, 184, 195
Fénélon, la Mothe, French ambassador, 141, 161, 211, 223
Fiennes: Edward, lord Clinton and Saye, earl of Lincoln (d. 1572), lord admiral,
    86, 98, 141, 153, 166, 174; Elizabeth wife of Edward, 156; Sir Henry, later
    earl of Lincoln and Clinton (d. 1616), 153
fisheries, 66
FitzAlan: Henry, earl of Arundel (d. 1580), 32, 35, 37-9, 90-3, 95, 98, 110-11,
    118, 120, 124, 134-5, 141, 147, 150-2, 155-7, 160-2, 164, 166-7, 191, 195, 197,
    224; Lord Henry, son of Henry (d. 1555), 33; Jane, daughter of Henry. *See*
    Lumley; Mary, daughter of Henry. *See* Howard, Mary
Fitzgarret, Edward, 164-5
Fitzroy: Henry, duke of Richmond (d. 1536), 5, 9; Mary, duchess of Richmond
    (daughter of Thomas third duke of Norfolk, d. 1557), 5, 9, 13-18; as guardian
    of Thomas Howard, 24-31
Fleming, John, lord Fleming (d. 1572), 135, 210
Flitcham, co. Norfolk, 212
Flower, William, Norroy, 42, 246
Flowerdue, Edward, 185
Fludd, Robert, of Norwich, 188
Foix, M. de, 211
Foster, Nurse, 129, 216
Forster, Sir John, 140, 163, 174
Foxe, John, 25-6, 29, 47-8, 164-5, 238-9, 253, 256
Framlingham, co. Suffolk, 160; castle, 7, 27, 31, 122, 128; church, 133; park, 70
France, 96; wars with, 11-12, 34, 40, 83; war in Scotland against, 53-62
Francis II of France, 52-3, 136
Froude, J. A., 138, 270n. 10, 272n. 14, 273n. 19
Fulmerston, Richard, 76
Furse, Thomas, 133

Gardening by Scotsmen, 223
Gardiner, Stephen, bishop of Winchester, lord chancellor, 9, 13, 18, 28-30, 32
Gargrave, Sir Thomas, 170
Gates: Sir Henry, 170; Sir John, 14
Gawdy: Bassingbourne, 31; Thomas, serjeant at law, 24, 26, 55, 163, 179, 185, 188
genealogy, study of, 42
Gerrard: Gilbert, attorney general, 123, 184, 228, 233, 235; Sir Thomas, 209-10
Gilbert, Edmund, 111
God, John, 111
Goodere, Henry, 208, 211, 223
Goodman, Jane, 32, 216
Granvelle, cardinal, govenor of the Netherlands, 83
Greenwich Palace, 99, 118, 155
Gresham: Sir Richard, 18; Sir Thomas, 109-10
Grey: Sir Arthur, 63; Lady Catherine, duchess of Hertford, 84-5; Lady Jane, 27, 114; William, lord Grey of Wilton, 54-5, 57-61
Greystoke, co. Cumb., castle, 174, 191-2
Guise: Henry of, 53, 57; Mary of, Regent of Scotland, 53, 57, 61

Hall, John, of Tynedale, 210
Hampton Court, 9, 84, 95, 143
Harleston in Redenhall, rising at, 181-2, 188
Harper, Sir William, 82
Harris, Robert, 76
Hartlepool, co. Durham, 173
Harwich, co. Essex, 104, 200, 204
Hastings, Henry, earl of Huntingdon (d. 1595), 124, 151; claim to throne, 83-5; custodian of Mary Queen of Scots, 161, 190
Hatfield House, co. Hertford, 36
Hatton, Sir Christopher, 229, 246
Hayward, Sir Rowland, 125
Heath, Nicholas, archbishop of York, 34
Heneage, Sir Thomas, 92, 98
Henry VIII, 2, 8, 9, 11, 12, 13-14, 16, 18-20
Henry II of France, 52-3
Henry Valois, duke of Anjou, later Henry III of France, 196, 201, 204, 211-12
Hepburn, James, earl of Bothwell (1536-78), 128, 138, 142, 149, 155, 201, 205, 225
heralds and heraldry, 37, 40-3, 52-3, 59, 96-7
Herbert, William, earl of Pembroke (d. 1570), 40, 84, 93, 99, 102, 118, 124, 147, 149, 156, 160-2, 164, 166, 191
Herle (or Erle), William, spy, 206, 232
Herries, lord. *See* Maxwell
Hertford, earl of. *See* Seymour
Heydon, Sir Christopher, 18, 163, 177-80, 214-15, 241
Higford, Robert, Norfolk's secretary, 119, 166, 190, 211-13, 217-19, 235-6, 243

Hobart, James, of Hales Hall, 180, 188

Holdyche, Robert, 14

Holland: Brian, 180-1; Elizabeth, 3, 15-17, 32

Holmes, William, 182

Hopton, Sir Owen, lieutenant of the Tower, 218, 232-3, 238, 250, 252

Horsham, co. Sussex, 3, 76-7, 108

Howard:

Anne (or Nanne), daughter of Thomas lord Dacre, married Philip earl of Arundel, 116-17, 119-20, 127, 241, 243-4

Catherine, Queen, 5, 10, 83

Charles, later lord Howard of Effingham (1536-1624), 24

Elizabeth, wife of Thomas, third duke of Norfolk (d. 1558), 3, 27-8, 34, 127

Elizabeth, third wife of Thomas fourth duke of Norfolk (relict of Thomas lord Dacre), 126-8, 168, 206

Elizabeth (or Bess), daughter of Thomas lord Dacre, married lord William Howard, 87, 116-17, 119, 123, 127, 216, 245.

Frances, countess of Surrey, (wife of Henry earl of Surrey, married Thomas Steynings, d. 1574), 1, 4, 22, 27, 30-1, 248.

Sir George, 39

Henry earl of Surrey (1517-47), 1, 6, 7, 9; marriage, 4; poetry, 6, 11; escapades, 10-11; dislike of 'new men', 10-11, 15-16, 19-20, 49; as soldier, 11-13; portrait, 13; children's lack of affection for, 12; treason, 14-19; trial and execution, 19 -20

Lord Henry, later earl of Northampton (1540-1614), 4, 6-7, 120, 133, 178

Jane, married Charles earl of Westmorland (1537-93). *See* Neville

Katherine, married Henry lord Berkeley (1539-96). *See* Berkeley

Margaret, second wife of Thomas fourth duke of Norfolk (daughter of Thomas lord Audley and, relict of lord Henry Dudley), 34-8, 40, 43-4, 46, 48-9, 87-8, 107

Margaret, married Henry lord Scrope (1543-91). *See* Scrope

Margaret, daughter of Thomas fourth duke of Norfolk, married Thomas lord Buckhurst. *See* Sackville

Mary, first wife of Thomas fourth duke of Norfolk (daughter of Henry earl of Arundel, d. 1557), 32-4, 120

Mary, duchess of Richmond. *See* Fitzroy

Philip earl of Surrey, later earl of Arundel (1557-95), 34, 119, 214-16, 239-42, 246-9; estates settled on 119-22; marriage, 120; establishment for, 122

Thomas, third duke of Norfolk (1473-1554), 1, 10-11, 13, 16, 19-23, 28, 46, 75, 109, 165, 240, 251; letter from, 2; builds Kenninghall, 2-3; as soldier, 8-9; political outlook, 9, 25, 29; in the Tower, 20, 27; restored to honours, 27-8; wealth, 2, 32; will, 2, 32; death, 31

Thomas, fourth duke of Norfolk (1538-72):

Early Life; (1538-58): birth, 1-2; childhood at Kenninghall, 5-7, 12, 21; effects of father's death on, 22-4, 256; under John Foxe, 25-7; (1553) created K. B., 28; restored in blood as earl of Surrey, 29; under bishops Gardiner and White, 29-30; (1554) succeeds to dukedom, 31; a gentleman of the chamber of Philip II, 31; (1555) marries Mary FitzAlan, 32-3; (1558) marries Margaret Audley, 35

Howard—*contd.*:

Public Affairs (1559-68): (1559) created K. G., 40; duties as Earl Marshal, 37-43, 52, 81, 134; (1560) as lieutenant-general in the North, 53-64, 107; breaks the 'Auld Alliance', 56-7; investitures by, 63; high stewardships, 46, 75, 88-9; (1561) admitted to Gray's Inn, 81; freeman of London, 82; in his county, chapter five; patronage, 75-9; (1562), admitted to Privy Council, 85; (1563-8) supports scheme for Elizabeth to marry Archduke Charles, 86, 88, 92-5, 97-103, 126, 129-32; (1564) honoured by Cambridge University, 89; (1566) spokesman for the lords, 101-3, 126; knight of the order of St Michael, 95-7, 100; (1567) marries Elizabeth Dacre; (1568) honoured by Oxford University, 133; friendship with Cecil, 61, 63-4, 92; dislike of Leicester, 48-51, 60-1, 81-2, 86-8, 90-8; friendship with Sussex, 91-2

Attempted Match with Mary Queen of Scots, (1568-72): first suggested as husband for Mary, 90; (1568) as commissioner at York, 135-40; befriends Mary, 134-6; re-action to Casket Letters, 137-9; at Westminster Conference, 141-4; Elizabeth's hints, 141; concordat with Murray, 144; decision to marry Mary, 138-9, 141, 145, 152; (1569) attempted removal of Cecil, 146-9; alliance with Leicester, 149-50, 155-9; Elizabeth's warnings, 155-8; Elizabeth places him on his allegiance, 159; misses Sussex's advice, 155-6; leaves the court, 160; escapes in fear to Kenninghall, 161; his nerve fails him, 162-4; submits to Elizabeth, 164-5; sent to Tower, 165; relations with Northern Earls, 158, 165, 173, 175-6; (1570) examination, 189; correspondence with Mary, 190-2; writes submission to Elizabeth, 192-4; released to Howard House, 194; renews negotiations for Mary's hand, 196, 219-25; (1571) enmeshed in Ridolfi Plot, 197-205, 219-25; returns to Tower, 213; confessions, 218, 225; examinations, 221-2; (1572) trial, 232-7; degradation from Garter, 246-7; penitence, 247, 257; last days, 238-53; execution, 253-4

Letters of, quoted, 47-8, 58-61, 63, 93-5, 130-1, 136-7, 140, 158, 161, 196, 239-49

Financial Affairs: acquires the Charterhouse, 114; arranges for settlement of Arundel estates, 120-2; as landlord, 26, 66, 79, 113; creates trustees for Howard inheritance, 119-20; debts, 106-8, 124-5; estates, 32-3, 104-25, 241; exchange of lands, 108, 113; loans, 107-9, 112, 195; private franchise, 64, 104-6, 114, 119-21, 230; taxation, 50, 107, 124; will, 122

Characteristics: aloofness, 82, 88; ambition, 64, 145, 255, 259; appearance, 33; courage, lack of, 162-3; deceipt, 193, 212, 222; dislike of the court, 22, 80, 155; health, 63, 128-9, 163, 190, 209, 249-51; indifferent scholarship, 7, 48, 85, 89; love of field sports, 6, 83, 153, of tennis, 45, 69, 91, 115; popularity, 48, 70, 79, 161, 178-9, 229, 257; pride, 49, 159; religion, 25-6, 29-30, 132, 242, 256; stubbornness in love, 222

Thomas, lord Howard de Walden, later earl of Suffolk (1561-1626), 46, 87, 119, 243, 246

William, later lord Howard of Naworth (1563-1640), 87, 119, 245

Hunsdon, lord. *See* Carey

Huntingdon, earl of. *See* Hastings

Ireland, 91, 99

James VI of Scotland, 99, 136, 144, 203
Jernygan, John, of Somerleytown, 180
Jewel, John, bishop of Salisbury, 48, 130
jewellery, 15, 43, 112, 248
Junius, Hadrianus, 6-7, 12, 21

Kenninghall, 24, 123; manor, 37; palace, 1-7, 14-17, 22-3, 27, 31, 45-6, 63, 82-3, 92, 98, 104, 122, 127-9, 161, 163, 165, 169, 178, 212, buildings, 2-4, 43-4, bathroom, 44, ransacked, 21-2, Princess Mary at, 22-3, closed down, 215-16, staff of, 3-4, 17, 68, 105-6, 113, Howard's affection for, 5, 43-4, 61; rising at, 177-9; St. Mary's church, 24, 44, 177, 179
Ket: Thomas, 182; William, 182
Ket's Rebellion, 26, 66, 73
Knollys: Sir Francis, 139, 163, 165-6, 229, 231, 233; Henry, 190; Lettice, viscountess Hereford, 92
Knox, John, 53
Knyvet: Sir Edmund, 16-17; Henry, 55

Lambeth, co. Surrey, Howard House in, 17
Laughton, George, 216
Lee, Sir Henry, 253
Leicester, earl of. *See* Dudley
Lennox, countess and earl of. *See* Stewart
Leith, 55, 208; siege of, 57-62, 138
Leslie, John, bishop of Ross, 135-44, 149, 152, 154, 161, 166, 176, 182, 197, 202, 204-11, 219, 221, 223-5, 235-6, 243
L'Estrange, Sir Nicholas, 18, 46, 60, 75, 81, 119, 166, 223
Lethington. *See* Maitland
Lewes, co. Sussex, 76
Leyburne, Sir John and lady, 126-7
loans, 107, 111-13
London, 47-8, 66, 83, 94, 126-7. Places in or near: Aldersgate Street, 221; Arundel Place (or House), 33, 121, 228; Cecil House, 228; Chapel Royal, St James's, 37; Charterhouse (or Howard House), 35-6, 112, 114-16, 135, 155-6, 188, 194, 197, 214, 218-19, 222-4, 229, 234, improvements to, 115-16, 125, 134, 196; Charterhouse Square, 114, 211; Clerkenwell, 107, 114; College of Arms (Derby House), 41-2; Cree Church Place, Aldgate, 35, 37, 48; Durham Place, 85-6; Ely House, Holborn, 209; Fleet Prison, 192; Gray's Inn, 81-2, 113; Guildhall, 19, 82; *King's Head*, Bridge Street, 82; Marshalsea, 203, 206, 228; Mountjoy House, Knight Rider Street, 24, 27; Paget House, 125; Pardon Churchyard, 114; St Clement Danes, 33-4; St Paul's Cathedral, 74; St Paul's Churchyard, 184, 195; Somerset House, 37; *Three Cranes*, Vintry Wharf, 233; *Three Tuns*, Newgate Street, 232; Tower, 7-8, 14, 18-20, 23, 27, 36, 75, 79, 83, 120, 160, 165, 177, 184, 188, 190, 207, 213, 218-26, 232 seq., mint in, 112, 198; Westminster Abbey, 28, 37-8; Westminster Hall, 28, 37-9, 230, 232-7, Star Chamber in, conference at, 141-3; Whitehall Palace, 34, 36, 39-40, 58, 93, 96, 98, 230

Lopham, co. Norfolk, 105, 113, 122
Loseley, near Guildford, co. Surrey, 157
Lowther, Norfolk's official in the north, 211, 238
Lumley: Jane, wife of John lord Lumley (daughter of Henry earl of Arundel, d. 1574), 33-4, 120-1; John, lord Lumley (d. 1609), 110-11, 120-2, 144, 147, 150-2, 161-2, 166-7, 195, 197, 202, 206, 221, 224, 228
Liggons, Norfolk's messenger, 144, 223
Lincoln, earl of. *See* Fiennes
Lisle, lord. *See* Dudley
Lynn, King's, co. Norfolk, 46, 66, 75, 101, 185, 209, 214-15

Maitland, William, of Lethington, 56, 90, 138-9, 143, 149, 155, 166
Manners, Henry, earl of Rutland (d. 1563), 40, 83
Manship, Henry, of Great Yarmouth, 74
Markenfeld, Thomas, 172
Marie de Medici, 88
Markham, Sir John, 27
Marsh, John, merchant adventurer, 110
Martin, Gregory, 133, 216
Mary, Queen, 27-8, 32, 35-7, 41; as Princess, 23-6
Mary Queen of Scots, 52-3, 56, 59, 62, 84, 90, 93, 99, 119, 126, 128-9, 152, 154, 166-8, 176, 192-5, 197, 205, 217-28, 235, 247, 251-3, 256-7; takes refuge in England, 134; commissioners to investigate charges against, 135-45; plans to rescue, 158, 160, 163, 173, 197, 209-10; letters to Norfolk, 190-1; tokens to and from Norfolk, 222, 236; epitaph on Norfolk, 257
Massey, Elizabeth, 218
Mather, Edmund, 231-2, 248
Mautravers, Henry, lord Mautravers, 120
Maximilian II, Emperor, 98, 129
Maxwell, John, lord Herries (d. 1583), 135, 210-11, 222
Melville, Sir James, 99, 137, 142
Mildmay, Sir Walter, 168, 233, 248
monasteries, dissolution of, 1, 5, 67-8
Monluc, bishop of Valence, 61
More, Sir William, 157
Morton, earl of. *See* Douglas
Murray (or Moray), earl of. *See* Stewart
music, 39, 44
Mynne, Nicholas, 34-5, 76

Naworth, co. Cumb., 117; castle, 174, 191-2
Neville: Charles, earl of Westmorland (d. 1601). 81, 83, 99, 111, 143, 147, 150, 152, 162, 165, 169-73, 175, 177, 195; Sir Henry, 165-6, 189-90, 195-6, 212-13, 223; Jane, wife of Charles (daughter of Henry earl of Surrey, 1537-93) 4, 6, 30-1, 165, 171-2, 179
new draperies, 70-3, 180-1
Newcastle upon Tyne, co. Northumb., 54, 61
Nolloth, Anthony, of Great Yarmouth, 181

Norfolk, county: description of, 65-8; government and administration of, 47, 49, 77-9; Parliamentary representation of, 75-7; risings in (1569-70), 176-88; recusant in, 165, 188
Norfolk, duchy of, 65-6, 104-6, 114, 119-21, 230; dukes of. *See* Howard
Norfolk peerage: early history of, 7-8; later history of, 258
Norris, Sir Henry, 231
North: Edward, lord North (d. 1564), 36, 114; Roger, lord North (d. 1600). 98, 114-15
Northampton: earl of. *See* Howard, Henry; marquess of. *See* Parr
Northern Rebellion (or Rebellion of the Earls), 169-76, 226
Northumberland: duke of. *See* Dudley; earl of. *See* Percy
Norton: Christopher, 172; Richard, 172
Norwich, 68-73, 75, 78-9, 87, 128, 130, 183; alien immigrants in, 70-1, 180-2; castle, special sessions at, 18, 184-7; cathedral, 30-1, 68; clothing industry, 47, 70-3, 163; *Crown* Inn, 69, 185; ducal palace, 5, 23, description of, 45, 68-70, 215, playhouse, 45, tennis court, 45, 69, Christmas entertainments, 45-6; gaol, 178, 182-3; Mousehold Heath, 26, 69, 73; Mount Surrey, 5, 13, 17, 21, 26; rebuilding, 68; religious houses in, 5, 68; risings in, 180-8; river trade to, 67, 69, 72; shirehouse, 32; Surrey House (St Leonards), 5, 26, 108
Nowell, Alexander, dean of St Paul's, 238-9, 249-50, 253-4, 256
Nuthurst, co. Sussex, 108

Oglethorpe, Owen, bishop of Carlisle, 38
Orkney, bishop of. *See* Bothwell, Adam
Ormes, Edmund, 229
Osborn, Peter, 77
Owen, Hugh, Arundel's servant, 160, 209
Oxford, earls of. *See* Vere
Oxford University, 98, 133

Paget, William, lord Paget (d. 1563), 13, 19, 20, 46
Papacy, 35, 189-204. *See also* Pius V
Paris, 52, 223
Parker, Matthew, archbishop of Canterbury, 93
Parliament: of 1547, 20; of 1553, 28-9; of 1555, 32; of 1559, 40; of 1563, 86; of 1566, 100-3, of 1571, 208, charge of breaking up, 221, 227-8; of 1572 demands Norfolk's execution, 251
Parliamentary elections, 75-7
Parr, William, marquess of Northampton (d. 1572), 40, 81, 83, 93, 102, 118, 147-8
Parry, Sir Thomas, 80
Paston: John, 188; Sir William, 18
Paulet, William, marquess of Winchester (d. 1572), 36, 78, 84, 101-2, 147
peerage, the Elizabethan, 124, 258
Pembroke, earl of. *See* Herbert
Percy: Sir Henry, 60, 209; Thomas, earl of Northumberland (d. 1572), 81, 83, 99, 147, 150-1, 160, 162, 165, 167, 169-73, 175, 177, 219
Perth, Convention of, 155, 158

Philip II, as Mary's consort, 31, 34; as King of Spain, 50, 54, 82, 86, 100, 152, 161, 199-200, 204-5, 208-9, 227; ambassadors of. *See* de Quadra; de Silva; de Spes
Pius V, Pope, 176, 196, 198-203, 205, 209, 220, 223, 227
plague, the, 2, 194-5
plate, sales of, 112-13
Plater, Christopher, 88
Poole, Arthur and Edmund, 194
prices, rise in, 2, 110, 268n. 9
public lottery, 74

Radcliffe: Frances, wife of Thomas, 242; Thomas, earl of Sussex (d. 1583), 80, 89, 91-2, 97-9, 129-33, 135-41, 149, 155-6, 162, 166-7, 169-73, 175, 197, 233, 248
Railton, Gregory, 56
Ramboilliet, M., 96-7
Randolph, Thomas, agent in Scotland, 91
recognisances for debt, 109
Redman, George, of Cringleford, 180, 186
Reigate, co. Surrey, castle, 24-6, 76, 104
Richard III, 7, 41, 43
Richmond, duke and duchess of. *See* Fitzroy
Richmond Palace, 156
Ricote, co. Oxford, 24
Ridolfi, Roberto, 110, 136, 167, 195-205, 208, 220-5, 227, 230-1, 247
Ripon, co. York, 172
Rizzio, David, 99, 128, 136
Robsart, Amy, wife of Robert Dudley, 49, 81, 95, 180
Rochefoucauld, Charles de, sieur de Randau, 60
Rogers, Edward, 16, 18
Rolleston, Francis, 210
Ross, bishop of. *See* Leslie
royal arms, 17, 19, 20, 52-3
Ruthven, William, lord Ruthven, later earl of Gowrie (d. 1584), 56
Rutland, earl of. *See* Manners

Sackville: Margaret, wife of Robert earl of Dorset (daughter of Thomas, fourth duke of Norfolk), 87, 123, 242, 244; Robert, earl of Dorset, (d. 1609), 87; Thomas, 110; Thomas, lord Buckhurst (d. 1608), 213
Sadler, Sir Ralph, 53, 135-41, 161, 169, 213, 229
Saunders, Sir Edward, chief baron of the Exchequer, 233
Sawston, co. Cambridge, rising at, 79, 229
Scotland, 8, 55, 58, 140, 174; war against French in, 53-62; ending of 'Auld alliance', 56-7. *Also* James VI; Mary Queen of Scots; Stewart, James
Scrope: Henry, lord Scrope of Bolton (d. 1592), 81, 111, 134, 140, 153, 174; Margaret, wife of Henry (daughter of Henry earl of Surrey, d. 1591), 4, 30-1, 134, 138

Seymour: Edward, earl of Hertford, duke of Somerset, Protector (d. 1552), 9, 13, 15, 18, 20-2, 49; Sir Thomas, lord Seymour of Sudeley (d. 1549), 13, 15
Shoreham, co. Sussex, 76
Shrewsbury, earl of. *See* Talbot
Skipwith, Sir Henry, 225, 239, 249, 252
Smith: Edward, of Oxnead, 182; Sir Thomas, 92, 210, 212-13, 217, 229
Soham, Earl, co. Suffolk, 30-1
Solempne, Anthony de, of Norwich, 186
Somerset, duke of. *See* Seymour
Southampton, earls of. *See* Wriothesley
Southwell, Sir Richard, 14-15
Spain, embargo on trade with, 146-7, 152. *See also* Philip II
Stanley: Henry, earl of Derby (d. 1593), 81, 99, 124, 204; Sir Thomas, 99, 209-10, 224, 229
Stewart: Henry, lord Darnley (d. 1567), 82-3, 85, 90, 93, 97, 137-8, 142, 225; James, earl of Murray (or Moray), Regent of Scotland (d. 1570), 128, 135-8, 140, 142-4, 149, 153-5, 158, 163, 166, 190; Matthew, earl of Lennox, (d. 1571), 209-10
Steynings, Thomas, 30-1, 160
Stirling, 54, 144
Stow, John, 115
Strynger, Anthony, of London, 107
Sturbridge Fair, co. Cambridge, 66
Surrey, earls of. *See* Howard
Surtees, Christopher, of Durham, 175
Sussex, county, Howard properties in, 76, 104
Sussex, earl of. *See* Radcliffe
Swinburne, John, 172
Sydney, Thomas, 214-15
Symondes, Sir Henry, 14

Talbot, George, earl of Shrewsbury (d. 1590), 36, 99, 124, 145, 158, 161, 217, 225; as lord high steward at Norfolk's trial, 232-7
tapestry, 44-5
Tattershall, co. Lincoln, 153
Tempest family, 172
Temple Newsam, co. York, 82
Thetford, co. Norfolk, 14, 24, 47, 68, 75-6, 117-18, 122
Thirlby, Thomas, bishop of Westminster, 21
Throgmorton: John, 180, 186-7; Margaret, wife of John, 187-8; Sir Nicholas, 52, 63, 144, 149-50, 157, 165-6, 231, 149-50, 157
timber, 72, 108-9
Timperley, Thomas, 55, 106, 119
Titchfield, co. Southampton, the court at, 159-60
Topcliffe, co. York, 165, 170
trade, 66-7, 70-3, 163, 191

Vere: Edward de, earl of Oxford (d. 1604), 119, 230, 246; John de, earl of Oxford (d. 1562), 45, 124

Wallop, Sir John, 11
Walsingham, Sir Francis, 77, 192-5, 214; discourse on Norfolk's proposed marriage to Mary Queen of Scots, 167-8
Ward, Edward, 112
wardship, problems of, 31-2, 98, 106-8, 116-20, 125, 127-8, 241
Warner. Sir Edward, 17
Warwick, earl of. *See* Dudley
Welles, John, of Kenninghall, 177-8
Wem, co. Salop, 222
Wentworth: Paul, 165; Thomas, lord Wentworth (d. 1584), 24, 77, 165, 184
Westmorland, county, lands in, 117
Westmorland, earl and countess of. *See* Neville
White, John, bishop of Lincoln and of Winchester, 29-31, 38
Wilbraham, Thomas, attorney of the Wards, 223, 235
Wilkes, John, 229
Williams, Sir John, lord Williams of Thame (d. 1559), 24
Wilson, Dr Thomas, 210, 212-13, 217, 225, 229, 233, 248
Wilton House, co. Wilts., 160
Winchester, marquess of. *See* Paulet
Windsor, co. Berks, castle, 161, 164-5, St George's chapel in, 40, 98, 246-7
Wingfield, co. Derby, Mary Queen of Scots at, 154, 158, 160-1
Winter, William, admiral, 54-5
Woller, a papist in Suffolk, 188
Wood, John, 142, 166
Woodhouse: Francis, 55; Sir Roger, 26; Sir William, 18, 73, 78, 163
Wootton, North, co. Norfolk, 108
Wootton, Dr Nicholas, 21, 61
Wriothesley: Henry, earl of Southampton (d. 1581), 159, 166, 224; Thomas, earl of Southampton (d. 1550), 13-14, 20
Wrothe, Sir Thomas, 214
Wymondham, co. Norfolk, 49; manor, 37

Yarmouth, Great, co. Norfolk, 46-7, 67, 73, 75, 181-2, 187; harbour, 67, 72-5
York, co. Yorks, 153, 170, 173-4, 235; Conference at, 135-40, 224-6, 228, 257; dean of, 141
Young, Thomas, archbishop of York, 133